The Caribbean Since 1900

PRENTICE-HALL

POLITICAL SCIENCE SERIES

Schuyler C. Wallace, Ph.D., Editor

A Syllabus in American Governmental Organization, *by* A. Gordon Dewey, Ph.D., Brooklyn College, New York.

Politics, Pressures, and the Tariff, *by* Elmer E. Schattschneider, Ph.D., Wesleyan University.

The Caribbean Since 1900, *by* Chester Lloyd Jones, Ph.D., University of Wisconsin.

Other titles in course of preparation

The Caribbean Since 1900

BY

Chester Lloyd Jones
Professor of Commerce and Political Science
University of Wisconsin

NEW YORK
PRENTICE-HALL, INC.
1936

PRINTED IN THE UNITED STATES OF AMERICA

TO MY WIFE

CAROLINE S. LLOYD JONES

Contents

CHAPTER I

The Caribbean and the United States

SINCE the opening of the twentieth century, the international relations of all states have become of greater significance than they have been at any previous time. Development of commerce has made domestic industries more dependent upon supplies from abroad and upon foreign outlets for their products. Better facilities of communication have shrunk the world, brought contrasted civilizations into closer contact, and made the privileges and obligations of neighborhood more intimate.

Expansion of interest has not in this period meant political conquest or loss of great territories such as were transferred from nation to nation in the three centuries following the discovery of America, nor has it been concerned with the establishment of such highly nationalistic controls of the course of trade as were common when the great maritime powers sought to monopolize the commerce of their colonies for themselves. But foreign relations have intimately influenced the lives of more people than ever before and have influenced them in unprecedented degree. Trade beyond national boundaries has reached amounts and values never before known. Capital has sought investments abroad in totals heretofore unapproached. The life of the world has been shot through with interrelationships so far-reaching that no country is "foreign" to others, as it might have claimed to be in past generations.

No nation has been more strikingly affected by the new outlook than has the United States. In the closing years of the previous century it was already growing rapidly in population and in its commercial relations with other countries. Between 1890 and 1930 the number of its inhabitants almost doubled and the value of its foreign trade rose almost fivefold. Exports increased from $1,394,483,000 to a peak of $5,240,-995,000 and imports from $849,941,000 to a high point of $4,399,361,000. In the same period, the policy of the nation swung from the isolation which had formerly characterized it to intimacy with events in the Far East, active participation in European affairs during the World War, and a steadily growing connection with developments in Latin America.

The international contacts of the United States have now become world-wide. During two crises, one rising in the Far East and one in Europe, the nation has played an outstanding role in developments in the Old World. But its greatest interest in foreign affairs and the most persistent of its problems in international relations have been in cisatlantic developments and especially in the countries bordering the Caribbean Sea. Though the growth of this relationship has been most striking in the last generation, its beginnings go back to the earliest years of British settlements in North America. An appreciation of the close connections which have come to exist and of the responsibilities which the various areas bear to each other can be obtained only by visualizing the long-time political and commercial interests which have made them associates.

Even before the first British settlements were established on the North American coasts, adventurers from the countries of northern Europe had made attempts to break down the monopoly of trade which Spain sought to maintain in the territories she claimed in the New World. Sir Walter Raleigh visited Trinidad in 1595, British seamen landed in Barbados in 1605, and Englishmen were established on St. Christopher in 1625. These were followed by other efforts to set up island bases for British settlements and for attacks on Spanish commerce. The mother country had, at first, only shadowy control over these outposts from which commercial ventures of legal and illegal nature were carried on. The activities of those who questioned Spanish control in America, however, were quite in line with their country's ambitions, and the Caribbean colonists, whatever the nature of their undertakings, could count on the complaisance if not the support of the home government.

The profits from successful voyages might be great. They attracted British interest not only in the home country, for the settlements in Virginia and New England were little more than established when there arose in them, also, the desire to share in the West Indian trade. From practically the beginning of British settlement in North America, therefore, the Caribbean region has had a special interest for those living northward.

Between 1631 and 1635, shipments were made from the Colonies on the North American continent to the Caribbean. The cargoes included grain, pork, fish, leather, Indian corn, pipe staves, and lumber. These commodities were long to be characteristic West Indian imports.[1] Cotton, sugar, tobacco, indigo, and silver were brought northward. By 1676, Colonial merchantmen were already engaged in the triangular trade to the coast of Guinea. They took New England rum to exchange for slaves in West Africa, brought the slaves to the West Indies and sold them for sugar and molasses, and then sailed homeward to dispose of their molasses cargoes to those for whom the product was the raw material for making New England rum.

The direct trade southward grew steadily. Colonial skippers did not confine their dealings to legal channels. They greased the palms of customs officials in the British island ports to induce them to allow dealings forbidden by the regulations of trade. They did the same thing in foreign harbors. They entered the ports of enemy nations in times of war or used convenient neutral islands as halfway stations to conceal trade legally forbidden. Officers of the home ports were lax in enforcing British legislation. They allowed foreign ships to enter under false papers, or sold them such documents as

---

[1] For details of the early trade to the Caribbean, see Frederick, John H., *The Development of American Commerce*, New York, D. Appleton and Co., 1932, pp. 1–10.

they lacked. Trade with privateers, who were often little if any better than pirates, was looked upon with complacency.

The small vessels of the time did a "huckstering" business with the West Indies. They loaded the typical exports, such as provisions, whale oil, candles, soap, horses, cattle, lumber, and even ready-cut houses and peddled their wares from one West Indian port to another. There were no great trading companies which monopolized the business. Nor was the commerce confined to a few specialties; it lay, rather, in the hands of a large number of small enterprisers and touched many lines of local production. These circumstances emphasized to the Colonists the close relation of southern sources of supply and markets to the prosperity of the average citizen.

It is not surprising, therefore, to find the Colonists represented in the later attacks which Great Britain made upon the Spanish possessions in the Caribbean.[2] In 1739 a certain Hamilton urged the conquest of Cuba by Colonial troops, for thus might be secured for British subjects "the whole Trade of the Spanish Empire." In the period from 1739 to 1741, an attack on the Spanish colonies was made by the British Admiral Vernon, who was joined at Jamaica by some 3,600 men drawn from nine of the North American Colonies. Among these was Colonel Lawrence Washington, half-brother of the man who was later to lead the Continental armies. Mt. Vernon was later named after the leader of this expedition. During the Seven Years' War, Governor Pownall, of Massachusetts, urged that the British attack Cuba; and at the capture of Havana in 1762, Colonial troops were again represented in the British forces.

So intimate had been the connection of the Colonies with the Caribbean that it is easy to understand their desire, once they became independent, to assure themselves that their position in its trade should not become less favorable. This ambition was increased by a realization that the trans-Alleghany region depended for its commercial outlet upon the route down the Mississippi and out through the Gulf.

---

[2] For greater detail, see Callahan, J. M., *Cuba and International Relations,* Baltimore, Johns Hopkins Press, 1899.

Considerations of this sort complicated the affairs of the United States even before its independence was formally recognized and continued to do so afterward in the long-drawn-out dispute concerning the freedom of navigation on the Mississippi.

In 1801 some 58.3 per cent of the exports of the United States went to the south. Of the $46,377,792 worth of export trade, 21 per cent went to the British West Indies, 19 per cent "to the Spanish West Indies; . . . 2.2 per cent . . . to the Danish West Indies, and 1.3 per cent . . . to the Dutch West Indies."[3]

Shortly after, in 1803, came the sale of the Louisiana Territory by France to the United States. Trade down the river, formerly possible only under treaty with Spain, which held territory on both sides of the mouth of the Mississippi, would no longer be dependent on the favor of a foreign power. For the immediate future, the trans-Mississippi area would, of course, contribute no appreciable part to the total; but the trade would grow and the necessity for keeping free access to markets through the route between Florida and Cuba for the commerce of the "western world" would be greater than ever.

The acquisition of Florida in 1819 strengthened the position of the United States, for one side, at least, of the straits of Florida thus fell under national control; but even this did not give complete security, for Havana, it was still felt, "lay at the mouth of the Mississippi."

By this time, the population was rapidly increasing west of the Alleghanies, and the need for good market routes was becoming steadily greater. In 1810 there were about one million people in the Western states and territories, but before the end of the next decade more than two million were living there.

The nature of the settlements which the Westerners made and their distance from the rest of the civilized world forced them to be largely self-sufficient. Livestock could be driven fairly long distances to market, but few other goods could

---

[3] Chandler, Charles Lyon, *Inter-American Acquaintances,* Sewanee, Tennessee, University Press, 1917, p. 23.

bear the cost of land transportation. The trade down the river, though expensive, was indispensable. Flatboats carried cargoes of corn, pork products, flour, whiskey, and cattle down to New Orleans for the world market, but effective exploitation of the national resources could not exist until better transportation facilities should be established. These would bring lower marketing costs and facilitate the opening of the back country.

For this reason, the appearance of the steamboat on the Western rivers marked the beginning of a new era. The first one had gone up the Mississippi from New Orleans to the Ohio in 1816, but by 1842 there were 450 steamboats on the river and its tributaries. The total value of the trade at New Orleans had risen since 1807 from five million dollars to over fifty million.

Other new methods of transportation were meanwhile helping to open up the West and increasing the products that it sent to market. Canals and railroads were beginning to stimulate development and to modify the practical monopoly of downstream trade in the exports of the Western country. By 1850 the passenger fare by lake and rail from Chicago to New York was $17. Twelve years before it had been $74.50. Freight rates had declined similarly.[4]

Though the East-West commerce which was coming into existence tended to diminish interest in the Caribbean, the annexation of Texas, the war with Mexico, and the new holding on the Pacific coast emphasized it. Railroads did not yet tap these more distant territories, and access to the Pacific overland was so difficult that the routes through Nicaragua and Panama across the isthmus attracted the attention of those who stayed at home almost as much as those of the pioneers who set out on new westward adventures by land.

Even before the middle of the century, a Caribbean policy had begun to develop. Indeed, it had been one of the causes of the issuance of the Monroe Doctrine. The incidents marking increased interest in the area centered largely about Cuba.

---

[4] Bogart, Ernest Ludlow, *The Economic History of the United States,* New York, Longmans, Green and Co., 1925, p. 230.

Concerning that Spanish colony the American minister to Spain in 1827 flatly declared that it was "the settled principle" of the United States "that the island must in no event pass into the possession of, or under the protection of, any European power other than Spain."[5] Nine tenths of Cuban commerce was then, he asserted, with the United States. Subsequent developments only continued to emphasize the growing connection, political and economic, with Cuba and with the territories surrounding the Caribbean Sea which the United States felt.[6]

During the Civil War, the activities of the blockade runners illustrated the relation of control of the coast to the Caribbean islands. Had the Union forces been in possession of an outlying port from which to operate, the blockade would have been much easier to maintain. Efforts were made, but without success, in the years following the close of the conflict to acquire a naval base in the Dominican Republic and to buy the Danish West Indies. Then, as the country recovered, exports to Latin America passed the fifty-million-dollar mark and imports reached twice that amount. Commercial interest in the trade with Caribbean areas and with the republics still farther to the south supplemented the more distinctively political interest. Merchants and manufacturers began to dream of a canal at Panama.

Before the war with Spain, the value of United States exports to Latin America exceeded $100,000,000, and imports were worth two and one-half times as much. To be sure, in the total exports, Latin America had not held the percentage it possessed in 1870,[7] and imports were no more impressive; but enthusiasm was keen about the possibilities of rapid expansion of commerce in the "undeveloped countries."

---

[5] Everett, A. H., Minister to Spain, in a communication published by the United States Congress. *House Executive Document 121,* 32nd Congress, 1st Session, p. 21.

[6] The development of the interest of the United States in Cuba is covered in Chadwick, French Ensor, *The Relations of the United States and Spain, Diplomacy,* New York, Charles Scribner's Sons, 1909.

[7] Of total exports, those to Latin America were 11.2 per cent in 1871–1875 and 8.7 per cent in 1896–1900. Imports were 27.6 per cent in 1871–1875 and 23.4 per cent in 1896–1900. *Statistical Abstract,* 1933, p. 412.

In the last quarter of the century, the share of manufactures in our exports had increased over that of crude materials and foodstuffs, while in the import trade the opposite tendency had shown itself.[8] A country which was undergoing rapid "industrialization" and which was so favorably located for trade southward as was the United States might well look to Latin America and especially to the Caribbean region as a great field for economic expansion as well as one which would continue to play an important part in its foreign politics.

The conflict with Spain in 1898, which, to the minds of many, seemed to open a new chapter in the development of the political and economic policy of the United States in the New World, was thus only an incident which emphasized and broadened an interest in the areas to the southward. This interest had its beginnings long before the United States was established as a nation—commencing, in fact, almost at the time of the earliest British settlements on the Atlantic coast.

The years since the opening of the century have only accentuated the long-standing connections. They have brought to the United States the possession of no new territory except the Danish West Indies, but the political involvement of the country in the affairs of the neighboring states, the special position which it has come to occupy under treaties with certain of them, the close relation which all of them have to its program of national defense, the great increase in commercial exchanges, and the heavy investments of American capital have made the United States by far the greatest of Caribbean powers.

In this period, a number of branches of American policy, in most cases not new and not always distinct from each other, have had further growth. All emphasize the increasing intimacy of the relation of all the units of the Caribbean to each other and to the United States.

Cuban developments continue to claim attention because of the strategic position of the island, economic and political developments within it, and the special treaties which have

---

[8] See tables in *Statistical Abstract,* 1933, p. 411.

bound it to its northern neighbor in relations of "peculiar intimacy."

A Canal policy has come into being because of the relation of the great waterway to the naval position of the United States and to its coastwise trade and merchant marine, and because of its connection with all problems involving the defense of Caribbean countries.

Broader than the interest in Cuba or in the Canal, but not unconnected with both of them, has been the Caribbean policy of the United States. The political phases of this policy have developed from the inability of the weaker states to maintain normal conditions within their own borders and in their relations with other nations. Its economic features, like those of the Cuban and Canal policies, touch the problem of the safety of the United States.

Underlying all these grounds of special interest in degrees varying at different times has stood the "America for Americans" policy. Like the other policies mentioned, it does not lend itself to exact definition and at times it has been subject to shifting interpretations. It has had peculiar application to the Caribbean because it is apt to be questioned only when life and property are endangered by disturbance of public order in weak states, and the weaker states of the New World are chiefly in the Caribbean area.

Obviously, in the generation which has passed since the Spanish-American War, the Caribbean countries and the United States have come to share the same problems and to be bound together in political interest to a degree equalled by few other regions of the world.

Increase in common economic interests has paralleled the increase in common interests in political affairs. The Caribbean republics are consumers of the products of the fields and factories of the United States, and the United States receives from them and through the nearby waters far the greater part of its imported food supplies and an important share of its raw materials. Imports into the United States from the Caribbean in 1900 had a value of $76,600,000. In 1929 they totalled $582,700,000. Exports in the same period rose from

$62,300,000 to $481,300,000. The United States' exports to the Caribbean republics in the latter year equalled over three-fifths of all the products that they bought abroad, and to the United States they sent almost as great a share of their own exports. In the depression years following 1929, both branches of foreign trade suffered heavy declines, falling in the case of a number of countries to less than a fourth of the total attained at the peak; but the relative position of the United States in Caribbean commerce suffered no material change, and the amount and value of this commerce can hardly fail to rise again as the world works its way back to more normal conditions.

The Caribbean republics, in their public finance, have relied heavily, especially in the period after the World War, in which the United States has been a creditor nation, upon capital from the northern republic. Their chief development activities to a high degree are the result of American enterprise and rest upon American financial support. From less than $300,000,000 in 1912, the United States capital investment in the region rose to an estimated total of $2,517,000,000 as of December 31, 1933.

Whether the countries sharing the territories of the Caribbean region be considered in their historical relationships or in their present-day political and economic dependencies, it is clear that they share a common fortune.

Their common interests have not eliminated the clash of national ambitions. Neighborhood does not of itself insure mutual understanding and co-operation. Sharing of responsibilities may accentuate contrasts of policy which but for the closeness of association might create little conflict of opinion. It does, however, create for governments and individual citizens the obligation to seek to understand the conditions which confront neighbor states, and it puts upon them a duty to contribute to the growth of public opinion, which, through adjustment of policy to circumstance, may minimize conflicts and contribute to the development of a basis of co-operation in the common interest.

CHAPTER II

Cuba Becomes a Republic

CUBA, greatest of the Antilles, outranks all other Caribbean states in contribution to the economic life of the world and in political importance. Its foreign trade in prosperous years has reached over half a billion dollars—over twice that of rapidly advancing Colombia with an area more than ten times that of the island and a population twice as great. It is well supplied with ports; its railways are better developed than those of any of the other republics, and the traffic they carry far exceeds in amount and value that in any other of the units. Through its geographical position it commands on the west the straits of Florida and the Channel of Yucatan—the entrances to the Gulf of Mexico. It lies at two of the great entrances to the Caribbean Sea—the Channel of Yucatan and the Windward Passage—and thus dominates two of the great routes leading to the crossroads at Panama.[1]

---

[1] STATISTICS OF THE LARGER CARIBBEAN AREAS *

	Colombia	*Cuba*	*Venezuela*	*Nicaragua*
Area (sq. miles)	444,100	44,164	352,143	49,500
Population .... (thousands)	7,851 (1928)	3,962 (est. 1931)	3,262 (est. 1932)	750 (est. 1929)
Population .... (per sq. mile)	17.7	87.9	8.2	15.2
Imports .... (millions of dollars)	60.6 (1930)	162.5 (1930[a])	87.4 (1929)	8.2 (1930)
Exports .... (millions of dollars)	108.8 (1930)	167.4 (1930[b])	150.3 (1930)	10.9 (1929)

[a] 278.1 for 1921–1925.
[b] 362.7 for 1921–1925.
* Compiled from tables in *Commerce Yearbook*, 1931, Vol. II, *Foreign Countries, 1931*, Department of Commerce, Washington, 1931; and from tables in *Foreign Commerce Yearbook, 1933*, Department of Commerce, Washington, 1934. (*Footnote continued on next page.*)

Cuban developments, therefore, are a consideration for any country the safety and economic development of which are affected by events in the middle region of the New World.

For a long time after the discovery of America, Cuba occupied a position in Caribbean affairs much less prominent than it has come to hold in our time. Discovered by Columbus, October 28, 1492, a little over two weeks after his first landfall on the twelfth at the island he named San Salvador, it was the first of the major islands of the Antilles known to Europeans and the major discovery on the famous first voyage. But the first attempts at settlement went elsewhere. By 1515, however, seven settlements,[2] including Santiago and Habana—later relocated—had been made. Within a few years Negroes were being imported to supplement the unsatisfactory and already diminishing supply of Indian labor. This seemed an auspicious beginning. Consistent development, however, did not take place. The riches of Cathay, it was soon evident, were not in Cuba, and the conquistadors turned their attention south and west. Cuba became a "jumping-off place" for explorers looking for richer returns than the island could give. Even the few settlers who had established themselves tended to slip away for adventures farther afield. Cortes, then Alcalde of Santiago, sailed off in November, 1518, on the expedition which was to conquer Mexico. De Soto set out from Cuba with an army of six hundred in 1539 on what proved to be three years of wandering through what is now the southeastern United States. Many others of the conquistadors either set out from Cuban towns or used them as ports of call.

But economic development in the island itself lagged. The

STATISTICS OF THE LARGER CARIBBEAN AREAS (*Cont.*)

	Colombia	*Cuba*	*Venezuela*	*Nicaragua*
Per Capita Foreign Trade (dollars)	21.9 (1930)	88.8 (1930)	73.1 (1929)	30.2 (1929)
Railways (miles)	1805	3064	587	166
Freight (1000 metric tons)	3,136 (1929)	28,469 (1929)	457 (1929)	115 (1929)

[2] In 1513 Hispaniola (Haiti) already had seventeen chartered towns.

King of Spain had approved an *asiento,* or contract, in 1517 allowing the introduction of 300 Negro slaves to Cuba; but few, if any, actually arrived. The island was too poor to allow their purchase. A few Negroes were gradually introduced, but their employment in gold mining proved unprofitable. As late as 1532 there were only some 300 Spaniards on the island, and these were in wretched circumstance.

Not till 1547 was the first small sugar mill set up by men brought from the more prosperous colony in Haiti. Only occasionally did vessels put in at Habana. In time, stock raising began to pick up, and sugar production, in spite of alleged continued discrimination against Cuba in the supplies of Negroes, increased, especially in the eastern part of the island.

A century and a quarter after the discovery, some thirty-seven *trapiches* [3] were reported from the eastern towns Santiago and Bayamo. Cattle ranches were plentiful—some with six thousand head. Habana, in the west, where sugar and tobacco production were increasing, had a population of over four thousand. But this, at best, was by no means a brilliant showing. The sixteen hundreds and the first half of the following century saw no great change in Cuban development. Other areas continued to attract greater attention, and Cuba was still hampered by the nationalistic trade policy and by inability to secure adequate supplies of African slaves. Even the growing contraband trade did not balance these disadvantages.

The outlook bettered somewhat as the seventeen hundreds advanced. Spaniards had by this time been forbidden to bring slave supplies from Africa, but an agreement was made authorizing a French company to do so. The tobacco industry in the Habana province began to prosper. Later, the rules in the slave trade were relaxed, and larger numbers of blacks came in as contraband. After the middle of the century, a more enlightened colonial policy was adopted. The

---

[3] Small sugar mills.

short English occupation of Habana in 1762 brought in 10,700 Negroes from Africa in its first five months.[4] The home government adopted more liberal rules as to commerce, and better methods of sugar making were introduced. The export trade, which went in three ships before 1762, required 200 in 1778.

By the end of the eighteenth century, Cuba was still, in population, far behind the other major divisions of the Spanish empire in the New World,[5] but it was no longer a neglected and almost forgotten island. Slave supplies, still considered inadequate, had been greatly increased; indeed, Cuba and Puerto Rico a quarter-century later were estimated to have about as many Negroes as all the other Spanish colonies combined.[6] Tobacco production flourished and coffee planting increased. Sugar was becoming rapidly more important in the export trade and the British colony of Jamaica was surpassed as a sugar producer. The winning of independence by the United States emphasized the importance of trade interchange with North America. The Negro revolution in Haiti already forecast the disappearance of serious French competition, and Cuba became the most important sugar-producing colony of the world. Additions of European stock to the population had been received from Jamaica, Florida, and French Haiti.

The nineteenth century, which was to bring the loss of Cuba to Spain, did not carry out in the island the promise of the years immediately preceding its opening. The wars of

---

[4] Aimes, Hubert H. S., *A History of Slavery in Cuba, 1511 to 1868,* New York, G. P. Putnam's Sons, 1907, p. 33.

[5] In 1788 Cuba and Puerto Rico together had an estimated population of 600,000; Venezuela, 900,000; Rio de la Plata, 1,100,000; Guatemala, 1,200,000; Peru, 1,700,000; New Granada, 1,800,000; and New Spain, 5,900,000. (Rippy, J. Fred, *Historical Evolution of Hispanic America,* New York, F. S. Crofts and Company, 1932, p. 106.) Leland H. Jenks, in *Our Cuban Colony,* New York, Vanguard Press, 1928, at pp. 22–23, gives the population of the island at the time of the American Revolution as "not more than 200,000, of which half were negroes and mulattoes." Later estimates are reported as follows: in 1804, 432,000; in 1846, 898,700; and in 1862, 1,357,000.

[6] Humbolt in 1823 estimated the population of Cuba and Puerto Rico as 800,000, including 389,000 Negroes. The other colonies were estimated to have 387,000 blacks. (Rippy, *op. cit.,* p. 107.)

the Napoleonic period made economic returns uncertain. On May 30, 1814, France and England agreed to work together against the African slave trade. The United States had renounced it. Only Spain and Portugal continued openly to support the traffic in black men, and even they had no uniform policy—indeed, Portugal shortly joined the northern powers, at least formally, in giving it up. Spain itself reluctantly consented to plan for the end of the slave trade in 1817 and by treaty with Great Britain agreed that it should cease in October, 1820.

Cuban opinion had been strongly opposed to these developments. Brazil still bought blacks from Africa,[7] and Cuba would now suffer in competition. The British, it was felt, had maneuvered Spain to abolish the slave trade in order chiefly to hamper the development of the greatest competitor of their own West Indian colonies. Freedom to trade with all nations, which had been granted in 1818, would not balance the disadvantage.

Contraband trade in slaves, in fact, continued[8] though Spain became apprehensive that the increase of the Negro population might bring a revolution comparable to that which had lost Haiti to France. Slave revolts did occur. The home country was in an unwelcome position. It wished to abolish the slave trade—but found itself opposed by those arguing that it was necessary for the economic development of the island. It wished to maintain slavery, though to do so might make Spanish control precarious. Meanwhile the economic development of Cuba was proceeding, political dissatisfaction with Spanish policy was increasing, and movements for "liberating" the island were taking form.

The prosperity of the closing years of the eighteenth century, so far as it involved Cuban sugar, was based on what now seems a comparatively small tonnage. Thereafter labor

---

[7] The continuance of this trade, largely in United States vessels, is discussed in Hill, Lawrence F., *Diplomatic Relations between the United States and Brazil,* Durham, N. C., Duke University, 1932, pp. 110–145.

[8] It was not entirely brought to an end until about 1867, but had ceased to be a factor two years before. See a detailed review in Aimes, *op. cit.,* pp. 219 and 242–248.

costs rose and sugar fell in price as European beet sugar producers brought more to market. The Cuban cane sugar crop averaged, from 1821 to 1825, only 57,710 tons. Planters successfully met the new conditions which they had to face. After 1827, better manufacturing methods, taken from European and Jamaican practice, were introduced. Horizontal rollers for crushing cane were set up, filters using animal charcoal were adopted, and in 1841 and 1842 the first crops were worked up with equipment using the new multiple-boiling process. After 1846 more liberal terms for the entry of Cuban sugar into Great Britain were secured. Coffee production was abandoned on many estates because of increasing competition from Brazil and because the hurricanes of 1844 and 1846 destroyed many Cuban *cafetales,* or coffee plantations. Under these circumstances Cuban sugar yield rose to average 279,400 tons from 1846 to 1850. By 1859 the production reached 536,000 tons; in 1866, 612,000 tons; and in 1894, the year before the outbreak of the final revolt against Spain, 1,054,214 tons.[9]

Increase of the trade with the United States came with the advance of the sugar industry. Restrictions on this commerce were relaxed in 1884 and in 1886 only to be increased in 1890, but were again reduced in 1891. Trade northward increased so rapidly that Spain was alarmed as to what might be the political consequences, and in 1894 the favorable tariff rates were brought to an end. These actions in no small degree helped crystallize Cuban opinion in favor of the final effort for independence.

Political relations of Cuba and the home country came to have more than local significance only in the nineteenth century. After the early period of neglect, the commercial policy in the latter half of the eighteenth century had been liberalized and the administrators whom Spain sent to the colony included a number of able men. The revolutionary propaganda which found ready acceptance after 1810 in the mainland colonies had only a faint reflection in the greatest island

---

[9] Tables of sugar production in Cuba are found in the *Census of Cuba, 1899*, Washington, 1900, pp. 524–528.

of the Antilles. The island continued to be referred to as "La Isla Siempre Leal"—"the ever-loyal island." But as the century advanced, contentment with Spanish rule waned.

A number of influences contributed to a growing popular unrest. Had Spain taken a lesson from developments on the mainland, opposition to continued colonial status might have been quieted or at least minimized. But disturbed conditions in the home country prevented the working out of a consistent and liberal colonial regime, and the loss of other American territories seemed to determine the Spanish authorities to tighten their control of the island possessions still held. Cuba was put under a captain-general with military powers equal to those of an officer in charge of a besieged town. Members of the local town councils were appointed and removed by this officer. Natives of the island were not accepted in the army. Strict censorship limited freedom of speech and of the press. The local population continued to be denied any significant role in their own government and trade policy after 1829 tended to become more restrictive. These conditions fostered ambitions for greater autonomy and, in the long run, for termination of the connection with Spain.

Supplementing the local desires were others involving a group of foreign nations which felt their own interests affected by those of Cuba. Mexico and Colombia, among the former mainland possessions, showed an interest in fostering revolution. France and Great Britain watched the fortunes of Spanish sovereignty in the island—each anxious that the other should not secure advantage from the course events might take and both apprehensive of the position in relation to the island which the United States might come to occupy. The latter had practically throughout its history felt that Cuba, lying close to its shores and commanding the Gulf of Mexico and the Caribbean, was an area having a very special relation to its foreign policy.[10] The "America for Americans" policy espoused by President Monroe in 1823 had reflected an atti-

[10] Charles E. Chapman, in *A History of the Cuban Republic,* New York, the Macmillan Co., 1927, p. 46 *et seq.*, gives a brief survey of the interest of the United States in Cuba.

tude toward European ambitions which was not unconnected with the control of the island and which was to receive growing support.

Cuban enthusiasts in the period before the Civil War in the United States often looked forward to freedom from Spain not as necessarily or even preferably involving complete independence. They dreamed of allying or annexing the island to some other Latin-American country—Mexico or Colombia—or, perhaps more frequently, to the United States. In 1822 an agent of one group of conspirators was sent northward to inform Americans of their plans for revolution and to sound the United States as to whether, if independence were secured, a proposal of annexation would be favorably received. The suggestion came too early, and the United States contented itself with being assured that no European power should become the successor of Spain.

Cuban leaders had to wait. They were too weak, most of them felt, permanently to maintain their independence, as some of them would have preferred, and had "no other recourse than to throw . . . [themselves] into the arms of the United States." [11]

As the years passed, however, the American willingness to allow affairs to drift disappeared. The Southern States came to look upon the acquisition of the slaveholding island as desirable for strengthening their position against the rapidly developing North. "Manifest destiny" pointed south as well as southwest. After the annexation of Texas, a number of moves toward purchase of the island from Spain were made, but only to meet with curt refusal. These plans failing, the more extreme turned to support projects of revolt in Cuba itself.

To keep alive among Cubans living in exile the enthusiasm for a "free Cuba," to arouse American opinion in its favor, and to collect funds for propaganda and eventually forcible resistance, juntas, or committees, were maintained in New York and other Atlantic coast towns. During the years fol-

---

[11] José Antonio Saco, writing in 1837, quoted in Chapman, *op. cit.*, p. 35.

lowing 1848 these societies devoted themselves to the development of a movement for annexation to the United States. In the same period occurred the expeditions led by Narciso Lopez. A Venezuelan by birth, he had become an enthusiastic advocate of "Cuba Libre"—which he hoped would later be received into the Union. Repeatedly he headed revolutionary movements, encouraged by support from the Southern States. In 1848 the American and Spanish authorities prevented the arrival of arms and Lopez fled to the United States. He offered the leadership of the next expedition to prominent southerners, Jefferson Davis, Robert E. Lee, and Governor Quitman, of Mississippi. Each considered the proposal seriously but declined. Late in 1850 Lopez was off for Cuba with a revolutionary force numbering almost six hundred, chiefly Americans. But the local population did not rise to his support, and, after an indecisive encounter, the expedition put back to the United States. Twice again in 1851 Lopez tried to call Cuba to arms. The first time, his sailing was prevented by the authorities of the United States; and the second, after landing with a force of about four hundred—again chiefly Americans—he found himself again without local support. His followers were finally overcome by the Spaniards. He himself was captured and later executed. Cuba was not yet ready to rise, not ready to fight for its freedom.

For a time interest in "free Cuba" lagged. A liberal movement in Spain raised the hope that better government might be granted—a hope soon disappointed. Gradually opinion against Spain was crystallized. The next move would not lack local support. On October 10, 1868, a declaration of independence was made at the Yara plantation in the poorly developed eastern province, Oriente. Thus began the Ten Years' War, carried on by a revolutionary government always in precarious circumstances and never possessed of a fixed capital.

The support it received and the American sympathy it aroused were far wider than in the Lopez adventures. The latter had had the sympathy of Creole slaveowners in Cuba and of the expansionist party in the southern United States. However, now that slavery had been abolished in the northern republic, the revolutionists in Cuba promptly declared for its abolition in Cuba—a move which won them many recruits from among the black men but cooled the support of propertied interests. Annexation to the United States was still hoped for by many, and Carlos Manuel de Céspedes, Provisional President, suggested to the Cuban agent in New York that it be requested and himself wrote President Grant to that end.

Military operations carried on by both sides were characterized by ruthless measures. The revolutionists were at an advantage in their guerilla campaigns because of the difficulty of communications in territory untapped by through railroads and ill-supplied with roads. They could live on the country, as the Spanish troops could not. The greatest of their military leaders was Maximo Gómez, a Dominican, later to become the commander-in-chief of the final revolt against Spain. American sympathy for the Cuban cause was keen throughout the struggle. Some citizens of the United States enlisted in the war, and more helped by subscribing funds; but officially the Government kept a neutral position in spite of incidents which might have been made the occasion of an active role.

Early in the war, the United States had sought to act as mediator to bring about the grant of independence. A number of Spanish leaders were willing to discuss it, and others would have been willing to transfer the island to the United States. Some Spanish newspapers argued that it should be ceded because Spain was badly in need of money and because the United States had never shown great enthusiasm for colonial possessions. Letting this opportunity slip, they held, might mean that this indifference would increase and that sale at a later time would not be possible. The efforts at adjustment, however, at no time brought a truce between the parties to the conflict. Attempts to secure help from European powers to induce Spain to yield also failed.

After long years of warfare of indecisive character, Gómez

met a severe defeat in 1875. Opposition gradually weakened and in 1878 was nominally brought to an end by the Treaty of Zanjón, which guaranteed a number of reforms in government. Irreconcilables carried on a losing fight until 1880.

But political unrest was practically uninterrupted from the end of the Ten Years' War to the outbreak of the revolution of 1895. Disputes between the colonists and the home country as to the rights to be granted the former continued to occur, and friction with the United States because of trade restrictions and claims was frequent. In both the island and the United States, annexation projects did not lack support. John Sherman declared that he found Cubans in 1887 almost unanimous in favor of annexation, and in the first term of President Cleveland purchase of the island was again suggested to Spain and again rejected.

On the other hand, as the time of the next effort to break the Spanish connection approached, annexation was less popular in both Cuba and the United States. In the former there grew confidence in the ability of the island to stand alone if independence were won or at least to stand alone with the benevolent protection of the United States. In the latter was growing the feeling that annexation of Cuba, with presumably the grant of statehood, might bring social, political, and economic problems difficult of solution.

The long-time grievances of the Cuban people against the home government broke into a new revolution with the *grito* at Banes on February 24, 1895. The outbreak began in the same month in which Spain passed a law which might have been a tardy first step toward greater Cuban home rule. The measure never went into effect, nor did its passage check even momentarily the plans of the revolutionists. Economically, the island was in the midst of the hard times caused by the panic of 1893. The sugar market was depressed. The favorable commercial arrangements with the United States had been canceled. Economic distress was reflected in rising political unrest.

Political clubs in the United States, intent on bringing a break with Spain, had grown in number, resources, and influence. There were sixty-one in Key West alone.[12] Cubans in exile and many Americans were regular contributors. Financial support and shipments of munitions from the United States could be counted upon to come forward in much greater amount than in the Lopez days. The propertied classes, the church interests, and most of the merchants continued to favor the Spanish connection or, that failing, some other which could guarantee public order. They were apprehensive of what might occur if independence were established. The poorer classes and at least a portion of the intellectuals were more sanguine, and among them possible annexation to the United States was now less in favor.

Spain signally failed to take advantage of this division of opinion. The revolutionists by carrying on campaigns with highly mobile forces minimized the Spanish advantage of numbers and were able, as they had not been in the Ten Years' War, to carry the contest into the better-developed western portion of the island. As in the previous conflict, the usual rules of warfare were often disregarded by both sides. Maximo Gómez, again the generalissimo of the opposition, gave orders forbidding trade with towns in possession of the Spaniards and any co-operation in the sugar industry. Thus, he would undermine economic activity and make the island worthless to the Spaniards. On the other side, General Weyler, who soon was put in command of Spanish operations—he also had fought in the Ten Years' War—established the "reconcentrado" policy. Under it the rural population was ordered into camps under penalty of death and confiscation of property. Between these programs the population stood to perish.

Public opinion outside the island rose in condemnation of Weyler's policy, which in practice herded the common people into small areas where, through lack of food and sanitary facilities, they died by thousands. Temporarily the fortunes

---

[12] An interesting account of the work of the Cuban revolutionary juntas in the United States by the American most closely connected with them is Rubens, Horatio S., *Liberty, The Story of Cuba*, New York, Harcourt, Brace and Co., 1932.

of war turned toward Spain in the west; but the demand for intervention on grounds of humanity became peremptory in the United States, and, under the storm of protests, Spain recalled Weyler late in 1897. It was too late. Though his moderate successor showed a desire for conciliation and though the revolution to many seemed to have spent its greatest strength, outside the island there were under way developments which were to bring Spanish control to an end.

The attitude of the people of the United States toward the revolution had radically changed since the outbreak in 1895. From his headquarters at the junta in New York, Tomás Estrada Palma had done effective propaganda work in collecting funds and arousing sympathy for the Cuban cause. In spite of efforts to stop the escape of expeditions carrying arms, ammunition, and money from the United States to the insurgents, enough had slipped through to keep the lifeblood of the revolution flowing. American sympathy with the cause had grown, especially as the sins of the Weyler regime came to public knowledge. On the other hand, not enough had been accomplished by the insurgents to justify their official recognition even as belligerents. Though Congress had passed a resolution granting that status if the executive should approve, President Cleveland to the end of his administration insisted that conditions did not warrant action.

In the party conventions of 1896 the Democrats declared "sympathy" with the Cuban cause and the Republicans felt that the United States "should actively use its influence and good offices to restore peace and give independence to the Island." During the campaign and following the election, public opinion in favor of a more active policy crystallized. In December, Cleveland, in his message to Congress, declared that duties to Spain might come to "be superseded by higher obligations." Weyler's operations were prejudicing the cause of Spain in the United States as much as in Cuba. A year later McKinley, the new President, declared that the contest as carried on was "not civilized warfare." In January, 1898, the ill-fated *Maine* was sent to Habana to protect American interests, and on the fifteenth of the next month was blown up by an explosion, with a loss of over 250 [13] men. Whether the disaster was from internal or external cause was later subject to conflicting reports by Spanish and American investigators, but public opinion at the time fixed the responsibility upon the unpopular Spaniards.

During the succeeding weeks, the United States administration sought ineffectually to secure an adjustment with Spain. On March 27, 1898, a demand for an armistice which was practically an ultimatum was dispatched, to be met by a counterproposal March 31. This was interpreted as merely a means to secure further delay, and McKinley turned the matter over to Congress, which, under the pressure of public opinion, was certain to declare war. The President's message was complete on April 10, when another communication from Spain announcing new concessions arrived, but McKinley only added a brief note to his previous statement and sent it to Congress on April 11.

He declared that the only hope of relief from the intolerable conditions was "the enforced pacification of Cuba." The war must stop "in the name of humanity, in the name of civilization, in behalf of endangered American interests which give us the right and the duty to speak and to act. . . ." He requested authority to use the Army and Navy "to secure in the island the establishment of a stable government, capable of maintaining order and observing its international obligations, insuring peace and tranquillity and the security of its citizens as well as our own. . . ." [14]

The joint resolution of April 20, 1898, giving the requested power, followed. In its course through Congress, phrases which have since caused long discussion and much hairsplitting were introduced. It was resolved: "That the people of the island of Cuba are and of right ought to be free and independent," and the so-called Teller Amendment stated: "That the United States hereby disclaims any disposition or

---

[13] The number reported lost varies in the official reports.

[14] Message of April 11, 1898. Richardson, James D., *A Compilation of the Messages and Papers of the Presidents, 1789–1905,* Washington, Bureau of National Literature and Art, 1907, Vol. X, p. 67.

intention to exercise sovereignty, jurisdiction, or control over said island except for the pacification thereof, and asserts its determination, when that is accomplished, to leave the government and control of the island to its people."[15]

What did these phrases, drawn in the heat of discussion attending a declaration of war, mean to those who drafted them, to those who voted upon them; and what should they mean to those who were later called upon to interpret them under the influence of conditions unforeseen and unforeseeable at the time when the resolution was adopted? There has been a wide variety of interpretations. It has been argued that, like the similar words in the American Declaration of Independence, the first clause quoted was not, when phrased, a statement of fact, and that whether it would come to be a fact depended on the outcome of the impending war, the circumstances at its close, and the agreements then entered. Further, it was pointed out the Declaration of Independence speaks of governments—"these United Colonies"—which "are, and of Right ought to be Free and Independent States." The joint resolution does not say "Cuba is and of right ought to be independent." The Senate, it appears, had been in favor of making such a declaration; but the House, at the express request of the President, refused to concur.[16] Still, it did say, "That the people of the island of Cuba are and of right ought to be free and independent." Was that a distinction without a difference?

The Teller Amendment has been argued to indicate that, "pacification" being accomplished, the United States bound itself to complete withdrawal. On the other hand, it is asserted that the declaration was not an agreement with anyone but merely a declaration of the understanding of Congress at the time and modifiable at the will of the United States in the light of circumstances which might later arise. No Congress could by such a declaration bind its successor. The war in contemplation was a war against Spain. The revolutionary

---

[15] *Ibid.*, pp. 72–73.

[16] See Presidential Message, December 5, 1898, in Richardson, *op. cit.*, Vol. X, p. 86.

authorities in Cuba were nowhere mentioned. The terms of peace when the war was over would presumably be in a treaty with Spain. Then only would engagements of a contractual character arise.

Whatever the intent of Congress at the moment of the passage of the resolution, it is clear that the executive was awake to the long-time interest of the United States in Cuba and desired to keep a free hand in dealing with situations which might arise. President McKinley in his messages had maintained that no conditions which made Cuba in fact independent, so that recognition should be granted, existed, and that it would also be inexpedient to recognize independence. Recognition might "subject us to embarrassing conditions" by making intervention subject to the approval of the local government and put us in "the mere relation of a friendly ally." When there should actually have arisen in the island a government with "the attributes of sovereignty," the "relations and interests of the United States with" it might be adjusted. Meanwhile, the intervention he contemplated would involve "hostile constraint upon both the parties to the contest." [17]

It is clear, too, that the enthusiasm of the Cubans for American aid was at the beginning and continued through the war and after to be by no means without qualification. Co-operation of American forces on Cuban soil was looked at askance. The American resolution passed on the eve of the war was curiously phrased. Did the statement mask a covert intent to deny real independence? Cuba was weak in opposition to Spain; it would be weaker if it had to stand against the United States. Perhaps, thought some, it would be best to keep any American part in local operations as restricted as possible.

Gómez wished no American troops, except perhaps artillery.[18] He would accept supplies and would welcome the interception of supplies for the Spaniards. When American troops landed, they received no enthusiastic welcome and by them there was no formal recognition of the Cubans as allies.

[17] *Ibid.*, pp. 63–64.
[18] Chapman, *op. cit.*, p. 91.

Even the military leaders received scant attention. They were not invited to be present at the surrender of Santiago, and General Wood was appointed military governor of Oriente without consultation of the local authorities. Establishment of American control was looked upon by the latter with anxiety. After all, would not imperialistic spirit sweep the people of the United States beyond the standard declared for in the resolution of April 20, 1898?[19] Through the war and after its close, Cuban suspicions of American intentions continued active.

The war which was precipitated by the joint resolution of April 20, 1898, was short and decisive. On May 1, a victory over the Spanish fleet in the Philippines had been won. Early in July the Spanish vessels which attempted to escape from the Cuban harbor at Santiago were overwhelmed. American troops were landed and the army at Santiago surrendered on July 17. Shortly after, Puerto Rico was taken over. Peace negotiations were begun in July and ripened into a protocol in August. The discussions for a definitive peace began in Paris in October and were concluded on December 10. On April 11, 1899, one year after the President's war message, the treaty was proclaimed.[20]

Once the war was at an end, the people of the United States resumed their habit of devoting their attention almost exclusively to domestic affairs. Realization that the outcome of the conflict had brought the country to face with new opportunities and responsibilities in the Far East and to the southward caused "anti-imperialism" to be an issue in the national campaign of 1900; but the far-reaching implications of the new national position were not then realized by the great mass of the people. Consequently, the adjustments following the war came to be made by the executive and Con-

---

[19] *Ibid.*, p. 126 *et seq.*

[20] Chadwick, French Ensor, *The Relations of the United States and Spain—The Spanish-American War,* New York, Charles Scribner's Sons, 1911, contains a detailed account of the war. See also Chadwick, French Ensor, *The Relations of the United States and Spain, Diplomacy,* New York, Charles Scribner's Sons, 1909, for a review of the diplomatic relations of the United States and Spain in the century preceding the war.

gress with only slight guidance by public opinion. Of the two, the executive, as was to be expected, was the more active in shaping the course to be adopted.

The point of view of the President continued to be that the United States had acted in the war without allies. It had dictated the terms of peace. Spain had relinquished "all claim of sovereignty over and title to Cuba." [21] The United States had refused to annex the island—the action which Spain would have preferred. It had agreed to discharge the obligations to protect life and property which resulted from occupation of the island as long as the occupation might last, and on retirement to "advise any government established in the island to assume the same obligations." Nowhere in the treaty did clauses appear committing the United States to recognizing any definite international status for Cuba.

Even before the treaty of peace was signed, however, the executive made it plain that the intent to set up an independent government in Cuba expressed by Congress before the war started was to be acted upon. "As soon as we are in possession of Cuba and have pacified the island," the President declared in a message to Congress on December 5, "it will be necessary to give aid and direction to its people to form a government for themselves." Relations between the two peoples should be "most friendly" and commercial connections "close and reciprocal." Military occupation would be continued until a government had been created.[22]

In the arrangements looking toward American withdrawal, it was made evident that, while the United States intended, as the resolution of April 20, 1898, had said, "to leave the government and control of the island to its people," it would take steps to make certain that its relations with the new government should assure the protection of the interests which had so long made the fortunes of Cuba of special significance to its neighbor.

---

[21] Text of the treaty in Malloy, W. M., *Treaties, Conventions, International Acts, Protocols and Agreements . . . 1776–1909, Sen. Doc. No. 357,* 61st Cong., 2nd Sess., 2 vols., Washington, 1910, Vol. II, pp. 1690, 1691, and 1695.

[22] Message to Congress, December 5, 1898. (Richardson, *op. cit.,* Vol. X, pp. 82, 97–98.)

On July 25, 1900, the President directed a call for election in Cuba of members of a constitutional convention. The military governor ordered the voting in September. Among the duties of the convention was that to "adopt a constitution . . . and as a part thereof to provide for and agree with . . . the United States upon the relations to exist between that Government and the Government of Cuba. . . ."[23]

In calling the convention to order on November 5, 1900, the military governor, General Wood, had again pointed out that when the convention had "formulated the relations" which it thought should exist between the two countries, "the Government of the United States would doubtless take such action on its part as would lead to a final and authoritative agreement between the people of the two countries to the promotion of their common interests."[24] Evidently the executive was still determined that American interests should not be neglected in the steps taken to set up an independent Cuba.

But the Cuban convention was not disposed to devote attention to the relations with the United States, definition of which had been indicated as part of its duties. While the sessions were still going on, Secretary of War Elihu Root wrote to Governor Wood outlining the character of the arrangements which Cuba would be expected to make. His comments were made known to the members of the convention when it met on February 15. The United States, he pointed out, had long maintained that it would not let any other foreign power but Spain hold the island. It had a vital interest in the maintenance of the independence which had been won for Cuba. Cuba could not defend itself against a great power. Its independence must depend on fulfillment of international obligations, maintenance of public order, and meeting any financial obligations assumed. The United States had, he argued, not only a moral obligation to establish a government which could assure these standards, but a substantial national interest in their observance. In conclu-

---

[23] Quoted in Richardson, *op. cit.*, Vol. X, p. 223.

[24] *Ibid.*, p. 224.

sion he cited five points which should be covered in the constitution. They touch the main features of provisions ultimately accepted by Cuba in the permanent treaty.

But this advice received no favorable consideration by the Cuban convention. The constitution was signed on February 21, 1901, without statements on the points to which the United States had called attention. There thus arose in the settlement of Cuban-American relations an impasse which continued until June 12, 1901, and was not finally adjusted until the "Permanent Treaty" was concluded on May 22, 1903.[25]

After the constitution had been signed, the convention appointed a committee which undertook to formulate the relations which should exist between the two republics,[26] but the apparent willingness to relegate relations with the United States to a secondary position was not acceptable to the American government. Certainly these relations had not been defined in the constitution, as the call for the elections of September had specified they should be.

The discussions in Washington which followed resulted in expansion of the principles which Mr. Root had laid down and their incorporation by amendment into the army appropriation bill of 1901. Thus became law on March 2, 1901, the "Platt Amendment," which was to be the basis of Cuban-American relations.

The terms of the law, in sum, provided that:

1. Cuba shall never enter any treaty with any foreign power which will impair or tend to impair its independence.

2. Cuba shall not assume or contract any public debt to pay interest and sinking fund charges upon which ordinary revenues, after defraying current expenses of government, shall be inadequate.

3. Cuba consents that the United States may exercise the right to intervene for the preservation of Cuban independence, the maintenance of a government adequate for the protection

---

[25] Text in Malloy, *op. cit.*, Vol. I, pp. 362–364.

[26] Machado y Ortega, Luis, *La Enmienda Platt*, Habana, Imprenta "El Siglo XX," 1922, p. 32. This volume contains a detailed criticism of the legal bases of Cuban-American relations.

of life, property, and individual liberty, and for discharging the obligations with respect to Cuba imposed upon the United States by the treaty with Spain.

4. Cuba ratifies all the acts of the United States during its military occupancy of the island.

5. Cuba will maintain and so far as necessary extend the measures for sanitation set up during the occupation.

6. The sovereignty of the Isle of Pines is to be left to later determination.

7. Cuba will sell or lease to the United States coaling or naval stations to enable the United States to maintain the independence of the island, to protect its people, and for its own defense.

8. The foregoing provisions will be put into a permanent treaty.

The United States proposed, in the words of the Joint Resolution of April 20, 1898, to "leave the government and control of the island of Cuba to its people" only when this standard of co-operation should have been adopted into the Constitution of Cuba and embodied in a treaty—the latter to assure that it could not later be modified by amendment of the constitution.

Opposition by the Cuban leaders, which arose at once, Secretary of War Elihu Root endeavored to assuage by declaring that the clauses were intended for the protection of Cuba and to assure its independence. The right of intervention would not mean "intermeddling or interference with the affairs of the Cuban Government" but formal action based on just grounds for maintaining "a government adequate for the protection of life, property, and individual liberty" and for discharging the treaty obligations of the United States in the treaty with Spain.

Opposition continued. The convention rejected the proposal by a vote of 24 to 2, and sent a committee to Washington to secure better terms. It failed to do so. The convention then voted acceptance by 15 to 14 votes and added an interpretation of its own. This the Washington administration refused to allow, and the convention on June 12, 1901, accepted the demands by 16 to 11 votes, four members being absent.

It is clear that the "Platt Amendment" was not freely accepted by Cuba but was approved because no better terms could be secured. To refuse would have meant further postponement of the withdrawal of the military government of the United States, an even less acceptable alternative. It is clear, also, in the light of subsequent experience, in spite of the assurances of strict interpretation given at the time when it was before the convention, that the terms of the engagement were such as could be given various interpretations. Some of the clauses were of transitory character, or at least were of a nature which made them of only occasional significance. Others, some Cuban writers continued to feel, cast a shadow on the sovereignty of the Republic even though its substance might not be touched. Some held that the "Amendment," as it continued to be called, particularly in its third clause gave ground for constant disagreement as to the extent of the authority of the United States, and would be made the basis of "intermeddling and interference" in internal affairs of the country such as those who drafted it would have disavowed.[27]

How the various clauses would work in practice no one could see, nor was this a major consideration once the standard insisted upon by the United States had been accepted. The leaders of the convention turned their attention to setting

---

[27] Cuban authorities differ widely among themselves as to the meaning of the clauses of the amendment and as to the alleged abuses committed in their interpretation. In the Machado regime, high officials defended, apologized for, and criticized its terms in turn. The following works of Cuban scholars give the terms of the measure and its interpretation detailed analysis: Machado y Ortega, Luis, *La Enmienda Platt,* Habana, Imprenta "El Siglo, XX," 1922; Leuchsenring, Emilio Roig De, *La Enmienda Platt,* Habana, Imprenta "El Siglo, XX," 1922; Sterling, M. Marquez, *Las Conferencias del Shoreham (El Cesarismo en Cuba),* Mexico, Imprenta Automática, 1933. These are critical of the amendment or of its interpretation. They stand in contrast to: Castillanos, Carlos Aurelio, "El Tratado de Monroe y El Tratado Permanente entre Cuba y Los Estados Unidos de Norte America," *Sociedad Cubana de Derecho Internacional, Anuario de 1922,* Habana, 1922, Vol. V, pp. 186–204, and Lendián, Evelio Rodríguez, *La Interpretación de la Enmienda Platt,* Habana, Imprenta "El Siglo XX," 1917.

up the new government under the Constitution. This government both they and the administration in the United States were one in desiring to have enter promptly on its functions.

Municipal elections were to be held and to be followed on December 31, 1901, by choice of a national government. Maximo Gómez, Dominican by birth, the generalissimo of the revolution, apparently might easily have had the presidential nomination of one or perhaps of more groups. A special clause had been inserted in the Constitution to make him eligible in spite of his foreign birth, but he declined to be a candidate. With him out of consideration, the strongest claim became that of Tomás Estrada Palma, veteran of the Ten Years' War and of the revolution of 1895, who received the support of Gómez and of the "Nationalist" and "Republican" parties. Before the election, his opponent, Bartolomé Masó, and his supporters announced that they would refuse to go to the polls because they had not been assured a part in supervising the elections. As a result, the Estrada Palma party had a walkaway, winning the presidency and all but a minor fraction of both houses of the Congress. On May 20, 1902, the long-awaited transfer of power took place amidst general patriotic rejoicing and General Wood left for the United States. The intervention was over and the newest of the American republics faced the future.

CHAPTER III

Political Development in Cuba

IN MANY respects, Cuba began its history under exceptionally favorable conditions. Freedom had been won at great sacrifice in men and resources but at much less cost in both than would have been the case had the islanders had to fight out their battle with Spain alone. Independence was guaranteed, owing to the relations established with the United States, and calls on the treasury for funds for national defense were therefore unnecessary. The country was practically without public debt, for the United States had refused to allow Spain to transfer a portion of her national debt to Cuba under the theory that sovereignty—and, therefore, the obligations of sovereignty—were being divided.

On the other hand, Cuba entered upon self-government with practically no political experience beyond that acquired during the brief months of the American occupation, a circumstance which did not promise the smooth running of public affairs. The educated classes might be expected to acquire familiarity with the duties of administration and legislation with promptness, but the common people, with whom the leaders would work and who might be controlled by the latter, were largely illiterate, unfamiliar with public problems, and, as a rule, uninterested in them.

Though these handicaps might be serious, Cuban and American observers found satisfaction in the accomplishments of the Estrada Palma administration. The President had a well-established reputation for honesty acquired during his long years of residence in Cuba and in his period of exile in the United States as an agent campaigning for funds for the

Cuban revolutionary cause. This good name he continued to justify. As his administration advanced, critics called him stiff-backed, penurious, and of narrow vision; but if these qualities were at times shortcomings, they were on the whole virtues for an executive of the period, because compromise, liberality with public funds, and ambitious political programs might easily have dissipated the advantages of the Cuban position. They proved to be features too little characteristic of Estrada Palma's successors.

The administration was uniformly successful in reaching workable adjustments in foreign affairs. Most important for the economic regeneration of the island were arrangements which would place the sugar industry in a favorable position. Sugar production had long been the leading economic activity in the island, and with the years it was to increase. Spanish unwillingness to develop favorable conditions for sugar export had been one of the causes of the revolution.

On May 5, 1902, before the Estrada Palma government was inaugurated, the chief beet-sugar-producing nations, at Brussels, had signed a convention which abolished export bounties, an action which would thus at least free the Cuban industry from competition with openly subsidized beet sugar. Tariffs in the beet-sugar-producing countries continued, however. It was of the first importance to secure concessions in the rates charged in the United States, the greatest consumer of sugar and a country which at that time had no great production of sugar within its own borders.

There was concluded on December 11, 1902, a treaty by which the republics guaranteed to each other the continuance of their existing free lists. All other Cuban products were given a reduction of twenty per cent from the existing United States tariff or any tariff subsequently enacted, and United States products of various classes were granted reductions from the corresponding Cuban tariffs ranging from twenty to forty per cent. Such an arrangement would assure Cuban sugar a steady market and an advantage over other foreign sugars in the United States that might almost equal a monopoly on the United States imports. The United States administration gave strong support to the convention, and, after delay, the Senate ratified it on March 30, 1903. It continued the basis of the commercial relations of the two countries to 1934.[1]

The naval or coaling stations provision of the Platt Amendment was adjusted. The United States had suggested grants at two ports on the north and two on the south coast, but it was brought to agree to leases of one on the north, at Bahía Honda, and one on the south, at Guantánamo, in the eastern province, Oriente.[2] The former was never developed. In 1912 an arrangement was signed by which rights at Bahía Honda were to be given up in return for extension of the area under lease at Guantánamo. Final adjustment on these lines is still incomplete.

The sovereignty over the Isle of Pines was by the Platt Amendment and the "Permanent Treaty" left to "future adjustment." This Cuba promptly sought to secure. In the treaty ending the war, Spain "relinquished" all title to Cuba and ceded "to the United States . . . Porto Rico and other islands . . . in the West Indies." Did the latter clause apply to the islands near Puerto Rico only, or did it include the Isle of Pines, or possibly all the islands lying off the coast of Cuba? Whatever the narrower meaning of the words, it is clear that Spain had long administered the Isle of Pines as a part of Cuba and that to hold that the treaty ceded to the United States all but the island of Cuba itself would have extended American jurisdiction to the some 1,360 islets and keys around the Cuban coasts. Such an interpretation could hardly have been intended.

On July 16, 1903, there was signed a treaty relinquishing to Cuba "all claim of title" to the Isle of Pines. But the Estrada Palma administration did not see the end of the matter. Opposition in the United States rested on strict construction of the treaty.

"Official" maps had been published in 1900 and 1901 show-

---

[1] Text in Malloy, *op. cit.,* Vol. I, pp. 353–357.
[2] Text in Malloy, *op. cit.,* Vol. I, pp. 358–361.

ing the Isle of Pines as American territory. Americans had settled there in the belief that it was such; and, through the activities of real estate operators, a large part of the land, estimated as high as nine tenths, was American property. In addition, certain groups in Navy circles were anxious that the island be secured by the United States as a base for defending its position in the Caribbean. None of these considerations, of course, operated automatically to transfer title to the island.

Ratification was long delayed. The original treaty expired because of non-action within the ratification period. A new one without a limited ratification date took its place on March 2, 1904. One American administration after another urged action by the Senate; but it was not until more than twenty years later, on March 24, 1925, that the measure, ratification having been advised by the Senate, finally became law.[3]

In domestic politics Estrada Palma worked under greater handicaps. The veterans of the revolution, having saved the country, "considered themselves entitled to all they had saved." A bonus bill so strongly backed that no president could have withstood it became the first great raid on the Treasury. In the carrying out of its provisions, flagrant abuses appeared. The army lists were padded, reported periods of service were lengthened, and the rank of favorites was raised to give them greater claim on the pension funds. Congress was more interested in jobs and favors than in legislation for the recovery of the country. Amnesty laws, excusing congressmen or others from suits for crimes, made their appearance. Measures of this sort were to become a standing abuse.

Bad features made their appearance not only in legislation. Government payrolls were padded. Many public officers became wealthy more rapidly than was possible from their sal-

[3] Text in *Treaty Series 709, Treaty between the United States and Cuba for the Adjustment of Title to the Ownership of the Isle of Pines* (United States Department of State). Discussions in the United States Senate reviewing the arguments for and against the treaty are in *Congressional Record,* Vol. LXVII, Part I, pp. 142–148, 156–185, 188–192, and 194–206.

aries. Customs frauds were common. Municipal and provincial governments were inefficient.

In spite of defects such as these, the first administration under the republic made a creditable economic record. The President, so his enemies said, had never seen a thousand dollars in his life before his election, and he continued for himself and, so far as he could, for the Treasury the economical habits to which he was accustomed. He was frugal in his personal life, kept his demands on the Treasury, and, so far as possible, those of all government departments, at a minimum. His first term closed with a sizable surplus—or probably with a balanced account, since the Treasury "surplus" was matched by outstanding floating debts. The showing made, in view of the public works financed, was highly creditable.

The improvement was the result of good management, so far as the President could assure it, higher customs and other taxes, and the recovery of industry. Economic activity, once peace was established, "came back" at a rate surprising to those unfamiliar with the quick reactions which often occur in semitropical monoculture countries.[4] As the four-year period came to a close, public revenues were running ahead of expenditures, and at least the better-to-do of the cities were rapidly raising their standards of living.

By the close of the first four years, there had appeared points of strength and weakness which would be exaggerated in later terms. Election abuses had come into evidence, the weakness of the legislature was demonstrated, and local government was more than inefficient. What success could be hoped for would depend largely on the vigor and probity with which executive powers were exercised. The inexperienced

---

[4] CUBAN SUGAR PRODUCTION IN CERTAIN YEARS *

In Thousands of Short Tons

Year	Tons	Year	Tons
1897–1898	342	1902–1903	1,151
1898–1899	376	1903–1904	1,239
1899–1900	336	1904–1905	1,332
1900–1901	712	1905–1906	1,403
1901–1902	976	1906–1907	1,599

* Compiled from *Statistical Abstract of Foreign Countries*, Great Britain, 1901–1912, p. 472.

Cuban electorate did not promise to create efficient popular government.

The mid-term elections of 1904 had already shown deficiencies in political organization. Party alignments were based on personalities, and not on professed support of political principles. This has continued to be the case. Quick regroupings of leaders occur. Some who are archenemies in one campaign appear as the closest associates in the next. Methods for defeating the intent of election laws promptly developed. Stuffing of the ballot boxes and fraudulent counting were prevalent. Whatever the political inexperience of the Cuban voter, his leaders showed no lack of ability to take over advanced methods of defeating the popular will.

At the national election of September 23, 1905, the "Liberals" brought out as their presidential candidate José Miguel Gomez of Santa Clara, while the "Moderates" backed Estrada Palma for re-election. The latter had hesitated to run, and after he agreed to do so was led into partisan appointments and loyalties from which he had formerly held himself apart. In the campaign, his managers used the power of the police, the executive dominance over municipal officers, and the whole range of extralegal influences to control the result. Abuses were by no means confined to one party, but the administration in power had the stronger hand.

Probably the Moderates would have won in a free election, but the leaders took no chances. They engineered a registry list comprising 432,313 voters,[5] some 150,000 more than could have been justified. Even the manager of the Moderate campaign later admitted the fraudulent character of the lists. The Liberals, convinced that they were to be cheated out of the election, refused to go to the polls on the day of election, and the Moderates had a walkaway.

This by no means meant acquiescence by the Liberals in the Moderate victory. It did mean that the Platt Amendment would come up for interpretation as to its extent. The Liberal leader, Gomez, came out for intervention to assure new

---

[5] These paragraphs are summarized from Chapman, *op. cit.*, p. 188 *et seq.*

and fair elections. It was, so he declared, the "duty" of the United States to take a hand. After the beginning of the President's second term on May 20, 1906, the opposition became frankly revolutionary. A *coup d'état* was to be staged. If it succeeded, the Liberals would be in power; if it did not, the United States would be forced to intervene and they might win the decision. In any case, intervention would not make their position worse.

The *coup d'état* never occurred. Armed conflict broke out in the provinces and rapidly spread. Most of the leaders of the conspiracy promptly took the field, or, like Alfredo Zayas, later himself to be president, scurried into obscurity and safety. By this time, whatever the case the previous autumn, the majority of the people were against the government, which evidently could not handle the situation. The leaders of the Veterans' Association sought to bring about a compromise by which new elections for all offices except those of president and vice president should be held. The conditions which had developed created dilemmas for both the government and the United States. Their counterparts were later to arise again to trouble both. If the government yielded, it would establish a dangerous precedent, encouraging those defeated in an election, whether a minority or majority, to go out in revolution to force a new election or some other compromise. If the government did not yield, it had to face a revolution which it was by no means sure it could subdue.

The United States might act to keep order under the Platt Amendment. If it did so, it would be expanding the narrow interpretation the Amendment had been given by its authors, thus giving ground for offense. If the United States supported the government in power, it would substantially be accepting an election in which there was a good measure of fraud. If it supported part of the contentions of the opposition, it would help establish the unfortunate precedent above cited.

Estrada Palma wavered and then decided to insist on the legalistic standard. His was the constituted government and he apparently expected the United States to support him. He also wanted intervention—in his favor. Acting through

Frank M. Steinhart, United States consul general, on September 6, 1906, he requested that two vessels be sent at once, as the Government could not put down the rebellion. Shortly, two ships were sent, while in a series of notes the United States protested its unwillingness to intervene and the Cuban administration urged its necessity. A formal request for intervention was made on the thirteenth. The administration proposed to resign, leaving the country without a government.

President Roosevelt urged that the Cuban factions get together. He would send the Secretary of War, William Howard Taft, and Robert Bacon, Assistant Secretary of State, to help compose differences. They arrived in Habana September 19 and promptly undertook conversations with representatives of the two sides. Both of the American representatives would have preferred to support the government in power, but it had lost credit with the people. They finally advised compromise of the sort which had been advocated by the veteranists' representatives. The revolutionists agreed to accept mediation but refused to lay down their arms, and this Estrada Palma and his counselors insisted should be a condition precedent to any settlement. He announced formally that his administration would resign rather than accept the compromise. This it did on September 28, and Cuba was without a government.

The next day, Taft issued a proclamation setting up a provisional government which was to be maintained until "order and peace and public confidence" could be restored. So far as possible, it was to be "a Cuban government," and it was to be under the Cuban flag.

Why had the elected administration broken down? What steps should be taken to assure that the provisional government should be succeeded by one less likely to fall? The answer to the first question might be the key to the latter—or might at least indicate the limitations under which any subsequent government would have to work.

No satisfactory answer can be given to either question. Cuban and foreign observers have emphasized as causes of this and later difficulties the lack of political experience, the high degree of illiteracy among the common people, the failure of a large part of the better-class Cubans to enter politics, the failure of immigrants of European stocks to become naturalized, the tendency of many of these to regard their residence as temporary and thus to refuse to identify themselves with the fortunes of the republic, and the formation of political groups around personalities rather than programs. All of these elements and many others doubtless contributed to the dissolution of 1906. Most serious perhaps is the last-mentioned. Because of it, the opposition of the "outs" to the "ins" takes on an acerbity not found in better-developed countries. Almost unbelievable realignments have occurred among the contending factions, and their "platforms," though they announce high-sounding principles, have never been programs of action.

The weaknesses of Cuban political life were such as could not promptly be eliminated by any provisional government such as was set up and continued in control from September 28, 1906, to January 28, 1909. The most that could be hoped for was that Cuba should be advanced in her political apprenticeship so that the republic might be relaunched in the direction of real self-government. The assumption of temporary authority by the United States was almost unanimously approved in the island. It was evident that the responsibility was accepted with great reluctance, and from the beginning it was clear that the desire was to make it of short duration.

Taft continued for a short time as governor. The revolutionists were disbanded and a general amnesty was given them. In October, Charles E. Magoon succeeded Taft. Cubans have condemned Magoon's administration of affairs with almost the same unanimity with which they recognized that the provisional government was unavoidable. Fair analysis does not justify their estimate. Magoon had a long and creditable though not brilliant record in private and public life. He acted in Cuba in a period following a crisis when harsh feelings still ran high. He had to lay new foundations for local political life and to meet at first hand the demands of political groups whose desires he was bound to disappoint. The charges that he was guilty of dishonest practices—that he wasted public funds and introduced the practice of padding Cuban payrolls—do not bear examination, though it does appear that he did distribute offices—some of them sinecures—among the factions in order to quiet political hostilities. The failure of much of the work which he undertook was not due to inherent defects but to later bad administration and to the refusal of the following Cuban congresses to pass the legislation necessary to put the program into effect.

The provisional authorities had first of all to carry on the ordinary functions of government, and this in a period a large part of which fell in years of economic distress. The new government undertook heavier expenditures than its predecessor in order to pay off the costs of the recent "revolution," to improve the general economic position of the island, and to relieve the distress of the less well-to-do classes. Yellow fever, conquered during the period of the military government, reappeared and was again stamped out, roads were built, streets were improved, railroads were extended, and adequate public buildings were constructed. In spite of hard times, customs house receipts rose, and up to the end of 1908 the public works were practically paid for up to date. Though the Provisional Government had undoubtedly spent much more generously than the Estrada Palma administration, it had lived in the main on its revenues and had given the republic a real return for the monies spent.

The Magoon administration made a notable record in legislation. The local Congress had not attempted to bring order out of the chaotic body of laws which it had inherited from Spain. To do this work, there being no legislature which could be called, there was created an "Advisory Law Commission," which revised the laws applying to municipalities, provinces, and the courts, created a civil service law, and, most important for setting up a new government, prepared an election law designed to eliminate the abuses which had appeared in previous voting periods. Contemporaneously, a census giving the basis for registration for the election of the new Cuban government was taken.

From almost the beginning of the Provisional Government, party leaders were working upon new groupings of politicians which would try their fortunes in the elections which would mark its close. Over lesser factions stood out the Conservatives and two branches of the Liberals: the "Miguelistas," followers of José Miguel Gomez, and the "Zayistas," supporters of Alfredo Zayas. The latter group made a poor showing in the municipal elections of 1908 and joined the Gomez forces for the national contest in November. For this trial of strength, the Conservatives put forward Mario Menocal.

The voting brought an easy victory to the Liberals, who won the presidency and vice presidency, all of the senatorships, and fifty-one seats in the House to the Conservatives' thirty-two. All parties agreed that under American supervision the first fair Cuban election had been achieved. Once more the United States was to retire from political control of Cuba. The date for this event was January 28, 1909. Then, for the moment amid great popular acclaim, Magoon sailed for the United States and José Miguel Gomez, Liberal leader of the revolution of 1906, became the second President of Cuba.

The new chief of state was far from the stubborn ascetic type of the first President. Like Estrada Palma, he was a veteran of the revolution of 1868–78—he joined in 1875 as a boy of 17—and of that of 1895; but he was a better politician than soldier. In the interval between the two revolutions, he had become boss of the province of Santa Clara, a position he maintained by a combination of cajolery, compromise, and high-handed methods. In politics he associated himself with a number of men who were to become, like him, prominent in the fortunes of the Liberal party. These included Gerardo Machado, Orestes Ferrara, and Carlos Mendieta, all later prominent in Cuban politics. When Spanish rule ended, he was made civil governor of Santa Clara under the United States military government.

Gomez had supported Estrada Palma for his first election

and had brought about the revolution of 1906 through opposition to his second election, an action "vindicated" by his recent triumph. Friends and enemies agree that Gomez had unusual power over men. He commanded respect because of neither his learning nor his ideals, but "he had a way with him." He was not quick in movement, either physically or mentally. Politically—like Caesar—he was ambitious, and, like Caesar, he wished it to appear that he was not; but there the comparison ends. An admirer characterized him as "a great leader of crowds." [6] Consistency never bothered him, nor did graft in public office, from which he came greatly to profit. His commission on contracts became the ground for his nickname, "Old Six Per Cent." He was now to have the opportunity to demonstrate his capacity for leadership.

On the whole, Cuba was to prosper under Gomez. The island enjoyed in his four years that greatest of all good fortunes for political leaders, good crops and good prices. For such or for lack of such the government in Cuba, as elsewhere, is praised or blamed—with even less justification in Cuba than elsewhere. With "good times" popular discontent disappeared and public income increased—so remarkably that for a time it kept ahead of the demands of the executive and Congress. Public improvements were extended. There was dishonesty in public contracts, to be sure; but some real benefits the President did insist should be gotten from expenditures, and, as money "was easy," criticism was not insistent. This was, the President insisted, a "business man's administration"; he would favor business, and business prospered as did the President himself. He had never been a man of fortune before his election—his enemies called him a bankrupt planter—but financial abilities of a sort he rapidly developed, for, at the end of four years in the presidency on a salary of $25,000 per year, he was reputed to have "saved" over $8,000,000.

Nevertheless, some definite advantages for the public came from the Gomez regime. Railways and telephone lines were

---

[6] Juan Gualberto Gomez, quoted in Chapman, *op. cit.*, p. 273.

extended, lower duties were granted on supplies to develop industry, and higher duties on other groups of products were adopted to encourage new lines of local enterprise. Even the items clearly most touched with graft had elements of public advantage in them. The "Arsenal" lands on the harbor front, belonging to the city, were exchanged for the Villa Nueva lands in the center of the city which had belonged to the United Railways. Moving a railway station from the heart of the business section could be defended, especially if, as later occurred, the space could be used to advantage for government buildings. Surrendering public control of the waterfront, however, might not be a clear advantage, and the graft which attended the transactions was, of course, indefensible.

On the other side of the ledger are heavy debits—not all to be blamed on Gomez, for many of the items were sponsored by Congress. But certain it is that the President made no serious effort to oppose some of the bad legislation and actively favored part of it. Payrolls were systematically padded with "deserving" Liberals, friends of the political leaders. This, to be sure, was "an old Spanish custom" but one which previously had at least not had free rein in the republic. Amnesty bills, by which favored individuals were freed of responsibility for even common crimes, continued to flourish. Cockfighting was re-legalized. The national lottery was set up. The latter, also, had its roots in Spanish precedent, but it was shortly to flower as the most flagrant means of corrupting members of Congress and others.

The army was greatly expanded in size and the number of officers and their pay were generously increased. From top to bottom, the army came to be made up of loyal Gomez men. "José Miguel" was not to be caught napping as "Don Tomás" had been. He would have an army which would assure that no one should do to him what he did to his predecessor! At least he was a realist. He was moving to make the executive stronger. In the Constitution there was outlined a balance of power among three departments of government, such as existed in the United States. But in Cuba and in all Latin America, conditions were different, as had been amply proved by experience. Would it not be preferable to recognize the facts?

As his administration approached its close, reasons for the President's believing in the virtues of executive predominance increased. The best of these involved the selection of the chief of state for the next administration, a question which presidents in all lands have a tendency to answer one way at the beginning and another way at the end of their terms. Gomez was not an exception to the rule.

When the Liberal factions agreed to support him in 1908, Gomez had pledged that he would support Alfredo Zayas in 1912. He long continued to assert that he was not a candidate for re-election. At the end of January, 1911, he still declared, "I wish to have the honor of being the first who is opposed to his own re-election; I wish to give that example to my people." But from early in the administration Zayas, and others less interested, felt such declarations to be insincere. Indeed, even in the first years of the term, there seem to have been cases in which men were persecuted or spirited away or even killed in cold blood because they did not fall in with Gomez' plans, and the public service had been promptly and thoroughly raided to give place to Gomez' partisans.

As the four-year period came to a close, two incidents arose to trouble the President and to threaten anew intervention by the United States. The veterans' groups, wooed by a rival presidential candidate late in 1911, took steps which caused the United States to indicate its "grave concern." Perhaps influenced by the desire to avoid a new suspension of local government, terms to keep the peace were reached by the government and the dissenters. Early the following year a "race war" broke out. Gomez had toyed with the leaders of the colored groups and, it appears, had even furnished them funds. What his purpose was is disputed. Some critics believe that he intended to let the Negroes have a free hand to develop their plans and then to turn on them, put down the opposition of the blacks, and thus forward his own plans for re-election, a course which he could present as one demanded by the public safety. Others think that the Negro leaders were in the plot, and that there was to be made only a show of revolution, which could nevertheless serve Gomez' purpose. If this was the intent, the revolution got out of hand or some of the leaders misunderstood the plans, for by May, 1912, talk of revolution was over all the island and serious outbreaks had occurred in the east. Much to Gomez' chagrin, the United States landed troops to protect foreign property.[7] The revolt continued to spread and, before it was crushed in July, authority to declare a state of siege in any part of the island had been granted to the President and over 3,000 colored persons had been killed.

Gomez' plans had not worked out as he intended. The Zayistas had not relied upon his promise. Zayas wanted the nomination, and some other leading Liberals, including Gerardo Machado, were supporting him. In the party convention in May, Zayas came out the victor. There was no patching up of party differences as there had been four years before. The Liberals engaged in harsh criticism of each other. Gomez protested that he had not been active for any candidate, but in fact he seems to have thrown his influence to the Conservatives, as did other prominent anti-Zayas Liberals. The Conservatives had renominated their candidate of 1908 —Mario Menocal—and with the advantage of a united front they won the election.

The term of "José Miguel" came to a close on May 20, 1913. He had not given an honest administration and had done much to reintroduce the traditional governmental abuses associated with the colonial regime. On the other hand, if graft had flourished and if he and his friends had become rich, the plunder of the public purse had been "reasonable." The people had something for their money. To the credit of the administration it is to be said also that it might have "controlled" the election. There was no such falsification of the

---

[7] This intervention, in fact, the administration in Washington apparently considered not one under the terms of the "Permanent Treaty" but action under the broader authority to protect foreign property in disturbed areas under the rules of international law. See Chapman, *op. cit.*, p. 311.

voting lists as had occurred at the second Estrada Palma election, nor did Gomez use his army, as he might have done, to influence either nomination or election. The voting was not "fair," but it was "fairly fair" and the government peacefully turned control over to the opposite party. The record of Gomez was not one of which to be proud, but that it could have been worse subsequent administrations were amply to demonstrate.

None of the presidents of Cuba have entered upon their duties with more general acclaim than did Mario Menocal. Born two years before the outbreak of the Ten Years' War, he had spent much of his youth abroad. As a baby he had been taken to the United States and later as a young boy to Mexico. His education had been completed in American universities. He had come back to Cuba and had enlisted in the revolution of 1895, in which he rose from private to major-general. The war over, he was for a short time connected with the United States military government and then was employed as engineer and manager of the Chaparra sugar plantation of the Cuban American Sugar Company. He entered the presidency with the confidence of labor and capital. To Cubans he seemed the best type of revolutionary patriot; to foreigners he was the product of American environment and education. To all he was a business man, rich in his own right and through his own efforts rather than through "politics." But great hopes were to meet great disappointments!

The eight-year period covered by Menocal's two terms, 1913 to 1921, was a period of tremendous upheaval throughout the world in both political and economic affairs. Perhaps in no other country was the ship of state to a greater degree whipped by the economic storm caused by the World War, carried farther from its normal moorings, and dashed more cruelly on the rocks at its close. In justice to Menocal it is to be said that an administration which could have held an even course under the conditions he had to face would have been superhuman.

Sugar prices, which are the index of Cuban prosperity and, to a degree, of domestic peace on the island, underwent extraordinary variations. In the last months of the Gomez period they were low, and they continued so during the first year under Menocal. Crops in 1912–1913 and the following two years were good, averaging over 700,000 tons more than at any previous time.[8] Prices began to pick up as the European war created an unusual demand and military operations paralyzed production in the beet-sugar-producing districts.[9]

Sugar sold at extraordinarily high prices, the average rising every year, with one exception, up to 1920. At one time Cuban raw sugar sold at 22.50 cents per pound.[10] Plantations were pushed to their greatest yield. The total crop rose from 2,719,961 tons in 1912–1913 to 4,408,365 in 1920–1921—the last year of Menocal's administration. New centrals were set up, chiefly with American capital, to profit from the green gold. They contributed to the "dance of the millions" which affected all classes of Cubans, though their greatest yield came only in 1921, after the bubble of the new era had burst. Foreign trade rose between 1913 and 1920 from $304,203,000

---

[8] CUBAN SUGAR PRODUCTION IN CERTAIN YEARS *

In Thousands of Short Tons

1907–8	1077	1915–16	3398
1908–9	1695	1916–17	3422
1909–10	2021	1917–18	3890
1910–11	1661	1918–19	4491
1911–12	2124	1919–20	4184
1912–13	2720	1920–21	4406
1913–14	2909	1921–22	4517
1914–15	2922		

* Computed from *Statistical Abstract of Foreign Countries*, Great Britain, 1901–1912, p. 472, for 1907–1908, 1908–1909, and from *Commerce Yearbook*, 1932, Vol. II, *Foreign Countries*, Washington, 1933, p. 677, for later years (crop years).

[9] The average price per pound in cents for raw sugar in Cuban ports was:

1913	1.95	1918	4.24
1914	2.64	1919	5.06
1915	3.31	1920	11.95
1916	4.37	1921	3.10
1917	4.62		

(Quoted from *Industria Azucarera, Zafra de 1930*, p. 109, in Wright, Philip G., *The Cuban Situation and our Treaty Relations*, Washington, Brookings Institution, 1931, p. 54.)

[10] Statistics of Willet and Gray quoted in Farr and Company, *Manual of Sugar Companies*, 1928, New York, Farr and Co., 1928, p. 50.

to $1,351,026,000,[11] of which over a billion dollars' worth was with the United States. The per capita trade was greater than that of any other country in the world.

Habana, under the influence of the flood of new wealth, became the most brilliant of tropical capitals. Millowners became millionaires almost overnight, *colonos* who had lived on the simplest standard of life blossomed out in the finest creations of London tailors and Paris *couturières*. The suburbs of the metropolis became dream cities—except where construction was still under way when the "crack" which brought the dream to an end came. Probably no other city of the world has shown the effects of sudden wealth followed by sudden economic disaster more spectacularly than did Habana during and immediately following the Menocal regime.

If irregularities in government appeared in the term of Gomez, it might be expected that they would grow in the high tide of extravagance which characterized what have since been called in Cuba "the seven years of the fat cows." With government income rising along with the income of individuals, both executive and legislature embarked on an orgy of spending. Quibbles between the President and Congress over appropriations and loans in the opening years of the period were forgotten. Only once in Menocal's term did Congress go through the formality of authorizing a budget, and in later years the President had resort to the simpler method of authorizing expenditures by decree. But the rapidly increasing public revenue could not keep up with the pace in spending which the administration established. Loans were contracted at home and abroad. In his eight years, Menocal spent about $600,000,000, besides creating a heavy floating debt. This does not include the expenditures of local governmental units. If these are included, the total may have been a billion.[12]

How were these funds disbursed? Menocal, unlike Gomez,

---

[11] *Commerce Yearbook*, 1926, Vol. II, *Foreign Countries*, Washington, 1927, p. 174.

[12] Chapman, *op. cit.*, p. 393.

it is said, did not profit directly from his position, though soft jobs were lavishly distributed among his extensive family connections. But whatever the amounts which went into these channels, they account for only a small fraction of the total disbursements. His defenders point to appropriations authorized for a long list of public works, including schools, hospitals, bridges, municipal improvements, waterworks, roads, and port improvements. Only a part of these, however, were actually undertaken. His enemies maintain that public services, far from being improved, steadily ran down. Large sums were spent for an elaborate presidential palace costing more than twice as much as the White House at Washington; heavy expenditures for other public works showed even less return.

A long list of "accomplishments" in legislation, involving small or no appropriations, are claimed for Menocal. They include reform of the currency, a real though not fundamental accomplishment. He declared for abolishing the lottery, but it continued. He opposed concessions for *jai alai,* the pelota or Basque handball of Spain, and for horse racing—but both were established. A concession for improvement of ports inherited from the Gomez administration, which had caused much criticism, was canceled by repurchase but under conditions which did not reflect credit on the administration.

Menocal's second term opened almost contemporaneously with the entry of the United States into the World War. Menocal promptly aligned himself with the Allies. German ships lying in Cuban harbors were seized. Red Cross activities were fostered and hospital units were sent to France. The army was strengthened, but no units were sent to Europe: it was used to maintain order at home, for Cuba could be of greatest service by assuring an adequate sugar supply. Restrictions on food consumption similar to those adopted in the United States were enforced.

But there is little of permanent value which can be credited by the people of Cuba to the eight years under her Conservative President. A period of unexampled prosperity had passed over the island but had left it little if any better off than it had been at the beginning. When the sugar prosperity bubble broke in the fall of 1920, most of the paper fortunes which it had created vanished with it. Work on the marble palaces of the cities, particularly that of the capital, suddenly ceased. The financial institutions faced bankruptcy, the sugar centrals could not meet the services on their mortgages, and the investments of citizens and foreigners "went flat."

Meanwhile, what were political developments in the abnormal Menocal period? They grouped themselves around the perennial problems of public order and the elections, both of which at times threatened to cause serious disturbance and to demand new "interventions" by the United States.

The President had been elected in 1912 possibly because of the split among the Liberal factions quite as much as by the strength of the Conservatives. In his first term he lent himself to developing the latter and to undermining the influence of his Liberal predecessor, who had contributed not a little to Menocal's success by his refusal to give support to the Liberal candidate Zayas. In the mid-term elections, the Liberals had won control of the lower branch of the Congress. But as the election of 1916 approached, the desire for another term overcame the President's declared intent to serve only for four years. In this change he was following the path of Estrada Palma and Gomez. But now the Conservative leaders were split in their allegiance, and Menocal secured renomination, it is asserted, only by manipulation of the membership of the convention and by falsification of the count of the votes.

The Liberals were even more divided, over half a dozen offering themselves as candidates to head the state in the fat years which were evidently coming. Gomez was a prominent candidate. So was Alfredo Zayas, unsuccessful running mate of Gomez in 1905, his successful running mate in 1908, and the unsuccessful presidential nominee of the Liberals in 1912. He won the nomination—but was denounced by Gomez and a number of other Liberals. Then dissatisfied groups in each party, as usual, deserted to the other.

Zayas and Gomez patched up their differences, and soon there was under way a heated campaign in which both sides were guilty of violence. The Liberals charged that Menocal would steal the election. They would have "Zayas or Revolution." Widespread abuses by both parties undoubtedly occurred in the voting on November 1, 1916. "It is said that there were over a million names on the voting lists and that about eight hundred thousand votes were cast. Yet, three years later the census was to show that there were only 477,786 eligible voters in Cuba. And the election was close!"[13] Menocal, it appears, was at first disposed to concede defeat but through control of the count of the votes "stole" the election. Would the Liberals go out in revolution as they had done when Estrada Palma "stole" the election from their candidate?

On the surface, affairs developed a curious parallel to those after the election of 1906. Would the United States Government again be forced to take a hand, and could the Liberals count on its again following the doubtful precedent then established? Zayas called on Menocal to guarantee fair treatment of the Liberals in supplementary elections which had been called in Santa Clara. If fairly conducted, they might have given the Liberals the election. But Menocal refused. The Liberals then declined to go to the polls and in February, 1917, went out in revolution—once more with Gomez at their head.

But the United States was not to follow the 1906 precedent. It had become clearer, perhaps, that the policy followed in 1906 might repeatedly put the defeated and disgruntled party in a position to force intervention practically at its own will. In addition—a practical consideration—it was already evident that the United States could not much longer remain out of the European war, for which a generous supply of Cuban sugar had importance. Further, while Estrada Palma had had no army on which he could rely, Menocal had a sizable force the majority of which stood

---

[13] *Ibid.*, pp. 353–354.

by him, and he was ready to use it. The army had, it will be remembered, been strengthened in the Gomez administration! Whatever the motive explaining the change of attitude, the United States did not intervene. It declared that it would hold the revolutionaries responsible for destruction of property, gave its moral support to Menocal, and sold him large supplies of arms.

Menocal on his side handled affairs with a high hand. Constitutional guarantees were suspended. A reign of terror had been established in the provinces, so the Liberals asserted, to control the supplementary elections which had been agreed upon; and, when the revolution got under way, the army was put into active operation. By May, opposition had been practically suppressed and Menocal's second term began.

The position which the United States had taken was, in this case, as in 1906, subject to widespread criticism by the losers. In both cases its action had been consistent in that it had earnestly sought to avoid intervention. It had been forced to come to it in 1906. Eleven years later it succeeded in avoiding it, unless supporting the government in power in itself be called intervention. In the first case, intervention came because the Cuban administration abdicated; in the second, it did not become necessary because the administration "stood by its guns." But at best, in both cases, the policy followed represented only a choice between bad alternatives. To have supported the government in power in 1906 would have been to support fraud against force—of the Liberal revolutionists. Was the support given in 1917 backing a government based on both fraud and force?

If the circumstances of the election in 1916 were bad, those attending that in 1920 were worse. Gomez and Zayas fell out again after the 1916 contest, but Gomez was again by 1920 the greatest influence among the Liberals. Zayas recognized that his influence among his former associates had declined, but his desire to continue his perennial campaign for the presidency was as strong as ever. It prompted him to consider making peace with Menocal, who might recognize that the chance for a Conservative victory in 1920 was poor and who might welcome a chance to split the Liberals and at least defeat Gomez, for whom he cherished a long-standing dislike.

Fusion of the "Popular" party, Zayas' new faction, and the Conservatives might turn the trick. By 1920 these highly contrasted factions had become associated. Meanwhile both parties had come to recognize that another election under the law in force in 1916 would almost certainly bring another threat to public order. An invitation was issued to General Enoch H. Crowder, who had had a prominent part in electoral reforms in the Magoon period, to assist in drafting a new electoral law, and one was on the statute books well before the election.

But laws were only paper under the conditions which the contest developed. Menocal had no intention of allowing a free election, and the Liberals in August threatened to withdraw from the voting, apparently hoping thus to force intervention. At any rate, they had no intention of being cheated of victory again. The United States on August 30 made it clear "that the Liberals had better go to the polls."[14] It would send "observers," whose presence it was hoped might minimize if not eliminate force and fraud in the choice. They were sent but were without power of control, and as a result Menocal proceeded with practically a free hand.

In the elections the army was widely used to intimidate voters, and pardoned criminals were used to the same end. In some districts the Liberals also were guilty of serious abuses. When the voting was over, the struggle was carried, under the provisions of the new electoral law, to the courts with unsatisfactory results. The Liberals suggested that a provisional government be set up by the United States to hold new elections. It was increasingly evident that this time, unless outside pressure were brought to bear, civil war was ahead.

There now began a far-reaching and continued intervention

---

[14] See Chapman, *op. cit.*, p. 402 *et seq.*, for detailed discussion of the means used to control the voting.

in Cuban affairs, though it was not then and has not since been formally called by that name. General Crowder suddenly reappeared as the representative of President Wilson. He pointed out that the disputes over elections must be expedited or the government in power would end its term before the choice of a successor. The cases in the courts were expedited. Elections in about a fifth of the districts were found fraudulent and new ones were ordered. The crisis might have passed quickly; but, as the new elections approached, the old party bitterness flamed up again, and the Liberals once more threatened to refuse to stay in the electoral contest. Such actions are not infrequent in Latin countries but are hard for those familiar with electoral contests in Anglo-Saxon communities to understand. The Liberals became convinced that they were again going to be cheated, and refused to go to the polls. As a result, the Conservatives, of course, carried the day. Had they voted, it is widely believed, the Liberals would have won; but, as they did not, they had only to declaim against another "stolen election." Gomez went to Washington to appeal for establishment of a provisional government and holding of new elections but without success; so Zayas, on May 20, 1921, at last achieved his often disappointed ambition. He was President of Cuba.

No other Cuban President has been so sharply criticized by Cubans and by foreigners as Alfredo Zayas, and of none has harsh criticism been easier to justify. In Latin-American countries the power of the executive is regularly so great that the record made by the government turns to a high degree about the abilities of the president. Zayas had perhaps the greatest opportunity of any chief of state in Cuba to render his country great service, and, by general agreement, no other President ever failed her so signally. In the first half of his term the character of the man was obscured through the fact that the veiled "intervention" headed by General Crowder continued and forced a "moralization" and "sanitation" in public affairs in spite of the local administration. In the last half, the crisis being past and the position of General Crowder changed, Zayas was free to show his qualities.

The term opened auspiciously. The President announced a program of economy and of long-needed reforms. At least part of the pronouncements are credited to Crowder's insistence. His attempts to help in assuring a fair election had been a failure, but at the moment he was in a position practically to dictate to the new President. This was a consequence of the fact that Cuba was in desperate financial straits and would clearly need generous help from outside the island if public credit were to be maintained. The control of the public purse, so far as the public purse depended on foreign assistance, lay not with the local government but with Crowder as representative of the country, without whose cooperation a foreign loan could not be secured. And, as a condition precedent for obtaining money, reforms could be demanded. Cuban critics later declaimed against the activity of the American representative in "forcing a loan on Cuba," but what actually occurred was that the local government was forced to take steps to improve its credit position and to abolish long-standing abuses as the condition of securing the funds which were essential to keep the country solvent.

Economic conditions were already bad when the Zayas administration began. Government receipts were still running high but the crisis of 1920 was hanging over the country. High prices were no longer received for sugar, most of the centrals were already in financial difficulties, and the banks which had extended credit accounts or had mortgage commitments with the sugar producers were embarrassed.

Business of all sorts had purchased heavily in the belief that the prosperity of the island would continue and now found itself overwhelmed through inability to collect outstanding bills. Merchants were carrying extraordinarily high stocks and were thrown into added difficulties by the arrival of large quantities of goods orders which had been placed at high prices in the boom days but which were no longer desired. The high level of imports into the republic, coupled with refusals to accept shipments, brought congestion at the ports, especially Habana, with the result that the customs administration broke down and commercial claims involving merchandise of value variously estimated at from sixty to eighty million dollars against the government arose. In addition, the suppliers of the government and those who had taken contracts for public works were clamoring for payment on their accounts, which were the greater part of a floating debt reported as over forty million dollars. Payments on the public debt service had temporarily gone into default and had been resumed only through an emergency loan advanced by bankers through the good offices of the United States.

Assistance in clearing up the confusion in public finance was the first essential, and Crowder was for the moment in a position to make demands which Zayas would be forced to grant. The floating debt was first attacked. It was honeycombed with accounts involving exaggerated claims for payment on contracts for public works part of which were fraudulent and some of which referred to construction which had not even been begun. Zayas unwillingly consented to an investigation and grudgingly permitted "squeezing out the water" from the floating debt account by the annulling of illegal contracts and by reduction of payments on others in which the contract prices were exorbitant.

Demands for a cleanup in lines other than public works followed in a series of memoranda from Crowder to Zayas. Among them were calls for cutting down current budget expenses, the elimination of graft in administrative departments,[15] and ascertainment of the actual total of all Government indebtedness. Without the latter information no basis for discussion of the terms of the proposed foreign loan existed. Other efforts, at the time less successful, looked toward the rehabilitation of the local banks which had broken down throughout the island, and the elimination or at least reduction of the abuses of gambling, prostitution, and blackmail.

For any effective "moralization" it became evident that the personnel of even the highest offices in the administration had to be changed. By June, 1922, Zayas had been forced to get

[15] See Chapman, *op. cit.*, p. 428 *et seq.* The commercial organizations of Habana added their influence to the demand for a thorough "sanitation" of the Government in all branches.

rid of his secretaries and appoint an "Honest Cabinet"—at least part of the members of which had probably been passed upon by Crowder. The co-operation of this group greatly strengthened the hands of the latter and explains much of the betterment which occurred.

In July, 1922, Crowder issued the thirteenth of the memoranda, in which his "advice" to the Zayas government had been outlined. It swept into a single document a review of evils faced and of the major steps which still demanded attention. Only this one of the series has been published, but even alone it furnishes a sad picture of the level to which the government of Cuba had sunk. Its printing let loose a flood of comment, some denouncing the government and some the "foreign dictatorship." For the rest of the year and for the first part of 1923, however, Zayas continued to grant unwilling co-operation. Even he recognized that the obtaining of a foreign loan—accepted as $50,000,000—was essential both for Cuba and for his administration.

The loan contract was signed early in 1923. The act marked the turning point in the administration. Zayas now "had the money" and Crowder no longer had the whip hand. Sugar crops turned out well and prices for sugar improved. Government income rose and happy days were on the way back. The President became the champion of "nationalism." Foreign influence was not to be tolerated. The "Honest Cabinet" was revamped by elimination of men recognized as its strongest members. Their successors were more pliant. Purchases of property for the government, notably that of the Santa Clara Convent, which brought handsome profits to the President and his associates, were arranged. The lottery was "reformed" with the same result.

Crowder was still in Cuba, but "circumstances alter cases." The local government no longer desperately needed assistance, and Crowder, after January, 1923, was American Ambassador to Cuba and limited in his actions by diplomatic custom. He did write some memoranda protesting against new abuses, but they fell on deaf ears. Possibly support from Washington, even such as could be given through diplomatic channels, became less consistent now that the real crisis was passed. Perhaps "forward action" became less popular because of the approaching Pan-American Conference, to be held in Chile from March to May, 1923, where any "interventionist" activity would be roundly denounced. At any rate Zayas soon realized that he could count on a free hand in developing his "nationalistic policy" to "save" Cuba.

A series of doubtful laws to favor railroad combinations as against groups using certain so-called private ports for sugar shipments was pushed to passage. A public statement charged that one of these laws had involved minimum payments of $6,000 to representatives, $20,000 to senators, and $500,000 to Zayas. Though nominally the legislation was part of a "nationalistic" program to help Cuban railways, the result was to strengthen the position of foreign interests, chiefly American, in control of Cuban transportation facilities.

These and other measures colored by graft were matched by minor peculations. Dozens of the President's relatives moved into the national palace. Large numbers received sinecures or soft contracts. Those in power managed to get an irregular income from the import of laborers for the sugar harvest, chiefly Haitians but including also Chinese—the immigration of whom was contrary to law. As the term drew to an end, and especially after it became evident that Zayas would not be re-elected, the enthusiasm for what "pickings" were left increased. An expropriation project on the Habana waterfront which brought fat "commissions" on the $2,247,075 ordered paid was put through. Comparable measures effected "improvements" in the provinces. Systematic levies on gambling houses and prostitution were perfected. This is not a list of the measures to "milk the cow dry" adopted in the closing years of the Zayas regime but merely a citing of examples of the low actions to which the administration stooped. No similar orgy of corruption had ever been known in Cuban annals.

To the credit of the better classes of Cuba must be put their reaction to the progressive degeneration which was occurring in their public affairs. They worked under patent disadvantages in attempting to stop the debacle. Civic organizations and the press put on a campaign demanding that steps be taken to stem the tide but without success. At bottom lay the handicap that the opposition, as has been regularly the case in Cuba, lacked unity of organization, a consequence of the personal basis on which politics run. Protests were not backed up by concrete programs of reform. Further, the United States had recognized the Zayas administration, and its policy was to recognize "constitutional" governments.[16] It would certainly not encourage revolution; in fact, it sold arms to Zayas to put down the revolutionary movements which did arise.

The better classes were thus to a large extent free to protest but powerless to act. The Veterans and Patriots Association and other extra-political organizations held meetings in which abuses were roundly condemned and a program practically paralleling that recently advocated by Crowder was supported. A general revolution was not infrequently threatened, but to the end no sizable outbreak occurred.

Elections came around again in 1924. Like his predecessors, Zayas had given a one-term pledge; and, like them, he changed his mind. Early in the year he announced his candidacy. He had deserted the Liberals in 1920. José Miguel Gomez was now dead and the leading Liberal was one of his former associates, Gerardo Machado, who had denounced the Zayas administration. The Zayas-Menocal combination of 1920 had weakened, and in the Conservative convention Menocal himself won the nomination. Could Zayas now shift his Popular faction to a coalition with the Liberals and become the nominee of both of these parties? It at one time seemed possible; but, by August, 1924, the President evidently realized that his record was so bad that re-election in a fair contest was impossible and that an unfair one would result in a general appeal to arms. He decided to support Machado.

[16] 1923 was the year of the Central American treaties favoring the same standards.

Gerardo Machado y Morales had much to recommend him. His record in the revolution of 1895–1898 was creditable if not brilliant. He had been a consistent Liberal, and Cuba has normally been Liberal to a far greater degree than the result of its elections indicates. Since 1917 he had been out of active politics and had built up a sizable fortune. He had an acceptable personality. For the moment, apparently as a political gesture, he declaimed against the Platt Amendment—always a good issue in Cuban campaigns. While his pre-election declarations against abuses in government lacked explicitness, he had no such record behind him as had Menocal, who was reputed so unpopular with the electorate that many Cuban writers believed that anyone could beat him. Thousands would vote the Liberal ticket for the privilege of voting against Menocal.

The election of 1924 was not free from disorder and casualties, though the degree to which the administration attempted to shape the result appears not to have been great. Far-reaching control was not necessary to assure a Liberal victory. After the contest the Conservatives made the usual claims that the election was stolen and talked revolution, but Menocal shortly acknowledged defeat—it is alleged, on the urgings of Crowder.

The record of the first Machado term in fair measure justified the forecasts made at the time he entered office. In foreign relations minor adjustments with the United States were made and no serious issues with other countries arose. The accomplishment in domestic affairs was less praiseworthy. The far-reaching "moralization" in government promised in pre-election announcements did not materialize. Padding of public payrolls continued, bribing of legislators apparently went on as before, and, as hard times became harder, popular dissatisfaction grew.

The administration had not created the crisis, and in fairness it must be said that it could do little to relieve it. Efforts were made to do so. The President backed a program to reduce the economic dependence on the sugar industry by diversifying agriculture through the re-establishment of crops formerly raised, such as coffee, and through the introduction of new ones—especially seasonal products which might find good markets abroad. Resort was had to tariffs to encourage local yield of corn, eggs, livestock, and other farm products. Another set of measures looked to the creation of light industries. Commendable progress was made in a large number of lines to the advantage of the Cuban trade balance. But general improvement through such a program cannot come quickly, and that which did occur was not sufficient to make the economic horizon bright.

Less success attended the efforts of Cuba, at first independently and later in co-operation with groups in other sugar-exporting areas, to limit the sugar crop in the hope of thus bringing about a rise in price. The public works program, long before advocated but now expanded and carried out, also brought disappointment. It did doubtless relieve the dissatisfaction rising from increasing unemployment, but it did not quicken general economic activity as it was expected to do. The chief feature in the plan was the building of the "central highway," which might in the long run, it is true, increase production in areas previously difficult of access but the effect of which would not be immediate. In addition, large amounts were spent on lines clearly nonproductive, such as an elaborate capitol. All in all, the public works program, though it did offer temporary relief, greatly increased the calls upon the taxpayers and the public credit at a time when neither of these could easily carry the increased burden.

At bottom, however, the economic program of the administration would probably have passed without criticism if it had brought about, or been contemporaneous with, the return of prosperity. But the Machado regime fell upon an unbroken series of unsatisfactory years. Estrada Palma had had the advantage of a recovering sugar industry, Gomez ruled in prosperous years, the Menocal period was that of high, wartime prices, and even Zayas, in the later years of his administration, had had the benefit of good returns for sugar. But Machado had none of these things. The sugar trade, the key of Cuban prosperity, was unprosperous.[17] A flooded world market brought an almost unbroken decline in the price of sugar which efforts to restrict production and export sales failed to check. Since the value of exports fell, imports declined and with them the income of the treasury.[18] The pub-

[17] The capacity of Cuban plantations continued high, owing to the increased facilities created in the boom and post-boom years. Restriction of the crop actually harvested and control of export sales were abandoned at the end of 1928. Control on an international basis in co-operation with other countries contributing to the world market was shortly attempted, but without favorable results.

STATISTICS OF THE CUBAN SUGAR INDUSTRY FOR CERTAIN YEARS *

Year	*Sugar Produced— 1000 Long Tons*	*Average Price per Pound— Cents*	*Total Value— Thousands of Dollars*
1922–23	3645	4.90	400,181
1923–24	4112	4.00	368,497
1924–25	5189	2.35	273,167
1925–26	4932	2.22	245,263
1926–27	4509	2.64	266,621
1927–28	4038	2.18	197,175
1928–29	5156	1.72	198,661
1929–30	4671	1.23	128,702
1930–31	3121	1.11	77,583
1931–32	2604	.72	41,981
1932–33	1995		

* Compiled from *Commerce Yearbook*, 1929, Vol. II, *Foreign Countries*, p. 189; *ibid.*, 1932, *op. cit.*, Vol. II, p. 404; *Foreign Commerce Yearbook*, 1933, p. 194.

[18] CERTAIN ECONOMIC CONDITIONS IN CUBA IN THE YEARS FOLLOWING 1924 *

Year	*Total Foreign Trade in Millions of Dollars*		*Value of Raw Sugar Exports in Millions of Dollars*	*Amount of Sugar Exports in Millions of Pounds*	*Government Receipts* [a] *in Millions of Pesos (Dollars)*	*Government Expenditures* [a] *in Millions of Pesos (Dollars)*	*Public Debt* [b] *in Millions of Dollars*	
	Imports	*Exports*					*Internal*	*External*
1924	289	434	374	8,750	96 [d]	93 [d]	21	94
1925	297	353	280	10,882	98	93	12	88
1926	260	301	237	10,299	92	88	11	82
1927	257	322	254	9,021	84	83	11	85
1928	212	278	199	8,302	85	83	10	80 [c]
1929	216	272	188	10,271	90	87	10	74 [c]
1930	162	167	92	6,566	77	81	9	68 [c]
1931	80	118	65 [f]	5,254 [g]	60	68	8	65
1932	51 [e]	81 [e]	...	5,991 [g]	47 [h]	44 [h]	8	60

* Compiled from *Commerce Yearbook*, Vol. II, *Foreign Countries*, for various years.

[a] For the fiscal periods ending in the years indicated. These figures are for the regular budgetary receipts. They do not include the public works and

lic works program by 1928 was increasing the national debt and was shortly to do so in much greater degree.

By the end of his first administration Machado faced widespread criticism. He was being denounced as a dictator who had broken down political opposition and connived at and even sponsored driving some opponents into exile and assassinating others. The rights of free speech and assembly no longer existed and justice was a farce. These charges were given blanket denial but steadily increased.

Political criticism was sharpened by the growing conviction that Machado intended to continue his control through a second term of four years or longer. Like so many other Cuban candidates for the presidency, he had loudly proclaimed his intention to accept but one term. In 1924, before his election, he stated: "A Liberal President cannot be re-elected. This is now a noble tradition—the most noble of this party." He would serve the office four years; "No power on earth," he announced, "will keep me in it one single day longer. . . ." In 1927 he would still stand by this pledge, for "a man who had never failed to keep his word, a man whose lips had never been defiled by a lie, would lower his dignity, and dishonor himself, if after . . . twenty-five years" of opposition to re-election, he should accept it.[19] But if he meant these words, he changed his mind. In fact, from early in his administration there had been taken steps which, if they were not in the beginning intended to favor the continuance of Machado in power beyond his first term, at least facilitated his keeping control when he did decide that he wished to do so.

---

certain other special funds. The entries for certain years in official documents vary in a number of cases.

[b] The dates to which these totals apply are not uniform within the years cited.

[c] Not including "public works serial certificates." The public works debt was reported as of February 29, 1932, as $93,750,000.

[d] *Commerce Yearbook*, 1925, Vol. II, p. 627.

[e] *Moody's Governments*, Apr. 22, 1933, p. 1346.

[f] Secretaria de Hacienda, Sección de estadística, año natural de 1931, Habana, 1932, p. 26.

[g] *Moody's Governments*, January 18, 1933, p. 1498.

[h] *Moody's Governments*, May 17, 1933, p. 1296.

[19] Quotations from Buell, Ramond Leslie, "Cuba and the Platt Amendment," *Foreign Policy Information Service*, April 17, 1929, New York, Foreign Policy Association, citing contemporary Cuban sources.

In 1925 the Congress changed the electoral code which had been adopted with General Crowder's advice in a way which made it difficult to reorganize old parties or set up new ones. Party control was put in the hands of the respective contingents in the Congress. Machado, it is asserted—he repeatedly denied the charge—thus became able to influence and did influence the leaders of all factions through the distribution to Congressmen of "collectorships" in the government lottery which gave the control over the sale of blocks of lottery tickets to those favored. From this control they could reap large supplements to their official salaries.

The next step taken in 1927 involved changes in the Constitution, some of which had long been discussed. The fundamental law could be altered through amendments proposed by Congress, which were to be referred to a constitutional convention which in turn was to adopt them or reject them—presumably without change. Congress suggested a long list of amendments the politically significant of which included proposals that the president should serve a single term of six years, and that the terms of representatives should be increased from four to six years and those of senators from eight to nine years. Thus far, the changes might be defended, but less disinterested were the clauses providing that the new rule should apply to those already in office, including the President.

The constitutional convention which was to pass on the amendments met on May 9, 1928. When the clause concerning the presidential term came up for consideration, the convention kept the six-year term and removed the provision for extending the administration of Machado for two years, but provided that the single-term limitation should not apply to the approaching election. The amendments were declared part of the Constitution on May 11, 1928. Thus, Machado was free to run for a second term. Indeed, the assembly had declared him "unavoidably bound to accept a new presidential period."[20] Thus besought, the President openly became a

---

[20] *Ibid.*, p. 40.

candidate. If elected, he might serve for ten years in all.

The amendments strengthened the already growing opposition to the President, for, their content having been altered by the convention, ground was given for arguing that the Constitution had been changed unconstitutionally and that all acts under the new provisions were therefore invalid. This position was at least partially sustained by subsequent decisions in the Cuban courts. But on May 20, 1929, Machado, having been "elected" by all parties, entered on his second term—to run six years.

Groups opposing the administration had no unity among themselves. They included part of the old Conservatives, led by ex-President Menocal, the opposition Liberals, leadership of whom had now fallen on the son of José Miguel Gomez, and an unrecognized group practically a party, the Unión Nacionalista, led by Carlos Mendieta. Less formal political oppositionists who later became increasingly active were a group made up of former professors and students in the University of Habana, which Machado had closed, the A.B.C., characterized as a terrorist organization composed largely of students or former students, and a nihilistic society known as the O.C.R.R.

As the second term ran on, the economic outlook continued to darken. Criticism of Machado tended to be expressed in open clashes with the police which were followed by new strong-arm measures of repression. Assassinations by both sides became frequent and the number of Cubans who fled to exile grew apace.

Both sides, or at least representatives of both sides, defended and criticized the United States and its policy. Machado at times sought to justify his actions by posing as the defender of Cuba against intervention, which would follow disorder. At other times he pointed to the fact that his government was "recognized" as proof that the United States backed him and relied on him to carry out the obligations of the Platt Amendment. At still other times he posed as the defender of Cuba and the United States against "Bolshevism." The opposition stand varied from declaring that the United

States ought to intervene under the obligations it had assumed under the Platt Amendment, to assertions that the anti-Machado group would create conditions which would force intervention to get rid of the dictator, and denouncement of the Platt Amendment as an insult to Cuban sovereignty and as the cause of Machado's remaining in power.

To outsiders it was evident that the United States would, as usual, go far to avoid interfering in Cuban internal affairs. Acceptance of the Root interpretation of the relations of the republics under the Platt Amendment seemed to be gaining over the broader meaning it had been given in more recent years. The ambassadors sent by the Hoover and Roosevelt administrations favored neither side, but within the scope of their authority were willing to give counsel looking toward peaceable adjustment among the factions.

President Hoover in 1929 made it known that he did not intend sending a representative who should undertake a veiled intervention such as had occurred under the leadership of General Crowder. At one time in 1930 revolution seemed imminent, but Secretary of State Stimson intimated that intervention would not be considered as long as it could possibly be avoided. Revolt did break out in August of the following year in three provinces, but Machado's well-paid and still loyal army brought it to an early end by the use of the new central highway, army trucks, machine guns, and airplanes. Again the policy of the United States was announced to be "no intervention till anarchy exists."

For two years more Cuban affairs, economic and political, continued to become more critical, but Machado held on. The change of administration brought no new policy in the United States. Locally, except for a brief period in 1933, opposition strengthened and the chance of compromise became dimmer, but President Roosevelt continued to show himself anxious to let Cuba work out her own problems.[21]

The rising tide of opposition was not to permit the conclu-

---

[21] The later political developments in the Machado administration are summarized from Fitzgibbon, Russell H., *Relations Between the United States and Cuba Since 1900,* Menasha, Wis., the George Banta Publishing Co., 1933.

sion of Machado's second term. In August, 1933, a general strike was called to try to force his resignation. The President, who was now generally decried as a dictator, proclaimed "a state of war," thinking to rely on the army to hold him in power. Dissatisfaction spread, however, even among the ranks of the soldiers, and Machado suddenly took the resolution to resign and fled the country by airplane to the Bahamas. A provisional government, headed by Carlos Manuel Céspedes, son of one of the Presidents during the war of 1868–1878, was installed. It was promptly recognized by the United States. Though his was a compromise administration including members of the chief groups dissatisfied with the Machado regime, it held power only to September 5, when another shift in control, due to dissatisfaction in the rank and file of the army, occurred.

Ramon Grau San Martin, a surgeon and professor of the University of Habana, was raised to the chief magistracy. President Roosevelt assured representatives of Latin-American countries at a White House conference that the United States was earnestly desirous of avoiding intervention. He did not recognize the new government, which refused to co-operate with other anti-Machado groups and which represented only a small group of public opinion.

The new administration held power, though with declining prestige, until January 15, 1934, when it gave place to a fleeting government under Carlos Hevia, which shortly yielded to another headed by Carlos Mendieta, old-time Liberal and associate of José Miguel Gomez. This group, which embraced representatives of the chief groups critical of the old regime, was promptly recognized by the United States on January 23 and addressed itself to the difficult task of regeneration.

On May 29, 1934, an important step in modifying relations with the United States was taken through the signing of a treaty, to securing which the Mendieta government had committed itself, superseding the political convention signed at Habana on May 22, 1903. The so-called Platt Amendment was to pass into history, to be replaced by a convention confirming the existing rights of the United States in the naval station at Guantánamo, the acts of the United States during its military occupation of the island up to May 20, 1902, and the rights acquired thereunder, and declaring the right of either Government to stop communications with any of the ports of either in which contagious diseases might threaten to become prevalent. Any intervention which might occur in Cuba in the future would rest, therefore, on the general rules of international law rather than on separate treaty provisions.[22]

Less easy of solution promised to be the economic problems which still beset the republic owing to the continued low price of sugar and the burden of the public debt, which had greatly increased during the Machado regime.

Cuban foreign trade had fallen sharply in value during the world depression, and the domestic policy of the United States, especially in relation to sugar imports, continued to be a serious handicap to the leading Cuban industry. The sugar problem was, of all those which the new government faced, by far the most serious. Cubans wished particularly to secure more favorable access to the sugar market of the United States than was now given the republic under the reciprocity treaty and the tariff legislation subsequently passed by the United States.[23]

A partial satisfaction of this desire was obtained in an agreement effective September 3, 1934, supplementing the commercial convention of 1902. By it each of the republics extended further concessions to the trade of the other on a long list of items. Substantial reduction was made on the rates on Cuban sugar, though action taken by the United States to limit the amount of sugar which would be admitted from Cuba made the advantages granted less than would otherwise have been the case.[24]

Serious also was the problem of the public debt. The in-

---

[22] Text in *Congressional Record,* May 29, 1934.

[23] See, for detail on the economic and political consequences of the restriction of the United States market, Wright, Philip G., *The Cuban Situation and Our Treaty Relations,* Washington, Brookings Institution, 1931.

[24] *Executive Agreement Series, No. 67,* Washington, 1934.

ternal and external funded public debt,[25] which on June 30, 1915, was reported as $70,204,000, had been reduced to $59,901,400 on December 31, 1933. But internal disorder and the reduced revenue which resulted from the declining economic activity of the country caused it to be less favorably situated to meet the interest on these obligations. In addition, other classes of expenditures, chiefly those for public works carried on in the Machado regime,[26] brought the total amount of public obligations to $158,567,060. The status of the public works debt, amounting to $80,867,000, became the basis of sharp division of opinion in the island. A partial default thereon occurred on June 30, 1933, and payments were completely suspended at the end of the year. The interest payments on the "regular external debt" were maintained throughout 1933, but sinking fund payments fell into arrears in 1934. Obviously, the task of the present Cuban administration was not only to build up for the republic more normal political relationships, domestic and international, but to work out an adjustment of an economic and financial situation of great difficulty.

In the long view, however, providing a market for Cuban products could be secured under satisfactory conditions, economic problems might decline in importance, and political difficulties might be made much easier of solution.

---

[25] The amount of the floating debt is not ascertainable. It was estimated by the Department of the Treasury of Cuba as about $50,000,000 on June 30, 1933.

[26] This item was reported as $80,867,000 on December 31, 1933.

CHAPTER IV

The Dominican Republic and the Establishment of Customs Control

THOUGH now less in the forefront of Caribbean relations than was the case a quarter of a century ago, the events in the Dominican Republic deserve special attention because it was there that some of the problems of international policy which still play a prominent role in the region first appeared in acute form, and because there some of the most marked successes and failures of the means adopted to solve them have occurred.

The island of Haiti—of which the Dominican Republic now forms almost exactly two-thirds—has a number of times swung into prominence in international affairs, only soon to fall back into insignificance.[1]

---

[1] The *Foreign Relations of the United States,* giving the official review of Dominican relations, contains fairly detailed entries only for the period from 1903 to 1917. The best secondary reviews of Dominican conditions are Welles, Sumner, *Naboth's Vineyard,* New York, Harcourt, Brace and Co., 1928; Schoenrich, Otto, *Santo Domingo,* New York, the Macmillan Co., 1918; Jacob H. Hollander in "The Convention of 1907 between the United States and the Dominican Republic," in *American Journal of International Law,* 1907, Vol. I, pp. 287–96; "Financial Difficulties of San Domingo," in *Annals of the American Academy,* 1907, Vol. XXX, pp. 93 ff., and "The Readjustment of San Domingo's Finances," in *Quarterly Journal of Economics,* 1907, Vol. XXI, pp. 405 ff., gives reviews of the adjustments of 1905 and 1907. A good description of the debt adjustment is in Schoenrich, *op. cit.,* pp. 350–408. Current economic developments are reported in *Annual Reports of the General Receiver of Customs of the Dominican Republic to the Bureau of Insular Affairs,* 1907 to date. (Title and place of publication vary.) The *Hearings Before a Select Committee on Haiti and Santo Domingo,* United States Senate, 67th Congress, 1st Session, Pursuant to S. Res. 112, Washington, 1922, gives a detailed discussion defending and criticizing American action in the republic. A critical review of the action of the United States is Knight, Melvin M., *The Americans in Santo Domingo,* New York, Vanguard Press, 1928. A comprehensive study of this subject from the Domini-

It was, with the exception of Cuba, the first of the major islands of the West Indies to be discovered by Columbus, and on it were made the first attempts at settlement. But after the initial glow of enthusiasm following the discovery of the New World, attention turned elsewhere—westward—to richer lands, especially those which yielded the precious metals. Only when the sugar trade came to hold the center of interest in the Caribbean did the island again figure prominently on the international stage—and then owing to activity in its western third, ownership of which had by that time passed from Spain to France. In the last part of the eighteenth century the French section became by far the most valued colony of the Caribbean region. At its close, a revolt which was to create the first free state in America south of the United States occurred. While the revolt was still in process, war broke out between France and Spain, and, when peace was made, to their astonishment the inhabitants of the Spanish portion of the island found themselves transferred to France by the treaty of Basle of 1795.

But French control was never firmly established. The use of Haitian Negro troops to put down attempts by the local population to resist the new authorities caused many to flee the country and aroused a fear of domination by the black race, an apprehension increased when the revolting French colonials shortly set up claim to the entire island. The forces of the latter were defeated with the aid of the French, against whom, in turn, the Spanish population then turned its arms. By 1810 the French were driven out, but the local population recognized its inability to defend itself against Haiti, which had now become independent. They asked Spain to take the colony back into its control—this at the very time when in the mainland areas the revolutions looking toward independence from Spain were rapidly making headway. Spain accepted. Thus, early in 1810 Santo Domingo, after being

can point of view is Ureña, Max Henriquez, *Los Yanquis en Santo Domingo*, Madrid, J. Pueyo, 1929. In preparation of this chapter, Welles' discussion has been made the basis for the earlier period of development. These volumes contain much documentary material not published in the *Foreign Relations of the United States*.

nominally under French control since 1796, once more became a Spanish colony.

But though rejoicing occurred on the return to the Spanish family, it soon passed. Local dissatisfaction with the policies of the mother country brought in 1821 a declaration of independence and the announcement of the desire to join the new Republic of Colombia. Before an envoy voicing these wishes could reach his South American destination, however, the government of Haiti decided to conquer the neighboring state. Its army met practically no resistance, and the life of the newborn "republic" was snuffed out.

The period from 1822 to 1844 is referred to by Dominicans as that of the "Haitian Servitude." The new rulers set about "stifling every form of culture." "Agriculture came eventually to a standstill; commerce was non-existent"; "all forms of intellectual progress . . . perished."[2] After more than five years of agitation by a devoted group of nationalists, the Haitian yoke was thrown off in 1844 and once more the leaders found themselves guardians of a sovereignty which they doubted their ability to defend. All feared the possibility that Haiti might re-establish its dominance, some were disposed to rely on local forces to uphold the newly won independence, and others wished that the republic should become a protectorate of some stronger power.

The history of the weak state for the next two generations is that of a nation dominated for most of the period by the ambitions of rival leaders swaying public policy this way and that, often by the employment of the most devious means, always in fear of another Negro domination, and as a rule anxious to save the country—or to assure their own continuation in power—by alliance with whatever power it seemed most likely could be induced to lend its aid.

No truly national policy existed. Three leaders, Buenaventura Baez, Pedro Santana, and Ulises Heureaux, the first

---

[2] Welles, Sumner, *Naboth's Vineyard*, New York, Harcourt, Brace and Co., 1928, Vol. I, pp. 51–52. The first portion of this volume gives a vivid picture of the excesses of the Haitians in Santo Domingo in this period and that preceding.

two intermittently and the last continuously from 1882 to 1899, played the leading roles in the republic from its re-established independence in 1844 to the end of the century. Those in power were buffeted by internal dissensions and by the foreign policies pursued by the agents and armed forces of Haiti, the United States, and European powers. Few, indeed, among local leaders or representatives of foreign powers left a record which can be pointed to with pride.

Projects of alliance or annexation were frequent. They seldom, if ever, had popular support, though by brazen control of the electorate the local leaders were not infrequently in a position to make them appear to have it. They hawked the sovereignty of the country on the international market in an announced endeavor to obtain national security—but in reality to fix themselves in power.

A study of Dominican relations in the period leaves a confusing picture of national helplessness, venality among those in high office, discreditable ambitions on the part of representatives of foreign powers—not one group came out with a clean record—and frequent acts by the governments whom these agents represented which would be met with universal reprobation if repeated at the present day. The story of the chief international maneuvers involving the Dominican Republic in this period illustrates not only the weakness of the local Government but the level to which the international jealousies of the time allowed the diplomatic practice of stronger powers to sink.

France, immediately after the winning of independence, flirted with the idea of establishing a protectorate with the covert support of Baez, who was repeatedly to act as President of the Republic. Santana, the first President, the longtime political rival and at times the associate of Baez, favored a French protectorate, or, that failing, a similar agreement with Spain.

Later a representative of the United States, which was then in the Manifest Destiny stage of its development, looked over the situation and reported to an apprehensive government that, if it did not act, some European power might do so.

In 1849, Haiti invaded the country and threatened the capital. The badly frightened local Congress passed a resolution begging France for a protectorate, but France was cold. Furthermore, England did not favor letting French influence increase. Neither was that plan acceptable to the Dominican President, who next approached the representative of the United States to inquire whether "the United States would allow this Republic to annex itself."

While the reply of France to the protectorate proposal was still uncertain, there arrived in Santo Domingo, in August, 1849, another representative of the United States, who reported that France and England were rivals for control of Samaná Bay. The local Government, he said, would grant it to either in return for guarantee against invasion by Haiti. He believed the Dominicans would favor an agreement with the United States. Shortly after, he was asked, on behalf of the President, "whether the Government of the United States would take the Dominican Republic under its protection, or, what they would prefer, annex" it. Great Britain, he was informed, had decided against assuming a protectorate, but would oppose annexation by France.[3]

France, Spain, England, and the United States all having shown no enthusiasm for new responsibilities, the Dominicans were faced by a serious situation, for the Haitians, now ruled over by Soulouque, who had created himself Emperor Faustin I, already had an army in the country, and there was fear that the "Black Republic" might again try to establish dominion over the whole island.

Out of this situation arose one of the most curious incidents of the history of the Caribbean. Early in 1850 the Dominican minister of foreign relations appealed to the representative of the United States for intervention "to end the cruel war which we [the Dominicans] have maintained against the Haitians."[4] The representatives of England and France at once objected. Neither of their countries wished to act alone

---

[3] Green to Clayton, August 27, 1849, quoted in Welles, *op. cit.*, Vol. I, pp. 99–100.

[4] *Ibid.*, p. 106.

or to allow the United States to do so. They would, it appears, have been willing to act jointly without the United States. The Dominicans next addressed to both the British and French notes similar to the one sent to the American representative.[5]

Daniel Webster had now become Secretary of State in the United States and adopted a more vigorous policy than his predecessor. In doing so he took a step which would almost certainly not be considered if like conditions should now arise. He decided to join France and Great Britain in mediation to bring peace between the two island republics. The instructions to Mr. Walsh, the new American representative, were to resist actions by the representatives of the European powers which might "trench upon the just rights" of the Dominicans and any demand by Haiti for extension of its territory or the assumption of any part of its debt.[6]

Promptly after his arrival at Port-au-Prince, where the negotiations were held, Walsh informed the Haitian minister of foreign relations that the United States was to co-operate with the European powers in bringing peace, and that it was convinced that it was "incumbent upon the Emperor to recognize the independence of Santo Domingo." The Haitian replied that the island was a unit by the "designs of nature" and by the Haitian Constitution of 1806. This constitution had been adopted, of course, before the establishment of Dominican independence.

The discussions of the representatives of the three powers with the local authorities were protracted and unsatisfactory, the representative of Soulouque insisting that His Majesty could not even engage to enter a truce without consulting the Senate, "his first duty being to God and to observe the Constitution."[7] At last the Congress was called in special session, but there was no decision. Soulouque refused to agree

[5] The support given by the British and French to the Haitian ambitions to re-establish control of Santo Domingo is treated in greater detail in Welles, *op. cit.*, Vol. I, p. 96 *et seq.*

[6] These instructions cited by Welles, *op. cit.*, Vol. I, pp. 113–115, are in a letter from Webster to Walsh, 18 Jan., 1851.

[7] Walsh to Webster, in Welles, *op. cit.*, Vol. I, p. 118.

to a truce or to recognize Dominican independence, and the representatives of the three powers departed empty-handed except for the promise that hostilities would not be renewed without notification to their governments. In fact, however, the Emperor had been made to realize that the time was not well chosen for renewed attacks on his eastern neighbor. Not till 1853, however, were assurances that England and France would continue to stand for Dominican independence received by the Dominican Republic.[8]

The decade following brought to Santo Domingo experience which did much to confirm the apprehensions of those who felt it folly to put their faith in princes or in any governmental allegation of disinterested motives.

No definite guarantee of support by England, France, and the United States had followed the appeal for protection. Perhaps the mother country, so some of the leaders again began to think, might be a better guardian. Whatever Spain might be disposed to do could hardly be more unsatisfactory than what had been granted by the other powers or what was soon to be suffered at their hands. But Spain once more was hesitant. It feared that assumption of an active role might awaken "the jealousy of the United States" and alienate "the sympathies of the Cuban slaveholders." It would not even grant recognition to the Republic.

Thus rebuffed, Santana, now President, turned again to consider what could be done with the other powers, but he was shortly to meet discouragement there too. Two French subjects of suspicious character had been expelled. The French consul, supported by a warship, forced the Dominicans to pay damages for this expulsion and demanded the removal of certain officials objectionable to him. France continued to play the Haitian game and was jealous of the growing prestige of Great Britain. The latter still did not want further responsibilities in the Caribbean but would oppose assumption of a more prominent role by France—and perhaps by the United States.

---

[8] *Ibid.*, p. 135.

The northern republic once more seemed to be the country from which most could be hoped. It was now represented by a not too meticulous expansionist, William L. Cazneau, who had won the support of the Secretary of State and the President of the United States for ambitious projects which might fit in with similar schemes of the Dominican leaders.

There now opened a chapter of American diplomacy creditable to none of those who played its leading roles. This was the time, Cazneau reported, for the United States to establish close relations with Santo Domingo. No American nation had by treaty recognized its independence.[9] There were many valuable concessions which would be open to exploitation by American investors once a protectorate was established. A first draft of a treaty was drawn in the island and was later modified in Washington expressly to include the grant to the United States of rights in Samaná Bay.

Cazneau, who brought the treaty to the United States, shortly returned with Captain George B. McClellan. He reported that distrust of the motives of the United States had developed, fostered by the European consuls. The people feared that their territory was to be seized; the native whites, it was said, were to be ousted from control and the blacks enslaved. Anxiety was increased by the surveys undertaken by McClellan before negotiations had begun and by his recommendations that the United States ask for an increase of the territory to be given over for the use of the American Navy.[10]

Nevertheless, Santana went ahead in spite of open opposition by the representative of Great Britain, and on September 8, 1854, the treaty was ready for signing. The same day, a British war vessel arrived. The British and French representatives put pressure on the President not to sign the treaty. Santana, fearing that the withdrawal of their support, problematical though it was, would precipitate a Haitian attack, asked that the convention be changed and then rushed through

---

[9] Cazneau's activities are detailed in Welles, *op. cit.*, Vol. I, p. 136 *et seq.*, and in the historical sketch in Schoenrich, *op. cit.*, pp. 45–80.

[10] Cazneau to Marcy, July 24 and Aug. 8, 1854, *ibid.*, p. 148.

before the British and French could mature their plans. Cazneau agreed, and the treaty was signed and the congress called to consider its ratification.

But the British and French representatives were still distrustful and soon had additional warships—both British and French—to support their demands. The Dominican administration hesitated. A French representative, recently arrived, declared he had come to block the treaty and that France would do so by force if necessary. His British colleague toured the country declaring that ratification of the treaty meant enslavement of the Dominicans. The strength of the opposition was sufficient. Santana agreed to let the Europeans revise the treaty, and Cazneau reported that, as finally submitted to the Congress, it had "offensive mutilations and additions inserted upon the margin of printed copies . . . in the handwriting of the British Consul." Thus changed so as to be unacceptable to the United States, it was ratified by the local Congress on December 5, 1854.

The check to the forward policy of the American administration and the domineering position taken by the British and French were followed by another of the always threatening invasions from Haiti, where His Imperial Majesty Faustin I had been aroused by the Europeans concerning the possibility that a slaveholding power, the United States, might become the dominant influence on his eastern border.

Three armies, numbering some 30,000 all told, invaded the Dominican Republic, which found that the often-repeated suggestion that the Europeans would protect them against Haitian ambitions amounted to nothing at all. But Santana, relying on local forces only, roundly defeated the Haitians and once more turned to discussion of an American treaty, this time, however, without the clauses granting a naval station. That was to be covered in a separate agreement to be taken up later. But in this form the treaty again failed to meet the approval of the American Senate, and the United States gave no indication that it was disposed to follow the matter up by further negotiations. The British and French then declared that their governments "would never permit the people of the United States to have a foothold in the Dominican Republic" and obliged the Dominicans to request the withdrawal of the treaty from further consideration.[11]

The Spanish Chargé d'Affaires on this turn of events became the most active foreign representative and did his best to increase anti-American feeling and discredit all who had had any connection with the negotiation of the American treaties. Santana himself was forced to go into exile in St. Thomas in January, 1857.

Santo Domingo was still a weathercock, blown this way and that by the rivalries of European and American foreign offices, which now helped to plunge the country deeper into revolution and economic distress. The Spanish representative overplayed his hand and gave offense to his European colleagues, whose governments showed themselves disturbed by his actions. He was suddenly recalled. Baez, who had for the moment established himself in power, had flooded the country with paper money, quantities of which he had sold to the Spanish, French, and British consuls at bargain rates—an action which was to plague the republic after he himself was no longer its head.

The economic unrest soon ripened into a new revolution, headed as soon as it was well under way by Santana, now returned from exile. Though the British, French, and Spanish consuls continued their support of Baez and even obtained French and Spanish officers to aid him in his military operations, the opposition continued to gain strength. The government forces were cooped up in the capital, where they were steadily reduced by deaths, disease, and desertion. For a year they held out against the increasing forces of the revolution, spurred by the thought of the vengeance which would follow surrender. Finally, in June, 1858, the contest was brought to an end through mediation of the commander of a United States warship, which had been sent to protect the American agency and to relieve the starving Americans in the city. Unwillingly Santana agreed not to persecute the defenders of

---

[11] *Ibid.*, p. 171.

the capital, and Baez, in turn, was allowed to go into exile.

Santana was soon again in the presidency and, like his ousted rival, got under way negotiations for a foreign protectorate, without which he was still convinced that the now more than ever prostrate republic could not maintain itself. How, moreover, could he otherwise assure himself that he could remain in power in his own declining years?

France he continued to suspect of Haitian leanings. Toward the United States he was more favorably disposed; but the anti-American feeling recently aroused was still to be reckoned with, and past experience had not given ground for hope of decisive action from that quarter. Should he try Spain again? Negotiations with Spain were started secretly as early as October, 1858. They met at first with little success—a fact which was the more disquieting because other European powers proceeded to coerce the republic to make reparations for alleged injuries done to their nationals.

Denmark demanded payment to owners of Danish vessels taken over by Baez. The European consuls who had been given special facilities to speculate in Baez' paper money demanded that it be redeemed at a higher rate than that offered by the government in power. In this they sought, but did not obtain, the support of the American representative. Their demands being refused, they left the country, but returned in November on warships with instructions to act together to force the Government to settle their claims. Before the crisis came to a head, however, the representative of the Spanish Government, with which negotiations of another sort were now giving some promise, withdrew his co-operation.

The conditions in Santo Domingo in these years preceding the outbreak of the Civil War in the United States give a truly sorry picture of the morale of international politics of the time. A fit companion to his European colleagues was now reappointed by the United States to bear its representation. Cazneau, after the failure of his negotiations in 1854, had left the service but returned to the island, where he had continued his schemes from an elaborate plantation, the Estancia Esmeralda, of which he had become owner. He now, in April, 1859, once more became the representative of the United States and promptly revived his schemes.

The negotiations with Spain were already far advanced, and by March, 1860, arrangements for a protectorate were practically complete. As Spain developed willingness to assume responsibility, Santana increased the functions he sought to transfer. On April 27—when the Democratic convention at Charleston was foreshadowing the coming Civil War in the United States—he announced the desire to avoid the tribulations which the republics of South America were going through and besought Spain "to draw more closely the bonds" uniting both peoples.[12] By the middle of the year, Spain had agreed to garrison the republic and troops and munitions were arriving. Santana was persuading his associates that a protectorate was less desirable than annexation. By October the leaders were committed to annexation, but Spain was still apprehensive of the effect of such action on "the other nations of the New World." Annexation would be accepted promptly, however, if necessary to check advance by the United States and provided "that the act be, and appear to be, completely spontaneous in order to safeguard absolutely the moral responsibility of Spain." [13]

While the plans for annexation developed, only a few protests were made by patriotic persons unable to take steps to arouse an apparently apathetic public. No strong protests were made by "the other nations of the New World"—with one exception: that by Haiti, not, in fact, because of violation of the general principle of "America for Americans" but because of local ambitions which caused the republic "to reserve to itself the right to employ any means within its power to assure its own best interests." The United States contented itself with a belated formal dissent.[14]

On March 18, 1861, the results of the long-drawn-out negotiations were made public. Santo Domingo was proclaimed a Spanish colony. In the United States, six States had joined

---

[12] *Ibid.*, p. 203.
[13] *Ibid.*, p. 207.
[14] *Ibid.*, pp. 222–223.

South Carolina in the secession movement, in just two weeks Lincoln would become President, and within a month hostilities at Fort Sumter were to waken the Nation to a crisis in its own affairs which for years would distract attention from what otherwise might have been a major issue in foreign policy.[15]

In Santo Domingo floated the "glorious Spanish flag . . . which for more than three centuries waved over . . . this Antillian Island, favored by Isabel I, loved by Columbus, and from now on under the protection of Isabel II, the Magnanimous. . . ."[16] The official announcements detail the general popular rejoicing accompanying the "political transfer." This was, read the proclamation, "a unique example in the history of other countries, but not so in our country which has already given to all unique examples of perfect fidelity and love at all periods. . . . May Divine Providence sanctify this splendid union. . . ."

Spain had stipulated that there must be a spontaneous and unanimous call for the resumption of its control. How far the people would have favored the reannexation had they been consulted it is not possible to say. Exhausted by civil and international conflicts, betrayed by one coterie after another, with commerce and industry at a standstill, tried by the jealousies of stronger nations, with a population overwhelmingly illiterate and ignorant of both domestic and international affairs, Santo Domingo had developed little public opinion which could be consulted. Whatever the result of annexation, it might be argued, it could not be worse than the experience under the republic.

In any case, it is clear that such public opinion as did exist was given no real chance to express itself. Santana sent out explicit directions as to how the ceremony of ratification in the

---

[15] The "America for Americans" doctrine had not infrequently been questioned in the period. The aggressive actions of France and England in Santo Domingo have already been cited. They followed forward policies in Central America. The French-English-Spanish action in Mexico was soon to be on the horizon.

[16] Quoted from the official *Gaceta de Santo Domingo,* March 21, 1861, by Welles, *op. cit.,* Vol. I, pp. 211–212.

localities was to be carried out and received satisfactory reports as to the "unanimous" desires of the provincial populations, reports which were subsequently accepted by the Spanish authorities. The decree of annexation was signed by the Spanish Queen on May 19, 1861.

The President's ambition had been achieved and for the moment Spanish pride was gratified. Neither condition was to last for long. Revolts broke out almost at once in spite of the "unanimous" vote. Prominent Dominicans became disgruntled as Spaniards replaced islanders in high military and civil positions. The hoped-for economic regeneration did not come. Tariffs were manipulated for the benefit of Spanish exporters rather than for that of local industries, and public expenditures were pushed up far beyond receipts. Santana himself, who had looked to Spain as a guarantor of his control of the island found that the fraction of the offices granted to Dominicans frequently went, not to his friends, but to the friends of Baez.

Before a year was out, dissatisfaction was widespread throughout the colony and it would not down. By 1863, armed opposition had to be faced by a Spanish army already badly thinned by yellow fever. The excesses they committed in attempting to repress opposition only fanned the flame, and by September a provisional government had set up a new republican government. Santana, still loyal, though disillusioned, headed the operations against the revolution, but his followers one by one deserted to the Nationalist cause. He himself, exasperated by his treatment by the Spaniards, turned over his troops to his lieutenant and went to the capital to put himself at the disposition of the Spanish captain general, who had charged him with mutinous acts. The day after his arrival, he died suddenly from causes unascertained.

The revolution continued, weakened by jealousies among its leaders but aided by the poor equipment of the Spanish troops, their unfamiliarity with the terrain, and, most of all, by the climate and the susceptibility of the Spaniards to fever, which carried them off by thousands. Before the beginning of 1865 Spain recognized that further opposition was hopeless, and early in the year a project authorizing evacuation of Santo Domingo was presented to the Cortes. Spain had acted in the belief—so it was stated in the preamble of the law—that "all the inhabitants of the Dominican Republic were begging, imploring and soliciting with impatience their reincorporation in the Spanish Nation . . ."; but now the world saw "an entire people in arms ungratefully treating as tyrants the same individuals who believed that they had been called to come to them as their saviors. . . ."[17] To continue would be to wage a war of conquest "not free from the necessity of *dangerous explanations*."[18] With this the condition or with the condition thus explained, the Cortes voted the "disoccupation" by a large majority. On May 1, 1865, the Queen approved the law revoking the annexation of May 19, 1861.

Whether aversion to a war of conquest, the "dangerous explanations," the popular feeling against carrying on a losing contest, or other factors were most influential in bringing about the decision is not clear. In any case it cannot have escaped the Spanish authorities that the Civil War in the United States was drawing to a close and that a large navy and army already in being would be at the command of the American administration. Lee had surrendered on April 9, 1865. By July, the last Spanish troops were leaving Santo Domingo.

If the establishment of Spanish authority had disappointed those who longed for peace and the orderly development of the country, so did its withdrawal. Local rivalries kept the revolutionary pot boiling. Baez, who had spent most of the years of the occupation in Spain and in its pay, resigned his post when Spanish retirement was imminent. He now returned, proclaimed by his newspaper as "the angel of peace," and became for the third time President.

Politically, Baez had now a freer hand. Santana, his old rival, was dead. Cazneau, who during the American Civil War had first lived in Santo Domingo, where he flirted with the Confederacy and worked with the abolitionists to found colonies of free Negroes in the island, was now back again as

---

[17] Quoted in Welles, *op. cit.,* Vol. I, pp. 287–288.
[18] *Ibid.,* p. 288.

a private citizen and anxious to resume his devious activities in concession brokerage and other lines. He had now a certain shifty Colonel J. W. Fabens as his partner.

Events at the moment could hardly have shaped themselves more to Cazneau's liking. Baez was in an insecure position: he had been anti-American, but foreign help from elsewhere than the United States was now unlikely. In Washington, Secretary Seward, anxious to rehabilitate the Monroe Doctrine, was disturbed by rumors that Napoleon III wished to work through Baez for annexation of the republic to France, as well as by a British proposal that the United States join in declaring Samaná Bay neutralized—an "entangling alliance." A similar declaration had been suggested to both Great Britain and France by Haiti. Further, the Civil War had pointed out how great would have been the advantages had the United States possessed a naval base in the Caribbean.

Seward decided to review conditions on the ground. He arrived with his son at Santo Domingo on January 15, 1866. The American representative was "incapacitated" to receive him, and Cazneau seized the opportunity to establish relations between Baez and Seward. Baez became pro-American, and Seward thought he could use Cazneau to forward his plans. Shortly after the Secretary's return, advance was for the moment checked by the overthrow of the island President; but in the fall of 1866 the new government was again asking for a treaty and desiring to know whether the United States would consider granting a money loan and "a number of pieces of heavy artillery." [19] Orally, through the American commercial agent, the possible willingness to grant possession of land on Samaná Bay if aid of more substantial amount were forthcoming was suggested. The secret suggestion, like similar ones before and later, was one made by a hard-pressed government which hoped through the aid requested to consolidate its position.

Seward promptly followed up the lead. His son, Assistant Secretary of State, went southward with a draft of a treaty

---

[19] Dominican Minister of Foreign Affairs, Nov. 8, 1866, *ibid.*, p. 323.

providing for the lease of territory on Samaná Bay.[20] If cession of the territory could be secured, he would be permitted to offer up to $2,000,000, half in cash, half in munitions. If only a lease were agreed upon, a nominal rental would be paid. The upset of previous negotiations by the interference of European powers was recalled, and the representative was cautioned that negotiations were to be carried on with "caution, secrecy, and dispatch" and was admonished to find out whether the consent of the Dominican Congress would be necessary to make the agreement valid.

The younger Seward arrived in Santo Domingo on January 19, 1867, and promptly began the negotiations. He urged that a lease or purchase would be preferable to a loan, for loans between governments made it difficult "to preserve independent sovereignty and peaceful relations." [21] He found the Cabinet split as to the policy to be followed. Further absolute cession was prohibited by the Constitution. Compromise measures were discussed, but opposition developed in the local Congress and Secretary Seward decided to turn elsewhere to find his proposed naval base, though he did not indicate that the Dominican plan might not be again taken up if local opinion became more favorable.[22]

Rising opposition to the government in power in Santo Domingo and assurances by various leaders, military and civil, that they would approve a lease of Samaná resulted before the end of 1867 in a renewal of discussions with the Washington administration, but Seward was now less enthusiastic about a lease. "A transfer . . . of the Peninsula of Samaná to the United States" on the other hand would have been, he continued to think, "a harbinger of independence and prosperity" to the ceding republic.[23]

Actual negotiations were again under way early in 1868, this time at Washington, and before the end of January an agreement was arrived at for a ninety-nine-year lease of Sa-

---

20 Seward to Seward, December 17, 1866, *ibid.*, p. 324.
21 Seward to Seward, January 20, 1867, *ibid.*, p. 327.
22 Seward to Smith, July 1, 1867, *ibid.*, pp. 332–333.
23 Seward to Smith, December 13, 1867, *ibid.*, p. 338.

maná, in return for which the United States was to pay $1,-000,000 in cash and $1,000,000 in munitions when a treaty had been ratified by both governments. The agreement came too late to help the local authorities, however. The day after its signing, the government fell; and Baez, now granted the title of "Great Citizen" by the Assembly, was soon again in the presidency.

Baez' return did not mean a crash of the plans as to Samaná. He recognized that without foreign aid he, now as previously, could not long keep himself in power; in fact, he was hardly inaugurated when revolts made their appearance. He was willing not only to support the lease convention but even to cede the entire Samaná peninsula. Cazneau, as usual, was a willing aid, and the failure in the United States Senate of the treaty for annexation of the Danish West Indies seemed to make prospects brighter for a renewed Dominican proposal. But the rising opposition made it plain that, if Baez was to put one through, action must be prompt. He now suggested a sale on substantially the same terms as had formerly been discussed for a lease. The Secretary of State of the United States might draft the agreement, and three war vessels should be sent to help keep the government of Baez in power while the agreement was going through the houses of the two governments.

As his position became less secure, his desire for quick action increased. The sale could be put through at once, and payment, which would need action by the United States Senate, could be arranged later. If no action could be expected, he would be forced to make a similar offer to a European power. Meanwhile, the fact that negotiations were in progress leaked out and a flood of letters of protest from revolutionary leaders, many of whom had formerly supported the lease projects, reached the Secretary of State. These individuals said that they would recognize no acts of the Baez government.

Cazneau and his partner, Fabens, who was now carrying on the negotiations at Washington, kept urging the agreement on Seward, who continued to keep the proposal under consideration. As 1868 came to a close, Baez became desperate.[24] He asked Seward to issue a decree putting the republic under the protection of the United States and to send vessels of war to take possession of all strategic points. If a protectorate were proclaimed, the Dominican Republic would apply to be admitted to the Union.

Such a program outran even the elastic measures Secretary Seward had been considering, and on November 17, 1868, he authorized the American representative to read to Baez confidentially a letter stating:

> The Congress of the United States are always disinclined to foreign military conquests, perhaps more so now than at any time heretofore. It seems unlikely, therefore, that Congress would entertain any other proposition for the annexation of Dominica than one which should originate with and have the sanction of the Dominican people, expressed in a regular Constitutional manner.[25]

Nevertheless, he said, the subject was "a very important one," and he reserved further consideration of it until Congress should have assembled.

Baez was not to be discouraged. He would undertake to get popular approval in any form Seward wished, but the United States should send a war vessel at once with a convention and $300,000 in cash! Seward had the full sympathy of President Johnson, his chief, in his plans for an expansionist policy, but the relation of the President to Congress placed decided limitations on what support he could secure. Measures looking toward advance in Dominican relations met defeat, and annexationist ambitions lay in abeyance until after the inauguration of President Grant.

The story of the action of the Grant administration in relation to Santo Domingo is one of the least admirable in American diplomacy. Unskilled in either domestic or international affairs, the head of the government was easily influenced and led by advisers whose qualities an executive politically more astute would have soon learned to distrust. They were too

---

[24] This account is summarized from Welles, *op. cit.*, Vol. I, p. 350 *et seq.*
[25] Seward to Smith, November 17, 1868, *ibid.*, p. 352.

often fit associates of such men as Fabens, Cazneau, and Baez, who promptly set about winning the administration to support their projects.

Less than a week after the inauguration, Fabens saw Hamilton Fish, the new Secretary of State. The Dominican government, he argued, was disposed to enter the Union as a free and sovereign state. Fish was favorably impressed. Fabens made a hurried trip to the island, nominally to secure information for a report on conditions, and was promptly back again to urge the Samaná lease, which could now be secured for an annual payment of $100,000. Grant was won to support the project and sent one of his satellites, General Orville E. Babcock, to secure "full and accurate information in regard to the disposition of the government and people of the Republic toward the United States." Babcock was also to report on the character of the government, its stability, the public debt, and any other conditions he might think pertinent.

Babcock, accompanied by Fabens, sailed to Santo Domingo, where Cazneau was waiting to give them welcome. The partners kept Babcock constantly in their company and so far as possible out of contact with the resident American commercial agent. From their conferences with Baez sprang a most remarkable document in which, among other things, Babcock engaged on behalf of President Grant that the President would use his influence to popularize annexation among members of Congress. More remarkable still, President Grant, on Babcock's return, approved what had been done.

Next the American commercial agent, who had been indiscreet enough to report Dominican conditions as they were and who was unacceptable to Cazneau and Fabens, was replaced by a man more in sympathy with the policy of the administration, R. H. Perry. Babcock was then sent back to finish the negotiation of the annexation treaty, which Perry was to sign on behalf of the United States. If the treaty were concluded—the already prepared draft was handed to him with his instructions—Babcock was "to take steps to carry out the agreement of the United States . . . to protect the people of . . . [the] Republic against foreign interference while the nation is expressing its will" as well as to protect the rights which the United States might obtain. At the same time Babcock received "a draft on New York for $100,000 and also a quantity of arms and ammunition valued at $50,000." [26] The Navy was to help in carrying out the agreement arrived at and, on proper occasion, to take over the lands involved in the Samaná Bay lease.[27]

Babcock returned to Santo Domingo, where again he was closely supervised by Cazneau and Fabens; and on November 29, 1869, a treaty of annexation and a convention for the Samaná lease were signed—the latter to be used if annexation should fail in the United States Senate. Babcock then proceeded to Samaná, where possession was taken in the name of the United States and the American flag raised. Naval forces were instructed to help in putting down revolutionary movements that might appear and to warn Haiti not to interfere.

Baez distrusted his ability to stay in office till the agreement was put through, and he appealed to Washington for help, this time not in vain. By the end of February, 1870, seven American vessels of war were cruising in Dominican or Haitian waters, their commanders, by order of the Secretary of the Navy, directing their operations in accordance with the indications of the President of the Dominican Republic.[28]

With such assistance Baez now felt that the time was ripe for the plebiscite he had promised. His decree of February 19, 1870, provided that voting booths should be open in all the provinces "in order that the inhabitants may come one by one to cast their votes, expressing definitely their desire to be united to the great Republic of the United States of America." The government paper commenting upon the issue proclaimed, "Santo Domingo gains everything and loses nothing. . . . Annexation means salvation because it will oblige Haiti to respect Dominican rights . . . and because it will persuade

---

[26] Fish to Babcock, November 6, 1869, *ibid.*, p. 376.
[27] Fish to Babcock, November 6, 1869, *ibid.*, p. 377.
[28] *Ibid.*, p. 383. The texts of the agreements are in Welles, *op. cit.*, Vol. II, pp. 977–984.

all Dominicans to renounce political disputes."[29]

That there was no free voting was evident to everybody. Even Major Perry reported that Baez had told him "that if any man opposed annexation they would either shoot him or send him his passports." "The people were not permitted to express any opposition to annexation." There were only about 16,000 votes cast, and only eleven, cast at the suggestion of the President, were against annexation. The result was triumphantly reported to the United States by the minister of foreign affairs. "This country," he wrote, "almost unanimously is burning to see the conclusion of its annexation to the United States."

The scene of greatest activity now shifted to Washington, where facts and rumors concerning the sorry Dominican episode gradually became matters of general discussion. The President still stood by the annexation treaty. Its chief opponent was Senator Charles Sumner, chairman of the Senate Committee on Foreign Relations. He had been a stanch friend of the President, but he broke with him on the Dominican policy, which he found contrary to his sense of justice and to foreshadow an aggressive policy toward Haiti. In the latter his abolitionist principles gave him a special interest. The administration used all its influence to secure ratification by the Senate, but the treaty failed by a vote of 28 to 28—two-thirds being necessary for ratification. Grant still sought to keep this favorite project alive; but, though in Congress a large party stood loyally by the President, at least in the desire to defend his personal integrity which he felt had been impugned, the proposal gradually fell out of attention. Babcock for some years continued in the favor of his chief, but the American war vessels were gradually withdrawn from Dominican waters and the archconspirators, Cazneau and Fabens, fell back into unnoticed obscurity.

Frequent and often justified have been the criticisms of the United States Senate in reference to its functions of advice and consent to the ratification of treaties, but there can be no

---

[29] Quoted in Welles, *op. cit.*, Vol. I, p. 385.

doubt that in defeating the treaty with the government of Santo Domingo headed by the notorious Baez it defended not only the rights of the Dominican people but the fair name of the United States.

Not till their close did the last thirty years of the nineteenth century bring to Santo Domingo any such critical issues in foreign relations as those raised by this project of annexation to the United States, but the character of local politics showed only occasional improvement. Civil war, clashes with Haiti, financial embarrassment, and new Samaná Bay projects continued to embarrass the government. Baez, as pro-American as formerly anti-American in sympathy, continued whether in or out of power to be a disturbing influence while he lived. Foreign debts into which he had led the country were an increasing cause of confusion, political and economic, and the curse of far-reaching and conflicting concessions fastened itself upon the republic.

The last fifth of the century was the period of another dictator, Ulises Heureaux, who became President on September 1, 1882. With one exception, he was the first President to be elected and installed by the rules laid down in the Constitution; but this auspicious circumstance did not forecast a period of constitutional government. His rule was to be one in which the republic slid steadily from a bad to a worse position and one in which there developed abuses which made the Dominican Republic in the early years of the twentieth century the center of far-reaching international complications threatening the continued existence of the nation.

Heureaux was of obscure and apparently illegitimate origin. His father is alleged to have been a Haitian and his mother a Negress of St. Thomas. His education was limited and was early forsaken for the more exciting career of a soldier, in which he rose steadily. Abstemious in diet, immaculate in dress, he was astute, fearless, cruel, and sensual. Once in power, he was to dominate Dominican affairs for almost seventeen years, whether in or out of the presidency.[30]

---

[30] He was continuously President from January 6, 1887, to his death, on July 25, 1899. See Schoenrich, *op. cit.*, p. 68 *et sqq.*

Domestic affairs were well in hand soon after his inauguration. He professed enthusiasm for increasing immigration from abroad and for promoting the development of the national resources through public improvements and the grant of concessions to foreign capitalists. In fact, however, no increase of immigration occurred, the loans secured by mortgaging the resources of the country went only in minor degree to the purposes for which they were announced, and the concessions for development which were granted to foreigners seldom brought any appreciable result.

In foreign relations Heureaux professed to be pro-American and showed in this respect a consistency in contrast to the vacillation of his less able predecessors. Also, until his long-drawn-out regime was drawing to a close, he could boast that the independence of the country was not seriously questioned. On the other hand, the financial commitments into which he drew the public treasury were of such a nature that foreign complications did become increasingly threatening; and when he passed out of control, the country faced the most serious political whirlwind of its history.

Heureaux inherited from previous administrations an already compromised Treasury, and current budget deficits from the beginning increased the floating debt. Loans from local merchants at usurious interest rates proved an expedient which could not be indefinitely relied upon. Increased taxes on imports did not bring in adequate public revenue. Loans from abroad might help. They were sought in the United States and in Europe, in the former case once more in connection with Samaná Bay schemes. But Cleveland was cold to adventures such as had aroused Johnson and Grant. Private financial interests in New York showed unwillingness to risk money in another proposal for a bond issue, the service of which they were to secure by collecting thirty per cent of the Dominican customs.

Borrowing in Europe also was difficult. Baez in 1869 had pledged the resources of the country to Hartmont and Company—English bankers—by a contract of such extravagant nature that its terms suggest an enterprise of a Munchausen rather than an engagement between a government and responsible financiers. As finally agreed upon, the loan had a total of £420,000. The bankers were to receive, among other advantages, a commission of £100,000. As security, the Government pledged the property and revenue of the republic—specifically, the customs revenue of the chief ports and the revenues from guano, coal and other minerals, mahogany, and other forest products.

Nominally, the loan was to promote roads and railways; actually, the money received was used for other purposes by Baez, and in total the cash which reached Santo Domingo was only $150,000.[31] The Dominican Senate had voted to cancel the contract in 1870, but the Hartmont Company insisted that such action was illegal. They had issued and sold bonds totalling £750,000, and they insisted that no further loan could be made by the republic until this one was settled. The interest payments had gone into default in 1872. Further default in Heureaux' administration met increasing objection by the British Government.

The agents of Heureaux succeeded in getting from Westendorp and Company, of Amsterdam, a new loan of £770,000 at 6 per cent, by which the outstanding securities of the Hartmont loan were retired at one-fifth of face value and other amounts made available for paying the floating indebtedness and as fresh money. The Westendorp interests were given a fresh lien on the customs revenues, which were to be collected after November 1, 1888, by agents of the creditor. The balance of collections after the loan services were met was to be turned over to the Government.

In the long view this contract could hardly fail to be unfortunate. Objection to it could be made on several grounds. It was by no means clear that the shady Hartmont loan should be redeemed at even one-fifth of its face value, and the floating debt claims might be questioned. Stronger pro-

---

[31] See Schoenrich, *op. cit.*, p. 350 *et sqq.*, and Hollander, *op. cit.*, *passim.*

test could be made against any increase in the public debt, especially when it was practically certain that any new money would not be wisely devoted to public uses.

But the best argument as to why the loan should not have been made lay in the agreement about the collection of the customs. Such provisions were by no means a new expedient in loan contracts with weak governments. Nor was the share of the customs income which would be required for the loan service, about thirty per cent, unusually high. Properly safeguarded, indeed, such arrangements might be a means to stimulate national advance.

But when made with an irresponsible dictator who would probably dissipate the funds without advantage to the public and whose acts his successors would almost certainly be disposed to disavow, such an agreement had in it at best little advantage to the borrower, no satisfactory security for the conservative lender, and the probability of serious political consequences should the lender secure the support of his government in an effort to enforce payment. Mortgages which involve governments, like those which involve individuals, bring advantages to all concerned when the conditions under which they are negotiated are normal—and not otherwise. Unfortunately, this loan contract pointed the way toward further steps to compromise the national position in public finance. *Facilis est descensus.*

There followed another period in which Heureaux showed himself anxious to secure close relations with the United States. There was negotiated and ratified a reciprocity treaty which caused a flare-up of European opposition and an anxious request for assurances, which were tardily given, that the United States would support the Dominican Republic in maintaining its position. The Samaná discussions were renewed, for the Harrison administration having been disappointed in efforts to secure a base at Môle Saint Nicholas, Haiti was now ready to consider an alternative. It leaked out that negotiations were going on, and popular opposition flared up. Heureaux then officially denied that any proposals had been made. The trouble, he told the American consul, was with the American press. "Whenever a Dominican editor writes anything objectionable . . . I put him in jail. That settles it. In the United States, the writers abuse their privileges and your ruling men do nothing. That article in the *Gaceta Oficial* will quiet the people." [32]

At first Heureaux did not want a money payment for the rights to be granted but only an "offensive and defensive alliance," especially if his government should get into trouble with Haiti. Later his position on this point changed.

The President was again short of money. The first Westendorp loan had been followed by another, a "railroad loan" the bonds of which were for £900,000 with interest at 6 per cent guaranteed by a mortgage on the railroad and a second lien on the customs. But now this money was also exhausted. Government credit was not good and the Samaná lease might bring in cash. The President would engage to call a special session of Congress and "to cause legislative ratification of the Samaná contracts," if money payment might be expected immediately thereafter, because a revolution was to be expected as soon as the agreement was acted upon.[33]

Mr. Durham, the consul of the United States, received final instructions as to the proposed Samaná agreement on August 6, 1892. He was told that the United States Congress had made the appropriations of the initial payment "and that the money had been placed at the disposal of President Harrison." If Heureaux was ready to act "under the terms agreed upon," he was to sign the convention. But when the matter was presented, Heureaux already had domestic troubles on his hands and public opinion had been aroused by reports that "the Westendorp loan was to be transferred to the Government of the United States." The President stated that he was sick and did not feel able to go ahead with the plan. Once more Samaná fell into the background.

But the need of money could not be so easily laid aside,

---

[32] Durham to J. W. Foster, July 22, 1891, Welles, *op. cit.,* Vol. I, pp. 479–480.

[33] Durham to Blaine in a private letter dated April 25, 1892, quoted in Welles, *op. cit.,* Vol. I, p. 486.

and the Westendorp Company would not advance any more money. As early as March, 1891, its superintendent had "confessed that his company's affairs were almost hopeless and that they wanted to get out." [34]

Fresh money was essential if the Heureaux administration was to get a new lease of life. The President secured it in May, 1892, from a new company, the San Domingo Improvement Company of New York, which agreed to make two new loans, one of $2,035,000 to refund old obligations and another of $1,250,000 to meet other "debts" which, however, in fact totalled only $438,000. The new company was to continue to collect the customs but, if default occurred, a committee of representatives of the governments of the United States, Great Britain, France, Holland, and Belgium was to take charge. Shortly after, still another loan similar to the second was added to the obligations of the republic. Already the future had been heavily mortgaged and the end was not yet.

The dictator's life had still several years to run. They were clouded by domestic troubles and international complications, political and financial. Haitian relations were troublesome. Controversies which would have been only amusing, had they not been seriously supported by France, resulted in the sending of French war vessels to compel payment of damages. American naval vessels opportunely appeared off the coast intent on "gun practice." There followed an amicable but expensive adjustment by the Dominican Republic and profuse thanks to the United States. Borrowing from the San Domingo Improvement Company was no longer possible. Paper money issues in large amounts were a hypodermic to the treasury—but brought widespread unrest in their wake. In 1897 the refunding loan of 1893 went into default. Public credit fell farther. The San Domingo Improvement Company decided to "throw good money after bad" and consented to still another loan—on hard terms. The republic's debt by 1898 was ten times its total at the time of the first Westendorp loan.[35]

---

[34] Durham to Foster, July 1, 1892, *ibid.*, p. 487.
[35] *Ibid.*, p. 527.

The dictator was now in desperate straits. He must have money. He made a settlement of claims against Haiti by which he was paid $400,000 and gave a receipt for $1,000,000.[36] The Spanish-American War was approaching; perhaps he could revive the Samaná Bay project with the McKinley administration or possibly get support other than financial from the colossus. Speaking about Samaná Bay to the American consul, he declared, "Let your Government come and take it . . . you understand me."[37] That, he said, was what other strong powers did. Later he sought to hasten action by reporting a rumor that Spain intended to seize Samaná and suggested that a secret cession be negotiated and the United States take over possession on the pretext of satisfying claims of American citizens. He needed, he said, $300,000 to assure a friendly local reception for such a move.

The only reply received was that the United States had no imperialistic design but would consider a lease convention similar to that of 1892. Next Heureaux asked that the United States immediately establish a formal protectorate. The Department of State returned a blunt refusal and reprimanded its officer for having forwarded the proposal. The career of the dictator was now drawing to an end. There had grown a widespread association having as its object his definite elimination. He was assassinated on July 25, 1899.

For a time it was felt that the passing of Heureaux might usher in a period of orderly government; but the debts with which he had saddled the republic, plus dissensions among the local leaders, dashed such hopes. French demands for immediate payments of the overdue balances of claims met the reply that the government was without funds. It asked time to arrange payments by installments. The consul threatened that if his demands were not met within three days, French war vessels would blockade the ports. The President then appealed to the nation. The popular subscriptions which were collected, in spite of the widespread poverty, enabled the government to meet the French demands. The French

[36] *Ibid.*, p. 528.
[37] *Ibid.*, p. 528.

consul then declared that the presidential appeal was an insult to France. Three French men of war arrived in port, but three days later an American warship, again on "gun practice," came into port. The French attitude became conciliatory and the incident soon blew over. Apprehension that the French action would be followed by similar steps by other nations was removed so far as the United States was concerned by instructions received by its minister not to press for immediate payment of American claims.

The position of the San Domingo Improvement Company was highly unsatisfactory to all parties. It wished to retire from its responsibilities, and the Dominican Government wished to speed its withdrawal. The problem was where to find some security which would allow the company to withdraw without sacrificing the interests of its owners. Efforts to do so resulted, in 1900, not in withdrawal, but in a recast arrangement to which some of the bondholders, especially the French and Belgians, refused to agree. Belgium announced that the company no longer represented Belgian interests, and the United States indicated that negotiations which the Dominican Government might undertake would not prejudice the interests of its citizens. Soon financial affairs were further complicated. The Dominican Government claimed that the company had not lived up to its contract. By a decree its right to collect the customs was terminated.

New proposals for purchase of the company necessitated adjustments to meet the views of the local administration, the various groups of bondholders, and the Congress. While they were still under discussion, the country fell into a welter of revolutions which was to have long-drawn-out consequences. In the course of the disturbances, the capital was reduced practically to a state of siege, and the foreign consuls cabled for protection of their national interests.

On April 2, 1903, United States troops were landed to protect American interests and a German warship landed 150 men to protect the German and British consulates. Italian and Dutch ships entered the harbor.[38] This crisis blew over,

[38] *For. Rel.*, 1903, p. 391.

but the rivalries of the creditor powers did not.

The agreements which had been made in efforts to solve the country's problems had been disregarded and were now almost beyond unraveling. The French and Belgian bondholders had been given a lien on the customs of Santo Domingo and San Pedro de Macorís. Without these the Government could not maintain itself. Various specific claims attached to the income from other ports. The French, Spanish, and Italian governments had secured definite pledges for payment of their claims, and the Germans had, through sending a warship, forced an agreement to pay $325,000 on claims for which $212,500 had originally been demanded. The export tax on cacao was mortgaged to Italy. There were other revenues that were allotted to foreign creditors—a revenue sometimes being repledged to various claimants.

On October 17 Belgium put in a new set of demands and suggested that that government and the United States should take over all the customs houses and, after rationing the Dominican Government, divide what was left of the income through an international committee representing the creditors.[39] Meanwhile, various revolutionary bands were operating practically throughout the entire country. Toward the end of 1903, American, French, and Italian forces were again landed to protect foreign interests.[40]

Out of the confusion at last arose Morales, a military leader who had not before played an important part in public affairs. He has been characterized as "a man of greater energy than intelligence, greater ambition than conscience,

---

39 These claims are outlined in greater detail in Welles, *op. cit.*, Vol. II, pp. 602–604, from which they are here summarized.

40 Tulio M. Cestero, in *Estados Unidos y las Antillas*, Madrid, Compañía Ibero-Americana de Publicaciones, 1931, p. 62, states that, in addition to the above landings, troops from Dutch and German vessels to protect foreign interests were ashore in October, 1903. Early in 1904, American marines were landed to protect German interests. (*For. Rel.*, 1904, p. 267 *et sqq.*) Reviewing the possible clash of United States and German interests, the Peruvian diplomat Francisco García Calderón says, in his *El Panamericanismo, su pasado y su porvenir*, "Panamericanism or Germanism, such seems to be the unavoidable dilemma for our democracies. . . . Between two dominations, between two dangers to the fragile independence of distracted republics, we must prefer North American hegemony, the preëminence of a liberal Republic." Quoted in Cestero, *op. cit.*, p. 187.

erratic and impulsive far beyond the border line of sanity." [41] From the beginning of his revolution, he had sought the intervention of the United States. He became Provisional President and late in 1903 outlined an agreement by which the United States should become protector of the republic for fifty years with supervision over its public finance and be granted a special trade position and the control by lease of Samaná and Manzanillo Bays.[42] The head of a rival group in February, 1904, proposed a secret treaty allying the republic with "the German Emperor, to whom the United States of America are commercial enemies." [43]

The Morales faction finally got the upper hand, and its leader became President on June 19, 1904. His position was insecure, however. Belgian, French, and Italian claims for which the revenues of certain ports had been pledged had for the moment been postponed but would shortly be pressed, as presumably would those of other countries. Further, an arbitral tribunal to which one of the recent fleeting governments had referred the case of the San Domingo Improvement Company had handed down an award by which its claims were secured on the receipts from all the northern ports, and, under the agreement, a financial agent of the United States had been placed in charge of the customs house at Puerto Plata. The government could not raise funds to support itself, and already new revolutions were in being.[44]

There had arisen one of those complicated situations which sometimes come into human affairs in which any decision taken for its solution would be a bad one. The country had been brought to extreme exhaustion through the abuses of a long dictatorship followed by a succession of civil wars, the end of which was not in sight. If foreign powers decided to keep hands off and to deliver over the lives and properties of the Dominicans and foreign residents to the mercies of whatever local governments might succeed each other, the

---

[41] *Welles, op. cit.*, Vol. II, pp. 606–607.

[42] Powell to Hay, December 17, 1903, *ibid.*, p. 612.

[43] Powell to Hay, February 26, 1904, *ibid.*, p. 613.

[44] For these developments, see *For. Rel.*, 1904, pp. 270–285.

prospect was one of indefinite struggle between factions with the further destruction of the economic basis of national prosperity and the prejudice of the chance of political regeneration. But the action of a number of powers was such that it was clear that they had no intention of sacrificing their national interests to the caprices of local politics.

As far as the United States was concerned, it was suggested, and has since been suggested in similar cases, that it should have declared that it would not intervene to protect the rights of its citizens and would oppose any intervention for a similar purpose by any other power. On the other hand, it has been argued that to take such a stand would be a highhanded assumption of a right to change the rule of international law. While Latin-American approval of the standard of nonintervention might be presumed, explicit assumption by the United States of the right to dictate what the standard of international action in the New World should be would in the long run arouse widespread resentment among other American states and would certainly not be accepted by non-American powers.

Another possible course of action would have been the assumption of some degree of control by concerted international action on the part of a group of American powers or of American and non-American powers. Such an arrangement had apparently been contemplated in one of the contracts of the San Domingo Improvement Company and apparently had at one time been given consideration in the then recent Venezuelan debt dispute. Aside from the fact that such a control might be one slow to act, expensive, and possibly inefficient because of conflicts among the different national interests, an arrangement of this nature would be unacceptable to the United States because of its policy of avoiding "entangling alliances."

The United States might take no forward action itself; but, reserving the right to protect the interests of its own citizens in any arrangement made, it might allow some non-American power or powers to establish some degree of control, such as the administration of the customs houses. Such a move had at one time been dicussed by European powers during the Venezuela dispute.[45] But that adjustment would have been unacceptable because it would to a degree have involved, or might so develop as to involve, at least a temporary extension of control by a non-American power over American territory, and certainly would have meant, for a period, a degree of control by that power over the destiny of the "occupied" power. Latin-American countries would hardly have found such an arrangement more acceptable than would the United States.

Finally, the United States might have thrown over the traditional policy of "America for Americans" and have declared that it would no longer oppose the extension of non-American political influence in the New World on the ground that the experience of almost a century had shown that the weaker republics were not able to develop governments which could assure public order and protect life and property. Such a solution, however, would have run counter to the sentiment of all but a negligible fraction of American public opinion and would have produced in Latin America a degree of ill feeling toward the United States compared to which the allegations of "imperialism" which have arisen as a result of the policy actually undertaken would have been a whisper.

A modification of this action by which the United States would have declared that the states of the New World had now developed to such a point that they would be held individually to defend their rights under the general rules of international law might have flattered Latin-American susceptibilities at first, but in the long run—and, indeed, in the crisis then to be faced—would have had an effect on the Latin-American attitude and on European action little different from a frank avowal of abandonment of the Monroe Doctrine.

The course which the United States would take would

---

[45] Bartholdy, Albrecht Mendelsohn, and Thimme, Friedrich, eds., *Die Auswärtige Politik des Deutschen Reiches, 1817–1914,* 4 vols., Berlin, Institut für Auswärtige Politik, 1928, Vol. II, p. 371.

doubtless continue to be influenced by the larger aspects of the "America for Americans" policy, which it had been championing, with varying degrees of insistence, for two generations. But the Government would be moved also by new considerations of national interest running to a high degree parallel with the established policy but which in the early years of the century were rapidly shaping standards of action which would have come to acceptance even if the earlier policy had never existed. Circumstances were developing a Caribbean policy.

The Spanish-American War had brought to the United States an increased political influence in the Caribbean region. The Panama Canal project was now well advanced. It had already foreshadowed the importance which the region off the southern coast of the United States would have in national defense and in the development of the country's now rapidly expanding industry and foreign trade. The positions which the United States took in Venezuelan and Cuban relations also were forecasts of a new but rapidly developing national policy not bounded by the Monroe Doctrine though it might be championed under its aegis. It was not a development prompted, at least in any but minor degree, by any enthusiasm for abstract standards of continental solidarity as against the rest of the world nor by any enthusiasm for popular or republican government, but one arising from the desire to strengthen the national position, political and economic. It was definitely opposed to complicating Caribbean affairs by allowing therein an expansion of European territorial control, permanent or temporary. In this respect it overlapped the long-established Monroe Doctrine.

Under these circumstances President Roosevelt came to decide on the forward action which was one of the most significant steps in the growth of the subsequent much-developed and much-criticized Caribbean policy of the United States. Morales, for the moment in power in Santo Domingo, was anxious that the United States should take the lead in attempting to solve what had already become for the local government an unsolvable problem. On December 30, 1904, Secretary of State Hay [46] telegraphed the American representative that one European government strongly intimated that it might resort to occupation of Dominican ports to secure payment of its claims, and that there appeared "to be a concert among" European powers. He was instructed to ascertain whether the Dominican Government "would be disposed to request the United States to take charge of the collection of duties and effect an equitable distribution of the assigned assets among the Dominican Government and the several claimants."

Morales was in favor of the project, as was the cabinet after a preamble emphasizing the importance of avoiding "the exigencies of foreign creditors" had been amplified to include a declaration by the United States that it would itself "respect the complete territorial integrity of the Dominican Republic." [47]

A protocol providing that representatives of the United States should collect the customs was, after a number of drafts, signed and submitted for the approval of the governments on February 7, 1905, but was not acted on by the United States Senate. Pending final action on the treaty, there was then put into force, on March 31, a *modus vivendi* under which American officials for collecting the customs entered on their duties and the danger of intervention by European powers was eliminated. Morales soon disappeared from the scene, but the benefits of the *modus vivendi* were soon evident and his successor could announce that the government was running without a deficit, for the first time in history.[48]

Though the arrangement was working successfully, opposition to the proposed treaty in the United States Senate grew, and its terms were changed to limit the functions to be dis-

---

[46] *For. Rel.*, 1905, p. 298.

[47] The negotiations are outlined and the texts of the draft agreements are printed in *For. Rel.*, 1905, pp. 298–324. See also *For. Rel.*, 1905, pp. 334–342, for the characteristic message of President Roosevelt transmitting the agreement to the United States Senate.

[48] *Ibid.*, 1905, pp. 355–390, especially Minister Dawson's Report to the President, July 1, 1905, pp. 355–391.

charged by the representatives of the American Government. The new convention was signed on February 8, 1907, and then sent out for ratification. It was approved by the United States Senate on February 25 and by the Dominican authorities on May 3.

In the interval between the negotiations of the *modus vivendi* and the ratification of the treaty, the Dominican authorities, on the suggestion of the United States, adjusted the claims urged by the various creditors. These claims nominally amounted to over $30,000,000, but conditional adjustments brought them to about $17,000,000. There was proposed a bond issue of $20,000,000 at 5 per cent, the yield of which, along with certain moneys received for the benefit of the creditors, was to be devoted to paying off outstanding accounts, the extinction of concessions and monopolies, and specified public improvements.

The treaty provided that the President of the United States should appoint officials to collect all the customs duties, which should be applied in order by their chief, the General Receiver, to pay the expenses of the receivership, the interest on the bonds, and amortization items and to cancel bonds acquired by purchase by the Dominican Government. Amounts remaining were to be paid over to the local Government. If in any year the customs receipts exceeded $3,000,000, one-half of the surplus was to be applied to the sinking fund for the redemption of the bonds.

The United States was to give the officials it appointed the protection necessary for discharge of their duties, and the Dominican Republic was not without previous agreement with the United States to modify the customs duties or increase the "public debt." The meaning of the latter phrase was later to be the subject of serious controversy.

In the actual debt adjustment which followed, the island republic paid off the greater part of the foreign bond claims at 50 per cent of their face value, the claims of the San Domingo Improvement Company at 90 per cent of their arbitrated amount, and the other obligations at from 10 to 40 per cent of what had been asked. Private concessions and monopolies were brought to an end and the economic and political horizon became probably more favorable than it had been at any previous time.

Uninterrupted peace did not follow, but the government was in a stronger position to cope with rebellion than before. The discontented elements no longer had possible control of the customs houses to whet their willingness to rise in revolt—though the increase of the amounts turned over by the collector general for local purposes tended to make control of the treasury itself a greater prize.

CHAPTER V

The Dominican Republic after the Customs Treaties

THE customs collectorship in the years following its establishment discharged satisfactorily the duties entrusted to it. Income went up, debts went down. Except in the regions along the Haitian border, its officers met no problems of a serious sort. A breakdown in its prestige came in the Wilson administration when, in contrast to the previous practice, the man at its head, who had had previous training in similar work in the Philippines, was replaced by a "political" appointee and the representation of the United States fell into the hands of Mr. James Mark Sullivan, whose chief recommendation was that he had been a loyal supporter of the party in power.

There are few better examples of well-intentioned blundering in international affairs than those furnished by the history of the relations between the United States and the Dominican Republic in the years beginning with 1913. It is, however, also to be borne in mind that the problems which here, as elsewhere, confronted the Wilson administration involved peculiar difficulties which it is not by any means sure that a better-chosen set of officials could have overcome.

President Wilson had announced that it would be the policy of the United States to treat Latin-American governments on the basis of equality, to try to bring into existence a spirit of solidarity on the basis of mutual appreciation, and to let them work out their own destinies. These soon proved to be standards subject to various interpretations. The new American minister was appointed in September, 1913, when a revolution was already in progress in Santo Domingo. Secretary Bryan, in his instructions intended to help in restoring peace, told him to inform the rebels that the United States, under the treaty of 1907, would not allow the Dominican Republic to increase its debts to pay revolutionary expenses and claims, that it would look with disfavor upon new taxes to pay such items, and that, if the revolution succeeded, it would not be recognized nor would any portion of the customs receipts be turned over to the leaders.[1] Certain features of such a program did not seem to be covered by the treaty of 1907 and were not evidence that the United States was allowing the Dominican Republic to work out its own destiny. To insure a fair election, Mr. Bryan next proposed American co-operation in Dominican elections.[2] No provision for such activity was found in the treaty, but, though this fact was pointed out, over thirty Americans were sent to assist in taking the vote. Following other demands showing a desire to exercise increasing functions in the direction of local affairs, Mr. Bryan finally asked that the Dominican Republic accept a financial adviser whose functions in connection with revenue and expenditures would assure budget balance and avoid, if possible, any further addition to the public debt—for increase of public obligations had already been heavy, owing to expenditures in defense of public order. To this demand the government in power yielded under the threat that otherwise it would be given no more funds from the office of the collector of customs.[3]

Such agreements would not of themselves put down revolution, and President Wilson now took a hand directly in an effort to bring about a solution in a situation already prejudiced. After setting out the altruistic purposes of the United States, he declared, "It is absolutely imperative that the present hostilities should cease. . . ." He suggested that

---

[1] Bryan to Sullivan through the American Consul at Santiago de Cuba, September 12, 1913, *For. Rel.*, 1913, p. 427.

[2] *Ibid.*, pp. 435–454. This action was also against the wishes of the Dominican Government.

[3] *Ibid.*, 1914, pp. 193–236.

the leaders get together to choose a provisional president. Later there should be held an election under American supervision. If satisfied that the election was fair, the United States would recognize the resulting government; if not, another election would be held. Thereafter, the United States would feel at liberty to insist that revolutions cease and that all later changes be in accordance with the rules of the Constitution.[4]

This plan, like the earlier projects of Secretary Bryan and Minister Sullivan, seemed to fail to meet the standard of letting Latin-American nations determine their own destinies, especially since, though the statement was couched in terms of counsel, the special commissioners whom President Wilson had now appointed were instructed as follows: "No opportunity for argument should be given to any person or faction. It is desired that you present the plan and see that it is complied with." [5]

In substance the procedure outlined was followed by the Dominican leaders. An election was held with American supervisors, but not without fraud. The President chosen was inaugurated in February, 1915, and Mr. Bryan next sought to have him confirm the intent to continue the American financial adviser accepted by his predecessor. Both candidates in the recent election had confidentially promised to do so if elected. The demands of the United States were now increased. The financial adviser was to "provide a budget" which was "to be rigidly adhered to," and no payments from government funds were to "be valid unless countersigned by" him. Internal revenue was to be put under the receivership, public works were to be put under American supervision, and American aid in setting up a constabulary to replace the army was to be asked.[6] But when these pro-

---

[4] This document, remarkable for its declaration of confidence in political processes and far-reaching in its assertion of prerogatives not covered by treaty, is found in *For. Rel.*, 1914, pp. 247–248.

[5] Bryan to Gonzales for the Commissioners, August 13, 1914, *ibid.*, p. 247.

[6] It is interesting to compare these demands with the provisions of the Haitian agreements shortly after entered. The development of the American demands is presented in *For. Rel.*, 1915, p. 297 *et sqq.*

posals were submitted to the Congress, they were rejected by a large vote.

Mr. Bryan gave way to Mr. Robert Lansing as Secretary of State on June 19, 1915, and a change occurred in the American representation in Santo Domingo, though not in American policy. The new American minister, Mr. W. W. Russell, early in the fall was instructed to call the attention of the Dominican Government to the fact that it was increasing its debt in violation of the agreement of 1907. Such a practice, if continued, would defeat the object of the treaty. These statements were a preface for a return to the demand that there be accepted a financial adviser "who shall be attached to the Ministry of Finance to give effect to whose proposals and labors the Minister will lend all efficient aid." [7] The constabulary proposals were also repeated.

Both demands were again rejected because they were outside the treaty of 1907, and were almost unanimously opposed by the people. Whichever way he turned politically, the Dominican President now met an impasse. With rising discontent in the country, he could not long maintain himself except by money secured by loan or otherwise. But the debt could not be increased without the consent of the United States, and evidently the United States would not now give its consent unless the financial adviser were accepted, which in turn it was impossible to do because of popular opposition. The situation furnished a fine example of the vicious circle. Opposition to the President continued to grow, and on May 1, 1916, he was impeached by the Congress.

Events now moved rapidly and brought an intervention the far-reaching consequences of which none of those active in the individual incidents could have foreseen. The United States continued to support the President,[8] who, however, refused to ask the assistance of American forces. American marines were landed to protect foreign interests and additional warships arrived in the ports.

---

[7] *Ibid.*, p. 333 *et sqq.* See also, for the general negotiations on finances, *For. Rel.*, 1915, pp. 297–339.

[8] See *For. Rel.*, 1916, p. 220 *et seq.*

On May 7 the President resigned, in preference to facing the responsibilities which would come with the intervention. The American minister was given wide powers by Secretary Lansing. Additional American troops were landed. The minister was instructed that no candidate for the presidency was to be approved unless he were willing to accept the "reforms" proposed by the United States.[9]

Progressive occupation of the chief towns of the country by American troops meanwhile was in process. Under instruction of the American minister, the collection of the internal revenues was undertaken by the collector general's representatives. Later, a similar control was established over expenditures, and it was decided not to recognize the new President who had now been chosen and to withhold all disbursements of Dominican funds to local authorities until the American demands were accepted.[10] These demands it was now proposed by the United States to crystallize into a new treaty, though the Dominicans declared that this could not be done without violating their Constitution. On September 30 it was proposed that the President agree to the American demands by decree—an action which would, of course, be subject to the same objection.[11] The Dominican officials declared themselves willing to accept a compromise which would not impair Dominican sovereignty, but none proposed was accepted.[12]

A crisis was now at hand. Dominican officials, by order of the United States, had not been paid for four months.[13] Demoralization in the service resulted. Secretary Lansing informed President Wilson that "revolution and economic disaster" were imminent[14] and recommended placing the country

[9] *For. Rel.*, 1916, p. 235, Lansing to Russell, August 26, 1916. The same position had been intimated in previous instructions, *ibid.*, 1916, pp. 254–255.

[10] Russell to Lansing, August 18, 1916, *ibid.*, p. 252.

[11] *Ibid.*, 1916, p. 254.

[12] An interesting presentation of the compromises suggested by the Dominicans is found in Ureña, Max Henriquez, *Los Yanquis en Santo Domingo,* Madrid, J. Pueyo, 1929, pp. 135–151. At one time the suggestions as to a financial adviser practically met those of the United States, but the demands as to reorganization of the army were found less acceptable.

[13] The "aviso" announcing this policy, dated August 18, 1916, is published in Ureña, Max Henriquez, *Los Yanquis en Santo Domingo, op. cit.*, p. 129.

[14] *For. Rel.*, 1916, p. 240.

under military occupation, "basing this on the interpretation which the United States has given to the Dominican Convention of 1907 and also upon the . . . unsettled conditions in the Republic. . . ."[15]

President Wilson on November 26, 1916, replied to Mr. Lansing's suggestion, stating, "It is with the deepest reluctance that I approve and authorize the course here proposed, but I am convinced that it is the least of the evils in sight in this very perplexing situation."[16]

The proclamation issued on November 29, 1916,[17] by Captain Knapp, commanding the American forces, based the action of the United States wholly on the treaty of February 8, 1907, and particularly on the clauses referring to the public debt, which it had been stipulated should not be increased "except by previous agreement between the Dominican Government and the United States." This provision, it was asserted, had been violated "on more than one occasion." Such "violations" Santo Domingo had explained by the necessity of incurring expenses to put down revolutions. The United States had urged the adoption of measures which would enable the Dominican Government to avoid further violations, but that Government had been unwilling to adopt such measures. As a result, public order was disturbed and future observance of the treaty was not assured. The United States had determined that the time had come to take measures to insure observance of the treaty and to maintain peace. Therefore, military occupation of the island was to occur. But it was declared, "This military occupation is undertaken with no immediate or ulterior object of destroying the sovereignty of the Republic of Santo Domingo. . . ." The object was rather to aid in establishing order, the observance of the treaty, and the duties of the republic "as one of the family of nations."

The Dominican interpretation of the treaty of 1907 came

---

[15] *Ibid.*, 1916, p. 241.
[16] *Ibid.*, 1916, p. 242.
[17] *Ibid.*, 1916, p. 247.

into conflict with that of the United States particularly as to what was meant by the phrase "public debt"—which was not to be increased without a joint agreement. There is no doubt that the obligations of the Dominican Treasury had been increased and that the credit of the nation and its ability to keep public order had thereby been compromised.[18] If this could continue indefinitely, there might arise conditions in which local credit would be exhausted, and there would then be no recourse but to resort to a foreign loan, to which the United States would be practically forced to consent, thus destroying the evident intent of the treaty. On the other hand, it was argued that the words of the treaty could not have meant that it was necessary to consult the United States every time expenditures for keeping the peace outran income. The phrase "public debt," the Dominicans contended, was clearly not used in the treaty with the intent to cover internal debts forced on the country by revolutions. They recognized that long-continued local disturbance might result in suspension of the service of the foreign debt; but, they argued, that had not occurred, and therefore the provision of the treaty could not become operative.[19] The debts referred to in the treaty were only "contractual debts or those resulting from loans." If there were divergence of opinion on this point, the natural recourse would be to arbitration, not to arbitrary action by one of the parties to the treaty.[20]

Failure to come to an agreement on this issue and the continued refusal of the Dominican Government to accept the

---

[18] The American argument on this point is set out in detail in the note of Mr. W. W. Russell, American minister, to the Secretary of State of the Dominican Republic, November 19, 1915, of which a Spanish translation appears in Ureña, Max Henriquez, *Los Yanquis en Santo Domingo, op. cit.*, pp. 71–78. This volume is a comprehensive exposition of the Dominican point of view and has been freely drawn from in the following paragraphs.

[19] See Ureña, *op. cit.*, pp. 113–119, quoting Dr. Francisco Henriquez y Carvajal. In fact, in the Dominican discussions, "public debt" was occasionally used to cover all obligations of the treasury, *ibid.*, p. 142. See the argument in the Dominican protest of December 4, 1916, and other Dominican documents, *ibid.*, p. 191 *et sqq.*

[20] Summarized from a letter of the Dominican secretary of foreign relations to Secretary Lansing, *ibid.*, pp. 194–197.

reforms upon which the United States insisted brought the military occupation of the Dominican Republic, extending into eight years.

As is to be expected, opinions as to the record of the military government during this period show wide contrasts according to the backgrounds of those testifying. The American minister, who was continued at his post, soon reported that "disappointed petty politicians were the only people dissatisfied" [21] and that "a feeling of security obtains not experienced for some time." [22] After the United States had entered the World War, the Department of State gave less attention of Dominican affairs and Navy officials were given greater responsibility. At one time the Navy officials even counseled that conversations between representatives of the Department of State and certain Dominican leaders were inadvisable and that plans be laid for control extending over "a minimum period of twenty years." Such standards, however, in view of the opinions of leading Dominicans which continued to be expressed and in view of opinion in the home country and Latin America, became less and less acceptable to the Department of State, and after 1919 its efforts were definitely devoted to bringing the anomalous position of the United States to an end.

In their relations with the people, the military forces were, as was to be expected, not altogether happy. After the period of establishment of control, during which minor clashes with dissatisfied elements occurred, peace was fairly well maintained in the greater part of the republic. Censorship of the press, established at once, became increasingly rigorous and public criticism of the government was not tolerated. Disarmament of the people was carried out except in the east, where clashes continued to be frequent. Cases of injustice and maltreatment occurred in a regrettable number. Such are not easily avoided in any military occupation. They were more numerous than otherwise would have been the case because of the character of the country and the unfamiliarity of

---

[21] Russell to Lansing, December 14, 1916, *For. Rel.*, 1916, p. 249.
[22] Russell to Lansing, January 5, 1917, *ibid.*, 1917, p. 707.

the occupying forces with the Spanish language. Abuses tended to increase, especially after the entry of the United States into the World War, when many of those more experienced in handling situations such as were to be met during the occupation were sent across the Atlantic into the major conflict.[23]

On the other hand, the forces of the occupation accomplished much which is to their credit. In education, sanitation, and public works, especially the building of roads, notable advance was made. Claims against the government amounting to over $12,000,000 were scaled down to about $3,500,000 and paid from a $5,000,000 bond issue of 1918. Less marked success attended the efforts to bring order in a highly confused land title system. It is clear, however, that the advances made were most important in the period immediately after the establishment of the occupation. Later, the Navy Department, like the Department of State, gave its attention primarily to developments across the Atlantic, and Dominican affairs were handled in a more autocratic and less constructive manner.

Dominican opinion, so far as it was able to find expression, was throughout the occupation critical of the action taken by the United States. Such action, it was asserted, involved encroachment upon the national sovereignty and was unjustified in international law, violative of the principles of the treaty of 1907, and contrary to the broader implications of the "America for Americans" policy and Pan-Americanism —both of which principles the United States had championed. In addition, the occupation, in the opinion of Dominican spokesmen, was a failure because it did not effectively forward the creation of conditions which would remedy the weaknesses of the national life, which they freely recognized.[24]

---

[23] The reports of the Navy officials concerning their activities following the occupation are in *For. Rel.*, 1917, pp. 709–720. The abuses charged to the military forces are discussed in *Hearings Before a Select Committee on Haiti and Santo Domingo,* United States Senate, 67th Congress, 1st Sess., Pursuant to S. Res. 112, Washington, 1922.

[24] A good review of Dominican opinion on these points is found in Ureña, *op. cit.*, pp. 217–241.

With the termination of the World War, the desires of Dominican leaders began to be more freely expressed, public opinion elsewhere became more critical, and the Department of State was freer to devote its attention to cisatlantic affairs. In 1919, plans for "disoccupation" began to be formulated. On Christmas Eve of the next year, the military governor was sent instructions to announce that the "friendly purposes" of the United States in using its military forces had been "substantially achieved" and that the time had arrived when it might "inaugurate the simple processes of its rapid withdrawal."

But retirement from responsibility proved, as is often the case, neither so simple nor so rapid as its assumption. To the surprise of many Americans, in the republic there arose a widespread protest against any co-operation looking toward the withdrawal of American authority. The radical demand was for "evacuation, pure and simple." [25] The impractical character of such a demand was evident to the more serious Dominicans, but the Wilson administration came to an end and its successor was long in office before local public opinion was disposed to consider a compromise course.

The Washington authorities, after the entry of the Harding administration, reflected an increasing desire on the part of the American public for return to normal conditions in relations with the Dominican and other Latin-American governments. On June 14, 1921, there was made an announcement following the tenor of that issued six months previous and outlining in detail a program of evacuation in a period of eight months. It met no more favorable a reception than its predecessor. Under these conditions, another announcement to the effect that the military government would continue at least until July 1, 1924, was made.

Soon after this position was taken, local public opinion began to change. An American commissioner sent to the island was effective in convincing many that the evacuation program involved no compromise of the vital interests of the republic.

[25] The developments here outlined are summarized from Welles, *op. cit.*, Vol. II, p. 829 *et seq.*

On September 19, 1922, a final draft of the evacuation convention was signed, and in October a provisional government was installed. The choice of a regular government did not take place until March 15, 1924, when in orderly manner about 110,000 votes were cast, half again as many as in any previous presidential contest. The new President was inaugurated on July 24, 1924, when the Dominican flag replaced the American flag after an interval of almost eight years.

Even before this, negotiations had been undertaken for a revision of the much-controverted convention of 1907. They resulted in the convention of December 27, 1924, which set out the special engagements which are now in force between the two republics.

During the period of the occupation, two new issues of Dominican bonds had occurred: one of $5,000,000 in 1918, the other of $10,000,000 in 1922. These, with the undischarged obligations of the 1908 issue, constituted the national foreign debt for which the new treaty was to make provision. Certain of the terms of the bond issues had been found onerous and required greater drafts on the customs revenues than were considered advisable or necessary. The new convention stipulated that the older issues were to be refunded and a balance for public improvements and other purposes secured through a new issue to total $25,000,000 and to be conditioned on the continued acceptance of the co-operation of the United States in the collection and application of the customs duties.

Financial functions are, according to the new treaty, to be carried on under rules practically identical with those established by the convention of 1907. Each month, one-twelfth of the interest and amortization charges on the foreign loans is to be paid, and the remaining collection of the last preceding month is to be turned over to the local Government or otherwise disposed of as it directs. In the case that in any year the annual income is over $4,000,000, one-tenth of the surplus above that amount is to be applied to the sinking fund for redemption of the bonds. This provision is more liberal than that in the 1907 convention, which required that one-half of any surplus above $3,000,000 be thus used. The provision as to a joint agreement in case of increase in the public debt remains unchanged and that concerning modification of the cutoms duties is substantially the same as before. So far as any statement in the treaty is concerned, the old controversy over what constitutes an increase in the public debt might, it appears, again arise.

One new article which is included, however, had it been in the treaty of 1907, might possibly have avoided the public debt controversy. It stipulates that any controversy which may arise between the parties in the carrying out of the convention shall be settled by arbitration.[26]

The ten years following the new adjustment of its relations with the United States brought to the Dominican Republic a period of peace and prosperity followed by one of economic distress due to the world-wide depression. The President inaugurated on July 12, 1924, Horacio Vasquez, sought to introduce reforms which might lessen the danger of new financial difficulties, and in 1929 a commission of United States experts headed by Charles G. Dawes visited the island and submitted a budgetary system, which, however, the Government has not proved able to follow without exception.

In 1928 the President had his term extended for two years and announced his candidacy for a second term in 1930. Revolutionary activity then revived, but an adjustment was peacefully arrived at through the friendly intercession of the United States minister. President Vasquez resigned and, after an interim government, was succeeded by a military man, Rafael L. Trujillo, for the term to end August 16, 1934. Trujillo was chosen for another term through an election on May 9, 1934, characterized by the opposition as "farcical."

The world-wide economic depression beginning in 1929 promptly found reflection in Dominican affairs. Foreign trade suffered heavy declines and a disastrous hurricane in September, 1930, complicated local problems. Public income seriously fell off. It became impossible for the administration to meet the obligations on its foreign debts and at the same time main-

---

[26] A collection of the texts of the agreements between the Dominican Republic and the United States is found in Welles, *op. cit.*, Vol. II, pp. 939–1024.

tain the minimum public services.[27] The Dominican Government thereafter informed the United States that it proposed to adopt emergency measures in violation of its obligations to the bondholders and of its conventions with the United States. By legislation of 1931, the customs receipts of three of the more important ports, up to $1,500,000 annually, were to be taken over temporarily to supplement the other available island revenues. Interest payments on the bonds would be continued, but it would be impossible to keep up remittances for amortization.[28] A financial adviser, an American citizen who had been put in office by the Dominican President, was appointed special emergency agent to handle the emergency funds thus made available.[29] Though the arrangement was irregular, obviously vital functions of government must be maintained even at the cost of temporary disregard of the claims of creditors of the republic. Indeed, the interests of the bondholders themselves would not be forwarded by insisting on payments which would put in danger the maintenance of such elemental services as the public order, public health, and communications.

The emergency legislation continued in force until August, 1934, when there was adopted a modification of the previous agreement which stipulated that the payment of interest on the external debts should continue as before but that the amount to be paid in amortization should be reduced. The last payments on the principal of the debts may thus be postponed from 1942 to 1970. The functions of officers appointed by the United States under the previous treaties are to be continued until the debts are paid.[30]

---

[27] Actual revenues were $15,385,843 in 1921, but fell to $7,311,417 in 1931. They were $8,415,432 in 1933.

[28] Department of State, *Press Releases,* November 14, 1931.

[29] Details of these arrangements are in *Dominican Republic, Report of the Special Emergency Agent for the period October 23, 1931 to December 31, 1932,* Santo Domingo, 1933. See also, for current developments, the annual *Report ...... of the ...... Dominican Customs Receivership,* published by the Bureau of Insular Affairs, Washington.

[30] *Report of the 28th Fiscal Period, Dominican Customs Receivership, Calendar Year 1934,* Bureau of Insular Affairs, Government Printing Office, Washington, 1935, pp. 6–9.

It is interesting to attempt to estimate the effect of the long-standing customs control upon the social, economic, and political life of the Dominican Republic. No agency of this sort operates independently of others in the body politic, and therefore causes and effects cannot be sharply traced. All the efforts made by the local population and its government to improve the conditions under which they live contribute to the result, and it is impossible to tell what would have occurred if any one of them had been lacking.

It is clear that the customs control and the various financial arrangements which have attended it have not fulfilled the hopes of their most sanguine friends. They have not brought the disappearance of movements disturbing public order and have not proved to be the key to uninterrupted, or at least steady, national advance. On the other hand, it seems fair to believe that they have been a stabilizing influence which has practically eliminated threat to the national sovereignty through interference on the part of other nations seeking to defend the rights of their citizens in disturbed areas of the country. They have also been accompanied by great improvements in the national economic position, though they alone have not been its cause.

Foreign trade has shown great variations in value and amount, as is always true in tropical countries dependent on world markets for staple crops; but, over the period from 1905 to the present, great advance has occurred. The aggregate value of imports and exports rose from $9,632,926 in 1905 to a peak of $105,257,117 in the boom year 1920. In post-war years up to 1929, it averaged well over $50,000,000 but sank in 1932 to $18,958,614, the lowest figure since 1914. They were $23,468,980 in 1934.

Public revenues have greatly increased. For the year preceding the *modus vivendi* of 1905, they were $1,864,775, being almost entirely customs revenues and port dues. In 1905 they rose to $2,806,379 and thereafter increased irregularly to reach a high point of $15,385,000 in 1929. They dropped to $7,424,650 in 1932. Over this period, revenues other than customs also have grown. From a negligible amount in 1905, they averaged above $750,000 in the period from 1910 to 1915 and reached a high point of $10,390,265 in 1929. Then they declined sharply to $4,708,420 in 1932.

Customs receipts pledged for the foreign debt service have varied fairly regularly with foreign trade, rising from $3,416,-201 in 1908 to $6,273,740 in 1920. They sank in the world depression to $2,716,232 in 1932, the lowest point reached since the control has been in operation. In 1934 they totaled $3,189,200.

The foreign debt service itself has risen and fallen as old debts have been paid off and as new ones have been assumed. The original 1908 issue of $20,000,000 in five-per-cent fifty-year bonds was entirely paid off in 1927, thirty-one years before maturity. The next large issue, that of 1918, totalling $4,161,300 and for 20 years, was retired in 1925. The $10,-000,000 issue authorized in 1922 is still in part outstanding, as are parts of the series of 1926. All told, the external funded debt on December 31, 1934, was $16,292,500. This, in view of the advance which the republic has made, is a much less serious obligation than the $20,000,000 issue of 1908. It is to be noted also that, owing to the guarantees provided by the convention, the terms of the current obligations are certainly much more favorable ones than could have been obtained had it been necessary to borrow these monies on the credit of the local government in the open market.

CHAPTER VI

Haiti and the Treaty of 1915

THROUGH much of the period since 1915, the center of political interest in the Caribbean has been Haiti. Here developed the most comprehensive and most criticized attempt by the United States to promote political stability in the region. The steps taken have been closely watched. The Haitian governing class jealously defended the national sovereignty, which it feared might not again emerge from the limitations to which it was temporarily forced to submit. Public opinion in the United States split on Haitian policy perhaps more sharply than on any other Caribbean question. Latin-American nations considered the plans followed by the United States in the republic the spear point of a new imperialistic advance, and European observers felt that local developments were a barometer not only of the southern policy of the greatest of American powers but of the relation of this policy to the Pan-American movement, of which the United States was and is the leading advocate.

Haitian affairs involve a number of factors of climate, resources, race, class feeling, education, public health, enterprise, economic development, and international ambitions which have made conflict of opinions and interests so sharp that impartial discussion of public conditions and public policy is rare both in the republic itself and elsewhere. In spite of the fact that a large body of facts concerning Haiti has become available, larger perhaps than that on any other Caribbean community except Cuba, most of the opinions expressed continue to lack the perspective given by the history of the republic and by the knowledge of the conditions which must be faced by the local population.

The island of Haiti lies almost directly south of New York on the eastern side of the Mona Passage, which separates it from the eastern tip of Cuba by somewhat over fifty miles. Its area is about 10,204 square miles, slightly more than twice that of Connecticut, or about half that of the neighboring Dominican Republic.[1]

The more northern of the two peninsulas which form the westward portion of the republic was sighted by Columbus on December 6, 1492, on his first voyage. He entered the harbor now known as Môle St. Nicholas, coveted in later days as a naval base for the American Navy, and thence coasted eastward.[2]

Colonization of the island was, practically from the beginning, identified with the cultivation of sugar and with Negro slavery. Sugar cane was introduced from the Canary Islands in 1506 and sugar soon became an important factor in local economy. These developments were pushed by the Spaniards with disastrous results for the population, which had welcomed them on their arrival. The natives did not furnish a sufficient labor supply, even in the early fifteen hundreds. Indians were imported from the Bahamas but in insufficient numbers to fill local demands. The summary estimates of the time reported the native population as 60,000 in 1508 but only 14,000 six years later. Negro labor had begun to be imported even at this early date, and the slave trade was given formal recognition by 1518.[3] As the years passed, the aboriginal population steadily fell in numbers, and dependence on Negro labor increased. Within a generation, the Indians ceased to be a factor.

The later settlement of the portion of the island which is

---

[1] For additional statistical data showing current developments, see the *Commerce Yearbook,* Vol. II, *Foreign Countries,* United States Department of Commerce, Washington (annual), and the annual reports published by the Haitian and American Governments elsewhere cited.

[2] H. P. Davis, in *Black Democracy,* New York, Dial Press, Inc., 1929, pp. 8–35, gives a good review of the colonial history of the region.

[3] See Jones, Chester Lloyd, *Caribbean Backgrounds and Prospects,* New York, D. Appleton and Co., 1931, Chap. II.

now Haiti was due to the efforts of other Europeans to break down the Spanish control of the newly discovered lands. The advance of these other nations in the region did not occur until a century and a third after the Spanish first sighted the territory. In 1629 a Spanish fleet drove English and French interlopers out of the small island of St. Christopher. A few settled in Tortuga, off the north coast of Haiti, where they were later joined by some Dutch expelled by Spain from Santa Cruz and still later by British expelled from St. Nevis. These *boucaniers*, not originally freebooters, the Spaniards tried repeatedly but unsuccessfully to dislodge.

France through the seventeenth century gave such support as she could to the settlement. Another French colony farther eastward at Samaná was removed to the present site of Cap-Haitien. New French refugees from other settlements sought to break down Spanish control in the West Indies, and finally, by the Treaty of Ryswick, in 1697 Spain recognized the right of France to the western part of the island.

The advance of the French colony, St. Domingue, came to be without precedent in the New World. Indigo, sugar, and cacao became important crops. The population grew rapidly under the influence of steady importation of blacks and widespread miscegenation. Slavery produced its worst abuses. The Negroes were so hard driven that in spite of a high birth rate it was reported that in the areas where production was most pressed they would not have maintained their numbers but for the new supplies brought by the slave ships. There were 2,000 slaves in 1681, when the colony was still unrecognized by Spain, 20,000 in 1701, and 50,000 in 1728. In 1754, plantation Negroes were estimated at 172,000 but another estimate for the same year reports 230,000 slaves. "A very conservative estimate for 1798 would be not less than 450,000." There were then about 32,000 whites and 24,000 freedmen in the colony.[4]

---

[4] The figures in this paragraph are from Davis, *op. cit.*, pp. 23 and 303. It is to be remembered, of course, that these estimates do not have official character. It is believed by some students that they understate the actual Negro population, at least in the later years.

In the period covered by these figures, the economic return from the French colony had also greatly increased. Just before the outbreak of the revolution against France, there were reported to be over 3,000 indigo plantations in operation, about as many plantations raising coffee, and almost 800 sugar and 800 cotton estates. Sugar was the greatest product. "The commerce of the colony with the mother country comprised over a third of the total foreign trade of France." [5]

In the community with this racial and economic background, revolt broke out in 1791. During its course the white, mulatto, and Negro inhabitants and the French forces sent to crush opposition were all guilty of excesses probably equalled in no conflict of modern times. British and Spanish forces held for a time portions of Haitian territory but were expelled by the brilliant Negro leader Toussaint l'Ouverture. Attempts by the forces of Napoleon to re-establish French authority failed, and by 1804 the power of France in the island was definitely at an end. The white population—with the exception of an insignificant minority—had perished or gone into exile. Twelve years of warfare had reduced the prize American colony of France to ruins and had set up the second republic of the New World.

The history of independent Haiti has been a troubled one. Except for the period of the American intervention beginning in 1915, it has figured only incidentally in international politics, and the prominent place which it held in Caribbean commerce at the end of the colonial period has never been regained. Sugar production for export practically disappeared in the period following independence, and in some years sugar

---

[5] *Ibid.*, p. 25. The actual amounts of sugar shipped from the West Indian areas in even the most prosperous years of the colonial regime were insignificant compared to those which enter international commerce in current years. In 1791, a year of high yield, St. Domingue shipped to France only 88,630 short tons. This is much less than is now produced by many individual sugar mills in Cuba.

In order to appreciate the position of sugar in the international politics of the colonial period it is necessary to remember the amount then entering all international trade, the role of sugar as a diet luxury of the time, and its high value per pound as compared to foods produced in temperate climates. Cestero, *op. cit.*, pp. 210 and 224, gives figures of Haitian production and export at various periods.

supplies actually found a place in imports. Other cultivated crops also declined in importance. Coffee gathered from trees growing in a semiwild state became the chief item in the export trade and still continues to be so.

Even in the opening years of the twentieth century, when foreign capital and enterprise were finding their way into neighboring lands, Haiti continued out of the current of world developments. Resident foreigners also were few. They were until 1918 incapable of acquiring real estate, owing to a constitutional provision adopted in 1804. They were found chiefly in the seaports, engaged in import and export trade. Instability of government and the backward character of economic life limited the role which outside influences could play in national development.

The domestic affairs of Haiti in the more than a century and a quarter which have passed since its winning of independence make a record of turmoil and tragedy. The population in 1804, it is estimated, was ninety per cent of African origin and it had been repressed under a slavery system which denied it all but the minimum of subsistence and gave it no opportunity to develop individual initiative or experience in public affairs. It came into possession of a country impoverished by the ravages of a long and destructive war. Public credit did not exist. Few if any states have started with greater handicaps.

It is not surprising that under these conditions national advance has been discouragingly slow. The basis of a national political life was lacking at the beginning of the history of the republic and has continued to be so. Control of the Government has been determined by ability to dominate the army and the customs—the latter traditionally the chief source of public income. With few exceptions, the dominant figures in Haitian life have been military men. Among the Presidents, there have been a few sincerely desirous of improving the position of the country; but, in the great majority of cases, personal rather than public interests have controlled politics.

As a result, the history of Haiti has with minor exceptions been that of a series of dictatorships in which the army influence has named the man in power, kept him in power, and determined his successor by either revolution or control of the election. Popular government, in the sense in which the phrase is used elsewhere, has never existed.

An indication of the troubled character of the history of independent Haiti may be given by a résumé of the fate of its chief executives from 1804 to 1915. The first ruler of independent Haiti, Jean Jacques Dessalines, made himself governor general for life in 1804. Later he assumed the title of Emperor Jacques I. He was assassinated in 1806. His successor, Henri Christophe, ruled as President of the "State of Haiti"—in fact, only of the north, for the country had become divided into two "republics"—from 1807 to 1811, when he became King of Haiti under the title Henri I. He shot himself in 1820. Both these rulers were Negroes. The list of Presidents of the Republic of Haiti from 1807 to 1915 includes two whose periods were partly contemporaneous with that of Christophe. The second of these brought the north and south of the country again under a single control.

Of the twenty-four Presidents in this period, twelve are listed as Negroes, six as Negroes with a dash of white blood, and six as mulattoes. Jean Pierre Boyer held office for almost twenty-five years and two others, for over eleven years each. Of the latter, one, Faustin Soulouque, after two years as President made himself Emperor with the title Faustin I. Two others held office for over eight years. On the other hand, eleven Presidents out of the twenty-four had terms of less than one year.

Only two Presidents in the list for this period lived out their terms and retired. Five died in office, "one at least by poison, one in the explosion of his palace, one on the eve of his overthrow by revolutionists." Seventeen were deposed by revolutions, and of these a number were exiled, one was murdered in prison, and one was seized in the French Legation and murdered by a mob. After 1908 the wheel of Haitian politics was in almost continuous revolution. Election to the presidency was for seven years, but in the seven-year period between December 17, 1908, and the corresponding date in 1915, "seven presidents were 'elected' and deposed" and an eighth was in the presidential office and receiving the support of United States forces to maintain public order.[6]

In the period from the time independence was secured up to 1915, economic advance was as little marked as was political stability. Statistics giving a satisfactory picture of the value of Haitian production and export are not available for either the colonial period or the period following it. The sugar, coffee, cotton, indigo, molasses, and dyewoods exported in 1791 at "present market values" one author estimates would be worth more than $50,000,000.[7]

Fair comparisons of figures such as these with those for later years are difficult not only because of changes in market values and in the value of money but because the world markets have changed enormously with developments of new cheap sources of supply and because industrial changes have destroyed the market for some articles formerly prominent in Haitian production—such as indigo, in the above list. It is indicative of the decline of importance of Haitian exports in world markets, however, that in recent years, when Haitian products have been sold at exceptionally favorable prices, the total exports have not reached a value of $25,000,000.

Revolutions, it is to be recognized, though a check to economic progress, affect the economic life of a country of few and simple products much less than might be supposed. World market conditions, in fact, influence Haitian export values probably quite as much as and perhaps more than do

[6] This summary is compiled from tables published in Davis, *op. cit.*, pp. 340–341. Of the Presidents in the seven years beginning December 17, 1908, Simon was deposed by revolution, Leconte was killed by an explosion in the palace, Auguste is said to have been poisoned, Oreste was deposed and exiled, Zamor was deposed and later murdered. Theodore was deposed and exiled, Sam was murdered by a mob, and Dartiguenave, who closed the seven-year period, was elected after the American intervention. See also Leger, J. N., *Haiti,* New York, the Neale Publishing Co., 1907, *passim,* and Crichfield, G. W., *American Supremacy,* 2 vols., New York, Brentano's, 1908, Vol. I, p. 158.

[7] Davis, *op. cit.*, p. 25.

domestic conditions.[8] The character of Haitian products is such that economic stability is not greatly affected by local disturbances,[9] although the economic basis on which the political life of the republic rests is a narrow one and, it seems, must continue to be so.

Political disturbance does not seem to have had a greater influence on the growth of population. No census has ever been taken in independent Haiti and reliance must be on estimates. Some of these indicate a very slow rate of increase up to about 1870 and a steady and rapid one thereafter. In the fifty-six years between 1870 and 1926, the population apparently increased about fourfold. In 1929 it was reported as 2,550,000. Other estimates seem to show a fairly steady in-

---

[8] The reported values of exports (in some cases estimates) in certain years were:

1900...	$13,328,000	(*Commercial Relations of the United States,* Washington, Department of Commerce, 1901, Vol. I, p. 145.)
1901...	12,300,000	(*Ibid.,* 1902, Vol. I, p. 93.)
1903...	8,585,687	(*Ibid.,* 1905, p. 303.)
1904...	17,874,926	(*Ibid.,* 1905, p. 303.)
1906...	4,100,000	(*Ibid.,* 1906, p. 147.)

These were years of comparative peace. In 1910–1913, a period during which four Presidents held fleeting control, the value of exports was $14,538,000. (*Commerce Yearbook,* 1926, Vol. II, *Foreign Countries,* Washington, 1927, p. 288.)

[9] The character of the chief exports in the colonial period, before the intervention and at present, is indicated by the following table.

CHIEF HAITIAN EXPORTS

In Thousands of Pounds

	1791*	1904†	1929‡
Sugar	177,230	......	10,427
Coffee	73,944	88,964	62,956
Cotton	6,820	3,017	10,482
Indigo	1,009	......	......
Molasses	29	......	......
Dyewoods	6,788	155,572**	46,066**
Cacao	......	5,124	3,011
Honey	......	......	1,297
Goatskins	......	......	502

* Davis, *op. cit.,* p. 25.
† *Commercial Relations of the United States, op. cit.,* 1905, p. 303.
‡ *Commerce Yearbook,* 1930, Vol. II, *Foreign Countries,* Washington, 1930, p. 280.
** Logwood and logwood roots.

crease ever since the republic's independence. The increase has been due practically exclusively to the African and mulatto population present in the island at the end of the colonial period. No immigration of any importance has occurred since that time.[10]

Before tracing the political developments in Haiti since 1915, it will be useful to survey local conditions as they then presented themselves to an observer interested in estimating the social, economic, and political endowment of the republic.

Transient visitors frequently carry away exaggerated impressions of the resources of tropical countries, a fact illustrated by many estimates of the possibilities of development in Haiti. Here, the visitor is prone to conclude, are 10,204 square miles of tropical lands whence once came the world's greatest sugar supply. Coffee, corn, cotton, cacao, tropical fruits, honey, dyewoods, and a long list of less developed products can be produced in far greater quantities than now reach the market. Livestock here may graze the year around.

---

[10] ESTIMATES OF HAITAIN POPULATION AT CERTAIN PERIODS

	Total
End of colonial period*	536,000
1870†	572,000
1880†	800,000
1887†	960,000
1901†	1,294,400
1909†	2,029,700
1926†	2,300,200
1927‡	2,550,000

* Davis, *op. cit.*, p. 24. Apparently 1798.
† *Commerce Yearbook*, 1926, *op cit.*, Vol. II, p. 288.
‡ *Commerce Yearbook*, 1930, *op. cit.*, Vol. II, p. 277.

Estimates cited by various authorities have a wide range. A note in Millspaugh, A. C., *Haiti Under American Control,* 1915–1930, Boston, World Peace Foundation, 1931, p. 13, says, "The population in 1824 or previously was estimated at figures ranging from 351,716 to one million. President Geffrard put it at 900,000 in 1863. St. John, writing in 1888, believed it had probably doubled since 1825. . . . Johnston in 1910 thought 2,700,000 a modest estimate and was inclined to put it at 3,000,000. . . . The general estimate in 1922 was 2,000,000. . . . Gen. Smedley D. Butler's estimate in 1922 was 2,500,-000. . . . The Senate Committee of Inquiry fixed the population in 1922 at about 3,250,000. . . ."

See other estimates in Cestero, *op. cit.*, pp. 222–223.

Labor is cheap. The land is on the route to the Panama Canal, the commercial crossroads of the world. Access to foreign markets from the seacoast is easy. All that is lacking is well-maintained public order, capital, and enterprise. If the first be obtained, the others will follow and what is now a neglected and backward republic will become a tropic paradise. Such visions of the future of tropic areas in the Caribbean and elsewhere have too frequently raised hopes destined to bitter disappointment. The tropics will continue to increase their yield for the world's benefit, but the problems of their exploitation are in large measure still unsolved and the development of their resources is still, as it has been in the past, much more difficult than the development of the riches of more temperate regions.

To this generalization Haiti is no exception. Highly fertile spots there are in the island. They give an extraordinary response to cultivation—but they cover only a small fraction of the total area. Haiti, taken as a whole, is highly mountainous. A very large but unascertained portion is unsuited to agriculture. In some districts, the land is too irregular to allow cultivation in more than small, scattered garden plots; in others, rainfall is insufficient, though expensive irrigation works might bring good yields under skillful management. Livestock raising, which has fair promise, is backward, owing in part, at least, to lack of initiative and to the fact that in a country which suffers from frequent revolutions livestock ownership is precarious, since cattle are "army supplies which carry themselves."

Large-scale agricultural operations are, in the greater part of the country, impractical because of the accidented character of the land. Where they could otherwise be carried on, they are hindered by the difficulty of getting good title to land—though some observers have pointed out that this is a handicap found also in many other countries of Latin America—and by the very large number of small holdings by peasants throughout the country. Large numbers of these plots are on public land and are held by squatters, who under Haitian law cannot, since 1864, acquire title against the state by prescription.[11] But dispossessing these holders would in practice create hardship and awaken widespread unrest.

Rapid change is not to be expected in Haiti because of the character of the population. There are two sharply defined classes—the elite, living in the larger towns, chiefly in Port-au-Prince, and the common people of the interior. Tourists who pay a short visit to the capital and who learn to know the upper class seldom appreciate how small is its percentage in the total population.

The number of the elite, the class which speaks for Haiti to the outside world, is variously estimated up to 50,000.[12] They are a group predominantly of Negro ancestry. They are sophisticated, race-conscious, and often well-educated—many of the better-to-do families send their children abroad to be educated. Their intellectual interests are French and their speech is French. They make up the office-holding and professional class. Persons of unmixed white blood, it appears, cannot rise high in Haitian affairs; at least, none do.

Back of this small ruling oligarchy is the great mass of the Haitian people, indigent, carefree, of low industrial initiative, often cultivating even the small plots on which they live in only intermittent, haphazard manner, seldom interested in continuous employment, and generally content to live on a low standard of life.

These are in point of numbers the typical Haitians, dependent but little on the outside world. Illiteracy among them is variously estimated at from 75 to 98 per cent. They are, on the whole, uninterested in politics except as they are inveigled, stampeded, or dragooned into the support of this or that aspirant for political honors.

Between the politically vocal minority and the unleavened mass of Haitian citizenry there is little connection or sympathy. The desire to raise the countryfolk to a higher standard of life, to give them better educational facilities, to make

---

[11] Millspaugh, *op. cit.*, p. 17.

[12] Millspaugh and a number of the officials of the occupation period were disposed to think that the elite numbered not more than 5,000. See also the class divisions given by Cestero, *op. cit.*, pp. 217–226.

them more active in contributing to national wealth, to bring them to share public duties and responsibilities, which is marked among political leaders and the upper classes in a number of other Latin-American countries, seems lacking among the better-to-do Haitians.[13]

As a result of the division of the nominal electorate, political leadership has fallen to the better-educated, class-conscious minority. Had its members developed within their own group a sense of political solidarity, stability in public affairs might have been won. The history of Haitian administrations does not show progress in that direction. The period preceding 1915, for example, saw a rapid succession of dictatorships in which one military leader after another proved his ability to overthrow the President in power but was unable to establish himself firmly in office. The elite, members of which were regularly in prominent positions in all the governments, does not appear to have been split into well-knit partisan factions of permanent character supporting this or that candidate. Successive new pretenders to power gathered a few influential friends, declared against the government, aroused an "army" among the country population, usually in the north, and marched on the capital, living on the country and such financial support as could be secured by blackmail and loot of commercial interests on the way south. Against such forces the government in power was at a disadvantage. It could seldom count on the loyal support of even those in the capital, it had only very restricted public funds at its disposal, and the lack of roads made it difficult to concentrate forces promptly to put down disorder. As a result, the country was in a condition of "permanent unstable equilibrium."

That conditions of this sort should be of long standing and not bring Haiti into serious difficulties in its international relations is at first sight surprising. In explanation, many reasons are cited. Foreign interests developed little. There were few resident foreigners. They could not hold real estate

---

[13] See a discussion of the shortcomings of the Haitian educational system, based chiefly on Haitian authors and public documents, in Cestero, *op. cit.*, p. 219 *et seq.*

and the commercial opportunities were restricted by disorder, the low level of initiative in the local population, and the character of the natural resources. When the more developed countries of the world became interested in economic and colonial expansion outside their own borders, their attention was attracted to Africa, the Near and Far East, and the stabler regions of North and South America. In addition, political expansion in the New World would involve general opposition from its republics, especially, as the years passed, from the United States. With the development of the Caribbean interests of the latter country in the period following the Spanish-American War, forward action on the part of any non-American power became less likely. The degree to which influences such as those cited may have contributed to keep Haitian foreign relations free from embarrassing complications must be a matter of opinion.

Occasionally, there arose conflicts which threatened to draw the country in controversy. Relations with France early raised difficult questions involving indemnity for damages to colonists whose properties were destroyed or confiscated. Later, disputes continued over the service on French loans. Border disputes with the Dominican Republic were long-drawn-out. On occasion, British forces bombarded Haitian fortifications in retaliation for the violation of a consulate, and German warships appeared off the coast to avenge alleged piratical acts against German shipping. But during more than a century, in spite of its revolutions and the general instability of its government, the cases in which serious conflict with foreign powers has been imminent have been surprisingly few.[14]

[14] An incident at the end of the century illustrates both the continuing powerlessness of the Government before any demands made by an advanced nation and perhaps the increasing impatience of the world with such impotence. In December, 1897, in the same month in which Bismarck had denounced the "extraordinary insolence" of the Monroe Doctrine, occurred the "Lueders Case." Lueders, a German, had a dispute with a Haitian policeman and was arrested, jailed, convicted, and sentenced to one month in prison. On appeal, he was retried under a Haitian law which denied the right of appeal to defendants, and was fined $500 and sentenced to imprisonment for a year. The German representative protested to the Haitian Government against this

The active intervention of the United States in Haitian affairs, which began in 1915, did not, however, occur without forewarning. Many factors contributed to its coming. Foreign interests, though still few, had increased in number and importance in the period after 1900. The possibility that they might be a subject of controversy was increased by what appeared to be the progressive decline of the ability of the Haitian administration to keep public order.

For some time, the Government of the United States had shown a desire to put itself in a position which would insure that, should a crisis develop, its general policy of opposing the extension of non-American control over American territory would not be brought into question. Negotiations looking to this end had not been successful, and when the breakdown in the local Government came in 1915, intervention followed. The interrelations of the influences which brought about the result merit more detailed discussion.

Among foreign interests in Haiti, those of France had always been prominent. "Haiti's foreign loans and the bonds of the National Railroad were held in France; the National Bank of Haiti was originally a French concession, and the French owned a cable monopoly. . . ."[15] In commerce and shipping, German interests were dominant. Britons owned part of the stock of the railroad. Americans had taken over

---

action and then to the German foreign office. Germany then had presented orally at a public reception to the Haitian President demands that Lueders be freed, the judges who convicted him be removed, the policeman with whom the dispute started be imprisoned, and Haiti pay $1,000 a day for the imprisonment in the first trial and $5,000 a day for that in the second.

The President refused to receive the verbal communication, and shortly two German warships appeared and issued an ultimatum requiring that an indemnity of $30,000 be paid, that Lueders be allowed to take up his business again with guarantee of his safety, and that an apology be made to the German representative, and relations with Germany should be promptly reestablished. Under this pressure, President Sam promptly yielded. See also Moore, J. B., *Digest of International Law,* Washington, United States Government Printing Office, 1906, Vol. VI, pp. 474–476; Keim, Jeannette, *Forty Years of German American Political Relations,* Philadelphia, W. J. Dornan, 1919, pp. 276–278; and Tansill, Charles Callan, *The Purchase of the Danish West Indies,* Baltimore, Johns Hopkins Press, 1932, pp. 378–381.

[15] Millspaugh, *op. cit.,* pp. 20–21. The following paragraphs are based on this author's analysis.

certain enterprises formerly held by Germans, including a sugar mill and concessions for a wharf, an electric light plant, a tramway, and a railroad.

It may be argued, of course, that irregularities in the local management of public finance are not matters which need concern foreign interests. If, however, they become so marked that default on the service of foreign debts occurs, foreign interests are affected. That such conditions developed in Haitian public finance is beyond dispute. "Political and personal plundering of the treasury had been so flagrant, so customary and so shameless that it may best be characterized as unmoral rather than immoral."[16] "Loans were floated on onerous terms to meet recurring deficits and to satisfy the rapacity of successful revolutionists and their followers." Customs duties were pledged for debt services and export duties were created and pledged. In 1912–1913, the deficit was almost a quarter of the receipts. It was covered by an internal loan and a loan from the National Bank of Haiti. The next year, the deficit was sixty per cent of the receipts. It was covered by the issue of paper money. "About 80 per cent of the government revenue was required for debt service." "In June, 1914, another internal loan was floated."[17] By the end of August, 1915, the external and internal funded debt and fiduciary currency amounted to $32,105,843.68.

Since 1903, no amortization payments had been made on the public debt of 1875, and since 1914, none on that of 1896. Interest payments had been kept up. They went into default first on November 15, 1915—after the intervention.[18]

---

[16] *Ibid.*, p. 17.

[17] *Ibid.*, p. 18.

[18] The facts about Haitian finance have been subject to frequent distortion. There can be no doubt that the public finance of the republic was in bad position for a long period previous to intervention, that foreign loan contracts were not being observed, and that there was widespread and serious pilfering of public receipts by the local officers both under the forms of law and otherwise. Under the conditions that were created by the World War, it seems clear that Haitian bonds must have gone into default even as to amortization payments and that they would have done so if the war had not occurred. Critics of American policy have made much of the fact that "Haiti never defaulted [on interest] until the United States intervened."

While this situation was developing, the Government became involved in contracts with foreign interests, two of which were to figure prominently in the crisis of 1915 and subsequent adjustments. One involved a highly unfortunate railway project, the first concession for which was granted "under dubious circumstances" in 1904. It later passed into the hands of Americans and assumed its final form in 1910. Two unfinished lines were to be united and operated under a fifty-year concession. The railroad company was to "issue bonds at the rate of $20,000 per kilometer of constructed track." The Government guaranteed interest on the bonds at six per cent and after January 1, 1916, a one-per-cent sinking fund. The enterprise was a dismal failure, contributed to by the mismanagement of the entrepreneurs and by the difficulties of the Government. By 1914 the Government was threatening foreclosure.[19]

The banking arrangements were to bring even more acute complications. A fifty-year concession to operate a national bank to act as the government depository was granted to French interests in 1880. At the time of the new loan in 1910, there was unearthed a scandal involving large thefts from the Government. Indictments were brought against the French director of the bank, two Germans, and "several very prominent Haitians"—among whom were an ex-President and three Cabinet ministers. They were convicted but not punished; in fact, the Cabinet ministers were in turn later elected to the office of President of the Republic. As a result, however, the bank was reorganized.[20]

In the reorganization, citizens of nations other than France came to hold shares. The French continued to hold about three-fourths, a portion went to three New York banks with

---

The default was precipitated by restrictions on imports during the war in France, where the chief Haitian market lay, and by shortage of ocean shipping. The full foreign debt service was resumed in 1920, when all arrears of amortization and interest were taken up.

[19] See, for greater detail, Buell, Raymond Leslie, "The American Occupation of Haiti," *Foreign Policy Association Information Service,* New York, 1929, Vol. V, Nos. 19–20, p. 334 *et seq.*, and Millspaugh, p. 21 *et seq.*

[20] See Davis, *op. cit.*, pp. 137–138, 143 *et sqq.*, Millspaugh, *op. cit.*, p. 22, and Buell, *op. cit.*, p. 335 *et sqq.*

German affiliations, a smaller fraction to a German bank, and a still smaller one—five per cent of the total—to the National City Bank of New York.

These new arrangements occurred when the series of quick changes in the government which preceded intervention was already under way and the Government was in hard straits to meet current obligations. The new contract, under the circumstances, could hardly be expected to work smoothly. "The bank was the sole treasury of the government: it received all government funds; it was further empowered to hold such funds intact until the end of the fiscal year; and it was in no way legally obligated to make advances." By the contract, also, certain funds were to be kept in the custody of the bank for monetary reform.

As the difficulties of what has come to be known in Haiti as "the period of ephemeral governments" increased, the bank was increasingly drawn into the local political contest. The Government passed a law suspending monetary reform; but the bank, alleging its obligation under its contract, refused to surrender the funds reserved for the purpose. By 1914 the bank, relying on its contract, was contemplating refusing to continue to make advances to the Government to meet its running expenses. The Haitian Chamber of Deputies proposed an issue of paper money. The bank protested that this would violate its contract and later that it would not recognize such money as legal tender. The Government then had a law passed authorizing the issue of fiat money and claimed that the bank had forced it to do so by refusing to continue its advances.

These and subsequent actions by the parties to the dispute brought the Government of the United States into the tangle. In December, 1914, the Haitian Government was informed that the United States would not recognize the proposed paper money as legal tender. The bank requested that the Department of State arrange for transfer of a portion of the funds held for currency reform to New York on an American warship. The transfer of the funds to the wharf would be unsafe, it was alleged, "owing to the state of mind of the people." Unarmed marines were landed December 7, 1914, at the siesta hour, when few of the inhabitants were in the streets, and the money was embarked without incident on the United States gunboat *Machias*.

The relations of the bank and Government continued to become strained. The Government, under a court decision, removed some of the bank funds, passed legislation for a new Government bank and an internal loan, and started printing paper money. It transferred the treasury service from the bank to a group of local merchants. Protests against these actions by the United States authorities led to offers, unaccepted on the part of Haiti, to arbitrate all differences.[21]

Protests were now made by the bank that its contract was being violated—protests supported by the United States. They brought a sharpening of American attention to Haiti, contributed to the development of the American plans looking toward the establishment of stabler conditions in the republic, and led, along with the local political crisis, to intervention.

Haiti had, up to the end of the first decade of the century, played no prominent part in American foreign policy. In 1850 and 1851 an American representative, in co-operation with agents of Great Britain and France, had sought without success to secure a promise that Haiti would not interfere in the affairs of the neighboring Dominican Republic.[22] Only in 1864, after slavery ceased to be an issue in American politics, was the independence of the country recognized.

At various times, naval vessels had visited the coast in periods of political upheaval or for the defense of the rights of American citizens. Desire for control of Môle St. Nicholas as a naval base had resulted in discussion of the lease of the port.[23] Later, American financial interests in the bank had momentarily attracted the attention of the Government. On the whole, however, American interposition in Haitian af-

[21] Millspaugh, *op. cit.*, p. 24.

[22] See Welles, *op. cit.*, Vol. I, p. 112 *et sqq.*, and above under the discussion of the Dominican Republic.

[23] See Davis, *op. cit.*, pp. 135 and 317–318 *et seq.*, for a description of incidents in 1889 involving Môle St. Nicholas.

fairs seems to have been less frequent than in a number of other weak states in which lack of public order had come to affect the interests of foreign powers.

Local developments in the period before 1915 did not give assurance that American or other foreign interests would continue to have only incidental cause for complaint. Nevertheless, so far as published documents indicate, no effort was made by the United States Government to develop a program. The administration in office was of the party associated in the popular mind with opposition to the expansion of American influence and responsibility in outlying areas. Its leaders had strongly expressed themselves in favor of letting the weaker states work out their own destinies. They committed themselves to action only under the influence of developing circumstances as specific incidents involving protection of foreign interests and the danger, real or imaginary, of interference by non-American powers in Haitian affairs presented themselves. The widely held opinion that powerful American financial interests operating in Haiti were able to influence and direct the policy of the administration seems to have no justification, though vigorous presentation by these interests of their wrongs, real and apprehended, cannot have been without influence in shaping the policy of the Government.

Looked at in retrospect, also, the policy developed by the Wilson administration after it came into power on March 5, 1913, does not seem to have been based on clear comprehension either of the local conditions existing at the time or of the long-time problems which must be solved in any attempt to improve these conditions. Step by step, the Government found itself led into support of a policy which stood in strong contrast to the standards of noninterference which both President Wilson and Secretary of State Bryan had consistently advocated. The facts, or what they believed to be facts, did not fit theory, and, in the conflict between facts and theory, the administration went forward to take a position more extreme than had ever before been assumed in relation to any other Caribbean government.

Before its first year had passed, the Wilson administration was already deeply involved in Haitian affairs. As a result of the local disorders, American warships had been despatched to the island. American marines had been landed "to cooperate with forces from British, French and German vessels in the protection of foreign interests." [24] Protests had been made against "the seizure of customs houses by the revolutionists"—action which violated the national obligations in "assignment of customs funds for the payment of definite debts" [25] and the United States had indicated its willingness "on account of the vested interests of American citizens" to lend its aid in any practical way to the Government of Haiti if such were desired. In June, 1914, the American minister reported that those directing the bank hoped that its refusal to continue advances to the Government would force the Government to ask assistance from the United States and result in American supervision of the customs collection.

In July the Department of State sent to its minister a proposed draft of a customs convention similar to that which was already operating in Santo Domingo, including in addition provision for a financial adviser whose functions, however, were described only as those of "a comptroller of accounts." [26] What degree of control the United States would seek or be willing to assume was still indefinite; but as the instability of local government continued to make itself evident, Secretary of State Bryan in October counseled an increase of naval forces for the protection of foreign interests and as evidence of the intention of the United States "to settle the unsatisfactory state of affairs which exists." Later in the year, an election supervised by American authorities was discussed as a means of bringing local political conflict to an end. Resort had been taken to such an expedient in Santo Domingo, and similar procedure was to continue to have support in other Caribbean areas.

The American program gradually became more definite.

---

[24] Millspaugh, *op. cit.*, p. 25.
[25] *For. Rel.*, 1914, pp. 335–337.
[26] *Ibid.*, pp. 347–350.

After the victory of the forces led by Davilmar Theodore, who headed the Government of Haiti three and a half months, came a statement that the United States would recognize a new government provisionally if it would agree to the establishment of a receiver of customs and financial adviser, as before proposed, settle the disputes about the railroad and the bank, protect foreign interests, engage not to lease any territory to a European government, and settle American claims by arbitration.[27] The Haitian reply accepted most of these proposals and indicated willingness to grant to Americans concessions and preferential privileges which had not been asked for but demurred on customs control.

There followed a period in which the United States wavered as to what should be its policy. Recognition was now not to be conditional but to be "considered on its merits," and customs control would be assumed only if Haiti desired it.[28] Shortly after this, Secretary Bryan informed the Haitians that the United States wished to help establish stability rather than to secure "special concessions to Americans." [29] This was the condition at the end of 1914. A new revolution was now in process and was closely watched by United States naval forces. On February 22, 1915, Theodore fell from power, to be succeeded by Guillaume Sam.

Two special missions sent from Washington now tried without success to bring an adjustment. The proposals made by the second of these showed that the United States was still uncertain as to the course to be pursued, or at least willing to consider alternatives to the previous suggestions. It was suggested that a treaty under which the United States should protect Haiti from outside attack and internal disorder be made. Haiti was to agree not to give rights in Môle St. Nicholas to foreign governments or nationals and to arbitrate foreign claims. The reply favored accepting protection from foreign aggression and the provisions as to Môle St. Nicholas.

---

[27] *Ibid.,* p. 359.

[28] *Ibid.,* p. 367. Millspaugh, *op. cit.,* at pages 29–30, suggests that the change of policy may have resulted from the influence of President Wilson.

[29] *For. Rel.,* 1914, pp. 370–371.

The co-operation of American capital to develop the country would be welcomed, as would measures for strengthening its financial position. But American official activity within the country continued to be regarded with apprehension. Haiti would agree to employ only dependable persons in the customs, and those who loaned the Government money might be consulted as to the choice for certain positions. Haiti might agree to accept help in putting down local disorder, too, but American forces should be withdrawn at once when that was demanded. This was the stage of negotiations when the breakdown of the Haitian Government in the middle months of 1915 brought intervention followed by acceptance under duress of terms which diplomacy alone had not been able to arrange.

To this point only United States-Haitian influences leading toward intervention have been discussed. The possibility that incidents which will cause European intervention may occur is always a factor determining the American attitude during times of Caribbean unrest. What may constitute such an incident depends on a variety of factors, such as the character of the alleged violation of foreign rights, the prospect that the local Government will promptly redress the wrong, the state of public opinion in the damaged state, the political relations of the latter with other states, the temper of public opinion in the United States, and, in turn, the general political position of this country in relation to other powers.

For reasons such as these, arguments minimizing the possibility of forward European action have usually found little support in administration circles. The official attitude tends to be: If action is taken to insure that non-American intervention be unnecessary, the evidences of non-American willingness to defend violated rights will be lacking, but this is not equivalent to saying that, should the United States not act to insure protection of foreign interests, other powers will not do so.

In Haitian affairs, indeed, European groups had not failed to make it evident that they had a lively interest. Whether that interest would have resulted in active and extended intervention if the United States had not acted cannot be deduced from the public documents published, but that the declarations made by these groups had a direct influence on American action seems beyond doubt.

European forces had been ashore and the war vessels of at least three European powers had been following Haitian developments early in 1914.[30] German merchants had advanced money on internal loans,[31] and their claims might be supported by the home country. American, French, and German interests in the bank were threatened as the Government position became weaker. French troops were ashore at Cap-Haitien to protect the consulate in March, 1915, and to protect the bank and other interests in June. The French representative in Washington had told the American Secretary of State that in any financial reorganization of Haiti "France should naturally be taken into partnership . . . because of the predominant importance of her financial interests in Haiti" and "ties of various kinds" in a land "formerly French."[32]

German interests also had importance. Germans held a minor part of the foreign loans, were active in business in the ports, and were the most important foreign owners of property. The United States Department of State "had good reason to believe" that "in the years 1913–14 Germany was ready to go to great lengths to secure the exclusive customs control of Haiti, and also to secure a coaling station at Môle St. Nicholas." The latter had been sought by a German private citizen in 1911 and its grant had been blocked by "the insistence of the then American minister." There is no published evidence that the German Government had asked the grant of a coaling station, although in 1913 and 1914 a German commercial firm stated to be backed by the German Government was reported to have negotiated for grants which would have permitted building coaling stations at Môle St. Nicholas. The contract was said to involve a loan to Haiti

---

[30] *Ibid.*, Jan. 30, p. 336.
[31] *Ibid.*, June 9, p. 345.
[32] *Ibid.*, 1915, Feb. 20, pp. 514–515.

and the grant of "control of Haitian customs by the concessionaire."

On July 25, 1914, the German Chargé d'Affaires wrote to the Secretary of State a memorandum referring to previous conversations with officials of the Department of State as to Haitian customs control. He referred to American opinion against participation by European powers in "customs control in Haiti." This prejudice he felt was due to "reasons of interior politics. . . . But the Imperial Government as well has to take into account the public opinion in their country. Considering our economical interests in Haiti and the part of the Banque Nationale which is owned by Germans, people in Germany would not understand, if my Government gave up their claim to participate in such a customs control."

No reply to this note was sent until after the outbreak of the European war. On September 16, 1914, Mr. Bryan reasserted the American policy of opposing non-American "control, either wholly or in part, of the Government or administration of any independent American State." The United States, he said, felt confident that Germany would not expect it to depart from support of that policy. Joint control would be a "serious departure" from precedent. Should the United States help Haiti to "escape the risks of default or disorder to her finances," it would be "planned for the benefit of all concerned." "Insistence upon an exclusive privilege in matters of this kind" would be "dictated by a desire for peace" and not by any motive unfriendly to any other nation.[33]

There was evidently ground for conflict of international interests, though that active European intervention was actually imminent is at least not clear.[34] Indeed, if an occasion had

---

[33] The letters above cited are quoted in a "Letter from Robert Lansing, former Secretary of State, to the Chairman of the Select Committee on Haiti and the Dominican Republic, May 4, 1922," in *Senate Report No. 794,* 67th Congress, 2nd Sess., p. 31 *et sqq.*

[34] Former Secretary of State Robert Lansing, in the letter cited above, gives an account of a screened landing at dusk by "a number of boatloads of German sailors with small arms and machine guns" at Port-au-Prince on July 31, 1914. Halfway down the dock, they turned back to their ship. The latter shortly after left the port and news was received by the *Connecticut,* the American vessel present, that war had broken out between Germany and

ever existed when the United States might have had to face the possibility of European intervention of a sort which would be contrary to its own policy, it passed before the time when American intervention occurred. The outbreak of the European war at once brought to an end any possibility of forward action in Haiti by non-American powers.

What was, then, the American policy just before the break which brought intervention? It was not well defined and did not contain many elements which at previous times had come under discussion officially or unofficially. It did not seek special trade privileges of the sort which had come into existence under the treaties with Cuba. It did not seek arrangements for special concessions to American enterprise—although these had at one time been offered by Haiti. It did not seek special advantages for American capital in the development of local resources. There was made no demand inconsistent with general equality of economic opportunity for foreigners. What right should be asked at Môle St. Nicholas was apparently still under discussion.

The positive elements in the United States policy as to Haiti which were now becoming more definite grouped themselves, in the main, about public order and public finance, both factors which, if regularized, would contribute to stability in the local government and to minimizing the chance of international complications. It was inevitable that in any program proposed the affairs of the National Bank of Haiti should play a prominent role. Originally a French interest, the French were still the majority and Americans and Germans minority stockholders. Loan contracts pledged the customs receipts "for the payment of definite debts." Because of the possibility that international difficulties involving these interests might arise, the United States had offered its aid to Haiti on February 26, 1914, "if such were desired." [35] Experience with provisions affecting the contracting of public debts and

---

Russia. "Thus," concludes Mr. Lansing, "the local situation was, by the outbreak of war, relieved of a conflict of interests which might have caused serious embarrassment." The only fault of the incident is its perfection.

[35] *For. Rel.*, 1914, pp. 339–340 (February 26, 1914).

collection of customs the United States had already had in Cuba and Santo Domingo—an experience which, before an agreement with Haiti was actually concluded, was to demonstrate weaknesses in the provisions applying in the latter country. The draft convention forwarded on July 2, 1914, had in part followed that in force in Santo Domingo. It included a provision reaching beyond customs collection to indefinite functions relating to "accounts."[36] Later in the year, a possible supervision of elections was under discussion.[37] Still later, arbitration of claims was added and clauses involving settlement of the bank and railroad controversies.[38] It was being made plain that the local Government would not be recognized unless it yielded to the demands of the United States. Still later, in the face of Haitian dissent, the policy shifted away from specific details—the United States, it was declared, wished to assist, even in customs control, only "in accordance with the wishes" of Haiti.[39] It seems clear that at the opening of 1915 the United States Government was still without a definite policy. It evidently aimed at the creation of stability in the local Government but had not worked out a plan by which it was to be secured. But in Haiti there were developing events which would make a program necessary.

A new revolution was under way in the north. The forces of General Guillaume Sam worked their way southward and occupied the capital on February 23, 1915. On March 4, General Sam became President, but peace did not come. Still another revolution, led by Rosalvo Bobo, was soon agitating the north, and by the end of July fighting had again reached the capital. On July 27 occurred a massacre of 167 prisoners alleged to have been taken as hostages for the safety of General Sam, carried out by General Oscar Etienne—whether acting at Sam's orders or not has not been explained.

Local opinion held Sam responsible. He took refuge in the French Legation, while Oscar Etienne fled to that of the

---

[36] *Ibid.*, pp. 347–350 (July 2, 1914).
[37] *Ibid.*, pp. 357–358 (November 4, 1914).
[38] *Ibid.*, p. 359 (November 12, 1914). See also pp. 355, 361–364.
[39] *Ibid.*, 1914, p. 367 (December 12, 1914).

Dominican Republic. The French Legation was threatened by a mob. The French minister cabled for naval support. The American representative asked that an American warship be sent to the capital to guard against eventualities. The *Washington* thereupon steamed toward Port-au-Prince. It was just arriving on the morning of July 28, 1915, when members of a crowd gathered about the French Legation, entered it, dragged out President Sam, and threw him to the mob over the iron gate at the entrance. He was promptly killed. The body was dismembered and portions were paraded around the streets. Oscar Etienne had met a similar fate at the Dominican Legation a few hours before.[40]

The Department of State on July 28 sent instructions to Admiral Caperton, now arrived on the *Washington,* "that American forces be landed at Port-au-Prince and that American and foreign interests be protected; that representatives of England and France be informed of this intention—informed that their interests will be protected, and that they be requested not to land." [41]

The American intervention apparently met the approval of the local public. Native leaders co-operated in the disarming of the soldiers and the populace. American marines arrived promptly, and disturbers were arrested or dispersed. Under instructions from the Navy, Admiral Caperton was to "conciliate Haitians to fullest extent consistent with maintaining order and firm control of situation" and to declare that the object of the Americans was only to protect Haitian independence and establish "a stable and firm government by the Haitian people." The Americans would stay "only so long as will be necessary for this purpose." [42]

Though the details of American policy were still unformu-

---

[40] The details of the chaotic events of the end of July were reported to the State Department by Admiral Caperton and Chargé Davis on July 27 and August 2. (*For. Rel.,* 1915, pp. 474–478.) An account based on information collected on the ground is given in Davis, *op. cit.,* pp. 161–179.

[41] "Inquiry into Occupation and Administration of Haiti and Santo Domingo," *Hearings before a Select Committee on Haiti and Santo Domingo,* United States Senate, 67th Cong., 1st Sess., p. 307. This publication is hereafter cited as *Hearings. For. Rel.,* 1915, pp. 475–476.

[42] *Hearings,* p. 313. See also *For. Rel.,* 1915, pp. 475–476, 481.

lated, it is clear that from the time of the intervention the American attitude became stiffer and that the policy to be adopted would be less influenced by local opinion. Two candidates now had pretensions to the presidency, Philippe Sudre Dartiguenave and Rosalvo Bobo, the leader of the revolution against Sam. Admiral Caperton believed that the former would be elected and reported that Dartiguenave recognized that "Haiti must agree to any terms laid down by the United States." [43] Dartiguenave, he reported, felt that the Legislature would "cede outright" Môle St. Nicholas and grant the right to intervene to keep order, customhouse control, and "any other terms."

The admiral proposed now to "permit" an election [44]—it had been delayed at his request. On August 9, 1915, the Department of State gave instructions that it be made clear to the local Congress that the United States "had no design upon the political or territorial integrity of Haiti" but wished only to establish a stable government and to maintain domestic peace. It should, however, "be made perfectly clear to candidates" in the election which the Congress was to hold "that the United States expects to be intrusted with the practical control of the customs, and such financial control . . . as the United States may deem necessary for an efficient administration." [45]

The election was held on August 12, 1915, "under protection of marines." The best opinion is that, while coercion of the legislative bodies in their voting did not occur, it is nevertheless clear that the result was assured by the position which the United States forces had come to occupy.[46]

The American proposals now took concrete form. A draft treaty which the Congress was to be asked to pass without modification was sent to the American minister. Thereafter, the newly elected government would be recognized. Meanwhile, the naval forces, under instructions, took charge of the customhouses and deposited collections with the national

---

[43] *Hearings,* p. 312.
[44] *For. Rel.,* 1915, pp. 478–479 (August 7, 1915).
[45] *For. Rel.,* 1915, pp. 479–480 (August 10, 1915).
[46] See Millspaugh, *op. cit.,* pp. 40–41.

bank. Admiral Caperton requested additional forces to allow more effective military occupation, which would be important in view of the "pending treaty negotiations." [47]

But the proposed treaty was not accepted without protest by the Haitian Legislature. The customs control was not acceptable. Opinion against the American suggestions was aroused, especially among the elite of the capital, who had dominated former governments. The attitude of the United States became more menacing, but discussion of alternatives to some of its proposals was granted.[48] The provision for a financial adviser of extended powers—now definitely included in the American demands—was especially criticized and other changes which would "concede all United States demands but . . . in a manner less humiliating to the Haitian people" and in ways consistent with the Haitian Constitution proposed.[49] Certain modifications proposed by the Haitian minister of foreign affairs were accepted and the treaty was signed on September 16, 1915. It was ratified by the Chamber of Deputies on October 6. A group in the Senate wanted further modifications, and in the north there was increasing disturbance resulting in expansion of the activities against the *cacos* by the Navy.

Under these circumstances and by direction of the Secretary of the Navy, Admiral Caperton on November 10 informed the Haitian Cabinet on his own authority that he believed that, if the treaty did not pass promptly, the United States forces would stay in the country and support the Government until it was accepted. The Senate then assented on November 11, 1915.[50] In the United States, the Senate voted to advise ratification on February 28, 1916. Ratifications were exchanged and the treaty proclaimed on May 3.

The terms of the treaty as adopted showed marked development of the program which had been outlined in July, 1914. They were not as definite in statement as the proposals ad-

[47] *Hearings*, p. 335.
[48] *For. Rel.*, 1915, pp. 439–440.
[49] *Ibid.*, p. 443.
[50] *Hearings*, pp. 394–395; *For. Rel.*, 1915, p. 458, notes the same action, Daniels to Caperton, November 10, 1915.

vanced in August, 1915, owing, it appears, to modifications adopted to meet Haitian objections. Some clauses had become vague and thus laid the ground for future dispute.

A preamble recites the desire of Haiti to remedy local economic and political conditions and the desire of the United States to assist to that end. The United States will help by good offices in the development of agricultural, mineral, and commercial resources and in the establishment of the finances of Haiti on a sound basis. The President of the United States will nominate and the President of Haiti "appoint a General Receiver and such aides and employees as may be necessary" to handle the customs receipts. Similarly, a financial adviser "who shall be an officer attached to the Ministry of Finance, to give effect to whose proposals and labours the Minister will lend efficient aid, shall be appointed."[51] This officer shall "devise an adequate system of public accounting, aid in increasing the revenues and adjusting them to the expenses, inquire into the validity of the debts of the republic, enlighten both governments with reference to all eventual debts, recommend improved methods of collecting and applying the revenues, and make such other recommendations to the Minister of Finance as may be deemed necessary for the welfare and prosperity of Haiti."

Both governments engaged to give "all needful aid and full protection in the execution of the powers conferred and duties imposed" on the officers mentioned.

Funds collected by the general receiver are first to be applied to pay the expenses of the services maintained under the receivership and the financial adviser, and then, in order, to be applied to the interest and sinking fund of the Haitian public debt and to maintaining a constabulary, to be created. The remainder is to be paid to the Haitian Government for current expenses. Reports of moneys collected are to be made to both governments monthly. Haiti is not to "increase its public debt except by previous agreement with the President of the United States," or contract debts or assume financial

[51] This phrasing has given rise to wide difference of opinion.

obligations beyond those for which service could be provided from ordinary revenues, or change the customs duties. To improve general conditions, Haiti "will cooperate with the Financial Adviser" in matters involving collecting and disbursing revenues and finding new sources of revenue. To keep the peace, a constabulary, made up of native Haitians but officered by Americans until Haitians can be made qualified for command, is to be created.

Haiti promises not to give any of the national territory to a foreign power by "sale, lease, or otherwise," or to enter any agreement with another power which will "impair" independence. Haiti will settle all foreign claims by arbitration. Sanitation and public improvements are to be under the supervision of an engineer or engineers nominated by the President of the United States and appointed by the President of Haiti.

Both parties pledge themselves to carry out the treaty, and, if necessary, "the United States will lend an efficient aid for the preservation of Haitian Independence and the maintenance of a Government adequate for the protection of life, property, and individual liberty." [52]

This was then the most far-reaching of the treaties of the United States with countries of the Caribbean. As might be expected, its terms show the influence of the agreements with Cuba and the Dominican Republic. The provisions on intervention to protect independence and "life, property, and individual liberty" and declaring against cession of territory and limitations on the public debt, adopt phrases used in the Platt Amendment. The major portion of the wording as to the general receiver, his application of funds, and his reports on work done recall provisions in the Dominican treaty of 1907, in which also appear the principles of the rule against modification of customs duties.

But the Haitian treaty went further in establishing a financial adviser. Some officer of this sort seemed to have been shown to be necessary by the weaknesses which had appeared

---

[52] *For. Rel.*, 1916, pp. 328–332.

in the Dominican agreement. The functions of the new official were set out in ambiguous language, perhaps in part to save Haitian susceptibilities, perhaps because it was felt that the exact boundaries which his authority should have could not be stated and should be left to be determined by experience. The provision for claims settlement, engineering services, and a constabulary to take the place of the army were also new.

Reading between the lines, it is possible to see fairly clearly the general object sought by the United States—which had, except for details, determined the form of the treaty. It was by no means clear how some of the provisions were to be fitted to the peculiar conditions of Haiti. As a result, the treaty had to be supplemented by interpretations more or less strained—a fact which did not uniformly contribute to its smooth working.

The American Government was put by the treaty in a dominant position in Haitian affairs. The agreement was not a convention entered freely by both parties. It was accepted by Haiti only under pressure. On the other hand, it did not give the United States a free hand; and in practice, even in the earlier period when military control was most emphasized, Haitian officials at times protested against and defeated American plans.

The period following the ratification of the treaty could hardly be expected to be without many difficult problems and irritating incidents. No country can take over such wide functions as the United States was assuming without mistakes and without at least occasional clashes with the local population. Further, the Department of State of the United States has never been organized for supervision and direction of functions such as the treaty put in the hands of American officers. At the time when the agreement was made, too, attention was concentrated on European developments, to the neglect of what were relatively less important fields.

CHAPTER VII

Haiti Under American Control

THE political developments in Haiti after the American occupation did not meet the hopes of those who expected rapid advance. The delays in deciding upon a program and the failure to secure the co-operation of the politically active portion of the Haitian people both limited what could have been accomplished. Even had neither of these handicaps existed, the hopes of the more sanguine would have been disappointed, for the economic, social, and political life of a country cannot be transformed in any period of ten or twenty years.

Philippe Sudre Dartiguenave occupied the presidency from August 12, 1915, to May 15, 1922. He sought to modify the Constitution of 1889 to make it accord with the regime now in control. The Constitution could be changed only by a National Assembly of the two legislative houses. A dispute with the Senate and later with the Chamber brought disregard of this provision by the election of a new Legislature—not under the terms provided in the Constitution—its dissolution, the drafting of a new constitution by the Haitian executive with the co-operation of American officers, and a plebiscite at which it was adopted. The voting was orderly, but the Gendarmerie had instructions to work for the adoption of the revised fundamental law. It was approved by an overwhelming majority.

A curious provision of the new constitution set out that the call for the first legislative elections should be by presidential decree in "an even-numbered year." Till the Legislature was called, the Council of State should legislate. Its members were appointed and removed by the President. President Dartiguenave did not call the elections in the first even-numbered year, and, through his powers to determine the membership of the Council, he was in a position to dominate legislation.

On the other hand, the new government was not a figurehead at the comand of the Americans. It showed a decided "independence." Shortly, it was in conflict with the American authorities because it refused to pass certain legislation including a contract for stabilizing the currency. Further, at least one provision of the treaty promptly became unenforcible under existing conditions. The clause as to the charges which should be met from customs receipts before any money should be turned over to the Government for current expenses was not carried out between 1915 and 1920, "for if it had been, little or nothing would have remained for salaries and other ordinary expenses of government." [1]

To bring an end to what were considered obstructionist tactics, the American authorities proceeded in 1920 to enforce strictly the provisions as to order of payment. This meant that there was no money available for salaries. The Haitian Government under this extraordinary pressure yielded and thereafter was practically in the position of having the Americans exercise a right of veto over its acts.

At the end of the first five years of the occupation, the politically active part of the local population, which continued highly critical of the American program, found its position strengthened. The European war had come to an end, the American public was giving greater attention to Haitian affairs, "the rights of small nations" were being widely discussed, alleged abuses by the American forces were aired, Latin-American nations were critical of the "aggressive" action of the United States, and a national election in the United States brought Haitian affairs into the field of partisan politics. A large number of investigators, official and unofficial, visited the republic.

---

[1] Millspaugh, *op. cit.*, pp. 79–80.

A Senate Committee of Inquiry began an exhaustive investigation in August, 1921, and brought in a report on June 26, 1922. It admitted some errors but generally approved the activities of both civil and military officers in the island, thought there was no occasion for modifying the treaty relation, and recommended changes, the most important of which was the appointment of a single representative of the United States—"a high commissioner" with diplomatic powers to whom the officers appointed under the treaty and the military stationed in the island "should look for direction and guidance . . ."[2]

Following the recommendation of the Committee, the United States established a high commissioner in Haiti on March 11, 1922, and the control of American activities was centralized. Almost contemporaneously with the establishment of the new American chief official, a new Haitian President came into office. Louis Borno, who had held office in previous governments, was chosen over Mr. Dartiguenave, on April 10, 1922, by a vote of the Council of State.

Peace had been established. American activities were under a single head. Borno was in friendly relations with the American officials. He was a man of force, and, through the power of appointment to the Council of State, he could control Haitian legislation. In addition, foreign trade picked up, making economic problems less insistent.

Popular assent, however, the new regime still failed to win. The upper-class Haitian continued to resent American control, the "unconstitutional" government, and the continued postponement of legislative elections. If Borno was on good terms with Colonel Russell, the high commissioner, he became identified with the occupation; if the officers appointed under the treaty were supervised and directed by the high commissioner, they also were not officers of Haiti and their work had the taint of the occupation. A sharp contrast developed. The work accomplished under the treaty steadily improved while the articulate portion of the Haitian population became in-

---

[2] For this investigation, see *Hearings* and *Senate Report No. 794,* 67th Cong. 2nd Sess., *passim.*

creasingly bitter against the foreigners and those of their co-citizens who co-operated with them.

On April 12, 1926, the Council of State re-elected Mr. Borno. When would come that "even year" spoken of in the Constitution in which popular elections should be held? Not in 1928,[3] though President Borno then indicated it would be in 1930. Later he indicated that not even then would the "even year" have arrived.

The repeated postponement of the legislative elections helped to crystallize opinion against the dictatorship and in favor of a modification of American activities. In June, 1929, prominent Haitians had petitioned President Hoover that the Borno regime be ended. In his message to Congress, December 3, 1929, Mr. Hoover asked approval of the appointment of a committee to study what steps should be taken to develop a "more definite policy" in Haiti.

The resulting "Forbes Commission" arrived in Haiti on February 8, 1930, and reported on March 26. After reviewing the accomplishments of the occupation, the Commission, among other things, declared for "increasingly rapid Haitianization" of the treaty services so that Haitians could take them over at the end of the treaty period, the recognition of a President properly chosen by a newly elected Legislature acting as a National Assembly, the appointment of a civilian minister to succeed the high commissioner, the gradual withdrawal of the marines, and the negotiation by the new minister of further modifications of the treaty providing for less intervention in Haitian domestic affairs and defining the assistance the United States would give in restoring order and maintaining credit.[4]

Under the arrangements made for re-establishment of repre-

[3] There was held in 1928, however, a nation-wide voting at which the people were asked to pass upon constitutional amendments on reformation of the courts, freedom of the press, jury trial, taxation, and the terms of certain public officers. Borno had set out at length the unpreparedness of the country population for popular elections, but he submitted this list of complicated constitutional questions to their suffrage.

[4] *Publications of the Department of State, Latin American Series No. 2, Report of the President's Commission for the Study and Review of Conditions in the Republic of Haiti,* March 26, 1930, Washington, 1930, pp. 1–43.

sentative government, a temporary President was chosen and inaugurated on May 15, 1930. On November 18 he was succeeded by Stenio Vincent, elected for a full term by the National Assembly. Also, in accord with the recommendation of the Commission, an American minister with supervision over the treaty services replaced the high commissioner.

In August, 1931, there was made an agreement by which, as of October 1, 1931, the treaty services involving public works, agriculture and industrial education, and public health (except the sanitation of Cap-Haitien and Port-au-Prince) were turned over to the Haitian Government. Only the offices of the financial adviser-general receiver and the *garde d'Haiti* continued under American control. Obligations assumed in connection with bond issues it was felt required the continuance of the first and the need to train Haitian officers for the Garde, or constabulary, the second. It was expected that Haitian officers would "be available to replace all American officers" by May, 1936.[5]

The Haitian administration soon showed itself anxious to speed still more the departure of the Americans. In September, 1932, there was signed a treaty looking toward the complete Haitianization of the Garde by December 31, 1934, and the reduction of the control over finance, but it proved unacceptable to the Haitian Legislature. On August 7, 1933, however, an executive agreement for withdrawal in October, 1934, of the United States military forces, complete Haitianization of the Garde, and limitation of the financial functions to be performed through American officers was signed.[6]

Study of the political developments may well be followed by an appraisal of the result of the far-reaching, long-continued intervention in Haitian affairs. The various features are reviewed here substantially in the order in which the treaty provisions referring to them occur.

---

[5] *Publications of the Department of State, Press Releases,* October 3, 1931. The issue for August 15 contains the text of the "Haitianization Agreement."

[6] *Haiti, Annual Report of the Financial Adviser-General Receiver, for the fiscal year October, 1932–September, 1933,* Port-au-Prince, p. 3. The last of the marines left Haiti under this convention on August 15, 1934.

The standards sought became clearer as the occupation continued. Policy and program, as was to be expected, underwent modifications as experience was gained. The organization of American activities after the treaty had been adopted proceeded as haltingly as the Washington administration had formulated its policy as to the control upon which it would insist. Advance, where experience is lacking, usually has that characteristic, but hesitance was accentuated in this case by the dispersion of authority over Haitian affairs among a number of authorities in Washington and in the island. The dominance of European affairs in American international relations drew attention from Caribbean developments which might otherwise have been a center of attention for the administration, Congress, and the public.

In the Department of State, in the first years after the treaty, there was no organization fitted to assume the unusual responsibilities which it created. The officers in charge of Latin-American affairs changed frequently. Naval officers active in Haiti conferred with officials of the Department of State but were not under its control. Some duties in Haiti were discharged through the Bureau of Insular Affairs of the Department of War. The American diplomatic representative in Haiti exercised no general authority over American military forces, and even his relations to "treaty officials" were not well defined.

In the period immediately following the treaty, the marine officers who organized the constabulary had wide, and, in practice, almost independent powers not only in military but also in civil affairs. Sanitation and public works activities were only after delay transferred to specially designated treaty officials. To add confusion to what was already an impossible "organization," the American officers on duty in Haiti were themselves often changed. The period from 1915 to 1922 was one in which the responsibilities undertaken in Haiti were sadly neglected.

After the report of the Senate Committee of Inquiry issued on June 26, 1922, activity in Haiti was put directly under the supervision of the Department of State, but a military man,

Colonel J. H. Russell, already in service in Haiti, was put at its head. Many felt that it would have been better to choose for the place a man unidentified with the military occupation and of experience in administration, commerce, and finance. Nevertheless this unification of authority brought a decided improvement both in the relations with the Haitian officials and in the work to be done under the treaty. The later re-establishment of a civilian minister at Port-au-Prince was followed by adjustments which relieved the tension between the occupying forces and the political leaders. Such a change was to be expected, in any case, with the modification of American policy.

Most criticized of the American activities in Haiti have been those involving the military forces in the years immediately following the treaty. Information as to what occurred is incomplete and seldom impartial. Long-continued military control of a civilian population can hardly fail to be irritating.

Promptly after the making of the treaty, efforts were undertaken to disarm the so-called *caco* bands still active in the interior. Some of these accepted the offers made. Some did not. The American authorities then sought to "pacify" the country through a campaign against all armed groups. The number of Haitians killed caused a bad impression on the Navy Department, which declared against "further offensive operations." [7]

Difficulties developed in 1917–1918 owing to the revival of the "*corvée*" law, under which men could be required to work on local roads for certain periods each year.[8] Road construction, it had been decided, was essential to effective maintenance of order. The work was undertaken by the recently organized Gendarmerie—the new Haitian force officered by Americans. Actual recruiting had usually to be delegated

[7] *Hearings,* p. 78.

[8] Similar laws are found elsewhere in Latin America; see that of Honduras discussed in *Commerce Reports,* November 23, 1931, Washington, United States Government Printing Office, p. 463.

to Haitian local officials or Haitian gendarmes. Work on the roads was unpopular, especially when the demands were extended to include labor outside the districts of the laborers' homes and lasting longer than the legally prescribed period. "Most of the mistreatment of *corvée* workers appears to have been by Haitian gendarmes." [9]

At the end of 1918, the *corvée* was stopped, but by that time there was under way an insurrection against American authority which, it was estimated, at one time came to involve one-fifth of the population. The gendarmes proved unable to handle the situation. The marines came to their aid, and by the middle of 1920 the opposition was crushed. Haitians declared that 2,250 casualties had occurred since the beginning of the occupation. American investigators estimated them at about 1,150. The "pacification" had been accomplished largely through small scouting parties, often made up of gendarmes led by marine privates.

It seems beyond doubt that during these operations the rules of civilized warfare went unobserved. Though investigation by Navy authorities and by the Senate Committee did not find that responsible officers had sanctioned the abuses and asserted that the Marine Corps deserved "admiration" for the way in which its men accomplished a "dangerous and delicate task," it is clear that the campaign heightened anti-American feeling in the island and aroused widespread prejudice elsewhere against the "Haitian adventure." [10]

On the other hand, the Marine Corps is to be credited with constructive work of no small importance. With the exception of the disturbance of public order above noted, Haiti under the occupation enjoyed peace to a degree unknown for a century. Property and person were given security. The American-officered Gendarmerie created to take over the function of maintaining order replaced the old army and police,

---

[9] Millspaugh, *op. cit.*, p. 89, and references cited.

[10] Details of the campaign are given in summary form in Millspaugh, *op. cit.*, p. 86 *et sqq.*, Buell, R. L., *op. cit.*, p. 349 *et sqq.* The testimony appears at length in *Hearings*.

became increasingly efficient, and developed an excellent *esprit de corps.*

The public works undertaken became an outstanding accomplishment. At first they were largely due to the marine forces and the Gendarmerie. Only in 1920 was an organization completed for the public works which under the terms of the treaty of 1915 were to be carried on under the direction of American engineers. Thereafter there was built up a staff of employees "capable of functioning with a minimum of Treaty supervision" and having permanence "similar to that of the Civil Service of the United States." The number of Americans in this service was always low and by 1930 was less than two-fifths of one per cent in a total of 6,162. Serving opposite the Americans were Haitian engineers or architects who were in training to take over active charge of the work. By 1930 half of the departments and districts had come to be under Haitians. Under the agreement of 1931 they became wholly so.

Roads usable at all seasons hardly existed in 1915. Bridges were few and dangerous and sidewalks were almost unknown. Until June, 1919, rapid clearance of temporary roadways was under the direction of the Gendarmerie, and 582 miles were made passable in dry weather. By 1923 many roads had been relocated, drainage had been improved, and sixty per cent of the roads had been graveled. By 1930 about 1,078 miles of road were open to automobile traffic. On 625 only, owing to lack of funds, was "fairly adequate" maintenance possible, however. Work on keeping open the principal "trails" feeding into these roads had been begun.

Until 1920 the lighthouses of the republic consisted of three kerosene lights at Port-au-Prince and one at Cap-Haitien. In 1930 there were fifteen of modern character. The wharves, except for a cement dock at the capital, were dilapidated timber piers at the beginning of the occupation. By 1930, five additional ports had reinforced concrete equipment. Similar advance had been made in the telegraph and telephone systems—the latter had practically been abandoned at the capital since 1911. Both now reach the important towns and the services are operated at a profit to the Government.[11]

One of the most striking advances made since 1915 has been in the construction of public buildings. A beginning had been made on the National Palace before the occupation, but in the years following, work was discontinued for lack of funds. After 1920 the structure was carried to completion. Schools, hospitals, rural dispensaries, barracks, customhouses, and other public buildings of modern sort have since claimed a large part of the funds devoted to public works. The pressing needs for construction have now been met.[12]

American activities for improving public health had marked success and were generally appreciated by Haitian critics. Prevalence of tropical and other diseases, the low individual income of the people, the absence of medical service in the country districts, and the slight attention formerly given to public health created conditions which called for drastic remedies. "The whole country teemed with filth and disease and Haiti . . . had reached a state that was pathetic indeed." [13]

Legislation putting health work on a satisfactory basis for carrying out the work contemplated in the treaty was secured only in 1919. "The few so-called hospitals," "miserable shacks to which more miserable human wrecks were brought to die," were replaced as rapidly as possible by modern equipment. At the end of 1929 there were in use eleven hospitals with a personnel of 2,222, of whom all but 1.72 per cent were Haitians. A nation-wide network of rural clinics was established. These clinics numbered 147 in 1929, when the total consultations and treatments for the year reached 1,341,596 in a population estimated at 2,550,000.[14] The widely prev-

[11] Summarized from Duncan, Commander G. A., *The Public Works of Haiti,* Port-au-Prince, Printing Office of the Service Technique, 1931.

[12] *Eighth Annual Report of the American High Commissioner,* Department of State, Washington, 1930, p. 25 *et sqq.*

[13] Melhorn, Captain K. C., *The Health of Haiti,* Baltimore, Waverly Press, 1930, p. 10. This publication gives an exhaustive review of health work in Haiti. See also Melhorn, Commander K. C., *Annual Report of the Director General of the Public Health Service for the Fiscal Year 1927–1928,* Port-au-Prince, 1928.

[14] This estimate is as of 1927 *(Commerce Yearbook,* 1930, *op. cit.,* Vol. II, p. 277).

alent diseases which claim major attention are yaws, malignant malaria, and diseases caused by intestinal parasites.

Public health activities included, besides treatment of patients, preventive measures such as quarantine regulations similar to those in the United States, refuse disposal, mosquito control, and water purification. Training of Haitians to do medical work of all grades was actively promoted.

The establishment of acceptable health conditions in Haiti was by no means accomplished—in fact, the work was only begun; but the creation of facilities to carry on the fight against disease is one of the most important benefits which Haiti came to enjoy as a result of the treaty of 1915.

Activity in promoting education in Haiti was limited in the early years of the occupation. The school system was not mentioned in the treaty and was brought into the field of supervised activity only through the treaty provision referring to the improvement of agriculture. Partly, at least, because of this alleged straining of the intent of the treaty, the undertakings met sharp criticism from the Haitian elite, who as a class have never sponsored a nation-wide school system [15] and have not looked with favor on the rise of a middle class which might upset their own position in public affairs. In addition, the local educational system in the urban centers had been of the formal cultural sort, and vocational and agricultural instruction had been neglected. The better-to-do classes had not been interested in instruction of a manual sort and they continued to oppose its extension.

---

[15] Tulio M. Cestero, in his *Estados Unidos y las Antillas,* Madrid, Compañía Ibero-Americana de Publicaciones, 1931, pp. 218–222, describes Haitian education. Common schools were created only in 1859. The number nominally established was 175 in 1860 and 775 in 1895. But Murat Claude, Minister of Public Instruction, in 1909 declared, "Primary education does not give as yet the hoped for results and the reasons are always the same, as the Department reports each year . . . the laxness of teachers, resistance of the parents and bad financial position of the country." Frederic Marcelin, sometime Secretary of the Treasury, declared, "Yearly, large sums are devoted in the Haitian budget to the support of schools. . . . This assignment is, pity 'tis, one of the most cruel farces to which the Haitian government subjects its people. . . . The funds appropriated for this splendid purpose find their way into the pockets of functionaries . . . or perhaps never leave the treasury." *Ibid.,* p. 220.

Because of the limitations of the treaty and the conviction that it was the best way to give the people of Haiti an economic and cultural background which would promote stability and a rising standard of life, American activity in education emphasized the creation of normal schools to train teachers for the country districts and the establishment of local schools teaching such subjects as agronomy, horticulture, animal husbandry, and dairying in addition to the usual elementary subjects of a more strictly cultural nature. In addition, experimental stations to promote diversification of crops and the spread of knowledge on the elimination of plant and animal diseases were established. Work in this field was developed only after 1923.

The effort to enlist Haitians in this work brought the total list of those employed in it at the end of 1929 to 476, of which only twenty-four were Americans. At the end of 1929, 11,430 students were enrolled—a good advance, but a pitiful number compared to the total of school age in the country.[16]

American efforts to set up an educational system in Haiti took form, however, with what appears to those not familiar with local conditions, unexplainable slowness. Haitian proposals for greater educational facilities were not lacking promptly after the occupation, but they failed of American support on the ground that revenues were insufficient at the time for support of any but elemental Government activities. Even projects for agricultural and normal education were disapproved. Objections were made to wider support of the existing schools because of alleged corruption in the handling of school funds and because the teachers appointed were incapable and sometimes political appointees who were themselves illiterate. Opposition to a Haitian program of education was alleged by the local leaders to be explained by the desire to oppose anything which would show that the Haitians were capable of doing something for themselves.

When, after a number of false starts, an American educational program got under way, it is clear that the plan out-

---

[16] *Annual Report, 1928–9, Bulletin No. 17, Technical Service of the Department of Agriculture and Professional Education,* Port-au-Prince, 1929.

lined was too ambitious for the island's resources. The American head of the educational system soon found himself the center of a political contest, and his successor, though personally acceptable, was refused confirmation in his office because of his association with the former head. There is no doubt that, creditable as the work done with limited means proved itself to be, what could have been accomplished was greatly lessened by the fact that the questions of education and who were to lead the work in it became a political issue which Haitians came to look upon as involving in essence the defense of that portion of the National Government which the treaty had intended to leave in their hands.[17] Meanwhile, the Haitian schools continued as a separate system. The funds granted them were inadequate, the teachers were poorly prepared, and housing, where it existed, was rudimentary. The management of the funds voted to schools under Haitian management, impartial observers admit, was not lacking in the defects alleged by the American administrative officers.

The failure to secure approval of the American educational program is especially to be regretted. Prompt establishment of schools even with the limited financial support which was available might have done something to lay the foundation for the rise of a middle class. If a demonstration of the advantages of more general education could have been made, the Haitian ruling class might have modified its traditional attitude. It might then have been disposed to continue the work initiated after American withdrawal.

The clash which occurred, however, stiffened the demand for the traditional "French" curriculum as opposed to the sort of education which it is clear would be of greatest use to the average Haitian; moreover, it so prejudiced opinion against not only the course of study but also the teaching personnel of the schools sponsored by the Americans that many of the teachers in these schools and many informed persons outside them came to believe that their employment

[17] Details of the earlier portion of this controversy are in Buell, *op. cit.*, p. 360 *et sqq.*

would promptly terminate with the ending of American control, a belief justified by the event.

No fair appraisal of the work done in the lines above discussed can fail to recognize that during the occupation advance unquestionably was made. It was uneven advance for a number of reasons. In some cases, co-operation on one side or the other was lacking. The Government at Washington did not uniformly appreciate the character of the task to which it had set itself, or at least it failed to develop promptly an organization fitted to meet the problems it was called upon to face. In addition, the limitations of the public treasury were such that only the most pressing demands could be met.

What has been accomplished in the field of public finance is less visually evident but even more fundamental for the future of Haiti. In the period before the occupation, unsatisfactory conditions in revenue and expenditure acted both as cause and effect. They brought revolution and they resulted in revolution. They were one of the main factors bringing tension in foreign relations and precipitating intervention.

In the last analysis, of course, the income of the government depends on the private income of the people at large. Changes in the latter in Haiti can be measured only imperfectly, for no census of the national wealth has ever been taken. Local activity—almost exclusively that in agriculture and the simplest of home industries—has presumably increased, but it has not done so in remarkable degree. The habit of life of the Haitian countryman has changed but little. He still continues to be nonindustrious, nonindustrial, and as a rule not highly dissatisfied with the low standard of life which the tropics yield in response to a minimum of effort. The products of his labor are few, and only a half-dozen of them affect in any important way the economic movements outside his own community.

Foreign trade, especially that in exports, furnishes some indication of the scale of local productive activity. It both shows an encouraging increase and illustrates the weak economic position of a country dependent on a few crops which must be sold in a world market where the total exchanges of the local offerings are hardly more than incidental. Exports were worth 44 million gourdes—a unit having a gold value of 20 cents—in 1916–1917. They were worth 113 million in the boom year 1927–1928 but fell to 36 million in 1931–1932, to rise to 51 million in 1933–1934.

Coffee, cotton, logwood, sugar, and cacao are the leading articles of export. Over the period 1916–1917 to 1929–1930, they made up 92.27 per cent, by value, of all shipments, a percentage which has tended to rise. Coffee and cotton alone make up over 81 per cent of the total. Four of these items in recent years have had to compete in oversupplied world markets. None, except coffee, has had special advantages in the period. The Haitian coffee crop sells regularly at higher prices than Brazilian coffee, especially in France; and, in the years before 1930, its market level was higher than usual because of the support of coffee prices in general by the Brazilian valorization activities. The quantities of coffee, cotton, and sugar marketed have shown an irregular tendency upward; those of logwood and cacao have tended downward. But neither in values nor in quantities have marked changes which promise to be permanent and to change the general outlook occurred in Haitian shipments. Whatever improvement has occurred has been caused by the maintenance of peace and by favorable price levels—until the world depression—rather than by new stimuli brought by the occupation.

No marked differentiation of exports has resulted from American activities in the island. This is, indeed, to be expected, for the efforts to improve Haitian agriculture were started late and had not time in their short duration to demonstrate what might be accomplished. The best that can be said is that whether Haitian agriculture can be diversified still remains to be proved.[18]

The taxing power has had to be exercised, therefore, on national wealth that is not rapidly expanding, and for the near future it will continue to be so. It is satisfactory to find

---

[18] The reports issued by the American treaty officers show optimism for the development of the production of pineapples, bananas, sisal, corn, and cashew nuts.

that even under these limitations public income has been increased,[19] chiefly by more efficient administration.

The collection of the customs revenue was by the terms of the treaty of 1915 to be put in charge of the general receiver. The internal revenue service was put in his hands by the law of June 6, 1924. Efforts were made under the latter authority to develop new sources of revenue and thus cut down the almost complete dependence on the customs which formerly characterized Haitian public finance.

Before the control of customs was established under the treaty, collections of revenue had become badly demoralized. The yield had fallen from the equivalent of almost 41 million gourdes in 1890–1891 to less than 10½ million in 1907. Thereafter it had risen to average over 24 million in the five years preceding 1916–1917.

After the establishment of American supervision of customs, the yield from duties rose to average 37 million gourdes for the five-year period ending 1929–1930. They were 30 million in 1933–1934. Internal revenues, the yield of which was declining before 1915, continued to yield decreasing amounts and in 1923–1924 showed less than 3 million gourdes. They were later developed by new legislation and better administration to yield over 6 million gourdes. They were 5,048,902 gourdes in 1933–1934. The percentage of total revenues derived from customs fell from 97.61 in 1915–1916 to 79.79 in 1929–1930. They were 82 per cent in 1933–1934. The total yield of all revenues in the same period increased from 18 million gourdes in 1916–1917 to over 50 million in 1927–1928. Thereafter, with the world depression the total fell to 28 million in 1931–1932, thereafter to rise to reach 36 million in 1933–1934. In other words, during the "occupation," the revenues devotable to state needs more than

---

[19] The tax system of Haiti has been modified by adjustments in the rate on imports, but these have increased the tax burden only slightly. Unlike most countries, Haiti derives a large part of its customs revenue from export taxes—38.76 per cent in 1929–1930. These are specific taxes which, while theoretically objectionable, have contributed to the stability of treasury income. See *Haiti, Annual Report of the Financial Adviser-General Receiver for the Fiscal Year October, 1929–September, 1930,* Port-au-Prince, 1930.

doubled in amount, but now they are below that level. Without this advance in income, of course, the greater expenditures for public purposes above outlined would have been impossible.

By the treaty of 1915, the payment of interest and amortization charges on the public debt are made the first charge on the public revenues after the expenses of collection. The protocol of October 3, 1919, pledges both the customs and the internal revenue for similar payments on the loans made under its authority. These pledges continue after the expiry of the treaty of 1915 until the loan is retired. The debt service has been fully maintained through the years of the world depression.

The total public debt at the end of September, 1915, was 153 million gourdes. During the war years, when Haitian trade and the national income were cut down, the debt grew to a high point of 177 million gourdes in 1918. The tide then turned, and total obligations fell to 91 million. They increased after the loans made under the agreement of 1919 and then again took a downward course, to reach 57,054,000 gourdes on April 30, 1935.

It is to be noted that practically all the material improvements in Haiti have been financed from current funds and not from loans. The latter have been used with minor exceptions to refund old debts and to liquidate claims and the floating debt. All in all, the strengthening of the national finances is the greatest accomplishment of the occupation.

It is easy in reviewing what has been achieved in improving the national position to overlook circumstances which raise problems as to its future. Order has been established, public improvements have been fostered, trade has been increased, public income has grown, claims have been settled, public credit has been strengthened, and public debt has decreased. These are all positive benefits.

On the other hand, the slight resources of the country have not been opened up to development in the degree that the sanguine had hoped might be possible. Agricultural yield has not been diversified so as to make the country less dependent on the price fluctuations in world markets of a few staple products. The standard of life of the people continues little above the minimum of subsistence. Expensive irrigation systems which could bring fertile areas into cultivation the Government has not been able to finance. Badly needed reforestation has had no attention because of lack of funds. Uncertainty of land titles continues to be a handicap. Public health, in spite of the improvement made, is still far from being in a satisfactory condition. Schools for the rural districts are lamentably few, with the result that all but a small percentage of the rising generation is growing up illiterate. Few of the people have even a rudimentary industrial efficiency. These are economic and social circumstances which will make the future of Haiti one full of problems for any government that directs its destinies. They are circumstances which will have far-reaching effects on the political progress which can be made.

As the governmental functions taken under American supervision in 1915 and subsequently are returned into Haitian hands, the literate portion of the Haitian people will take over opportunities and responsibilities greater than they have ever before discharged. They will have to assume public services involving greater financial responsibilities and more complicated functions than those of the period preceding 1915. Technical skills far beyond what Haiti then knew must be developed to maintain the administrative functions of the Government—police, public health, communications, education, and—key of them all—public finance. Ability to discharge these functions Haitian leaders must develop if they are to maintain what has been achieved and go on to the solution of the problems which the twenty-year-long American intervention and the still longer American financial control will have left unsolved.

CHAPTER VIII

United States Possessions in the Caribbean

Puerto Rico

ON his second voyage of discovery, Columbus, after visiting some of the southerly Leeward Islands, turned to the northwest and on the fourteenth of November, 1493, lay off what was later to be called *Saint Croix,* the largest of the Danish West Indies. Two days later he "discovered another island called Burenquen,"[1] *Puerto Rico,* as it is now known. The inhabitants, so he was told, were periodically attacked by the Caribbees and, like the latter, practiced cannibalism. Many of the men went ashore, though whether the admiral himself was among them does not appear. Those who did so were the first Europeans to set foot on the lands now under the United States flag in the Caribbean.

This oblong island, about one hundred miles long by thirty-five miles broad, Columbus named San Juan Bautista. It was settled soon after its discovery but, like Cuba, was for many years little prized. In 1508 Juan Ponce de León, better known because of his later explorations of Florida, after reconnoitering the coast, established a fort inland from the bay on which San Juan is now located. In the years following, other colonists and their families arrived. The natives were forced to labor for the settlers, and shortly, in 1521, the Spanish town was moved down to the shore of the "rich

---

[1] The modern spelling is *Boriquen.* The facts on the discovery are summarized from the account of Doctor Chanca, physician to the fleet, as reprinted in Herbermann, Charles G. (ed.), *The Voyages of Christopher Columbus,* printed for the United States Catholic Historical Society, New York, 1892, pp. 177–178.

port" and became known as San Juan Bautista de Puerto Rico.

But other New World areas held out more attractive prospects than Puerto Rico. Puerto Rico yielded no great quantities of gold. The alluvial washings were already considered exhausted by 1536, though only some $4,000,000 worth of gold had been won. The labor supply fell off, for the Indians perished under the hard conditions imposed by the white men and were carried off by diseases introduced by the Europeans and by the Negroes whom they brought to replenish the supply of workers. Carib attacks also continued to threaten the colony.

Agricultural crops began to be given greater attention by the discouraged colonists. Columbus had on his second voyage brought sugar cane to Haiti, whence it passed to the other islands. The first sugar mill in Puerto Rico dates, it is said, from 1523. The banana was introduced shortly after it had been brought to Haiti by Tomás de Berlanga in 1516. The coconut tree was introduced in 1549 from the Cape Verde Islands.[2] Nevertheless, the island continued unprosperous.

By the end of the century, the Indians had disappeared and the number of Spaniards in the island was less than 3,000.[3] The inhabitants beat off an attack by the English under Sir Francis Drake in 1595 but three years later were forced to surrender for some months to the Earl of Cumberland. The British shortly abandoned the island. Foreign attacks, diseases, and emigration had reduced the colony to a pitiful state.

The 1600's brought no better fortune. The Dutch had now joined the nations that were trying to break the Spanish hold in America and in 1625 made an unsuccessful attempt to take Puerto Rico. French, British, and Dutch established themselves in neighboring Caribbean islands and pillaged the fleets

---

[2] Van Deusen, Richard James and Elizabeth Kneipple, *Porto Rico, A Caribbean Isle,* New York, Henry Holt and Co., 1931, p. 67.

[3] See Rosario, Jose C., "The Porto Rican Peasant and his Historical Antecedents," in Clark, Victor S., and associates, *Porto Rico and its Problems,* Washington, Brookings Institution, 1930, pp. 537–546, for a discussion of the growth of population in the island.

carrying the silver from Mexico, with part of which Spain was maintaining the colony. In addition, the mother country did not adopt a liberal program to encourage local development. Its restrictive trade policy made the settlers take up contraband trade with the very enemies who wished to bring Spanish control to an end.

The Governor complained in 1662 that no merchant ship from Spain had reached the colony in eleven years. Sugar production had apparently declined. Except for the foodstuffs raised for local consumption, ginger, to be sold to Dutch contraband traders, was the chief crop. The population was apparently less at the end of the century than at its beginning. In 1700 San Juan had less than 2,000 inhabitants, even counting the slaves.

The next century saw no end to the attacks on Spanish sovereignty, but the mother country took greater interest in Puerto Rico and the economic prospects greatly improved. The English renewed their attacks in 1702, as did the Dutch in 1703. In 1765 and the years following, however, Spain increased the subsidy from the Mexican Treasury and made San Juan next to her strongest position in the Caribbean. As a result, renewed British attacks from 1797 to 1801 were again defeated.

The economic strength of the colony also increased in the century. In 1736 coffee had been introduced from Santo Domingo and it soon became an important item in the contraband trade through the nearby Danish West Indies. Sugar, cotton, and tobacco gave increasing yields, and the Spanish commercial policy was relaxed, with a favorable effect on the export trade. In 1795 Spain ceded Santo Domingo to France, and many of the Spanish inhabitants emigrated to Puerto Rico, thus giving a welcome reinforcement to the European population in the colony. In 1765 the first census showed a total of 44,883 inhabitants, which had increased by 1800 to 155,426.[4]

The nineteenth century brought to Puerto Rico great

---

[4] Capó, Claudio, *The Island of Porto Rico,* San Juan, the Globe Publishing Co., 1925, p. 57, and Rosario, *op. cit.,* pp. 541–542.

changes in its economic and political organization. In 1804 trade with foreign nations was legalized, and in 1811 five other ports besides San Juan were opened to commerce. Foreigners, especially British and French subjects, attracted by the freer conditions granted to commerce, established themselves in the island. Sugar, tobacco, and coffee production rose, the latter taking the lead and reaching in 1897 an export value of 12,222,595 pesos, three times that of sugar.

Politically the changes were more irregular. When revolts broke out in the mainland colonies, Spain in 1810 gave the local Governor absolute power to handle affairs in Puerto Rico, though no serious dissatisfaction had made itself evident. At times the island enjoyed representation in the Spanish Cortes but lost it again when less liberal regimes came into control in the mother country. From 1837 to 1873, indeed, the Governor-General held almost absolute power.

Dissatisfaction with the unprogressive policy of the governments at Madrid did not fail to grow as the century advanced. It came to a head in 1887 when an assembly at Ponce, while protesting loyalty, demanded a greater degree of autonomy. Thereafter, particularly as feeling against the Spanish policy rose in Cuba, Puerto Rican dissatisfaction with the local political status increased. When the Cubans set up their revolutionary juntas in New York, a Puerto Rican section was promptly created. Contemporaneously, a less extreme group again sought from Spain the grant of greater political freedom and won a fair measure of self-government.

The executive was still to be the Governor-General, now assisted by an appointive Cabinet. Legislation was to be entrusted, within specified limits, to two bodies, a Council of Administration of fifteen, seven to be chosen by the Governor-General and eight to be elected, and a Chamber of Representatives elected one for every 25,000 inhabitants. The new government never functioned effectively because it was hardly set up before the United States and Spain were engaging in the war which brought to an end the more than four hundred years of Spanish control.

The Cabinet had been organized under the new charter on February 12, 1898, and war was declared between the United States and Spain on April 25. The legislature began its first and last session on July 13. On the twenty-fifth, it abruptly adjourned on receipt of the news that United States troops had landed in the island. The naval and military operations of the Spanish-American War in Puerto Rico were brief and ceased on August 13, 1898, when news of the signing of the peace protocol on the previous day reached the island. The treaty which followed ceded Puerto Rico to the United States and provided that "the civil rights and political status of the native inhabitants" should "be determined by the Congress" of the United States.[5] On October 18 the United States flag was raised at numerous points throughout the island.

Little was known by the American public about the people whom the fortunes of war had brought under the national control, though popular opinion was enthusiastic about what "we could do with the island." Puerto Rico was reputed to be a "tropical paradise." It had been neglected by Spain, but by establishing a modern health service and an adequate school system the foundation could be laid for the rapid development of natural resources and for self-government comparable to that on the continent. Better communications would open up the interior, capital would flow into local industries, and a large trade would develop. Imports would be of products different from those imported by the United States and the exports to the island would be a valuable outlet for the products of American farms and factories. The new association, it was confidently believed, brought no difficult problems and should result to the advantage of both islanders and "continentals." Some of these sanguine hopes have been realized; some have been grievously disappointed. Puerto Rico under the United States flag has in certain lines developed far beyond any other Caribbean area. In others it continues to struggle with difficulties, some of which it shares with other tropic areas and some of which seem peculiarly its own.

[5] Treaty in Malloy, *op. cit.*, Vol. II, pp. 1690–1695.

For a year and a half after passing under United States control, the island continued to be governed by the Army. Constructive measures were rapidly undertaken. An insular police force was organized, changes designed to lessen the costs of litigation were made in the courts, taxation was reformed to distribute its burdens equitably, and departments of public health, education, and public works were created. In four centuries of Spanish control, only 165 miles of roads had been built. The total was more than doubled in eighteen months under the Army administration. The trade of the island during the period, however, was carried on under unfavorable circumstances. Shipments to Spain paid the duties charged against goods from foreign nations. Cuba, to which Puerto Rico had formerly sent large exports, charged her own tariff rates, as did, indeed, the United States itself.[6]

Army control came to an end through the establishment of civil government by the Foraker Act approved by President McKinley on April 12, 1900.[7] The new regime was inaugurated on May 1. Under it the executive power rested in a governor appointed for a four-year term by the President of the United States by and with the advice and consent of the Senate. The legislature consisted of two houses. An upper house, called the Executive Council and consisting of eleven members, all appointed by the President with the consent of the Senate, was created. Six of the number were the heads of the administrative departments in the island and five were to be native Puerto Ricans. A second body, the House of Delegates, had thirty-five members, five being elected from each of seven districts. The two houses together formed the Legislative Assembly of Puerto Rico. To become laws, all bills had to be supported by a majority of the members belonging to each house and approved by the governor. Veto by the governor could be overridden by a two-thirds vote in each of the houses. All legislation enacted was to be re-

---

[6] Richardson, *op. cit.,* Vol. X, pp. 178–179, Message of December 5, 1899, gives President McKinley's discussion of the commercial position of the island.

[7] *Statutes at Large of the United States of America, 1899–1901,* Washington, 1901, Vol. XXXI, Chap. 191, pp. 77–86.

ported to the Congress of the United States, which reserved the power to annul it.

This law, though its purpose was reported to be only "temporarily to provide a civil government," remained in force for seventeen years. It was criticized by Puerto Ricans as setting up a government less liberal than "Spanish autonomy" and was also unacceptable because it made Puerto Ricans "citizens of Puerto Rico" but did not give them full United States citizenship.

On July 25, 1901, free trade was established between the island and the United States; [8] but not until March 2, 1917, was a new organic law, the Jones Act, passed by Congress and approved by President Wilson.[9] Congress had become convinced that the experience in self-government acquired by the Puerto Ricans justified granting to them larger powers to determine the laws under which they should live. The United States Constitution was still not to apply fully to Puerto Rico, but its people were made citizens of the United States and were given a bill of rights similar to that in the Federal Constitution. All statutory laws except those inapplicable were to have force in the island unless Congress should otherwise provide.

The executive power remained in a governor appointed by the President of the United States with the advice and consent of the Senate. To assist the governor there were established four administrative officers, two appointed by the President of the United States with the advice and consent of the Senate and four appointed by the governor with the advice and consent of the Senate of Puerto Rico. A lawmaking body of two houses, which together are the Legislature of Puerto Rico, was created. The Senate, elected for

[8] The Foraker Act had provided that this standard should be observed when the civil government it contemplated should have been set up, but in any case not later than March 1, 1902. The act also established the same customs duties on goods entering Puerto Rico as on goods entering the United States, with the exception of duties on certain specified articles chief of which was coffee, which was to pay duty on entering Puerto Rico, though it entered the United States free.

[9] *Statutes at Large of the United States of America, 1915–1917,* Washington, 1917, Vol. XXXIX, Chap. 145, pp. 951–968.

four years, has nineteen members, two from each of seven districts and five chosen at large. The House of Representatives has thirty-nine members chosen for four years, one being chosen from each of thirty-five districts and four at large. All bills must be passed by an absolute majority of the members belonging to each house. The governor has the power of veto, which can be overridden by a two-thirds vote of all members of each house, in which case, if the governor still disapproves the measure, it is sent to the President of the United States. Only if the President approves does it then become a law. In financial bills the governor has the power to disapprove items while approving the rest. Finally, all laws passed by Puerto Rico are reported to the Congress of the United States, which has the right to annul them—a power which has not been used.

One popularly elected resident commissioner, who, like other territorial representatives, may speak but not vote, represents Puerto Rico in the Congress of the United States.

The qualifications for voting in elections are determined by the local legislature. Though the percentage of illiteracy is high—it was still 44.1 in 1932—there is universal manhood suffrage. Only women, who were first allowed to vote in the election of November 8, 1932, "are submitted to a literacy test." [10]

Under the powers granted to the local government, the people of Puerto Rico now enjoy a wide degree of freedom to determine its laws. Attention has often been called to the fact that the island has a degree of self-government greater than was given to the "incorporated territories" of the continent in the periods before they became States in the Union.

The legislation passed by Congress affecting public finance in Puerto Rico deserves special attention. In all Caribbean governmental units, the money which it has been possible to secure through the usual methods of local taxation has often been less than that needed to meet the legitimate needs of the government. The United States has recognized that this

---

[10] Beverley, Honorable James R., *Thirty-Third Annual Report of the Governor of Puerto Rico,* San Juan, 1933, p. 13.

is regularly the case in Puerto Rico, and laws have been passed to turn to local use funds which otherwise would have found their way into the National Treasury. This has been the practice from the beginning of American control.

A law approved on March 24, 1900, provided that all customs revenues collected in the United States on goods from Puerto Rico after the evacuation of the Spanish troops should be turned over to the President for the use of Puerto Rico.[11] Under the Foraker Act, the duties collected on goods passing between the two units before free trade between them went into effect were to be held in a separate fund and turned over to the civil government when it should be established. The customs duties collected on foreign goods entering the island are turned into the island treasury after the cost of their collection has been subtracted. In incorporated territory, this income would go to the Federal Government. In 1913 the United States income tax was extended to Puerto Rico, except as the local legislature might modify it, with the provision that the yield should be turned over to Puerto Rico.[12] By the Jones Act, similar disposition was made of the internal revenues collected in the United States on articles produced in Puerto Rico.

These various laws place the island in a particularly favored position. Puerto Rico pays no tax to the United States Treasury and a large part of the income which the island does receive comes to it by special legislation.

In 1933 almost forty per cent of the entire income came from three Federal taxes diverted to the island. If to the yield of these taxes be added the income from excises which would under the general laws in great part not accrue to the local treasury, the total is some $8,663,000 in revenue receipts of $9,374,358.[13]

---

[11] *Statutes at Large, of the United States of America, 1899–1901,* Washington, 1901, Vol. XXXI, Chap. 91, p. 51.

[12] *Ibid., 1913–1915,* Washington, 1915, Vol. XXXVIII, Chap. 16, p. 180.

[13] Beverley, Honorable James R., *Thirty-Third Annual Report of the Governor of Puerto Rico,* San Juan, 1933, pp. 60–61. For a similar calculation and comment, see "Letter of President Calvin Coolidge to the Governor of Puerto Rico, Feb. 28, 1928," in the *New York Times,* Mar. 16, 1928.

In spite of the extension of a wide degree of self-government to the island and the efforts to put it in a favorable position in its public finance and in its economic affairs, political groups in Puerto Rico continue to be dissatisfied with its relations to the United States. It is charged that the appointees to the governorship have been selected because of their political services to the party in power in the United States and often without reference to their fitness for the office. This, with some conspicuous exceptions, seems to have been true. The governor, others insist, should be a Puerto Rican, not a "continental." The power of the governor over appropriations is criticized as being too extensive, though the exercise of the veto over appropriations made by the local legislature has not been sufficiently vigorous to prevent building up a public debt which other island critics assert is a "serious problem." Greater autonomy continues to be a widely supported demand. A large group are anxious that Puerto Rico be accepted as a State in the Union. Probably only a small minority are enthusiastic advocates of complete severance of the relations with the United States.

Economic and social developments in the island since its acquisition by the United States present strong contrasts. Agricultural and industrial production have risen remarkably and have revolutionized local life. Sugar, coffee, and tobacco dominate developments, as they did at the end of the Spanish regime; but their relative importance has shown great changes.

Sugar cane, which had been successfully introduced into the New World in 1506, found its way to Puerto Rico shortly thereafter, and the production of sugar promptly became a staple industry. The yield never became large, however, in the Spanish period. It was less than 10,000 short tons in 1828; and in 1880, when it reached its peak for the Spanish period of control, it was only about 170,000 short tons, falling again to 40,000 tons in 1900.[14] Thereafter the industry rose spectacularly under the favorable conditions created through

---

[14] Beverley, Honorable James R., *Thirty-Third Annual Report of the Governor of Puerto Rico,* San Juan, 1933, chart facing p. 116.

free entry of island sugar into the United States market. Capital from outside Puerto Rico flowed into production, small mills gave place to large centrals, and production steadily mounted to 992,432 short tons in 1932.

The industry is to a degree artificial and a result of tariff protection, for Puerto Rico has no large areas of sugar land which can compete with better-favored regions such as Cuba. The sugar companies, since they are financed by other than local capital, send the major portion of their profits out of the island. Sugar production has disturbed the economic balance in local economic life also because of the seasonal character of the employment it offers and because the establishment of plantations has broken up the small landholdings upon which crops for the subsistence of the local population were formerly raised.[15]

Coffee, introduced about the middle of the eighteenth century, is produced under shade here as in other Caribbean countries. Like tobacco, it is a crop grown chiefly on small farms. The chief yield is from the interior mountainous districts. Unlike sugar and tobacco, this product has not profited by protection under the American tariff. The transfer from Spain brought to an end the advantages which Puerto Rican coffee formerly enjoyed in the Spanish market and in Cuba without creating a compensation in the American market, where all coffee enters free of duty. Hence, the Puerto Rican crop has there had to bear competition with the product of Brazil and other countries. It has been practically excluded from Cuba, where it formerly enjoyed at least the advantage of the United States reciprocity treaty with that republic, because of the efforts which Cuba has made to re-establish its domestic coffee production. In addition, the yield has in recent years been disastrously affected by hurricanes.

As a result of these influences, coffee has been a very irregular contributor to Puerto Rican income. In 1870 the export trade alone had reached almost 18,000,000 pounds. It rose irregularly to about 58,000,000 in 1915 and then declined,

[15] For further details, see Clark, Victor S., and associates, *Porto Rico and its Problems,* Washington, Brookings Institution, 1930, especially pp. 611–647.

chiefly owing to hurricane damage, falling practically to the vanishing point in 1930. Because of the heavy local consumption, Puerto Rico has in some current years been, if exports are balanced against imports, an importer of coffee.

Tobacco, indigenous to America, has been cultivated in Puerto Rico on a commercial scale since early colonial times and in 1898 was the leading product of the island. It has continued to prosper under advantageous access to the American market, though the yield has in recent years shown a tendency to become stationary. The highest production was reached in 1927 at 50,000,000 pounds. A sizable cigar and cigarette industry has also developed in the period of American control.

A number of other lines of agricultural production have been encouraged since the opening of the century by the position of the export trade under the American tariff and through private and public interest in new or neglected crops. Exports of fresh and canned fruit have had increasing importance. The citrous varieties and pineapples hold the leading positions. Vegetables for the winter market in the United States have given interesting returns. The lace and women's wear industry also contributes increasingly to the export trade.

The total value of the commerce passing in and out of the island ports has shown remarkable increases. Like the foreign trade of all other areas which compete in the world foodstuff and raw materials markets, that of Puerto Rico shows great changes in value as world prices rise and fall; but, over the period since the beginning of the century, the totals have shown great advance.

Exports rose in value from $8,583,967 in 1901 to $150,-811,449 in 1920 but declined owing to the world depression to $75,406,455 in 1933. Imports were worth $8,918,136 in 1901, $105,479,703 in 1921, and $54,745,711 in 1933. Over ninety per cent of the trade in current years is with the United States.[16]

Public works have been greatly extended. Government

---

[16] See Beverley, Honorable James R., *Thirty-Third Annual Report of the Governor of Puerto Rico,* San Juan, 1933, pp. 111 and 72. The reports of the Governor give a detailed exposition of commercial developments.

buildings of modern character have replaced the very inadequate colonial equipment. The rudimentary roads of the colonial period have been extended to total almost 1,200 miles of well-maintained highways.

Efforts to improve material conditions have been accompanied by other efforts to improve public education and public health. The advance in education is one of the most outstanding achievements of the Puerto Ricans in the American regime. In 1899, 85 per cent of the population were unable to read and write. At present only 44.1 per cent cannot do so—a large percentage still, but one which shows great advance when compared to conditions a generation ago.

In 1898 the maximum enrollment in the schools, government and private, was 29,182; it was 233,457 in 1933, though the population had increased by only some seventy per cent. School buildings have increased in number and in excellence. The per capita expenditure on education per year has risen from about thirty cents to about four dollars, and the curriculum has been expanded to include instruction in the practical branches which will prove of greatest value to the student in afterlife.

Public health conditions were given attention from the beginning of American control. Puerto Rico had suffered greatly for generations from the diseases which have handicapped the development of the American tropics and many of which, indeed, still are very serious obstacles to progress. Smallpox regularly took a heavy toll, tuberculosis was widespread, and yellow fever was endemic, as were also hookworm and malaria. Good headway has been made in many lines in improving local health conditions. Smallpox has been practically wiped out, and yellow fever has been conquered through the application of the methods first developed during the American occupation of Cuba. Hookworm, which so seriously cuts down the vitality of those afflicted, can now be eliminated through a treatment developed after identification of the parasite in 1899 by Bailey K. Ashford, of the Medical Corps of the United States Army, then stationed in Puerto Rico.

Nevertheless, in spite of these and other improvements, health conditions in Puerto Rico continue far from satisfactory. Endeavors both by the local government and by that of the United States to make the island the "tropical paradise" which many believed it would become under American control have been cruelly disappointed.

In 1897, shortly before the end of Spanish control, an authority on local conditions, Dr. Cayetano Coll y Teste, published a study on Puerto Rico which was later awarded a prize by the Economic Society of the Friends of the Country. In it he gave a picture of the condition of the country dweller of the time. The laborer, he said, was "one of the most unfortunate beings in the world, with a pale face, bare feet, lean body, ragged clothing and feverish outlook." He walked "indifferently, with the shadows of ignorance in his eyes. . . ." He lived in a "miserable cabin, hung on a peak like a swallow's nest. . . ." For food he had "putrid salt meat, codfish filled with rotten red spots, and India rice. . . ."[17]

The picture may not have been accurate, and certainly it is not descriptive of conditions in rural Puerto Rico at the present time; but it is far nearer the truth even now than those unfamiliar with Puerto Rican conditions realize. The plain fact is that, under American as under Spanish control, the people of Puerto Rico live at a desperately low standard of life and there is no early prospect of change in that condition. A number of circumstances contribute to this discouraging outlook. Some of them are common to other comparable areas in the American tropics, while some seem to be accentuated in Puerto Rico. Some had their beginning in the Spanish period but have become more serious in the years of American control.

Like many other tropical areas, Puerto Rico is specially adapted to certain crops, and these have tended to monopolize economic activity. It was primarily a coffee and tobacco area under Spain; it has become a sugar area under the United States. In both periods the tendency has been to

[17] The quotation from which these phrases are taken is in the letter of President Coolidge above cited.

neglect locally producible subsistence crops and to rely on imported foodstuffs. At present it is asserted that, though this is an overwhelmingly agricultural region, still only about one-tenth of the foodstuffs are locally produced. The tendency to rely on imported foods has been accentuated by the growth of the sugar industry, which has absorbed many of the smaller holdings. Good land has sold in prosperous years for as high as $800 per acre, a price far above what it is worth for subsistence crops. As a result, the former owners become landless or are forced back into the rougher country. Many become partially dependent on seasonal employment in sugar production.

Another factor contributing to the low economic efficiency of the people is the continuance of bad health conditions in spite of the great efforts made in this field. At first sight, this seems unexplainable, for Puerto Rico has an equable climate and, as Governor Theodore Roosevelt reported in 1930, "should be . . . a health resort." But the best use of the lower land levels requires irrigation, and the irrigation ditches are ideal places for the malaria-carrying mosquito to breed. Hookworm can be practically eliminated if the people wear shoes, for the disease enters the body through the soles of the feet. But, because of his low vitality, the peasant is economically inefficient and cannot earn the money with which to buy shoes. Since he has not shoes, he is economically inefficient. It is a vicious circle. Tuberculosis and a number of the other less prevalent diseases also continue to be difficult to conquer.

Governor Roosevelt reported in 1930 that there were then in the island 35,000 people suffering from tuberculosis, 200,000 suffering from malaria, and 600,000 suffering from hookworm alone. And this in a population reported as 1,543,913!

Purchase of sugar lands by large companies may have narrowed the economic opportunity of the average man. Poor health conditions are a drag on his efforts to improve his position. But neither of these is so serious a problem as the overpopulation which is the outstanding social phenomenon in the island. Overcrowding is not absent in a number of the other Caribbean units. In Salvador the population is dense, and in a number of the islands of the West Indies dense population limits the available food supply and makes anything but a low standard of life impossible. In no instance, however, does the combination of low income, poor health, and rapid increase of population stand out so sharply as in the case of Puerto Rico.

Conditions are exceptional also because here only, in the Caribbean, is the congestion found in a community of predominantly European stock. A very large percentage of the people of Salvador are of Indian or mixed Indian and Spanish ancestry; the smaller West Indian islands and Jamaica are overwhelmingly of Negro stock. But Puerto Rico in 1899 listed 61 per cent of its population as white, and 73 per cent were thus classified in the census of 1930. Costa Rica, Cuba, and Puerto Rico have the highest percentage of white blood in the Caribbean region.

Rapid increase of population began long before the period of American control. In 1765 there were still only 44,833 people in the island; but in the following years immigration, better trade connections with the outside world, and the money support from Mexico conceded by Spain created conditions in which the population increased at a rate seldom if ever duplicated in other regions of the world. In the fifty-nine years between 1765 and 1824, the population rose to 221,268—an increase of 394 per cent. In the next sixty-three years, from 1824 to 1887, the growth was 260 per cent; and between 1887 and 1932, forty-five years, it was over 100 per cent. The estimated number of inhabitants in 1932 was 1,597,500.[18]

The significance of this remarkable growth is emphasized by the figures of the density of population per square mile. It was 13 in 1765, 64 in 1824, 232 in 1887, and 465 in 1932. There are no signs that the rapid increase is approaching an end. It appears, in fact, that the activities to promote public health

[18] These calculations are based on figures in Clark, *op. cit.*, p. 548, Capó, *op. cit.*, p. 57, and Beverley, Honorable James R., *Thirty-Third Annual Report of the Governor of Puerto Rico,* San Juan, 1933, p. 133.

which have been undertaken may have accentuated the population problem, for, in the period since the establishment of American control, the death rate has fallen and the birth rate has shown a strong upward tendency.[19] Both of the ratios are high, but births exceed deaths to an extraordinary degree.

Clearly, the great problem of Puerto Rico is not political, but social and economic. A number of advanced countries whose people live on a much higher standard have populations of comparable density, but all of them have an industrial development depending on heavy imports of materials from other lands and heavy exports of manufactured articles. Puerto Rico, however, is a distinctively agricultural area, although only about one-tenth of the land is characterized as fertile. It is impossible for an average of 465 people to win a satisfactory standard of living on a square mile of Puerto Rican land.

Under conditions as they now are, there is a permanent oversupply of laborers, a large part of whom must eke out a meager existence from small landholdings and from seasonal employment paying low wages.[20] "More than 60 per cent of our people," reported Governor Roosevelt, "are out of em-

---

[19] POPULATION INCREASE IN PUERTO RICO *

	Births per 1,000	*Deaths per 1,000*	*Net Increase*
1900–04	28.99	26.39	2.60
1905–09	33.02	23.00	10.02
1910–14	36.57	21.75	14.82
1915–19	37.82	26.73	11.09
1920–24	38.33	21.70	16.63
1925–28	40.55	22.43	18.12
1929–32	39.08	21.65	17.45

* Compiled from Clark, *op. cit.*, p. 548, and Beverley, Honorable James R., *Thirty-Third Annual Report of the Governor of Puerto Rico*, San Juan, 1933, p. 133.

The comparable rates in the registration area in the United States in 1930 were: for births, 18.9; for deaths, 11.3. (*Commerce Yearbook*, 1932, Vol. II, p. 666.)

[20] Daily wages on coffee plantations range as follows: men, $.30 to $.75; women, $.22 to $.78; minors, 16 to 18 years, $.12 to $.37. On sugar plantations, in which the work is largely seasonal, the pay varies greatly with the type of work. The range is: men, $.30 to $6.16; women, $.30 to $.70; minors under 18 years, $.25 to $.60. Beverley, Honorable James R., *Thirty-Third Annual Report of the Governor of Puerto Rico*, San Juan, 1933, pp. 138–139.

ployment either all or a part of each year. The average yearly income of the working man or woman ranges between $150 and $200. Hundreds come to the government offices weekly with but a single request—work." [21]

The Danish West Indies

Discussion of annexation of the Danish West Indies to the United States began long before the acquisition of neighboring Puerto Rico. Re-establishment of European control in Santo Domingo and Mexico in the period of the war between the States had shown that questioning of the "America for Americans" policy was still a reality. Transfer of possessions of the weaker European powers to more aggressive ones might be equally disconcerting. Further, the advantage which a naval base southward would have given to the United States Government had been recently emphasized by the difficulties encountered in maintaining the blockade of Southern ports. The contest was hardly over before proposals for acquiring Caribbean outposts from which the Navy might operate to advantage became a favorite theme of diplomatic discussion.[22]

Shortly before his assassination in April, 1865, President Lincoln's attention had been turned by his Secretary of State, William H. Seward, to the possibility of purchase of the Danish islands. A suggestion to the Danes brought the reply that they were indisposed to consider sale at the moment but might do so in the future. Before the end of the year, however, Danish opinion shifted and Secretary Seward was inquiring about the price which would be asked for St. Thomas, St. John, and St. Croix. Negotiations dragged, the Danes expressing doubts as to whether the conflict between President Johnson and Congress might not endanger the success

---

[21] Roosevelt, Honorable Theodore, *Thirtieth Annual Report of the Governor of Porto Rico,* San Juan, 1930, p. 2.

[22] The following summary of the negotiations leading up to the annexation of the Virgin Islands is based upon Tansill, Charles Callan, *The Purchase of the Danish West Indies,* Baltimore, Johns Hopkins Press, 1932, and *The Virgin Islands of the United States, A General Report by the Governor,* Washington, 1928.

of the project, to which the President had given his support, and proposing that the negotiations include only the first two islands. St. Croix, it was felt, if it were to be disposed of, should first be offered to France, from which Denmark had bought it in 1733. In any case, Denmark would insist that a vote of the inhabitants be taken before any cession. This to Seward seemed unnecessary, but after hesitation he yielded the point. The price asked was the subject of many adjustments. On July 2, 1867, the Cabinet agreed to offer $7,500,000 for St. Thomas and St. John, and on these conditions a treaty was signed on October 24, 1867.

The sales plan promised to go through promptly, and Seward sent to the islands a special representative to arrange certain details with a Danish commissioner. These two had hardly taken up their discussions at Christiansted, St. Croix, when a severe earthquake and a tidal wave sent them scurrying to the hills for safety. It was an event which in the long run cut down the enthusiasm of the United States for annexation, but it did not diminish enthusiasm for a new allegiance among the inhabitants of the islands which were to be transferred. On January 9, 1868, a plebiscite in St. Thomas resulted in 1,039 votes for annexation to 22 against it. The next day a vote in St. John resulted in 205 votes for transfer to none against it.

The Danish Legislature promptly ratified the treaty on January 30; but, in spite of strenuous efforts by the administration, the United States Senate could not be brought to act. Though the project had been favored by President Lincoln, the fact that President Johnson favored it was in itself, for many, reason enough to oppose it. No better fortune awaited it in the Grant administration, in which an unfavorable report was made by the Senate Committee on Foreign Relations on March 22, 1870.

For a quarter of a century thereafter, the United States showed interest in the Danish islands only when reports of the possibility of their passing into control of some European power aroused apprehension. In 1873 fears that Denmark might cede the islands to Germany to secure the return of the portion of Schleswig taken by Prussia in 1864 were expressed. When in 1879 a French company undertook to build a canal at Panama, France became an object of suspicion—had it not two years before taken over the Swedish rights in St. Barthélemy in violation of the principle of the Monroe Doctrine, and would not acquiring the Danish islands strengthen its influence over the Caribbean? Later, Germany again fell under suspicion, and representatives of the Navy urged that discussions with Denmark be reopened.

Heureaux, dictator in the Dominican Republic, had in 1898 indicated willingness to arrange for a German naval station in that republic, and the German foreign secretary had inquired of his ambassador in Washington what the United States would think of such an arrangement. He had received a discouraging answer. Shortly after, certain high officials in Germany had flirted with a plan to buy up the property in St. John through Mr. A. Ballin, director of the Hamburg-America Steamship Line. Admiral Tirpitz had pointed out that, with the island in the possession of German capitalists, the ground would "be prepared for the actual possession of it," and certainly "in view of the proposed resumption of work on the Panama Canal" "a naval base in the West Indies" would be "of greater interest" for Germany. St. John seemed to have "all the requirements necessary." [23] Other German naval officers shared this viewpoint. But Emperor William II had not encouraged moves of this sort. The Dominican proposal had, indeed, been called to his attention, but he indicated that the offer would be declined. He "did not want to be at logger-heads with the United States." [24] The proposed backdoor diplomacy as to the Danish islands could not have been more acceptable. Through his Minister of Foreign Affairs, Von Bülow, Kaiser William declared, "We had nothing against the transfer of the islands to American

[23] Tirpitz to Von Bülow, January 7, 1899. MS. of the German Foreign Office, cited in Tansill, *op. cit.*, pp. 400–401.

[24] *Ibid.*, p. 397, and authorities cited.

possession and would find it quite natural if it should happen."[25]

Not until the period following the Spanish-American War, however, did the interest of the United States in the Danish islands again become serious. Unofficial representatives of Denmark then sought to reawaken American desires, and on January 29, 1900, Secretary Hay initiated negotiations through the American minister at Copenhagen for cession of all three of the islands.

The colony had long been a drain on the Danish Treasury, and the chance of its becoming self-supporting was slight. Perhaps on this account, the sum offered for all of it was reduced to $3,500,000. The Danes thought this too little and wished, as before, to make action conditional on a plebiscite in the islands. This the United States administration did not favor. After long-drawn-out negotiations, the United States agreed to pay $5,000,000 and consented that Denmark might hold a plebiscite in the islands as a part of its procedure of ratification. On these terms a treaty was signed January 24, 1902.

This time the United States Senate acted promptly, ratifying the agreement on February 17. The lower house of the Danish Legislature assented by a large majority on March 13; but the upper house refused to act, forced a new election, and then on October 22, 1902, defeated the treaty by a tie vote. The action, it was rumored, had been influenced by the desires of Germany; but this appears not to have been the case.

The period which followed was one of inaction in which occasionally intimations of Danish willingness to sell, American desire to buy, and alleged German activities continued to be cited. In both Denmark and the United States there grew the conviction that ultimately the islands would pass to the latter, and the outbreak of the World War in Europe strengthened the desire in the United States that the transfer should occur soon.

---

[25] Quotation in Tansill, *op. cit.*, p. 436.

Negotiations were resumed in 1915. High officials in the United States were becoming convinced that the United States would be dragged into the conflict in Europe. German opposition to transfer, if it did exist, could not be very effective during the war; but the possibility of advance by her in the Caribbean continued to give many Americans "a case of nerves." Further, if Denmark should be absorbed by Germany and Germany should be victorious at the end of the war, the islands might automatically fall to the victor.

Secretary Lansing informed the Danish minister at Washington that if Germany showed an intention of taking possession of Denmark or of forcing her to cede the Danish West Indies, "the United States would be under the necessity of seizing and annexing them . . . though it would be done with the greatest reluctance."[26] It would indeed have been a remarkable action by an administration which had been so shocked by the German violation of the sovereignty of Belgium! President Wilson on December 5 expressed "gratification" that Lansing had been "so frank with the Danish Minister," and the negotiations proceeded.

If the Danes felt their hands forced by Lansing's threatening remarks, they did not show it in the later negotiations nor in the price they asked for the privilege of being coerced. The payment for the islands, they suggested, might well be $27,000,000, which even the anxious Mr. Lansing thought "excessive." He preferred to talk on the basis of $20,000,000, which itself was a fair increase over the $5,000,000 which had been discussed at the beginning of the century. But the Danes realized that they were in "a seller's market," and President Wilson was disposed to consider $27,000,000 and would not haggle "on a question of money." A compromise was reached, however, at $25,000,000, with the provision that the United States would yield on a long list of items involving concessions of various sorts which Denmark had granted to individuals in the islands.

In addition, the Danes wished to insist on a plebiscite in

---

[26] Lansing, Robert, "Drama of the Virgin Islands Purchase," in *New York Times Magazine,* July 9, 1931, p. 4. Quoted in Tansill, *op. cit.,* p. 478.

the islands, the grant by the treaty of United States citizenship to the inhabitants, and the grant to the islands of free trade with the United States. But on those points they finally yielded.

A third treaty of cession was signed at New York on August 4, 1916, and ratification was advised by the United States Senate on September 7. In Denmark the new agreement again encountered opposition. Both houses on September 30 passed a bill submitting the question of sale to a popular vote in Denmark, which on December 14 resulted in 283,694 yeas and 157,596 nays. Promptly thereafter, both houses of the Danish Legislature approved the treaty, and ratifications were exchanged at Washington on January 17, 1917. On March 31 the formal transfer occurred at St. Thomas.

The three small islands which thus came under American control have an area of 133 square miles, poorly distributed rainfall, and limited resources.[27] Once important as a transshipment point and later in the bunkering trade, they now have limited commercial or naval value. This fact was recognized by the American authorities at the time of their acquisition. The chief advantage of their possession is that, now that the United States is in control, no other power can make them a base of operations. Since at least as early as 1867, they have been in economic decline.

The population, which totalled 43,178 in 1835, has steadily fallen. It was 26,051 in 1917, when the islands came into American possession. By 1930 it was 22,012—a decline of 15.5 per cent. Of the population in 1930, 78.3 per cent were reported as Negroes, 12.4 per cent as mixed, and 9.1 per cent as white. Efforts are being made to develop local industries, the most important of which is sugar production.

From the time of annexation to the United States until March 31, 1931, the Federal authority in the islands was ex-

---

[27] The following paragraphs are summarized from Brock, H. G., Smith, Philip S., and Tucker, W. A., "*The Danish West Indies,*" *Special Agents Series No. 129,* United States Department of Commerce, Washington, 1917; *The Virgin Islands of the United States, A General Report by the Governor,* Washington, 1928; and the *Annual Reports of the Governor of the Virgin Islands,* Washington.

ercised by the Navy Department through a governor assisted by two locally chosen councils. Since that date, a civil governor working under the Department of the Interior has been at the head of the executive authority.

A heavy deficit in local budgets, paid every year through subsidy from the United States, averaged in recent years about $400,000. There is little probability that this small area will soon become self-supporting. "The Virgin Islands were bought as a defense investment, as the key to the defense of the Panama Canal. The appropriation [for their support] is less than 25 per cent of the interest on the money invested in a battleship." [28]

---

[28] *Annual Report of the Governor of the Virgin Islands for fiscal year ended June 30, 1932,* United States Department of the Interior, Washington, 1932, p. 33.

CHAPTER IX

European Colonies

LONG after the period of the conquest, other European countries continued to look with envious eyes upon the Spanish possessions in America; but, for about a century, control over them was seldom successfully questioned. Then one after another point of vantage fell under the control of the peoples of northern Europe, and for over two hundred years the map of the Caribbean region became a shifting mosaic. British, French, Dutch, Danes, and Swedes all came to hold islands in the West Indies and to have disputes over their rights with the Spaniards and with each other. The first two for long periods looked upon the sugar colonies which they had acquired in America as their most valuable possessions; but the significance of these holdings for the mother countries was dimmed in the 1800's by slave revolts, the abolition of slavery, the rise of competing areas, and the development of the beet sugar industry.

By the end of the nineteenth century only Great Britain was still in possession of sizable holdings both in the islands and on the mainland. The Spaniards had been eliminated from the latter in the years following 1810. The Swedes had retired in 1878 by ceding their small holding on St. Barthélemy to the French—a technical violation of the Monroe Doctrine espoused by the United States. The Dutch and French pretentions had shrunk to mainland holdings and a few small islands, and the Danes held only their small group of unprofitable little islands which later, in 1917, were sold to the United States. European colonies in the Caribbean, except those of Great Britain, had become of historical interest rather than of political or economic importance. They were remnants left over from the struggles of previous centuries.

With the freeing of the Negroes came a fairly steady increase in the percentage of African blood in the local populations. Previously, in some of the sugar areas slave-driving had been so harsh that the number of inhabitants would have been stationary or would have declined but for fresh supplies regularly brought in from Africa. When the Negroes became free, however, though the economic yield of the island possessions fell off, the high birth rate among the blacks caused a general and fairly steady increase in the population which, with some exceptions, continues to the present time.

In the smaller British island colonies, the saturation point as to the population which can be carried seems to be approaching. In the Leeward group, the number of inhabitants has not increased appreciably since 1891; and, from 1911 to 1921, it declined. The Bahamas since 1911 have also in this respect been practically stationary. On the other hand, in some of the areas a marked increase has occurred in recent years, probably in part owing to the better health services now maintained. Since 1921 the Windward Islands, Barbados, Trinidad and Tobago, and Jamaica have all shown extraordinary growth.[1]

Comparable population increases are in process in the European island colonies other than the British possessions.

---

[1] AREA AND POPULATION IN CERTAIN BRITISH CARIBBEAN COLONIES *

	Area in Square Miles	*Population, 1921*	*Population, 1930*	*Density per Square Mile, 1921*	*Estimated Density per Square Mile, 1930*
Windward Islands	516	162,254	188,689	314	365.6
Trinidad and Tobago	1,976	365,913	413,119	185	209.1
Barbados	166	156,312	172,182	942	1,037.2
Jamaica	4,841	868,983	1,022,152	180	211.1
British Guiana	89,480	297,691	310,933[a] (1931)	3.3	3.5

* Compiled from *Commerce Yearbook*, 1932, Vol. II, p. 496, and *Statesman's Yearbook*, 1922, p. 338, 1933, p. 328.

[a] Census excluding aborigines.

In the small Dutch holdings, the oil developments now support much greater numbers than could live on local production. None of the mainland holdings shows a marked population increase.[2]

All of the island colonies, with the partial exception of the Bahamas, have in our day become black man's islands in which the population has increased to the point where the locally produced food supply is insufficient to meet the demand. In the mainland areas aboriginal stocks are still found in relatively large numbers, and in Trinidad and British Guiana there is a sizable representation of East Indians.

There have been no significant developments in the political life of the European colonies since 1900. Most of them have not had an economic development sufficient to allow collection of public revenues greater than are necessary for the maintenance of the minimum standards of order, communications, and public health. Roughly, half of the people are still unable to read and write, and the standard of life is so low that social organization is weak. Subsidies from the home governments are often necessary to enable the colonies to meet the normal public expenses, and they are imperative whenever extraordinary resources must be secured.

The government organization in the various units shows

---

[2] AREA AND POPULATION IN FRENCH AND DUTCH CARIBBEAN POSSESSIONS *

	Area in Square Miles	*Population, 1911*	*Population, 1921*	*Population, 1931*	*Density of Population per Square Mile, 1921*	*Density of Population per Square Mile, 1931*
Guadeloupe	532	212,430	229,822	267,407 (1932)	432.0	502.6
Martinique	385	184,004	244,439	234,695	634.9	609.6
French Guiana	34,799	49,009	44,202	47,346 (1926)	1.3	1.4
Dutch Guiana	54,291	86,233	113,181	155,888	2.1	2.9
Dutch West Indies	403	54,469 (1910)	54,963	71,769	136.0	178.0

* Compiled from *Statesman's Yearbook*, various issues, 1913–1933, and *Commerce Yearbook*, Vol. II, p. 431.

wide variety. None of the European colonies is self-governing. The degree of popular participation in government runs through a wide range. The executive is regularly appointed. As a rule, the balance of power in control of legislation is in the hands of persons appointed directly or indirectly by the home government, and such changes as have recently been introduced have not showed abandonment of this policy.

The Bahamas and Barbados have a lower house which is wholly elected, working with a nominated legislative council; Grenada, Jamaica, the Leeward Islands Federation, St. Lucia, St. Vincent, and Trinidad have legislative councils in which the minority—in some cases only a minor fraction—is elected. In British Honduras there are no elected members on the legislative council. In British Guiana a change in 1928 replaced the partly elective body formerly functioning by a legislative council consisting of the Governor, as president, and ten official and nineteen nonofficial members.

The French colonies have steadily sunk in relative importance. At one time, possession of the island of Guadeloupe was considered to have advantages comparable to those attending ownership of Canada. Benjamin Franklin argued at length in favor of retaining the latter rather than the former when the alternative was under consideration by the British at the close of the Seven Years' War in 1763. Neither politically nor economically are the French possessions at present of great value.

Guadeloupe and Martinique are under governors assisted in each case by a council. These islands, in contrast to the British colonies, have direct representation in the legislature of the mother country, each sending a senator and two deputies. A small garrison is maintained. French Guiana is under a governor, a privy council, and a council-general elected by the French citizens in Guiana. It sends one deputy to the French Chamber.

The Dutch islands, Curaçao, Bonaire, and Aruba, to which are added for administrative purposes the scattered holdings in Saba, St. Eustache, and the north half of St. Martin, the rest of which is French, are under an appointive governor with a garrison of about 100. Dutch Guiana has a governor and an assisting council nominated by the Crown.

There have, at times, arisen demands for closer relations with the United States even in such long-established British communities as Barbados and Jamaica. Anxiety not to do anything which might provoke tariff reprisals by the United States has been expressed even in discussions of closer economic connections with the northern British American possessions. But such dissatisfaction as has manifested itself has been economic rather than political in origin and does not reflect any deep-seated feeling against the established political regime.

The influences which have so changed the economic outlook of other Caribbean areas since the opening of the twentieth century have not failed to have a far-reaching effect on the European colonies. There is no satisfactory yardstick by which the advance which has been made can be measured. The amount of production and export of the staple products does not show the effect of increased yield on the local life because the values per unit vary with production in the world at large and with shifting demand. Values of production and export are unsatisfactory as bases of measurement because of the changing purchasing power of money. In addition, both weight and value standards may not reflect changes in the well-being of the inhabitants. Apparent advance in either may be counterbalanced by the increase which has occurred in the population.

Values of exports and imports do show the changes which have occurred in contributions to the commerce of the world, and in this respect there has recently occurred decided, though irregular, advance in most areas. Such improvement as has taken place has been greatly cut down in the period following 1929 with the fall in world trade.

In the smaller British islands, export trade showed in a number of the units spectacular increases to the peak of prosperity, which was reached irregularly by them between 1920 and 1929. Thereafter, the value of shipments declined sharply in all cases. The total contributions to world trade in none of these cases are large. If comparison be made with the showing in the years just before the World War, the trade values in late years are decidedly discouraging and seem to indicate, particularly if the increase in population be borne in mind, that the standard of life of the inhabitants has shown no improvement and may actually have sunk. The total exports in 1930 and 1931 were below, or only slightly above, the values reached in 1910 in Turks and Caicos Islands, Barbados, the Leeward Islands, the Bahamas, and St. Lucia.

In Jamaica and Trinidad, though the percentage of increase in exports over those of the prewar period is lower than in the smaller islands, the contribution to world trade at the peak is much greater in both quantity and value and the decline during the years following is much less marked. On the other hand, it is in these units also that the greatest addition has been made to the population, so that, as far as the standard of life is concerned, greater economic return may be counterbalanced by the greater number of mouths to be fed.

The mainland colonies of Great Britain also give no great promise. The value of exports in British Honduras is stationary, and, though British Guiana showed an encouraging rise in yield during the sugar boom, it ships goods in current years of far less value than those it shipped in 1910.

Each of the three larger colonies maintains its position through a single product: British Guiana by sugar, which in normal years makes up over one-half of the export; Trinidad by petroleum products; and Jamaica by tropical fruits. The government of the latter has in recent years diversified local products through a number of specialties, thus making the basis of the economic life more secure than it formerly was.

The French and Dutch possessions also are single-industry areas which show great variations in the amount of their products finding their way into world markets. The French islands, Guadeloupe and Martinique, increased the value of their exports fivefold during the sugar boom; and in 1930, when the total shipments had fallen to a third of what they had been five years before, they still exported goods worth

$18,000,000, or about as much as Trinidad or Jamaica. Their apparent strength rises from the highly favored position which they hold under the French sugar and rum tariff. French Guiana, never prosperous, now exports less than it did at the beginning of the century.

The Dutch colonies, like the French, consist of a poor mainland holding and a group of small islands the economic return of which in recent years is explained by special circumstances. In Dutch Guiana (Surinam) bauxite, which played no part a generation ago, leads the exports. Total shipments now reach a value less than those of 1900 and in some years are worth even less than those of French Guiana.

The location of the small Dutch islands off the coast of Venezuela has at times given them unusual importance. In Curaçao is the harbor of Willemstad, one of the best in the West Indies. It was long one of the centers of illegal trade to the Spanish colonies and later an entrepôt for trade to the north-coast republics. By the opening of the nineteenth century, shifts in trade routes had made the group almost valueless. Its fortunes have been revolutionized since the rise of the Venezuelan petroleum industry, which uses the local ports for transshipment and refining. The exports have risen under these influences more than one hundredfold. They were valued at $124,960 in 1900 and at $129,573,004 in 1931.

In the amounts of their foreign trade, the major European colonies rank well with the middle group of the other Caribbean units. The exchanges of either Trinidad or Jamaica equal those of the strongest of the Central American states but fall far below those of Cuba, Colombia, and Venezuela. Those of even the small French islands, Guadeloupe and Martinique, because of the favored position of their sugar trade, reach a similar level. The extraordinary nominal position which the Dutch West Indian group holds—it has in recent years outstripped even Cuba—is, of course, explained not by the development of local resources but by the transit trade.

The European colonies present some interesting contrasts in the degree to which their trade is with the United States. They send there only negligible parts of their sugar exports, because Cuba, through the advantages it enjoys under treaty, practically monopolizes shipments to the United States. American trade with the British islands is affected by steamship connections and tariff concessions recently arranged with Canada. The Bahamas send roughly half of their exports to the United States. Jamaica, which formerly did likewise, now, because of shifts in the fruit trade, sends only one-third in that direction. Somewhat less of the exports of Trinidad find the same destination. The United States as a rule continues to be the best market for these areas, though it does not hold as strong a position as it did formerly.

In imports, some of the British colonies rely heavily on the United States, though the tendency to do so has in this respect also uniformly declined in later years. In 1900 about half of the total came from United States ports, while at present the share varies from about a third in Jamaica, the Bahamas, and British Honduras to a fifth in Trinidad and even less in the smaller islands.

American trade with the French colonies is negligible—indeed, almost nonexistent. In Dutch Guiana over a third of the exports, chiefly bauxite, goes northward, as do roughly half of the heavy oil shipments from the island areas.

Taken as a whole, the European colonies play no important part in Caribbean affairs. They have no domestic political problems of significance, public order is seldom disturbed, and they influence international politics but little. Economically, with the exception of the larger British holdings, they are now of negligible yield from local resources and, so far as the future can be forecast, are not of great promise. European powers in Caribbean affairs hold only a secondary position.

CHAPTER X

Venezuela and European Policy

ON the third of his voyages to the New World, Columbus, in 1498, after discovering Trinidad and a number of smaller islands, came upon the mainland of South America in the region in which the Orinoco flows into the Atlantic. He was the first white person to come to lands which now lie in the Republic of Venezuela. The next year, Alonzo de Ojeda reached the coast, probably in what is now Dutch Guiana, and felt his way westward to Lake Maracaibo. He had skirted the entire seacoast of what has since become the republic. Amerigo Vespucci, who accompanied him, later came to have his name identified with the New World. He is said to have called the district he visited *Venezuela,* "Little Venice," because the natives built their villages over the water on piles driven into the bottom of Lake Maracaibo. This name was later to be that of a captaincy general and still later that of a republic.

The new land was shortly colonized. Pearl fisheries were developed and slave hunters exploited the Indians, but no great natural riches were discovered. The north coast region as a whole disappointed the continued hopes of its possessors. The trade restrictions of Spanish colonial policy were partly to blame, though their effect was mitigated, as time went on, by an increasing contraband trade, especially in the case of Venezuela, with the Dutch. No steady advance occurred. For long after the colony was "settled," for years at a time not a single ship sailed from Caracas to Spain. Immigration never was large. Even the more liberal standards adopted in the eighteenth century were not sufficient to bring local resources to a prominent position in trade.

Slow growth, however, did occur, and in 1773 Venezuela became a captaincy general. Local dissatisfaction with Spanish policy continued to increase and prepared the ground early in the nineteenth century for a revolt which from this and other centers spread over the continent and brought the great Spanish colonial empire to an end.

Venezuela claims the honor of being the first of the Spanish colonies to seek its freedom. A premature effort led by Francisco Miranda in 1806 met no popular support. On April 19, 1810, when the control of Spain had been seized by the French, the people of Caracas repudiated connection with the Spanish Government, encouraged resistance by other colonies, and later came out for independence in a declaration in part paraphrasing that issued by British colonies a generation previous.

This rising also proved unsuccessful. The Spanish forces developed unexpected strength. An earthquake at Caracas in 1811 was used by the clergy to persuade the people that resistance to the "mother country" met divine disapproval, and by 1812 resistance was practically at an end. Simón Bolívar, a Venezuelan who had already become identified with the revolution, kept the movement alive first in what is now northern Colombia. The war was carried back into Venezuela, and before the end of 1813 the revolutionists were in control of Caracas. In the merciless conflict which followed, fortune again favored the Spaniards, who had received heavy reinforcements, and by 1816 opposition again seemed crushed.

The "legitimate dynasty" had been restored in Spain, but it showed no desire for reconciliation and its arbitrary actions kept the spirit of opposition alive. Late in 1816, Bolívar was again at the head of an independence movement, led this time from the Orinoco Valley, whence entry to Colombia was made. On August 7, 1819, in the battle of Boyacá, near Bogotá, the royalist forces were decisively defeated. Spanish resistance in Colombia was shortly thereafter at an end. After fruitless negotiations, the war was carried back again into Venezuela, where a decisive defeat was inflicted on the Spaniards at the battle of Carabobo in 1821.

Colombia, Venezuela, and Ecuador, from which latter region also the Spaniards had been driven, were united on May 29, 1822, in the Republic of Great Colombia. Local ambitions and geographical disunity, however, soon brought its dissolution. Early in May, 1830, Venezuela declared its independence and shortly adopted a constitution.

The subsequent history of the state has been characterized by disturbed periods and dictatorships. The outstanding figures after Antonio Páez,[1] who established Venezuelan independence, have been Antonio Guzmán Blanco, who, in and out of office as President, was virtual dictator from 1872 to 1888, Cipriano Castro, dictator from 1899 to 1908, an irresponsible adventurer who embroiled his country with a large number of other powers, American and European, and Juan Vicente Gómez, who has dominated Venezuelan developments since 1908.

After the end of the colonial period, Venezuelan resources continued to have but slow development until well past the beginning of the twentieth century. The greatest activity occurred in the northwest, where coffee and cacao became important crops and where petroleum has in recent years brought about one of the most remarkable transformations found in any South American region. Less advance was made in the region north of the Orinoco—still chiefly valuable for its extensive but backward cattle industry. In the lands south of the Orinoco, conditions have changed but little since the time of the conquest.

Nevertheless, Venezuela has at a number of periods played a prominent part in international incidents which have contributed in no small degree to the formulation of American international policy, and the current developments in its industries and politics make it one of the regions of the Caribbean deserving of close attention.

---

[1] An account of this picturesque figure is given in Graham, R. B. Cunninghame, *José Antonio Páez,* London, W. Heineman, Ltd., 1929.

The closing years of the nineteenth century gave Venezuelan affairs for a time great prominence in international relations. A disagreement with Great Britain rose from the uncertainty of boundaries in the colonial period. At the end of the colonial regime, the line dividing Venezuela from the lands to the east, then Dutch possessions, was unsettled, and controversy continued after the acquisition of part of Guiana by the British from the Dutch in 1814 and after the winning of Venezuelan independence. When Spain finally recognized Venezuelan independence in 1845, the Republic received territory the boundaries of which were indefinitely described as "the same as those which marked the ancient viceroyalty and captaincy general of New Granada and Venezuela in the year 1810." [2]

The Venezuelan minister in London in 1841 proposed joint action in fixing a boundary on the Guiana frontier and stated that he had notice that British agents were surveying a dividing line. In later disputes, this came to be known as the Schomburgk line. Thereafter for a generation, rival claims were urged by the parties with rising bitterness.[3]

Feeling that it was making no progress, the Venezuelan Government on November 14, 1876, through its foreign minister wrote to Secretary Hamilton Fish calling on "the most powerful and the oldest of the Republics of the new continent" to lend its aid in "having due justice done to Venezuela." [4] The request was not explicit and did not result in positive action by the United States.

Further requests for settlement by arbitration or other means were made to Great Britain without success. In 1881 the case was again called to the attention of the United States Department of State by Venezuela on the occasion of the appearance of British warships at the mouth of the Orinoco near the disputed territory. Secretary Evarts responded that the

---

[2] Cleveland, Grover, *Presidential Problems,* New York, Century Co., 1904, p. 175.

[3] A review of these claims is given in Cleveland, *op. cit.,* pp. 177–189. The documents detailing the various steps in the controversy, upon which the discussion below is in large part based, are in *For. Rel.,* 1895, Part I, pp. 545–576.

[4] Quoted in Cleveland, *op. cit.,* pp. 192–193.

United States "could not look with indifference" on the forcible acquisition of such territory by England. His successors continued to show themselves interested in any settlement. In 1882 Venezuela was told that the United States would suggest arbitration by a third power if Venezuela wished. Two years later, the American minister in London was reminded of the continued interest of the United States in "all that touches the independent life of the Republics of the American continent" and was told to assist the Venezuelan representative by pointing out this interest to the British, though he was not, it appears, to raise specifically the issue of the application of the Monroe Doctrine to the Venezuelan claims. But no advance resulted. In 1887 the United States at the request of Venezuela tendered its good offices to Great Britain for arranging arbitration but found the foreign office not favorably disposed.[5]

The complaints of Venezuela against renewed British "encroachments" in the year following became more insistent, and the Department of State came to view developments with "grave disquietude" as involving extensions of British claims which, by taking over territory in fact Venezuelan, involved the principles announced in the Monroe Doctrine. The President and Congress also showed increasing concern, and the latter adopted a joint resolution recommending that the dispute be referred to "friendly arbitration." [6] But Great Britain, though now ready to arbitrate part of the claims, insisted that Venezuela should first agree to consider a large part of the territory in dispute as definitely British.[7]

With the appointment of Richard Olney as Secretary of State, the American policy became more energetic. There was sent to the American minister in London on July 20, 1895, a message passages in which have since become famous. The bearing of the Monroe Doctrine on the case was pointed out.

---

[5] The United States showed itself disposed to support the Venezuelan claims at various other times not here detailed.

[6] See *Joint Resolution Relative to the British Guiana-Venezuela Boundary Dispute,* 53rd Cong., 3rd Sess., Res. 17 (February 20), 1895, *Statutes at Large,* Vol. XXVIII, p. 971.

[7] See Cleveland, *op cit.,* p. 248 *et sqq.*

The British demand for acceptance of a tentative boundary as a basis of discussion was declared inacceptable. The American minister was instructed to read the dispatch to the British authorities and to declare that the circumstances called "for a definite decision upon the point whether Great Britain will consent or will decline to submit the Venezuelan boundary question in its entirety to impartial arbitration."

Lord Salisbury replied November 26, 1895. The Monroe Doctrine, he declared, was no longer applicable to international affairs. It was no part of international law. The United States had no right to insist that the disputed boundaries of European colonies in America be submitted to arbitration. However, Great Britain still hoped for "a reasonable arrangement at an early date." [8]

The Cleveland administration next committed itself to bringing a settlement. The President's message to Congress on December 17, 1895,[9] reaffirmed that the controversy touched policies which "can not become obsolete while our Republic endures." It involved the "Monroe doctrine," which was "of vital concern to" the people and Government of the United States. While it might not "have been admitted in so many words to the code of international law," still "every nation is entitled to the rights belonging to it," and, "if the enforcement of the Monroe doctrine is something we may justly claim it has its place in the code of international law as certainly and as securely as if it were specifically mentioned."

"If a European power," he continued, "by an extension of

---

[8] The flare-up of American opinion caused by the Venezuelan controversy which followed Olney's action took the British public by surprise. James Bryce heard of the "war scare" on a voyage back to England from South Africa. In a letter to Theodore Roosevelt dated January 1, 1896, he wrote, "Not one man out of ten in the House of Commons even knew there was such a thing as a Venezuelan question pending." He himself was astonished at the "sympathy with a corrupt military tyranny like that of Venezuela. . . . They are not a civilized government at all." (Letter printed in Fisher, H. A. L., *James Bryce,* New York, the Macmillan Company, 1927, Vol. I, pp. 318–319.)

[9] Richardson, James D., *A Compilation of the Messages and Papers of the Presidents, 1789–1897,* Washington, Bureau of National Literature and Art, 1897, Vol. IX, pp. 655–658.

its boundaries takes possession of the territory of one of our neighboring Republics against its will and in derogation of its rights, it is difficult to see why to that extent such European power does not thereby attempt to extend its system of government to that portion of this continent which is thus taken. This is the precise action which President Monroe declared to be 'dangerous to our peace and safety' and it can make no difference whether the European system is extended by an advance of frontier or otherwise."

It was suggested that Congress appropriate money for the expenses of a commission to be appointed by the executive which should make a report on what should be the boundary. "When such report is made and accepted," insisted the President, "it will, in my opinion, be the duty of the United States to resist by every means in its power, as a willful aggression upon its rights and interests, the appropriation by Great Britain of any lands or the exercise of governmental jurisdiction over any territory which after investigation we have determined of right belongs to Venezuela."[10]

Soon thereafter Congress by an almost unanimous vote supported the President and appropriated money for the commission. Five men were appointed "to investigate and report upon the true divisional line between the republic of Venezuela and British Guiana."

Meanwhile the United States once more urged Great Britain to accept a compromise and on March 3, 1896, received a reply in which Great Britain consented to arbitrate with Venezuela or with the United States acting on her behalf. Minimum territorial concessions were no longer insisted upon, but it was reasserted by Great Britain that long British settlement—fifty years, as finally agreed upon—should be accepted as evidence of title, a standard acquiesced in by the representatives of Venezuela. Thereupon, Olney informed the American commission that it might cease its activities.

A treaty for arbitration of all claims drawn up on this basis was signed on February 2, 1897. Negotiations for settlement

---

[10] *Ibid.*, Vol. IX, p. 658.

were begun at Paris on June 3, 1899. On the tribunal were two English judges, two American judges, and a president selected by these four. The decision was handed down on October 3, 1899. The greater part of the territory in dispute went to Great Britain, though Venezuela succeeded in maintaining her claims to the region near the mouth of the Orinoco River, which she had felt to be essential as the key to the development of the hinterland, and some territory east of the Schomburgk line was awarded to her.[11]

Thus closed with the century a controversy which in retrospect appears to many to have been given importance far beyond that of its subject matter. That the question of arbitrating a disputed boundary in territory of little value claimed by a third nation could have brought the two great Anglo-Saxon powers to a point where popular opinion was roused to war pitch seems, as we now look back upon it, almost unbelievable. The danger was doubtless more apparent than real. It was hardly to be expected that Great Britain would go to war in defense of the right to refuse to arbitrate, for she had been a defender of the pacific settlement of international disputes. The United States also at the last would consent to compromise rather than force a conflict on a technical issue. In fact, even assuming that the principle of the Monroe Doctrine applied to the case, it is evident that one of the bases of settlement actually adopted—that fifty years' occupation should constitute good title—does not necessarily mean that the result would not involve an extension of territorial holdings by a European power.

In practice, too, the possibility of the abuse of strength by European countries in the settlement of boundary disputes in Latin America is decidedly limited, for, with the exception of the Guianas and British Honduras, there are no mainland

[11] The American official correspondence on the controversy is found in *For. Rel.*, 1895, Part I. Short secondary discussions are found in Bingham, Hiram, *The Monroe Doctrine, an Obsolete Shibboleth,* New Haven, Yale University Press, 1913; Cleveland, Grover, *Presidential Problems,* New York, the Century Co., 1904, pp. 173–281; Henderson, John B., *American Diplomatic Questions,* New York, the Macmillan Co., 1901, pp. 411–444; and Mowat, R. B., *The Diplomatic Relations of Great Britain and the United States,* London, Longmans, Green and Co., 1925, pp. 258–272.

colonies in the area. That the extension of European control over minor disputed districts in any of these areas would constitute a threat to the interests of the United States can be maintained only with difficulty.

Technically, however, the case argued by Olney did not lack strength. The Monroe Doctrine, even if it was not international law, was an accepted policy of the United States. British claims had shown a remarkable elasticity and tended to follow the spread of mining developments in a way which seemed conclusively to prove that a boundary determined on a purely historical basis would not be willingly accepted. A colony which "apparently expanded in two years some 33,000 square miles" [12] can hardly be argued to be one which does not involve an extension of the European system to America and an attempt in some degree to control the destiny of the American state claiming the territory.

Whatever the technical merits of the controversy, Venezuelan affairs had served as the occasion for a vigorous restatement of the American position—a position which had become increasingly defendable with the appearance of a less forward British policy as to the Caribbean in the latter half of the nineteenth century. The declarations made by the United States were also a forecast of events which were soon to make the desires of this country an increasing factor in developments throughout the region and to affect its relations with both the Caribbean states and more distant American powers.

One of the declarations in particular was to have an unexpected repercussion in the Latin-American states. In developing his argument as to the position of the United States in relation to European powers, Mr. Olney stated that the safety of the United States was involved in the maintenance of the independence of every American state against European aggression. He insisted that all American states were friends and allies. If any should be subjected by European states, this happy condition would cease. After an ambiguous transition, the Secretary went on to say that in the last analysis

---

[12] For a full statement of the American position, see Olney to Bayard, July 20, 1895, *For. Rel.*, 1895, Part 1, pp. 545–562.

every state, if it is to have the "regard and respect of other states," must "be largely dependent upon its own strength and power." . . . "Today the United States is practically sovereign on this continent, and its fiat is law upon the subjects to which it confines its interposition." This he felt to be true "because, in addition to all other grounds, its infinite resources combined with its isolated position render it master of the situation and practically invulnerable as against any or all other powers. All the advantages of this superiority are at once imperiled if the principle be admitted that European powers may convert American states into colonies or provinces of their own." European powers would acquire military bases against the United States. South America might be divided up as Africa was then being partitioned. This would be disastrous to American prestige. "Our only real rivals in peace as well as enemies in war would be found located at our very doors." We would be forced to arm to the teeth, "with the powers of Europe permanently encamped on American soil." We should have to spend "a large share of the productive energy of the nation" in military activities. "The ideal conditions we have thus far enjoyed" could "not be expected to continue." [13]

This rather florid utterance announced an intention to defend both the policy of the United States and the independence of Latin-American nations. It resulted from action taken on behalf of Venezuela and by Venezuela's request. The later steps in adjustment were taken with Venezuela's co-operation and resulted to its advantage. The position was assumed against European powers. The Secretary had not at all in mind a statement of American policy as to other American states. Assertion that the United States "in addition to other grounds" was master of the situation because of its resources and its isolated position was, after all, little if anything more than a statement of fact, a statement justified perhaps more in 1895 than at the present time, for the development of the resources of other American states since then

---

[13] *Ibid.*, p. 558.

has been spectacular, and the isolation of the United States, along with that of other nations, has greatly decreased.

Nevertheless, phrases of the declaration taken out of their context have been given a meaning which their author could never have intended. Latin-American commentators and others have found in the pronouncement that the United States is "practically sovereign" in the New World and that it is a country whose "fiat is law" indication that the greatest of American nations covertly aspires to a leadership synonymous with domination and that such will to power must be taken into account, not only by all non-American states, but by all American states as well.

The decision in the boundary controversy on October 3, 1899, had not been handed down before political complications had again arisen. Venezuela was to continue in a prominent position during the quick succession of incidents which made the Caribbean so large a factor in international developments in the opening years of the current century.

As has already been shown, through much of its history Venezuela has been controlled by "strong men," "*caudillos,*" who have made themselves dictators. By their control of the Army, they have been able to keep all rivals in hand. Between these periods of more or less well-maintained peace, the country has been ruled by weaker men who have succeeded each other at short intervals, sometimes at intervals of only a few months.

The boundary dispute was put on the way to settlement by Joaquin Crespo, one of these less important presidents who had at one time been a collaborator of Guzmán Blanco. By the time the arbitral tribunal had given its decision, however, two new revolts against the government had occurred and the political fortunes of General Cipriano Castro were in the ascendant.[14] He declared himself "Supreme Chief" on October 20, 1899, and in spite of serious revolutions succeeded in keeping control of the government until the end of 1908.

---

[14] A calendar of political events in Venezuelan history is found in Crichfield, George W., *American Supremacy,* New York, Brentano's, 1908, Vol. I, pp. 13–78.

During his nine-year period of control, Castro found himself not only faced by domestic revolution but in controversy with a list of both European and American countries, including Belgium, France, Germany, Great Britain, Italy, Mexico, the Netherlands, Spain, Sweden, Norway, and the United States. He came to be called with justice *"l'enfant terrible"* of American international politics. Out of this maze of complications, two groups of claims rose to special significance. They were (1) claims involving the grievances of a group of European powers and (2) claims involving the grievances of the United States.

It became evident soon after Castro came into power that the damages arising from the revolution which put him into control would bring demands from foreign nations for settlement, and that other claims would doubtless be joined to the recent ones when adjustments were asked. The new claims alone totalled some 725. Foreign ministers at Caracas approached the American representative to ascertain what the attitude of the United States would be toward joint action to secure redress. The United States Department of State shortly after declared that it was not the policy of the United States to act with other governments in such matters.[15]

The complaints made showed wide variety. They included alleged damage to foreign interests resulting from the revolution of 1892 and subsequent domestic disturbances, damages from the civil wars of 1898–1900, including forced loans, confiscation of cattle, destruction of property, confiscation of vessels and plundering of their contents and maltreatment of their crews, summary expulsion of foreign residents, and false imprisonments. Other claims involved default in interest on public loans, nonpayment of interest and amortization charges on railway bonds guaranteed by the Government, violation of contracts entered into by the Government which had resulted in practical confiscation of property, infringement of the rights of diplomatic representatives, and other offenses against comity and international law.

---

[15] *For. Rel.*, 1901, p. 550 (June 30, 1901).

If these claims should be actively pushed by non-American powers, they would be sure to raise questions (1) as to the degree to which force could be used to secure redress for various classes of claims under the rules of international law, and (2) as to the attitude which the United States might assume toward the more extreme measures which might be proposed. As in the boundary dispute, policy might play a role quite as important as that of international law.

At the end of 1901 the German embassy sent the United States Department of State a *promemoria* stating that Venezuela was guilty of "a frivolous attempt to avoid just obligations," and that, if refusal to make adjustment continued, Germany would have to consider "what measures of coercion" to use.

"But," continued the statement, "we consider it of importance to let first of all the Government of the United States know . . . that we have nothing else in view than to help those of our citizens who have suffered damages. . . .

"We declare especially that under no circumstances do we consider in our proceedings the acquisition or the permanent occupation of Venezuelan territory." [16] Blockade of the principal harbors to cut off the customs income and foodstuffs on which Venezuela was greatly dependent was all that was contemplated. However, "If this measure does not seem sufficient, we would have to consider the temporary occupation on our part of different Venezuelan harbor places and the levying of duties in those places." [17]

---

[16] *Ibid.*, pp. 193 and 194 (December 11, 1901). Similar statements do not appear to have been made by Great Britain at this time; but, when the joint move against Venezuela was actually in progress, a somewhat broader statement was made in the House of Lords: "It is not intended to land a British force, and still less to occupy Venezuelan territory." (White to Hay, December 16, 1902, *ibid.*, 1903, p. 453.) See also *Die Grosse Politik der Europäischen Kabinette,* 1871–1914 (Johannes Lepsius, Albrecht Mendelssohn Bartholdy, Friedrich Thimme, eds.), Berlin, Deutsche Verlagsgesellschaft für Politik und Geschichte, 1924, Vol. XVII, p. 241, for the report of the German ambassador, Von Holleben, December 24, 1901.

[17] The German correspondence seems to indicate that the British also faced that possibility on November 17, 1902. (*Die Auswärtige Politik des Deutschen Reiches, 1871–1914,* Berlin, 1928, Vol. II, p. 371). On December 17, however, Lord Balfour declared in Parliament, "We have no intention, and have never had any intention, of landing troops in Venezuela or of occupying territory,

To this announcement the Department of State replied[18] by quoting a clause in the first message of President Roosevelt to Congress delivered only eight days before the date of the German message. In discussing the Monroe Doctrine, the President had said, "We do not guarantee any state against punishment if it misconducts itself, provided that punishment does not take the form of the acquisition of territory by any non-American power."[19] Though the note did not specifically declare opposition to temporary occupation, evidently such action would not be welcome.

Apparently, almost contemporaneously with the German note feeling out the attitude of the United States toward projects to coerce Venezuela into a settlement, there developed discussion of general action by Germany and Great Britain. What power initiated the movement is not clear.

A telegram of the German Chargé d'Affaires in London dated January 2, 1902, reported that it was possible that after an early Cabinet meeting joint action would be proposed.[20] That this was the case was called to the attention of the Kaiser by the Imperial Chancellor on January 20.[21] At a later date, when British public opinion was aroused against the Venezuelan developments, the German ambassador in London reported that it would create a difficult position for the Cabinet if it were officially stated that Lord Lansdowne had incited the affair. An announcement of this sort the Chancellor and the Kaiser agreed should be avoided.[22]

The indications in the German correspondence that the suggestion started with Great Britain is strengthened by the lack of preciseness in the British statements. The earliest reference as to the origin of co-operation is in a dispatch from

---

even though that occupation might only be of temporary character." (*Parliamentary Debates,* 4th Ser., Vol. 116, Col. 1489.)

[18] *For. Rel.,* 1901, p. 195 (December 16, 1901).

[19] Richardson, *op. cit.,* Vol. X, p. 441.

[20] *Grosse Politik,* Vol. XVII, p. 242.

[21] *Ibid.,* pp. 241–243: The Imperial Chancellor von Bülow to Kaiser William, January 20, 1902.

[22] *Ibid.,* pp. 288–289, February 4, 1903: The Ambassador in London, Count von Metternich, to the Imperial Chancellor Count von Bülow, and appended comments.

Lord Lansdowne to the British ambassador in Berlin on July 23, 1902, in which it is stated that in a conversation about Venezuelan affairs he had said that "we [the British] should be quite ready to confer with the German Government with a view to joint action." [23]

This, it seems, could not have been the beginning of the discussions. Later, when developments had become active, the British Government did not explain the origin of the co-operation but contented itself, in the Answer to the King's Speech on February 17, 1903, with saying that "when approached by the German Ambassador, whose country had similar causes of complaint," the Secretary of State for Foreign Affairs "informed him that His Majesty's Government were prepared to take joint action. . . ." [24] As the incident progressed, each of the parties became anxious to avoid assuming responsibility for its initiation.

It may be, too, that, during the preliminary discussions between British and German officials over the wrongs of their citizens, the possibility of joint action was brought into the conversations so gradually that the original suggestion could not be justly assigned to either side.

Among the means proposed to coerce Venezuela to recognize its alleged international obligations was the establishment of a pacific blockade. The standing of such a measure in international law was by no means generally recognized, though the German Imperial Chancellor stated to Kaiser William II that the foreign office informed him that it had in a number of cases been used with success, and had been accepted, in the practice of European states, at least, to involve practically the same factors as a warlike blockade except that ships breaking the blockade were sequestered till the end of the blockade instead of being confiscated. The United States had not, he said, taken a position as to the legality of pacific blockade; but its effectiveness against Venezuela prom-

---

[23] *House of Commons, Accounts and Papers,* 1902, Vol. 130, *Venezuela,* No. 1 (1902): Correspondence respecting the Affairs of Venezuela (cd. 1372), pp. 4–5.

[24] *Parliamentary Debates,* 4th Series, Vol. 118, Col. 5.

ised to be great, since it would shut off the customs revenue, almost the only source of Government income, and interfere with the entry of imported foodstuffs.[25]

Procedure on these lines, he later informed the Kaiser, would allow sequestration of the enemy warships without a declaration of war, as had been done "in many cases involving South American states." No opposition was to be expected from the United States and the action taken was to be carried out jointly with Great Britain. The Kaiser approved the proposal.[26]

The negotiations for common action proceeded smoothly as to the ends to be sought but not as to the means. On August 8, the Germans suggested a joint naval demonstration,[27] but the British did not look favorably on a pacific blockade. The Germans, however, continued anxious to avoid the establishment of a warlike blockade, which under their Constitution would require action by the Bundesrath. They suggested as a possible expedient the establishment merely of "a blockade" without specification of its nature.[28] To determine what might be the fate of such a venture, Germany asked the position of the United States and on December 12 was informed that the proposed pacific blockade could not apply to the United States vessels.[29] The British also decided that under English law a regular blockade was called for. Germany then acceded to the British plan.[30] Meanwhile, as

[25] Imperial Chancellor von Bülow to Kaiser William II, January 20, 1902, *Grosse Politik, op. cit.*, Vol. XVII, p. 241.

[26] Imperial Chancellor von Bülow to Kaiser William II, September 1, 1902 (with marginal notes by the Kaiser). *Grosse Politik, op. cit.*, Vol. XVII, p. 245.

[27] *House of Commons, Accounts and Papers,* 1902, Vol. 130, *Venezuela,* No. 1 (1902): Correspondence respecting the Affairs of Venezuela (cd. 1372), p. 5 (Foreign Office to Admiralty, August 8, 1902).

[28] *Grosse Politik, op. cit.*, Vol. XVII, pp. 257–258 (December 9 and 12, 1902). British freedom of action was limited by the fact that Great Britain had objected to enforcement against neutral ships of the French blockade of Formosa in 1884 involving circumstances comparable to those which Germany proposed to create in the Venezuelan case. (*Ibid.*, p. 255.) W. E. Hall, in *A Treatise on International Law,* 8th ed. (ed. by A. P. Higgins), Oxford, Clarendon Press, 1924, at pp. 437–443, discusses the chief instances of the use of pacific blockade in the nineteenth century.

[29] *For. Rel.*, 1903, p. 420 (December 12, 1902).

[30] *Grosse Politik, op. cit.*, Vol. XVII, p. 258 (December 12, 1902).

the season advanced, the governments had other details of the proposed action under consideration.

The early German note to the American Department of State had shown that the German Government had been willing to face the possibility of having ultimately to resort to more vigorous measures if the blockade did not bring the desired results. Great Britain wavered but was clearly in favor of avoiding any advanced program. Even the establishment of a warlike blockade, they had felt, had disadvantages, and in October they thought it would be better only to seize all the Venezuelan gunboats until the British demands were complied with.[31] About a month later they were reported to be willing, in case this measure were insufficient, to consider the seizing of the customhouses.[32] In December, however, Lord Balfour declared in Parliament that Great Britain never intended occupying territory even temporarily.[33]

As the year approached a close, the program turned toward establishment of a blockade on accepted lines, but the desire on the part of Germany to follow the British lead and the anxiety which the British Government felt in the face of growing criticism at home and elsewhere concerning the whole undertaking banished any consideration of more extensive operations.[34]

Meanwhile, apparently still doubtful about joint action, Great Britain sent "ultimata" to Venezuela without waiting for Germany. The first note of this sort was sent, indeed, as early as July, 1902. It made little impression on Venezuela.[35]

---

[31] *House of Commons, Accounts and Papers,* 1902, Vol. 130, *Venezuela,* No. 1 (1902): Correspondence respecting the Affairs of Venezula (cd. 1372), p. 10; and Foreign Office to Admiralty, October 22, 1902, *Grosse Politik, op. cit.,* Vol. XVII, p. 255.

[32] *Grosse Politik, op. cit.,* Vol. XVII, p. 255: The Chargé d'Affaires in London, Count Bernstorff, to the Foreign Office, November 17, 1902.

[33] *Parliamentary Debates,* 4th Ser., Vol. 116, Col. 1489, December 17, 1902.

[34] The ambassador in London, Count von Metternich, reported to the foreign office on December 13, 1902, that the press in England and elsewhere argued that Germany had proceeded with too great vigor and that there was no disposition in England to adopt drastic measures. *Grosse Politik, op. cit.,* Vol. XVII, pp. 261–262.

[35] Statement of Balfour, *Parliamentary Debates,* 4th Ser., Vol. 116, Col. 1274 (December 15, 1902).

After hearing it read to him, the Venezuelan minister of foreign affairs calmly remarked "that they were used to these communications." [36]

Co-operation now having been decided upon, both parties sought reassurance as to the attitude of the United States toward their project. The British inquired whether objection would be made to the use of force by European powers against Central and South American countries. Secretary Hay replied that, while such action would be regretted, no objection to steps to obtain redress for injuries would be made "provided that no acquisition of territory was contemplated." [37] Thereafter, the two powers entered active negotiations as to the way in which their "ultimata" should be presented.[38] On December 3, the American ambassador in Berlin reported a conversation with the German Under-Secretary in which the latter again brought out that "all Germany desired was that Venezuela should not shield herself behind the United States from fulfilling her just obligations." Two days later, Secretary Hay informed the ambassador of steps being taken by American bankers which if successful might avoid any exhibition of force by European powers; but, he said, if any such arrangements were made, the bankers would understand that they could not rely on the United States to give any moral or material guarantee to the agreement.[39] No development of this sort eventuated.

While the final demands were under discussion, Italy, on December 5, asked to be allowed to join in the British-German

---

[36] Hazard to Marquis of Lansdowne, *House of Commons, Accounts and Papers,* 1902, Vol. 130, *Venezuela,* No. 1 (1902): Correspondence respecting the Affairs of Venezuela (cd. 1372), in Dispatch of August 1, 1902, pp. 6–7.

[37] Herbert to Lansdowne, November 13, 1902. *House of Commons, Accounts and Papers,* Vol. 87, 1903. *Venezuela,* No. 1 (1903): Correspondence respecting the Affairs of Venezuela (cd. 1399), p. 147; 1902, Vol. 130, Correspondence respecting the Affairs of Venezuela (cd. 1372), p. 13, Memorandum, November 26, 1902.

[38] *House of Commons, Accounts and Papers,* 1902, Vol. 130: Correspondence respecting the Affairs of Venezuela (cd. 1372), p. 13, Memorandum, November 26, 1902.

[39] *For. Rel.,* 1903, p. 418 (Dodge to Hay, December 3, 1902, and Hay to Dodge, December 5, 1902). The position taken may be compared to that later adopted in similar circumstances in the Dominican Republic.

action. The British replied that it was probably too late to arrange it but that they had no objection in principle. Germany later also approved. Though Italy took no active part in the hostilities, the action became, thus, tripartite.[40] The next day, the ministers of the two powers turned over the protection of their national interests to Mr. Herbert Bowen, the minister of the United States, and left Caracas.[41] There followed a period in which all parties to the dispute resorted to extreme measures.[42] Castro proceeded to arrest all British and German subjects whom he could apprehend, including the German consul general and the chancellor of the German Legation. Many British subjects went into hiding. Bowen protested against the arrests and by December 10 was assured that all prisoners had been freed.

Castro had promptly come to his senses after the severance of diplomatic relations and was anxious for quick action to head off what he now saw might be serious consequences. He told Bowen on December 9 that he believed all the German and British differences could be settled by arbitration. It was too late. On their side, the naval forces of the European powers already off the coast also acted promptly. The British and German fleets captured all the Venezuelan war vessels in La Guaira.[43] "Two hundred and fifty sailors landed

---

[40] Lansdowne to R. Rodd, December 5, 1902 (No. 166), *House of Commons, Accounts and Papers,* Vol. 87, 1903, *Venezuela,* No. 1 (1903): Correspondence respecting the Affairs of Venezuela (cd. 1399), p. 165; and *Die Auswärtige Politik,* Vol. II, p. 372 (The Imperial Chancellor to the Kaiser, December 12, 1902).

[41] *For Rel.,* 1903, p. 789 (December 8, 1902).

[42] *Ibid.,* p. 789 *et sqq.*

[43] *Ibid.,* 1903, pp. 794–795 (December 9, 1902). The character of this conflict is set forth in *For. Rel.,* 1903, pp. 421–422. The Venezuelan men-of-war captured by the Germans were stated to be one vessel of 600 tons, which was manned by Germans and put under the German flag, and two small vessels of 137 tons each, which were not sufficiently seaworthy to allow crews to be put aboard to take them to Trinidad. Since towing them to port would weaken the blokading force and since they "had absolutely no value whatever," these two vessels were sunk. The naval action was a joint affair. The British report indicates that two of the Venezuelan vessels were brought out by the German ships *Vineta* and *Panther.* One was brought out by the British vessel *Ossun.* The British also took the machinery out of the Venezuelan destroyer *Margarita.* (*House of Commons, Accounts and Papers,* Vol. 87, 1903, *Venezuela,* No. 1 (1903), Correspondence respecting the Affairs

at La Guaira, rescued some British subjects, and took them aboard [a] British war vessel." [44]

Castro saw that he must yield.[45] He requested that the British and German claims be arbitrated and asked Bowen to act as arbitrator for Venezuela, but the storm could not now be stopped. The enemy bombarded the forts at Puerto Cabello.[46] The United States Department of State recommended that the powers arbitrate the issues,[47] but no reply came in till the 20th. The European powers then invited the President of the United States to arbitrate, and on the following day Castro agreed.[48] But the blockade was formally proclaimed and made effective. The British blockade was extended to the eastern ports and the mouths of the Orinoco, and the Germans shut up Puerto Cabello and Maracaibo.[49]

---

of Venezuela (cd. 1399), pp. 167 and 201.) The European ships which operated against Venezuela, as listed by the Germans, numbered fourteen, including eight British ships, four German ships, and two Italian ships. *Die Auswärtige Politik,* Vol. II, p. 372: The Imperial Chancellor to the Kaiser, December 12, 1902.

[44] *For. Rel.,* 1903, p. 790 (December 10, 1902). The British accounts of the operations of December 10, 1902, report two landings, one with 70 men and 2 officers, and the other with 74 seamen and other troops. *House of Commons, Accounts and Papers,* Vol. 87, 1903, *Venezuela,* No. 1 (1903) Correspondence respecting the Affairs of Venezuela (cd. 1399), pp. 201–202.

[45] *For. Rel.,* 1903, p. 793 (December 9, 1902).

[46] *Ibid.,* pp. 796–797: Documents of December 13–14, 1902. This also, to the later disappointment of the British public, was a joint undertaking. The British commander took the lead. The British vessel *Charybdis* and the German *Vineta* co-operated to avenge an insult to the British flag and to a British vessel. The authorities were told that the forts would be demolished if no apology were forthcoming. None came. Fort Libertador, which the British bombarded, replied by rifle fire only, as the guns were on the side commanding the town and could not be moved. Fort Vigia, object of the German fire, replied by a few shots and was then abandoned. The next day, the British and Germans landed forces which blew up the guns. *House of Commons, Accounts and Papers,* Vol. 87, 1903, *Venezuela,* No. 1 (1903) (cd. 1399), pp. 174, 202, and 204. The German documents report that a Venezuelan fort on the seventeenth fired on the German vessel *Panther.* It was destroyed by the *Panther's* fire on the twenty-first. (*Die Auswärtige Politik,* Vol. II, p. 377.)

[47] *Ibid.,* pp. 798–800 (December 16, 1902).

[48] Castro at one time proposed that "an American power" arbitrate the case. As to this, the United States minister in London reported that Lord Lansdowne considered arbitration by any American power except the United States out of the question. (*For. Rel.,* 1903, p. 466.)

[49] The text of the British blockade proclamation of December 20, 1902, is published in *For. Rel.,* 1903, p. 458. The similar German announcement is in

Venezuela was effectively shut off from the outside world, and Castro was anxious to have the blockade raised as promptly as possible. He was willing to grant Great Britain and Germany the customhouses as guarantee of payment.[50]

When Castro had first become persuaded by events that arbitration of the disagreements was to be desired, he had favored having the American minister act for Venezuela, and in the adjustments later undertaken Bowen did so. The appointment was not welcomed by the allies, and, as time went on, their feeling toward Bowen became increasingly unfriendly. When Castro's suggestion of arbitration had been received from the United States by the European powers, however, Germany desired that the offer be promptly accepted for fear that the United States might advance from the position of an intermediator to a more active diplomatic role. Acquiescence, it was felt, would assure the allies greater freedom of action than would be possible if the United States were allowed to develop a definite program of its own.[51]

To this end, after outlining reservations as to certain claims, the allies asked President Roosevelt to act as arbitrator; but they declared, "if he will not do so the governments will accept settlement by the Hague Tribunal." [52] The President declared for the latter course,[53] which Venezuela also shortly accepted "in principle," though previously The Hague had not been favored because of its expense and the slowness with which it would act.[54]

President Roosevelt, when declining to act, suggested a preliminary diplomatic conference at Washington. Germany was indisposed to approve such a meeting and Great Britain declared in favor of separate negotiation of the details of the

---

For. Rel., 1903, p. 425. See also *For. Rel.*, 1903, p. 424 (Tower to Hay, December 22, 1902).

[50] *Ibid.*, 1903, p. 803 (January 7, 1903).

[51] The Imperial Chancellor Count von Bülow to the Ambassador in London, Count von Metternich, December 17, 1902. (*Grosse Politik, op. cit.*, Vol. XVII, pp. 266–268.)

[52] The text of the memorandum, dated December 22, 1902, is in *For. Rel.*, 1903, pp. 427–428.

[53] *Ibid.*, p. 428 (Hay to Tower, December 26, 1902).

[54] *Ibid.*, p. 802.

further arrangements by Bowen with the representatives of the allies, who should, however, keep each other informed of developments.[55]

While these arrangements were being made, a collateral discussion was in process as to what claims should be arbitrated. Certain ones, "first line claims," the blockading powers insisted, involved factors which could not be arbitrated. Only the amount of the damage could be submitted to adjudication, but a cash payment would have to be made at once if the obligation were to be recognized in principle.[56]

These claims were, in the case of Germany, those involving damages arising from the civil war of 1898–1900. Great Britain considered to fall in this class "claims for injuries to the person and property of British subjects owing to the confiscation of British vessels, the plundering of their contents, and the maltreatment of their crews, as well as some claims for the ill-usage and false imprisonment of British subjects. . . ." Other claims would be submitted to arbitration or to settlement by mixed commissions. On the last day of the year 1902, Castro announced, "I recognize in principle the claims which the allied powers have presented to Venezuela." [57]

A settlement seemed now in prospect. Arbitration, except as to the "first line claims," had been agreed upon in principle. The actual amounts to be paid to recognize the special position of these "first line claims" had been by agreement greatly cut down from their original totals. All other claims were to be settled by amicable adjustment. President Roosevelt had declined to act as arbiter. Whether the actual settlement should take place at The Hague or elsewhere was still

---

[55] *Die Grosse Politik, op. cit.*, Vol. XVII, 271–272.

[56] The British position is outlined in White to Hay, December 18, 1902, *For. Rel.*, 1903, pp. 455–456, and a memorandum of December 23, 1902, *For. Rel.*, 1903, pp. 461–462. See Tower to Hay, December 23, 1902, *For. Rel.*, 1903, pp. 425–426, for the similar German statement, and also, Tower to Hay, January 13, 1903, *For. Rel.*, 1903, p. 436.

[57] *Ibid.*, 1903, p. 433. See also his elaboration of this acceptance, as of January 8, 1903, in *For. Rel.*, 1903, p. 435. Great Britain accepted Castro's statement with the reservation that it be interpreted to mean that he specifically accepted the reservations outlined as to arbitration. (Lansdowne to White, January 5, 1903, *ibid.*, p. 467.)

undecided, but no serious difficulty was to be anticipated on this account.

Agreement upon a principle is often far easier than agreement on the application of the principle to facts. It proved so in this case. Indeed, in a number of ways, the conflict became more acute after the agreement on arbitration than it had been at any previous time. Mr. Bowen, now acting on behalf of Venezuela, on January 20, 1903, asked for the general raising of the blockade before further negotiations, and for mixed commissions to sit in Venezuela and pass on the lower-rank claims, for only on the ground could these, he held, be effectively investigated. Such mixed commissions he found the allies disposed to accept provided their demands on certain items were specifically accepted and guarantees for the payment of the others were given. The powers made it clear also that they would expect a separate settlement including the claims of bondholders.

The Venezuelan representative declared that the republic wished the demands of all countries which had claims against it to stand on the same footing. Otherwise a premium would be given to powers resorting to force. The non-blockading powers would, if this program were not accepted, have to wait for years before their claims would be paid. He declared also that it was now too late for the blockading powers to ask for preferential treatment. On this point, however, the allies refused to yield.

As the discussions proceeded, the European negotiators became highly critical of Bowen's actions and reported that he had undertaken to break down their desire to act as a unit. They felt that Bowen had the support of the United States in his stand, that France was disposed to take the same position, and that other claimants might do so. Would it be best, they wondered, to put forth a claim for payment of the expenses of the blockade in place of that for preferential treatment? Or should President Roosevelt be asked to pass on precedence of payment? The Germans and British both felt that, if the last were done, the decision would be against them. They had doubts as to whether they could hope for much more from the Hague Court. Opinion in Central and South America, they learned, was crystallizing against the allies to the great advantage of the United States. The German ambassador in London was disposed to think that the demand for preferential treatment should be abandoned except for such installments of the payments as might fall due in a three-months period, which would save the principle.[58]

What was the best way out of a tangle which was creating a situation that the Germans now saw threatened the preferential treatment they felt public opinion at home greatly desired, which was reported to be already hurting the trade position of European powers in Latin America, and which was highly unpopular in Great Britain and threatened to bring the fall of the ministry if President Roosevelt should lose patience and demand the lifting of the blockade? The British ministry, so the German ambassador in London felt, could not stand up "against the American fetish in combination with the feeling against Germany."[59]

The blockading powers decided to take the risk of asking President Roosevelt to decide whether preferential treatment should be granted. He declined to act.[60] There followed involved negotiations which resulted in a protocol on February 13, 1903.[61] Venezuela recognized the justice of the allied demands. The "first line claims," as adjusted, were to be paid part in cash, part in securities of short term. The second-rank claims were to be passed upon by mixed commissions. They

---

58 The diplomatic papers on which the above summary rests date from January 20, 1903, to January 31, 1903, *Grosse Politik, op. cit.,* Vol. XVII, pp. 273–285.

59 The Ambassador in London, Count von Metternich, to the Imperial Chancellor, Count von Bülow, February 4, 1903, *ibid.,* p. 289.

60 The Special Representative in Washington, Freiherr Spec von Sternberg, to the Foreign Office, February 6, 1903, *ibid.,* p. 287.

61 Both Great Britain and Germany welcomed a solution. British public opinion against co-operation with Germany had grown steadily stronger, and the date of the reassembly of Parliament was approaching. Lord Lansdowne told the German ambassador that the Germans had insisted on a strong program, and that, if the two powers maintained the blockade, a misunderstanding would arise in England and the United States the consequences of which could not be foreseen. The ambassador felt that the situation might become critical not only for the government in England but also in Germany. *(Ibid.,* p. 290.)

were for less flagrant damages to individuals and companies. For both classes of claims, guarantees were to be given. The preferential treatment question was to be referred to The Hague if other means of settlement were not found. Finally, the third-rank claims—those of the bondholders—and the railroad claims were to be settled by a new agreement which was also to adjust the general Venezuelan foreign debt.[62]

The crisis was now past. The British raised the blockade of eastern Venezuelan ports at midnight February 14, 1903. The Germans followed their example in the west the following day.[63]

Whether the claims of the blockading powers should be given preferential treatment was finally referred to the Hague Court for decision under a protocol signed May 7, 1903, between Venezuela and the blockading powers and with the assent of other claimants, including Belgium, France, Mexico, the Netherlands, Spain, Sweden and Norway, and the United States. Venezuela, it was agreed, should undertake to set aside monthly thirty per cent of the customs revenues of La Guaira and Puerto Cabello, dating from March 1, 1903, for payment of the claims in question, and the Hague Court should determine how these revenues should be divided.[64]

It is interesting to follow the claims which had caused such a high degree of international tension to their final settlement even though doing so necessitates postponing a summary of the forces which brought about the protocol and of the developments in American and international policy following the debt controversy.

The mixed commissions to settle the second-rank claims met at Caracas in the summer of 1903.[65] The amounts claimed

---

[62] Imperial Chancellor Count von Bülow to Kaiser William II, February 14, 1903, *ibid.*, p. 289.

[63] *For. Rel.*, 103, p. 476 (British) and p. 437 (German).

[64] The text of the protocol is in *ibid.*, pp. 439–441.

[65] The protocol setting up the United States-Venezuelan Mixed Claims Commission, signed at Washington on February 17, 1903, provided that one member should be chosen by the United States, one by Venezuela, and one who should act as umpire by the Queen of the Netherlands. A curious provision, which did not become operative, referred to the alternative course to be followed if Venezuela failed to set aside the agreed-upon revenues to

and the awards made by the mixed commissions are indicated below. The contrasts between the two give ground for reflection upon the justice of many demands made upon governments and upon the injustice which may be involved in forcing their payment without the intervention of some quasi-judicial body.

SETTLEMENTS BY THE VENEZUELAN MIXED CLAIMS COMMISSION OF 1903 *

In Bolivars

	Claimed	*Awarded*
Belgium	14,921,805	10,898,643
France	17,888,512	2,667,079
Germany	7,376,685	2,091,908
Great Britain	14,743,572	9,401,267
Italy	39,844,258	2,975,906
Netherlands	5,242,519	544,301
Spain	5,307,626	1,974,818
Sweden-Norway	1,047,701	174,359
United States	81,410,952	2,261,402
Totals	187,783,635	32,989,687

* These figures are summarized from the discussion in Ralston, Jackson H., "Venezuelan Arbitrations of 1903," *Senate Documents*, 58th Cong., 2nd Sess., No. 316 (Serial No. 4620). The award to the United States is reported in dollars as $436,450.70, which is entered in the above table as bolivars calculated at par at $.193. There were, in addition to the above claims, others by France (see Ralston, p. 510) and by Mexico (see Ralston, p. 888).

The argument of the preferential claims case before the Hague Court broke new ground. "It was conceded on both sides that the law of nations afforded no clear rule for the decision of the controversy. No such case had ever before arisen. . . ." [66] The decision was unanimous [67]: "Great Britain, Germany, and Italy have a right to preferential treatment

satisfy the claims adjudicated by this and other commissions. It read, "In the case of the failure to carry out the above agreement, Belgian officials shall be placed in charge of the customs of the two ports, and shall administer them until the liabilities of the Venezuelan Government in respect to the above claims shall have been discharged." The text of the agreement is in *For. Rel.*, 1903, pp. 804 and 805. It is highly doubtful whether such a provision would be acceptable to the United States in a similar case arising at the present time.

[66] Summary of the Report of the Agent of the United States in the Arbitration of 1903 before the Hague Tribunal. (*For. Rel.*, 1904, pp. 509–516, at p. 511.)

[67] *Ibid.*, p. 509. The full report of the agent of the United States is in *Sen. Doc. No. 119,* 58th Cong., 3rd Sess. (Serial No. 4769).

for the payment of their claims against Venezuela. . . ."[68]

The payments to the blockading powers involved in "preferential treatment," totalling £684,330, were completed in August, 1907, before the end of the Castro regime. Payments to cancel the claims of the non-blockading powers, amounting to £835,900, then assumed first position. They were brought to an end in September, 1912.

Finally there were the "third rank" claims. Though the British Government had expressly stated in Parliament in the earlier debates that they were not acting in Venezuela in behalf of the bondholders, their engagements with Germany ultimately brought them to demand arrangements including these.

As a result of the Washington protocols, Venezuela undertook to enter an agreement to satisfy these accounts. The bond issue arranged to this end is known as the "Three per Cent Diplomatic Debt Issue of 1905." It took up also old loans of 1881 and 1896, the first at a discount. Payment of these new obligations was guaranteed by an assignment of twenty-five per cent of the customs revenue. Until the payments of the first- and second-line claims above discussed were discharged, this guarantee was to be substituted by one of sixty per cent of the customs at all ports except La Guaira and Puerto Cabello. The following year, the internal debt, largely held in Europe, was converted into a new issue guaranteed by the Government receipts from the liquor monopoly.

The considerations which influence foreign offices in composing international misunderstandings by no means always have full reflection in the diplomatic documents which they publish. They appear in an unusual degree in the documents dealing with the debt controversy.[69]

---

[68] *House of Commons, Accounts and Papers,* 1904, Vol. III (cd. 1949), p. 2. For the text of the decision, see pp. 2–5.

[69] The chief public documents relating to the Venezuelan controversy published are found in the collections listed below.

Germany:

Die Auswärtige Politik des Deutschen Reiches, 1871–1914 (Albrecht Mendelssohn Bartholdy and Friedrich Thimme, eds.), 4 vols., Berlin, 1928. (Exclusive, authorized, abbreviated edition of the German documents.)

Die Grosse Politik der Europäischen Kabinette, 1871–1914 (Johannes Lep-

In the adjustment of perhaps no other international dispute of our time has the influence of public opinion been so unmistakable. It was a public opinion keenly alive to national interests, not always well informed, but which on the whole earnestly desired a peaceful settlement.

The attitude of the United States toward forward action against American states by European powers is regularly one of apprehension. In the opening years of the century, the boundary dispute between Great Britain and Venezuela was still fresh in the public mind. It had shown that popular feeling in favor of defense of the long-established policy of "America for Americans" might easily be aroused to dangerous heights. Public opinion in Europe and America could not look lightly upon the development of circumstances which might cause this policy to become the subject of active international controversy.

The European chancelleries from the beginning of their negotiations recognized that this factor must be dealt with, and the event justified their judgment. The American press was critical from the start. Germany was considered the aggressor, but any action by European powers was looked on with increasing anxiety. Within a week after diplomatic relations with Venezuela were broken by the powers, Lord Lansdowne feared that popular resentment might develop before which the American Government might be helpless.[70] Two months later, when a German ambassador on special mis-

---

sius, Albrecht Mendelssohn Bartholdy, Friedrich Thimme, eds.), Berlin, Deutsche Verlagsgesellschaft für Politik und Geschichte, 1924, Vol. XVII, Chap. CXII, pp. 241–292.

Great Britain:

House of Commons, Accounts and Papers, 1902, Vol. 130, *Venezuela,* No. 1. (1902): Correspondence respecting the Affairs of Venezuela (cd. 1372).

House of Commons, Accounts and Papers, 1903, Vol. 87, *Venezuela,* No. 1: Correspondence respecting the Affairs of Venezuela (cd. 1399).

House of Commons, Accounts and Papers, 1904, Vol. III, *Venezuela,* No. 1 (1904): Award of the Tribunal of Arbitration (cd. 1949).

Parliamentary Debates, 4th Ser., Vols. 115 and 118.

United States:

Foreign Relations of the United States, Washington (Annual), 1901–1904.

[70] The Ambassador in London, Count von Metternich, to the Foreign Office, December 16, 1902, *Grosse Politik,* Vol. XVII, p. 265.

sion arrived in Washington, President Roosevelt informed him that "public opinion was in high degree irritated by the continuing blockade" and that a "critical situation" had been created. Congress might easily get out of hand. These statements were hardly news to the Europeans.

As far as local public opinion was concerned, Germany was in the easiest position of any of the parties—at least in the early phases of the controversy. Whoever suggested the joint enterprise, it is clear that, after it was launched, Germany, though she urged a stronger program than the British, nevertheless wished to follow the British rather than to take the lead herself,[71] and that German local opinion was not opposed to any strong stand that might be decided upon under such circumstances. Neither of the chief allies was sure, however, of what might happen in the United States. Both felt it important to avoid offending American susceptibilities. The German chancellor thought that the British were willing to take the lead because American suspicions would in that case be less aroused. This the Kaiser approved: "The more ships the English send," wrote he, "the better. . . . Hence our action stands in the background, theirs in the foreground. We go along with the English program. . . . Our flag is represented, let the British take the lead." [72]

This was the position of Germany at the time when the Venezuelan ships were sunk. It did not change, in spite of the fact that the Germans were in favor of a much stronger policy than the British. After the break, the German ambassador in London felt that the best plan was actively to push the blockade and thus bring things to a head, because "Public opinion . . . does not long occupy itself with accomplished things." He recognized at the same time that delays in accepting the American suggestion for arbitration might bring unexpected developments. Later, in urging cash payments on "first line" claims at their face amounts, in arguing for inclusion of bondholders' claims, and in insistence on preferential treatment, Germany was much more advanced in its

---

[71] *Die Auswärtige Politik, op. cit.,* Vol. II, pp. 370–371 (Nov. 12, 1902).
[72] *Ibid.,* p. 373 (Dec. 12, 1902).

position than was Great Britain. How much this attitude was one in response to nonofficial opinion in the empire does not appear in the official documents. There was not, so far as the published materials show, any demand, popular or otherwise, for adoption of an independent line of action or of one which would bring into question the general policy of "America for Americans."

Venezuela, it was argued, was endeavoring to escape its international responsibilities by pleading clauses in its domestic legislation under which all diplomatic appeal could be excluded. Attempts to secure consideration of redress had been futile. The Venezuelan authorities appeared to be of the opinion that Germans living in their country were without protection against arbitrary action. Strong action against them was, therefore, greatly to be desired in view of the position of the great German interests in Central and South America.[73] It seems fair to assume that this position had cordial support among at least the commercial classes.

As the dispute developed, however, it became clearer even in Germany that whatever the motives with which the adventure was entered, events following such entry might bring unwelcome complications. A new anti-European declaration by the United States might be forthcoming. Latin-American states might be forced to recognize the United States as their champion, however great their reservations as to the desirability of closer political association with the dominant American power might be. Further, prejudice against Germany in Latin America began to be cited as a detriment to German foreign trade and the national prestige. By the end of January, 1903, the Government was anxious to close the incident and wished only to assure that public satisfaction in its ending would be greater than the criticism which would follow if it "retired from Venezuela empty handed."

---

[73] Imperial Chancellor Count von Bülow to Kaiser William II, September 1, 1902, *Grosse Politik, op. cit.,* Vol. XVII, pp. 244–245. It has often been overlooked that legislation of the sort objected to by Germany is found not only in Venezuela but in many Latin-American countries, and that the position which Germany took in reference to it is substantially that taken by European nations generally and by the United States.

The position of Great Britain was far from enviable. Since practically the middle of the nineteenth century, its role in the Caribbean had been becoming less important. The period of its desire for increased responsibilities in that part of the world had passed. It was content if it could assure for itself equality of commercial opportunity and protection of the rights of its resident citizens. It had no quarrel with the established policy of the United States as to European activities in America. Nevertheless, in the case in hand, it felt British interests to be threatened and thought it necessary to defend them—with the least show of force which would bring results.

In the enterprise undertaken, it could act with better chance of not offending American opinion than could perhaps any other European power; but, even at home, opinion would be critical of any aggressive movements. Before matters came to a head, it found itself in association with Germany, whose motives would be viewed with more suspicion both in Great Britain and in the New World.

Independent diplomatic action had been tried by the British Government without success even before any agreement with Germany and had been continued even after joint action had been decided upon.[74] The German suggestion that bondholders' claims should be included in the settlement demanded from Venezuela was reluctantly accepted. The measures of aggression which Great Britain proposed showed the desire to keep action within the smallest limits.

Once the joint action was under way, it was evident that it was everywhere unpopular in Great Britain. After the sinking of the Venezuelan warships, the *Times* commented on the bad impression made by the action on public opinion. The affair had the appearance of a punitive expedition. It was hoped that the Germans, not the British, were responsible.[75]

---

[74] The Germans recognized that, should such action by the British result in a settlement, it would bring co-operation to an end. (The Ambassador in London, Count von Metternich, . . . to the Foreign Office, November 12, 1902, *ibid.*, p. 252.)

[75] As reported in The Imperial Chancellor Count von Bülow to Kaiser William II, December 12, 1902, *ibid.*, pp. 258–260.

The press felt that Germany was all too ready to adopt unnecessarily harsh measures. Drastic action had no advocates.[76]

Apprehension appeared promptly in Government circles. King Edward, so the German ambassador was confidentially informed, was displeased by developments.[77] The British minister of foreign affairs feared that coolness in relations with the United States might develop. He was disposed to accept arbitration. The criticism which had already been voiced in the British Parliament "was only a weak beginning" of what was to be expected.[78]

The British uneasiness, which the German ambassador had noticed, increased. In both houses of Parliament, the action of the Government was severely criticized. The Prime Minister hastened to declare that force had been resorted to only with great reluctance, that three "ultimata" had been sent before joint action had been undertaken, that there was no intention to land troops, and that the action was not for collecting of debts but because of assaults on British citizens and mistreatment of British ships.[79]

The criticism of the Government's action referred to the aroused state of both British and American public opinion. Arbitration of the issue had been suggested. It should be promptly accepted. The recently settled boundary dispute was recalled. Venezuela had asked arbitration then and Salis-

---

[76] The Ambassador in London, Count von Metternich, to the Foreign Office, December 13, 1902, *ibid.,* Vol. XVII, pp. 261–262.

[77] The Ambassador in London, Count von Metternich, to the Foreign Office, December 15, 1902, *ibid.,* Vol. XVII, p. 262.

[78] The Ambassador in London, Count von Metternich, to the Foreign Office, December 16, 1902, *ibid.,* p. 265.

[79] These declarations by Mr. Balfour were made in the House of Commons, December 17, 1902. See *Parliamentary Debates,* 4th Series, Vol. 116, Cols. 1488, 1489, and 1491. It appears, however, in a note from Lansdowne to Buchanan, November 17, 1902, No. 141, that this was not unqualifiedly the case so far as bondholders' claims were concerned. These, it is there stated, were not included in earlier British protests, but Lansdowne came to think that the British should support the German stand and "join in urging the Venezuelan Government to accept the proposed arrangement." The bond claims included ones pressed by the Disconto Gesellschaft and by the British Council of the Corporation of Foreign Bondholders. See *House of Commons, Accounts and Papers,* Vol. 87, 1903, *Venezuela,* No. 1 (1903), Correspondence respecting the Affairs of Venezuela (cd. 1399), pp. 149–150.

bury had refused. "Then America asked for it, and we granted it next day. We ate dirt," declared an opposition member, not without arousing protests. "We should do nothing of any kind, sort, or description," said the less extreme Lord Charles Beresford, "that would be in the least way provocative of irritation or animosity on the part of the United States." The Government, said another, had been "astutely cajoled . . . into a partnership" with Germany in an enterprise which the United States would never have countenanced if Germany had undertaken it alone.[80]

A month passed in negotiations concerning the claims which should be arbitrated and the conditions of arbitration during which British opinion crystallized. Balfour and Lansdowne urged the Germans to find "some sort of a means" by which their demands for payment of first-line claims could be adjusted.[81]

The German ambassador had a conversation with King Edward in which the British monarch frankly expressed his opinion. The report of the discussion as printed, with the notes made upon it by Kaiser William, reflects the anxiety felt in England and the Kaiser's amusement over British difficulties. King Edward, so the ambassador wrote, wished to end the affair as soon as possible. "It was much more important to end the incident at the earliest moment than to secure payment of the claims of the two parties." The Kaiser's marginal comments read, "His most serene highness is losing his nerve!" and "Grandmama would never have said that." [82]

The pressure of public opinion was too great to be resisted. Before the first month of 1903 had run its course, indeed, public opinion was demanding a peaceful solution of the dispute not only in Great Britain and the United States but also in

---

[80] *Parliamentary Debates,* 4th Series, Vol. 116, pp. 1254, 1258, 1274, 1278, 1286, and 1491. See similar declarations in *House of Lords, Parliamentary Debates,* 4th Series, Vol. 118, Cols. 12 and 14.

[81] *Grosse Politik, op. cit.,* Vol. XVII, pp. 278–279 (January 27, 1903).

[82] The Ambassador in London, Count von Metternich, to the Foreign Office, January 29, 1903. *Grosse Politik, op. cit.,* Vol. XVII, pp. 281–282. See also, on the attitude of the royal family, the Ambassador in London, Count von Metternich, to the Imperial Chancellor, Count von Bülow, February 4, 1903, *Grosse Politik, op. cit.,* Vol. XVII, pp. 288–289.

Germany. All three governments were ready to welcome a way out of an affair which might easily slip out of their control. The protocol of February 14, 1903, which made it possible for Von Bülow to inform the Kaiser on the following day that the Venezuelan difficulties had been brought to an end, that the blockade might be raised and the Venezuelan ships returned, was received with a feeling of relief in both Europe and the United States.

In the published official documents, there are only occasional references to the role of President Roosevelt in the settlement of the Venezuelan debt controversy. It is a subject which has given rise to much speculation and is still a matter of controversy among scholars.

No contemporary record of the conversations which the President had with representatives of European powers has been published. Not until after the outbreak of the World War was any statement purporting to set out his actions made. In 1915, certain details were given in William Roscoe Thayer's *Life of John Hay*. This story was questioned and Mr. Roosevelt wrote a letter to Mr. Thayer, the more important parts of which are quoted below from the full text as it appears in Mr. Joseph Bucklin Bishop's *Theodore Roosevelt and His Time.*[83]

Sagamore Hill, August 21, 1916.

My dear Mr. Thayer:

There is now no reason why I should not speak of the facts connected with the disagreement between the United States and Germany over the Venezuela matter, in the early part of my administration as President, and of the final amicable settlement of the disagreement. . . .

I speedily became convinced that Germany was the leader and the really formidable party in the transaction; and that England was merely following Germany's lead in rather half-hearted fashion. I became convinced that England would not back Germany in the event of a clash over the matter between Germany

[83] Bishop, Joseph Bucklin, *Theodore Roosevelt and His Time,* New York, Charles Scribner's Sons, 1920, 2 vols., Vol. I, pp. 221–226. The latter part of Mr. Roosevelt's letter contains correspondence by persons closely connected with the Venezuelan affair tending to substantiate his statements. This correspondence includes statements by Admiral Dewey and by persons in close contact with German representatives. It is not, however, contemporaneous with the crisis.

and the United States, but would remain neutral. . . . I also became convinced that Germany intended to seize some Venezuelan harbor and turn it into a strongly fortified place of arms, on the model of Kiauchau, with a view to exercising some degree of control over the future Isthmian Canal, and over South American affairs generally.

For some time the usual methods of diplomatic intercourse were tried. Germany declined to agree to arbitrate the question at issue between her and Venezuela, and declined to say that she would not take possession of Venezuelan territory, merely saying that such possession would be "temporary"—which might mean anything. I finally decided that no useful purpose would be served by further delay, and I took action accordingly. I assembled our battle fleet, under Admiral Dewey, near Porto Rico, for "maneuvers," with instructions that the fleet should be kept in hand and in fighting trim, and should be ready to sail at an hour's notice. The fact that the fleet was in West Indian waters was of course generally known; but I believe that the Secretary of the Navy, and Admiral Dewey, and perhaps his Chief of Staff, and the Secretary of State, John Hay, were the only persons who knew about the order for the fleet to be ready to sail at an hour's notice. I told John Hay that I would now see the German Ambassador, Herr von Holleben, myself, and that I intended to bring matters to an early conclusion. Our navy was in very efficient condition, being superior to the German navy.

I saw the Ambassador, and explained that in view of the presence of the German Squadron on the Venezuelan coast I could not permit longer delay in answering my request for an arbitration, and that I could not acquiesce in any seizure of Venezuelan territory. The Ambassador responded that his government could not agree to arbitrate, and that there was no intention to take "permanent" possession of Venezuelan territory. I answered that Kiauchau was not a "permanent" possession of Germany—that I understand that it was merely held by a 99 years' lease; and that I did not intend to have another Kiauchau, held by similar tenure, on the approach to the Isthmian Canal. The Ambassador repeated that his government would not agree to arbitrate. I then asked him to inform his government that if no notification for arbitration came within a certain specified number of days I should be obliged to order Dewey to take his fleet to the Venezuelan coast and see that the German forces did not take possession of any territory. He expressed very grave concern, and asked me if I realized the serious consequences that would follow such action; consequences so serious to both countries that he dreaded to give them a name. I answered that I had thoroughly counted the cost before I decided on the step, and asked him to look at the map, as a glance would show him that there was no spot in the world where Germany in the event of a conflict with the United States would be at a greater disadvantage than in the Caribbean Sea.

A few days later the Ambassador came to see me, talked pleasantly on several subjects, and rose to go. I asked him if he had any answer to make from his government to my request, and when he said no, I informed him that in such event it was useless to wait as long as I had intended, and that Dewey would be ordered to sail twenty-four hours in advance of the time I had set. He expressed deep apprehension, and said that his government would not arbitrate. However, less than twenty-four hours before the time I had appointed for cabling the order to Dewey, the Embassy notified me that his Imperial Majesty the German Emperor had directed him to request me to undertake the arbitration myself. I felt, and publicly expressed, great gratification at this outcome, and great appreciation of the course the German Government had finally agreed to take. Later I received the consent of the German Government to have the arbitration undertaken by The Hague Tribunal, and not by me.

The degree to which President Roosevelt's memory of what occurred served him cannot be exactly stated with the information at hand. By some this description of the incidents is considered an example of the coloring of the recollection of events by their outcome,[84] and at a number of points at least it must be admitted that the account is at least vague. On the other hand, examination of Mr. Roosevelt's statement, along with the German diplomatic documents contemporaneous with the Venezuelan controversy which have been published since the World War, makes it evident that, while the account may not be accurate in all details, the President did play a very active part in bringing about a solution.

Was Roosevelt's analysis of the German position in all respects correct? It seems clear that it was not. His belief that Germany was the instigator of the advance against Venezuela was, however, one that was widely held by the public in the United States and Great Britain at the time. It was strongly voiced in the British Parliament. It was probably a mistaken belief, but this does not mean that it was not the

[84] For an analysis concluding that the influence of Roosevelt in the settlement of the dispute has been exaggerated, see Hill, Howard C., *Roosevelt and the Caribbean,* Chicago, University of Chicago Press, 1927, pp. 106–147. J. F. Rippy, in his *Latin America in World Politics,* New York, F. S. Crofts and Co., 1928, pp. 182–199, gives a good review of the evidence.

basis of his actions nor that actions taken on the false premise did not materially influence the outcome.

Was the estimate of the position of Great Britain sound? The British Government went into the Venezuelan affair without enthusiasm. On December 15, 1902, the British took the initiative in urging on Germany acceptance of the Venezuelan proposal for arbitration sent through the good offices of the United States to London and Berlin on December 13. On the next day, the German ambassador reported that the parliamentary and press comment was critical. Later, when Bowen became the representative of Venezuela, Great Britain showed itself anxious that the Germans should compromise on the terms by which a solution might be achieved. It led in giving back captured Venezuelan gunboats. Lansdowne urged that bondholders' claims be not made a condition which would hinder settlement and counseled the reduction of the cash payments to be demanded. The King, and, indeed, all the royal family, stood out for speedy settlement. At the last, the British no longer insisted on preferential payment. All the details of these items could not have been known to the President; but, as the controversy advanced, some of them came to his attention through the press, some through diplomatic correspondence entering the Department of State, some —at least, so the allies believed—through Bowen. Roosevelt's conviction that Great Britain would not support Germany in a clash with the United States was justified. It was fair to assume that the latter would not "go it alone." [85]

Did Germany plan to acquire an American naval base? That she did so is hard to believe, though this is far from saying that an opportunity to acquire one would have been unwelcome or that a plan to acquire one might not have arisen if affairs in Venezuela had drifted in a direction to allow it. Both in the statements made to the United States and in

---

[85] The German diplomatic documents show that Von Bülow on November 3, 1902, called the attention of Kaiser William to the fact that Germany could "hardly count upon" vigorous English support in "a military action against Venezuela" if the latter gave determined opposition to the proposed demands. *Grosse Politik, op. cit.*, Vol. XVII, pp. 247–248.

the discussions with the British, disclaimers of territorial ambitions appear. The disclaimer to the former referred to "the permanent occupation of Venezuelan harbors" and the collection of duties there. Such language touched a sensitive American nerve. Roosevelt's conclusion that this "might mean anything" was one in which he would have been followed by many—probably most—Americans. There have been too many instances outside of America in which what seemed unportentous first steps of this sort have proved to be "the nose of the camel in the tent" for temporary occupation of American soil to be acceptable to the American public.

These are phases of the incident which came at its beginning. The position that Roosevelt later reported he had taken at that time, even though it may in part have been based on a mistaken premise, was in accord with American policy and one in which he could count on the vigorous support of American public opinion. It is, indeed, hard to see how his position could have been other than that which he later reported.

What were the relations which President Roosevelt had with the representatives[85a] of Germany? There is no published record of these conversations. The number explicitly cited in the German notes is only two; but, since the adjustment dragged over the period from December to February, there may have been several. Nevertheless, it is evident from

---

[85a] Roosevelt's letter mentions dealings only with Von Holleben. A change of German representatives occurred during the controversy. The last of the published documents from Von Holleben is dated December 16, 1902. Two days later, the Washington correspondence begins to be conducted by Chargé d'Affaires von Quadt, and by the end of January by Von Sternberg, Minister and Envoy on Extraordinary Mission. The latter became the head of the German representation on August 7, 1903.

Now on December 16, 1902, it appears by a dispatch by Von Bülow of the following day, Lansdowne was already urging the Germans to agree to have the affair arbitrated "if a good opportunity offered" (*ibid.*, p. 267). By this time—before arbitration had been formally agreed to—Von Holleben had ceased to sign the dispatches. It appears clear, therefore, that the settlement to which Roosevelt refers could not have been made through him. Later in Roosevelt's letter there is a reference to the arbitration by the Hague Tribunal. If this refers to the arbitration actually carried on before the Hague Tribunal, it must have involved the preferential treatment question. This was decided upon when Von Sternberg was in charge of German affairs at Washington.

the German diplomatic correspondence that the influence of the President was a very real factor throughout the incident and that it grew steadily up to the time of settlement.

The answer of the United States Department of State to the German preliminary inquiry in 1901 concerning the proposed blockade carried an expression of Roosevelt's opinions. A year later, when the crisis was approaching, Von Quadt, Chargé d'Affaires, emphasized the anxiety of Secretary of State Hay as to what might happen if Congress submitted to the President a resolution connecting the Venezuelan affair with the defense of the Monroe Doctrine. In the same communication, he also reported a statement by Hay that both he and the President had "full confidence" in the declarations which the Germans had made.[86]

On December 24, 1902, Germany agreed to arbitrate if Venezuela accepted certain conditions, and asked that Roosevelt arbitrate, but he declined.[87] Whether Venezuela accepted the German conditions was not yet clear[88] and on them she continued insistent.[89] On January 20, 1903, the Imperial Cancellor reported to Von Quadt that Venezuela had accepted the demands of the powers.[90]

The discussion now concentrated on preferential treatment, and the German correspondence reflects relations much more acute than those in the previous discussion over the general principle of arbitration. Germany continued more exigent than the British were disposed to be. Bowen, who, they felt, had "beyond doubt informed the Department of State in Washington concerning his negotiations,"[91] was defending the principle of equal treatment for all. The position taken by Bowen was supported by the American Secretary of State, so Von Sternberg, now in charge of German affairs at Washington reported.[92] The powers were discussing having Roosevelt

[86] Chargé d'Affaires in Washington Count von Quadt to the Foreign Office, *ibid.*, p. 269 (December 18, 1902).
[87] *Ibid.*, pp. 269–270 (December 24, 1902).
[88] *Ibid.*, p. 270 (December 28, 1902).
[89] *Ibid.*, p. 271 (December 30, 1902).
[90] *Ibid.*, p. 272 (January 20, 1903).
[91] *Ibid.*, p. 283 (January 30, 1903).
[92] *Ibid.*, pp. 283–284 (January 30, 1903).

arbitrate this question also, though they felt that they might be "riding for a fall" if he consented.

"The temptation offered to President Roosevelt," the German ambassador in London wrote the foreign office on January 30, 1903, "to give the blockading powers and Europe a snub and at the same time to pose as the lord-protector of South America . . . as well as to give a warning to Europe for the future may be too great to be resisted." [93] The next day he was convinced that the British had decided to throw their case into Roosevelt's hands.[94]

The same day there came also another telegram from Von Sternberg. The British and Italian ambassadors, he said, were urging their governments to compromise the preferential treatment issue. "The President," he continued, "had expressed the wish to see me immediately. He set out in what high degree it seemed to him desirable that the Venezuelan negotiations should come to an amicable settlement as soon as possible as they are beginning actively to irritate public opinion here and in Europe." [95]

Four days more passed, and Von Sternberg then telegraphed again. Bowen was putting pressure on the powers to yield on preferential treatment. The non-blockading nations were stiffening their position. "I have become convinced," he declares, "that in all circles on this side the question of preferential treatment is highly unpopular. . . . I am confidentially told from the best informed sources that the actions of the allies have been followed by a marked swing of sympathy in South and Central America in favor of the United States which promises the latter great advantages. The little sympathy which Germany still had in the United States has been sacrificed. Dewey's fleet has received secret orders to hold itself in readiness." He favored yielding to Bowen. Driving

---

[93] The Ambassador in London, Graf von Metternich, to the Foreign Office, January 30, 1903, *ibid.*, pp. 283 and 284 (January 30, 1903). The Olney declaration in the Venezuela boundary controversy was doubtless remembered.

[94] *Ibid.*, pp. 284–285 (January 31, 1903).

[95] The Ambassador on Extraordinary Mission in Washington, Freiherr Spec von Sternberg, to the Foreign Office, January 31, 1903, *ibid.*, Vol. XVII, p. 285.

the controversy farther would bring Germany "immeasurable damage in Central and South America and in the United States." [96] Roosevelt's actions, if not direct declarations, evidently were influencing the German communications.

The Imperial Chancellor promptly telegraphed his ambassadors in London and Washington. He referred to Von Sternberg's telegram, reaffirmed the determination to act with Great Britain, and gave instructions to Von Sternberg "to stand fully on the same line with" the British ambassador.[97] This was on February 4, 1903. On the sixth, Von Sternberg telegraphed the German Foreign Office that under instructions the British ambassador had proposed that President Roosevelt pass on the question of preferential treatment.[98] Roosevelt declined to act, with the result already discussed. This series of events has special interest when read in connection with the later paragraphs cited above from Roosevelt's statement.

One more German document, a letter from the German representative in Washington to the foreign office, should be cited to complete the account of Roosevelt's role so far as it is shown by contemporary evidence.[99]

On February 18, 1903, four days after the signing of the protocol, the German ambassador and the President had taken a long ride together. Roosevelt had shown himself in high degree pleased by the outcome of the Venezuelan affair. On Von Sternberg's arrival, so the ambassador reports, the President had urged "the pressing necessity of the quickest solution of the Venezuelan question" because "public opinion was in high degree irritated by the continuing blockade. The sinking of the Venezuelan ships and the bombardment of the forts during the negotiations had created at once sympathy

---

[96] The Ambassador on Extraordinary Mission in Washington, Freiherr Spec von Sternberg, to the Foreign Office, February 3, 1903, *ibid.*, Vol. XVII, pp. 285–286.

[97] The Imperial Chancellor, Count von Bülow, to the Ambassador in London, Count von Metternich, *ibid.*, pp. 286–287 (February 4, 1903).

[98] The Ambassador on Extraordinary Mission in Washington, Freiherr Spec von Sternberg, to the Foreign Office, *ibid.*, p. 287 (February 6, 1903).

[99] The Ambassador on Special Mission, Freiherr Spec von Sternberg, to the Foreign Office, February 19, 1903, *ibid.*, pp. 291–292.

for Venezuela and caused a critical situation. The German battleships of the blockade had looked at the fleet of Admiral Dewey as their next opponents.[100] Dewey's people on the other hand had considered Germany's ships as their next object of attack.[101] It was high time to make an end of these conditions."

This account, written shortly after the protocol and referring to a period preceding it, taken with Von Sternberg's dispatch of February 3, 1903, as to the orders to "Dewey's fleet," go far to substantiate the general thesis of Mr. Roosevelt's later account.

In details, Roosevelt's account at some points blurs the facts. Probably, during the controversy itself, Roosevelt felt the situation to be more critical than it was. It is evident, however, that the position taken was in accord with American policy and that developing circumstances made insistence on its observance easier. At the last the President stood on such firm ground that he risked little in putting pressure on the European allies. That this is the case, however, should not obscure the fact that the stand he had taken during the controversy was itself one of the factors in developing the situation which brought the solution.

Out of the action against Venezuela by the European powers rose a movement aimed at much more than the settlement of the controversy which had won so much notoriety. The international investment of capital was rapidly growing. So far as foreign money came to be placed in new countries or in countries in which political and financial stability were not well assured, questions similar to those in Venezuela might again arise; and, so far as these countries lay in America, the controversies with foreign investors would have an especial interest for the United States.

To what degree did international law justify the use of force in the collection of claims of pecuniary origin and claims of other sorts? Was the use of naval and military force the best way to secure settlement? Was the expense of such col-

---

[100] Marginal note by Kaiser William II, "it never entered their dreams."
[101] Marginal note by Kaiser William II, "very foolish of them."

lection out of proportion to the advantage secured from the payment? Did the bitterness following the use of such means overbalance the advantage obtained by defending in principle the rights of the damaged foreigners? Was the use of armed force a practice uniformly followed in enforcing rights against strong as well as weak states?[102] These and similar questions of international interest came in for wide discussion.

Adjustment of international claims is obviously more difficult than the settlement of ordinary domestic disputes in which both parties can seek judgment as to their rights before a national court. The foreigner who has been wronged or believes himself to have been wronged has an acute appreciation of the damages he has suffered. He, too, may take his case to the local courts, but he may be unable to secure just treatment from them, or at least he may be convinced that justice has been denied him. The foreign office of his own country to which he appeals for support, though it seeks to secure all the facts, has no satisfactory facilities by which to ascertain them.

On the other hand, the country against which the claims are urged tends to look upon the demands that foreigners' claims be settled as questioning the local sovereignty and disregarding the difficulties under which the local government may have been working during a period of civil disturbance or financial distress. These handicaps may have been so great as to make it impossible either to give full protection to the rights of foreigners or citizens or to make prompt redress for their wrongs. Under such circumstances, a state may

[102] On this point it is to be said, of course, that the fact that the use of force would in the case of stronger nations involve greatly increased expense and much more serious conflicts is not the only reason why coercive measures against them have less frequently been proposed. The stronger states have had better-established order, better courts, and less discriminatory legislation and administration. The cases in which foreigners have suffered damage giving rise to claims have been relatively fewer because of these facts, and such as have arisen have been more generally adjusted through the established courts or through diplomacy. The record of the settlement of claims against the stabler states is, however, much less subject to criticism than the record of the settlement of claims which weak states have been forced to make.

find it highly irritating to be forced to give special consideration to certain claims.

Even when exceptional factors of this sort are absent, it is obviously highly desirable that there be created facilities by which the conflicting points of view can be adjusted. This is one of the important fields in which diplomatic representatives work for the promotion of friendly international relations, and large numbers of claims are settled either directly by these representatives or through special commissions of a semijudicial nature which pass upon the merits of the controversies.

But diplomatic adjustment of claims does not always prove possible. What then? Is the state whose citizens have been damaged at the end of its resources and under the necessity of allowing the wrong to go unrighted? Should it wait in the hope that some future administration may be more disposed to do justice, or should it take strong-handed measures to force recognition of what it regards as a just obligation? Doing the latter may involve an expenditure far beyond the money value of the claim and may even result in the sacrifice of lives and the embitterment of international feeling. Using force to make a weak state comply with demands may constrain it to pay a claim which is baseless or at best exaggerated in amount, for the stronger state has no effective means to determine its justice. Payment may be exacted under circumstances which will weaken the power of the coerced government to assure order for other persons, citizens and foreigners. On the other hand, a decision not to use force may indicate that all foreigners, or at least other citizens of the claimant country, may be mistreated with impunity by irresponsible governments.

Out of this situation there had arisen at the beginning of the century an acute state of feeling as to international practice in the collection of claims, especially in Latin America. An authority on international law summarized the case as follows:

> Experience shows that it is particularly against the American states of Latin race that the European governments have found

> themselves obliged to adopt forcible measures for the defense of their claims. It is unfortunately incontestable that the domestic disturbances, the unexpected *coup d'état* and the changeableness of the governments of the American states have given ground, with great frequency, for armed interventions, bombarding of forts and ports and, finally, for the establishment of blockades more or less pacific. The most sincere friends of the states of Central or South America have had to recognize the absolute necessity of coercive measures, in order to obtain satisfaction for unheard of violations of established and incontestable rights.

It was, he confessed, nevertheless true that very often brutal measures had been adopted to support shady claims. The demands upon their governments, Latin-American statesmen declared, had given rise to "a system of regularly organized extortion." [103]

Claims urged by foreigners against governments of other states fall into two classes: first, a general class involving damages suffered through civil wars, failure of the local courts to give justice, and arbitrary executive action; and second, claims arising out of some contractual relation, such as the engagement given by a government to those who purchase its bonds that payments on principal and interest will be made at specified rates, or a government guarantee that the service charges due on an issue of public utility bonds, such as those issued by a railroad, shall be similarly paid at specified rates.

Neither class of claims had previously had the importance that such claims were to assume in the nineteenth century. This is not surprising. Before the nineteenth century, there were comparatively few who took up residence in territory not controlled by their own countries. In many colonial areas such residence was surrounded by restrictions, if it was allowed at all. International investments also were small before the nineteenth century. With the rise of the New World nations, what had been investments in the colonies became investments in independent countries. The Indus-

---

[103] F. de Martens, St. Petersburg, 1904, quoted in Drago, Luis M., *Cobro Coercitivo de Deudas Publicas,* Buenos Aires, Imprenta y Casa Editorra de Coni Hermanos, 1906, pp. 90–91.

trial Revolution and international trade, as they came to be characteristic of the life of the world, brought a widening of the field of enterprises beyond national borders in which capital was risked. The new governments also sought capital in the money markets of more-developed countries.

Direct investments and public loans were made in amounts before unapproached and under conditions not comparable to those of previous times. In addition, the number of those living under foreign flags became many times greater than had formerly been the case.

The rules of international law as to the claims which foreigners might make against the countries in which they were residing or in which they had invested their capital were not clear. That was to be expected, for well-defined standards of action could not, of course, arise until the subject matter to which they were to apply had itself come into existence.

Commentators varied and continue to vary widely in their opinion as to what the rules should be. Those who emphasize the principle that sovereign states have "complete independence" restrict sometimes almost to the vanishing point the right of foreign powers to influence the actions of any state within its own borders, no matter how arbitrary the restriction may be. Others argue that sovereign states, as members of the family of nations, have duties to each other as well as rights against each other, and that all states can properly be held to the discharge of such duties even if it be necessary to coerce them to do so. From these contrasted points of view there has arisen wide divergence of opinion as to the degree to which the use of force should be allowed in the settlement of international claims.

While the Venezuelan debt controversy was still going on, a distinguished Argentine statesman, Dr. Luis M. Drago, then minister of foreign affairs in his country, raised the question as to the degree to which certain contractual claims, which he described generically as "public debts," should be held subject to collection by force. It was a question the consideration of which was to be carried far beyond the then troublesome Venezuelan controversy. The discussion brought to the attention of the world the importance of making the settlement of claims a matter in which judicial procedure rather than brute force should play the leading part, and it gave rise to general declarations of world opinion which have at least lessened the chance that incidents such as those which had arisen in Venezuela will be repeated.

On December 29, 1902, shortly after the principle of arbitration had been accepted by the powers but while the controversy was still far from settled, Doctor Drago addressed to the Argentine minister in Washington an argument which the latter was instructed to bring to the notice of the United States.

Laying aside questions pertaining to other sorts of claims, Doctor Drago called attention to the fact that the powers were seeking to enforce payment on "certain services of the foreign debt of the state which have not been kept up in due course." Lenders to foreign states, he said, when making loans took account of the resources of the borrowing state and of the chance that payments would be made without interruption. Hence, governments enjoyed varying degrees of credit according to which favorable or exacting terms were received from those advancing the money. Persons lending money, too, entered contracts with independent governments, knowing that they were dealing with sovereign states which could not be sued. All states should pay their obligations, but using force to make them pay at a definite time might ruin the weaker ones and bring absorption of their governments by the stronger states. Governments should be left free to choose the time and means by which they would pay their debts. The creditor should rely on their desire to protect their honor and credit to make them do so. Collection of such debts by force, Doctor Drago felt, would constitute a dangerous precedent, for "it presupposes territorial occupation to make it effective,[104] and occupation of territory signifies the suppression or subordination of the local governments. . . ." Occupation of territory in the New World by

[104] It is not clear that this is necessarily true. Blockade of ports might prove effective.

European powers would be against the policy of American nations frequently proclaimed and especially against the Monroe Doctrine [105] defended by the United States and to which Argentina had given its adhesion.[106]

"The only thing," declared Doctor Drago in concluding the main part of his argument, "which the Argentine Republic maintains and . . . the principle which it would wish to see recognized, is that public debt can not give ground for armed intervention, much less to actual occupation of the soil of the American nations by an European power." [107]

The Argentine statement was the only one made by a nation outside the conflict during its progress which raised a question as to what should be the larger rule of international law in such cases. To it the United States made no reply until after the protocol by which the controversy was adjusted had been signed. Doctor Drago had not argued that the proposed rule was already international law. For the United States to have announced it as a part of its international policy, or with the other states of America to have made such an announcement, would have been for it to set up a new rule of "American international law" in conflict with the widespread practice of European nations both in the New World and elsewhere. It would have been an action the more questionable since it would have been a new rule set up for America limiting the rights of creditor nations and supported

---

[105] This interpretation would give the Monroe Doctrine a much wider scope than the United States has been willing to give it. In fact, if the Doctrine was to be held to prohibit the use of force for collection of claims involving public debts on the ground that such collection might result in territorial occupation, it might also extend to prohibiting the use of force in the enforcement of *any* claims, since these also might result in occupation of territory. Dr. Drago's argument does not, however, go this far. He expressly states that "European powers . . . have the undoubted right to protect their subjects as fully [in Latin America] as in any other part of the globe, against the persecutions or injustices of which they may be the victims."

[106] This adhesion is cited by Drago, in *Cobro Coercitivo, op. cit.*, p. 16, as follows: "Véase, Sarmiento, Obras y Memorias de Relaciones Exteriores, 1886; nota del ministro Quesada á la cancillería Americana de 9 de diciembre de 1885." The declarations on which rests the statement that Argentina had adhered to the Doctrine are in very general terms. The text is published in Drago, Luis M., *La República Argentina y el Caso de Venezuela,* Buenos Aires, Imprenta y Casa Editorra de Coni Hermanos, 1903, pp. 299–312.

[107] Drago, *Cobro Coercitivo, op. cit.*, pp. 20–21.

by nations the great majority of which were themselves debtors. Such action, indeed, the foreign office of Argentina had not requested; but it hoped that the United States would strongly declare for the principle.[108]

On February 17, 1903, after the protocal of settlement in the Venezuelan controversy had been signed, Secretary Hay sent a memorandum to the Argentine minister. Without expressing an opinion as to the doctrines which Doctor Drago had expounded, he set out that the practice of the United States was to resort to arbitration in claims involving "individual damages or national obligations." Thus, before "tribunals of impartial arbitrators . . . disputing nations, the weak as well as the strong, may appear as equals. . . ." [109]

The statement of the practice of European nations will bring out the contrast between it and the rule which Doctor Drago proposed and will show the bearing upon both of the policy favored by the United States. No government recognized that a request by a citizen that his alleged wrongs be redressed created an obligation to act. To act in defense of the rights of an individual might prejudice larger public interests. Support of claims, it was uniformly held, was discretionary. All governments, at least in theory, also followed the general rule that they would consider action only after all

---

[108] Drago, *La República Argentina,* p. x.

[109] Quoted in Drago, *Cobro Coercitivo,* pp. 29–30. The opinions expressed in the British Parliament were in strong support of the Drago doctrine, apparently because it was felt that any other standard would disturb the relations of Great Britain and the United States. See the texts in Drago, *La República Argentina,* pp. 57–112. James Bryce declared that the Argentine position had the support of "public opinion" in Great Britain. Opinion highly critical of Latin-American practice as to foreign claims was not, however, lacking in Great Britain. See articles from *The Nineteenth Century and After,* April, 1903, reprinted in Drago, *La República Argentina,* pp. 142–177, arguing that the defense of the Monroe Doctrine by the United States was the only thing which prevented Latin America from becoming divided among European powers as Africa had been in the late nineteenth century. Central America and northern South America were regions especially tempting. "To visit these countries is to despair of any internal regeneration in them." Great Britain would not be the aggressor because the Canadian border made it vulnerable, but Germany would risk less. Only the Monroe Doctrine is their "guarantee against foreign intervention. . . . a wall against the rapacity of which . . . [they] would [otherwise] have become the victims." The British press in general supported the Drago doctrine, as did also that of the United States. (*Ibid.,* pp. 177–294.)

the usual legal means of redress, such as appeal to the local courts, had been exhausted. It was recognized that claims in general could be supported by force.

But definite announcements of the principles on which the governments acted in cases in which they decided to support general damage claims of their nationals had not been made, and the policy as to the support of claims involving public debts of other countries was still less clear. Many in official positions continued to feel that foreign investments were of questionable advantage to the nation whose citizens invested their capital abroad, and that this was particularly true when the capital went into loans to foreign, especially weak, governments. Great Britain, then as later the greatest foreign lender, had announced as early as 1848 that claims of her citizens arising out of the debts of foreign countries might be made diplomatic questions. A circular issued to her diplomatic agents set out that on frequent occasions the Government had directed its representatives to support claims based on the public securities of foreign states, and that the Government had a just right to intervene in an authoritative manner in defense of such claims if it chose to do so. What action should be taken the Government would itself determine. It was a matter of policy, not of international law.[110] This position had been reaffirmed in 1880 and 1888.

But, by the opening of the century, the free-hand authority which creditors claimed in supporting the claims of their nationals had already been widely criticized, especially when the claims involved public debts.[111] The adverse opinion aroused by the Venezuelan incident, though formally voiced

[110] It is interesting to note that Great Britain had not given diplomatic support to such claims up to this time because it wished to discourage investment abroad or at least favored investment only in countries of well-established credit. The text of the announcement of Palmerston is in Walker, T. A., *The Science of International Law,* London, Cambridge University Press, 1893, pp. 153–154. W. E. Hall states that, a short time before Palmerston had declared that in certain cases force might be used in collecting foreign loans. (*Ibid.,* p. 335.)

[111] Russia had proposed at the first Hague Conference in 1899 that arbitration of pecuniary claims be made obligatory under stated circumstances. See Scott, J. B., *The Hague Peace Conference of 1899 and 1907,* Baltimore, Johns Hopkins Press, 1909, Vol. I, pp. 321 *et seq.* and 803 *et seq.*

by the Government of Argentina alone, was widely shared by other states and by authorities in international law in both the New World and the Old.

Even the farthest-sighted probably had only the vaguest of ideas as to the development which was just ahead in the international flow of capital. Creditor nations were to abandon their lack of enthusiasm over foreign investment. Some were frankly to encourage it. All were to become anxious to protect the rights acquired. In Latin America, indeed, there were already large investments of foreign capital in 1900. These investments increased greatly after the World War. In 1931 the total had passed thirteen billion dollars. Of this great amount, the larger part represented private direct investments; the minority was made up of holdings of Government securities.[112] Even at the beginning of the century, therefore, it was greatly to be desired that the degree to which creditor countries could use force in assuring the payment of public debts should be definitely agreed upon. From that time on, the importance of having a general rule was greatly to increase.

The Argentine authorities and some European commentators were disappointed that the United States did not more vigorously follow up the suggestion of Doctor Drago. They felt that the declaration by the United States in favor of arbitration to settle controversies of the sort in question was little more than an evasion of the issue.[113]

This opinion proved, in the event, to be mistaken. On March 22, 1906, Secretary Root addressed a letter to the committee for preparing a program for the Third Interna-

---

[112] These figures are only general estimates. The British and American investments in government securities were estimated as totalling about $3,350,000,000 in 1930. (William Manger in *Revista del Banco de la República,* Bogota, November, 1931.)

[113] See, for example, the message of President Roca to the Argentine Congress, May 4, 1903, quoted in Drago, *Cobro Coercitivo,* p. 31 *et sqq.,* F. de Martens, quoted in Drago, *ibid.,* pp. 81–122; and Jules Basdevant, in Drago, *ibid.,* pp. 136–152. The last author reviews the opinions of various authorities as to the legality of the use of force in the collection of public debts. See also, for contrasted points of view, W. E. Hall, *op. cit.,* pp. 333–336, and Calvo, C., *Le Droit International Théorique et Pratique,* 5th ed., Paris, Arthur Rousseau, 1896, Vol. I, sec. 205, pp. 350–351.

tional Conference of the American Republics, then shortly to be held at Rio de Janeiro. He recounted the successful efforts of the United States to have all the states of Latin America invited to the Hague Conference of 1907 and suggested that the American states might well consider at the Rio conference whether in the instructions to their delegates to the Hague Conference there should be included an item on the issue which Doctor Drago had raised. If acceptance of its principle could be secured at The Hague, he felt, an important step would have been taken "in the direction of narrowing the causes of war." [114]

The committee inserted in the program for the Rio conference a proposal to ask the Hague Conference "to consider whether it is admissible to use force for the collection of public debts, and if it is admissible, to what degree." [115]

In the discussions at the Rio conference, there appeared a strong demand that the claims of which it was proposed to ask consideration at The Hague include not only those involving public debts but all claims of pecuniary character. On the insistence of Argentina, this plan was modified so as to leave the discussion of public debts as the major suggestion.

The resolution, unanimously adopted, recommended to the governments of the American states that they consider asking the Hague Conference to "examine the matter of the forcible collection of public debts, and in general, means tending to diminish conflicts of exclusively pecuniary origin among nations." [116]

---

[114] Text in Drago, *Cobro Coercitivo,* pp. 153–157.

[115] *Ibid.,* p. 164.

[116] Text in Carbonell, Nestor, *Las Conferencias Internacionales Americanas,* Habana, Montalvo y Cardenas, 1928, p. 255. It is to be noted that some of the American states had already by treaty made broader agreements as to the means to be used in collecting pecuniary claims. See: Treaty adopted in the Second Pan-American Conference (Mexico, 1902), Carbonell, *op. cit.,* pp. 188–189, ratified by the United States, Mexico, Nicaragua, Guatemala, Salvador, Honduras, Peru, and Bolivia. This treaty was amplified at the Rio conference, and in the new form was ratified by Colombia, Costa Rica, Cuba, Chile, Ecuador, Salvador, the United States, Guatemala, Honduras, Mexico, Nicaragua, and Panama, and, in still broader terms, in the fourth conference (at Buenos Aires). In this form it was ratified by the United States, Brazil, Costa Rica, Ecuador, Guatemala, Honduras, Nicaragua, Panama, Paraguay, the Dominican Republic, and Uruguay. (Carbonell, *op. cit.,* p. 351.)

It was there presented by General Horace Porter on behalf of the United States delegation in a proposal for "an agreement to observe some restrictions on . . . the use of force in the collection of ordinary public debts arising from contracts." [117] Its essential part in the form finally approved ran:

> The contracting powers agree not to have recourse to armed force for the recovery of contract debts claimed from the government of one country by the government of another country as being due to its nationals.
>
> This understanding is, however, not applicable when the debtor state refuses or neglects to reply to an offer of arbitration, or after accepting the offer, prevents any *compromis* from being agreed on, or, after the arbitration fails to submit to the award.[118]

The adoption of this convention was hailed by some as "one of the most important achievements of the second conference and one of the greatest triumphs in the history of diplomacy." [119]

This estimate has proved to be oversanguine. The convention was not acceptable to all nations. It was not an unqualified adoption of the Drago doctrine. Doctor Drago, representing Argentina, made vigorous protest against it because in the opinion of the Argentine delegation in some ways it went too far and in others not far enough. Many other protests, largely from Latin-American countries, were made; but at the last it was approved by the delegations of thirty-nine states, including large and often creditor nations, such as Great Britain, France, Germany, Russia, and Austria. Five abstained from voting. Nine of the American states signing did so only with reservations.[120]

From The Hague, the convention went back to the individual states for ratification. It was open also to adhesion by states the delegations of which had not signed it. A fairly long list of states have now accepted its principles. While

---

[117] The substance of the argument of General Porter supporting the proposed restriction is found in Hull, William I., *The Two Hague Conferences,* Boston, Ginn and Co., 1908, p. 352 *et sqq.*

[118] Text in Scott, J. B. (ed.), *Texts of the Peace Conference at The Hague, 1899 and 1907,* Boston, Ginn and Co., 1908, p. 194.

[119] Hull, *op. cit.,* p. 491.

[120] *Ibid.,* p. 370.

the convention cannot be said to have established a new rule of international law, and while many of the Latin-American countries, including some whose delegations signed the instrument, continue dissenters, it is by no means a dead letter. The discussion which the convention brought forth visualized the disadvantages of the use of force in the collection of contract debts—indeed, in the collection of claims in general.

These discussions, with the treaty as ratified, have made clear the minimum standard of restraint to which a large part of the world is committed. The convention is, if not a part of international law, at least an important instrument of international policy. The standard established, it is widely believed, states at least a minimum which is not likely to be questioned in the settlement of debt controversies in the New World. It aims to assure that claims rising out of contract shall not be collected by force unless the defendant refuses arbitration or refuses to comply with a decision reached by arbitration. The new rules may properly be considered one of the most important results of the Venezuelan incidents of 1902–1903.[121]

---

[121] The convention is reported in force as of 1930, through ratification by the United States of America, Denmark, France, Germany, Great Britain, Guatemala, Haiti, Hungary, Japan, Mexico, Norway, Panama, the Netherlands, Portugal, Russia, El Salvador, and Spain, and through adhesion in China, Finland, Liberia, and Nicaragua. It has thus been accepted by the great lending countries. Among Latin-American nations, only six have ratified or adhered; and, of the six, all but Mexico are small Caribbean republics. The abstention of Argentina, Brazil, Chile, and a number of other Latin-American states is due, if the positions assumed at The Hague be taken as an indication, to divergent reasons.

Further material on the forcible collection of public debts is found in Drago, L. M., "State Loans in Their Relation to International Policy," in *American Journal of International Law,* Vol. I, pp. 692–726 (1907); Hershey, A. S., "The Calvo and Drago Doctrines," in *American Journal of International Law,* Vol. I, pp. 26–45 (1907); Higgins, A. P., *The Hague Peace Conferences,* London, Cambridge University Press, 1909, pp. 180–197; Latané, J. H., "Forcible Collection of Public Debts," in *Atlantic Monthly,* Vol. 98, pp. 542–550 (October, 1906); Moulin, H. A., *La Doctrine de Drago,* Paris, A. Pedone, 1908; Scott, G. W., "Hague Convention Restricting the Use of Force to Recover on Contract Claims," in *American Journal of International Law,* Vol. II, pp. 78–94 (1908); Scott, G. W. "International Law and the Drago Doctrine," in *North American Review,* Vol. 183, pp. 602–610 (1906); Scott, J. B., *The Hague Peace Conferences,* Baltimore, Johns Hopkins Press, 1909, Chap. 8; and *Revue de Droit International et de Legislation Comparée,* Vol. 35, pp. 597–623 (1903).

On the other hand, it is to be remembered that the advance made has not affected the degree to which claims other than those involving public debts may be collected by force. The United States has long stood for arbitration of all pecuniary controversies, and treaties between many states and groups of states both in the New World and the Old have adopted this standard; but no general convention similar to that adopted at the Hague Conference of 1907 yet applies to such cases. It is also to be borne in mind that controversies arising on other grounds may in their adjustment come to include both claims involving contracts of governments and other claims.[122]

The degree to which force may properly be used in the collection of claims continues to be a question on which authorities on international law and the foreign offices of the nations of the world are in wide disagreement. Debtor states, especially the nations of Latin America, continue critical of forcible measures for the collection of any international claims. Nations whose citizens have heavy investments in the less stable countries are still unwilling to abandon their citizens to whatever remedies the local courts may afford.

It is not too much to say, however, that the drift of opinion favors the position of the weaker states. Creditors are less sure of support from their governments in their demands for pressure to bring payment for alleged violation of rights than was the case a generation ago. The gradual establishment of better government—especially better courts—in the so-called "backward" nations will tend, it may be assumed, to reduce the number of cases in which appeal to the conflicting principles will be made. Nevertheless, up to the present, at least, the debtor communities continue firm in their contentions that the use of force in collection of international claims should not be sanctioned by international law.

---

[122] The conditions arising in the intervention in Santo Domingo, before the Hague Conference of 1907, and in Haiti and Nicaragua at later dates show that the rule may be much simpler than the circumstances to which it may apply.

CHAPTER XI

American Claims and Regeneration in Venezuela

VENEZUELAN relations with the United States had been, to the beginning of the twentieth century, almost uniformly friendly. The northern republic had shown its sympathy with its neighbor during the boundary controversy. It had not joined with other creditor powers to use force to bring payment of the claims of its citizens. It had acted as next friend of Venezuela in bringing the parties to the debt dispute to accept arbitration. The adjustments arrived at by the mixed claims commissions were by 1903 in process of friendly settlement. President Castro could announce in his message to the Congress of 1904, "Our relations with the United States are perfectly harmonious. Each day the deferential consideration which that great nation is showing us becomes more frank and affectionate." [1]

But the year was little more than half through before the relations of the two countries were far from amicable, and the United States found itself in many particulars in a position comparable to that which the European powers had occupied a few years before. The position was not unique, for, as has been indicated, the policies of the Castro government brought him repeatedly, before and after this date, into clashes with a number of European powers. In fact, the President still sought by obstruction to defeat foreign efforts to secure redress.[2]

---

[1] *For. Rel.,* 1904, p. 871 (dispatch of March 2, 1904).

[2] The details of these conflicts are not reviewed. Castro declared that he would make foreigners resident in Venezuela pay the money needed to

The cases which for the last four and a half years of Castro's regime compromised the relations between Venezuela and the United States show wide variety in merit and importance. They illustrate the difficulties to be met in attempts to determine what are the facts which justify a nation in supporting claims for alleged damages to its citizens, the desirability of some arbitral or other impartial review of conflicting arguments, some of the means which may be used for the peaceful adjustment of controversies, and the limitations which surround even arbitral settlements.

So harsh had Castro's policy toward foreigners become after the arbitrations of 1903 that Mr. Bowen, United States minister, who had acted as Venezuela's representative in the then recent adjustments, as early as July, 1904, urged strong action by the United States, the sending of warships, and the seizure of ports to stop the attacks on foreign interests.[3] "Castro," he later declared, "has now reached a point where he will only yield to force." [4]

---

satisfy the awards of the mixed commissions. (*Ibid.,* 1905, p. 928.) A few examples of the sorts of difficulties faced by foreigners may be mentioned:

In July, 1904, Castro was reported to have demanded 12,000,000 bolivars from the British railway at Puerto Cabello and the sale of another British road to the government at 1,000,000 bolivars. His agents were annoying Germans in the interior and attacking the French cable company. The only wealthy Italian landowner in the country was notified not to cut any wood on his land nor to raise any crops. (*Ibid.,* 1905, p. 921.)

Tariff charges were modified so that the revenue yield which was to pay foreign claims fell, and new ports were opened for the same end. Belgium was notified that its award would not be paid. (*Ibid.,* 1905, pp. 1008–1019.)

In 1906 France became exasperated by the mistreatment of her representatives and broke off relations with Venezuela. They were not renewed until 1913. (*Ibid.,* 1906, pp. 1432, 1450, *et seq.*)

In 1908, the minister of the Netherlands was given his passports. The Dutch sent a war vessel to Venezuela as a precautionary measure and asked the United States "whether the government of the United States would object to coercive measures in Venezuela should the national honor of the Netherlands require them." (*Ibid.,* 1909, pp. 630–631.) The reply was that it would not object to such measures if "not involving occupation of territory either permanent or of such a character as to threaten permanency." (*Ibid.,* p. 632.)

Subsequently, Castro seized five Dutch "vessels," and Dutch warships seized the Venezuela "guardships." No adjustment was arrived at until Gómez succeeded Castro, when Venezuela agreed to pay damages. (*Ibid.,* 1909, p. 633.)

[3] *Ibid.,* 1905, pp. 920–921 (July 22 and 24, 1904).

[4] Bowen to Secretary of State, *ibid.,* p. 928 (August 7, 1904).

The United States Secretary of State sought to have all the matters outstanding submitted to arbitration on their merits.[5] Such a standard, however, was not acceptable to Castro. It ran counter to the "Calvo clause," maintained by Venezuela, which denied the right of diplomatic intervention, and to provisions in Venezuelan laws and contracts with concessionaries stipulating that all cases arising under them should be decided without appeal in Venezuelan courts.[6] By these rules it was sought to make it impossible for any claim of a foreigner to become a "diplomatic question," and, relying upon them, Castro refused to arbitrate.

The United States took an equally uncompromising position. It could not agree with any government whatever to submit to a tribunal the function to pass on its exercise of the discretionary right of diplomatic intervention.[7] Later it announced that, if Venezuela continued to refuse to arbitrate, diplomacy might have to be abandoned for harsher means.[8]

In this statement, Castro saw a reflection on the integrity of the Venezuelan courts and asked to have the American Secretary of State informed "that this government [Venezuela] . . . needs to know at once . . . whether or not the Government of the United States respects and reveres the legislation of this Republic and the nobility of its tribunals. . . ."[9]

Almost two years passed after this interchange of amenities with no advance toward settlement. During this period Castro temporarily retired from active politics, to return amid

---

[5] Secretary of State to Bowen, January 28, 1905, *ibid.*, 1905, p. 1020.

[6] These principles are, as was declared by Mr. Frank Plumley, umpire of the British Venezuelan Commission, in discussing in 1903 the Aroa Mines Case, "in sharp and rugged conflict with the law of nations as understood and accepted by Europe and the United States of America." They are, however, widely supported in Latin America. At this time they found expression in the Constitution of Venezuela, Title III, Section I, Article 14, and in the law of February 14, 1873, republished by order of President Castro January 24, 1901. See review of this sort of legislation in Latin America in quotation from the arguments before the British Venezuelan Commission of 1903 in Crichfield, *op. cit.*, p. 48 *et seq.*

[7] Loomis to Bowen, January 30, 1905, *For. Rel.*, 1905, p. 1021 (paraphrased).

[8] Hay to Bowen, March 10, 1905, *ibid.*, 1905, p. 1028.

[9] Minister of Foreign Affairs to Bowen, March 23, 1905, *ibid.*, 1905, p. 1030.

popular rejoicing. On February 28, 1907, the United States again laid its case before the Venezuelan Government.[10]

The statement of the American position signed by Secretary Elihu Root sets out the facts of the cases and the American position—which paralleled that asserted by European powers —on a number of the legal issues arising in international claims. It merits study because it brings out the contrast between the position of these powers and that maintained by Venezuela and a number of other Latin-American states under their constitutions and legislation.

"Notwithstanding the repeated occasions upon which the United States has intervened," declared the Secretary of State, "as a friend in need to relieve Venezuela from disagreeable and dangerous complications with other foreign powers . . . the Government of Venezuela has within the past few years practically confiscated or destroyed all the substantial property interests of Americans in that country."[11] He states that this had been done sometimes in accordance with forms of law and sometimes otherwise, "until of the many millions of dollars invested by American citizens in that country practically nothing remains."

Consideration was asked for five cases:[12]

1. A. F. Jaurett, an American citizen, was notified after the close of business on Saturday, November 12, 1904, that he must leave Venezuela, on the ground that "he was notoriously prejudicial to public order." He had been an established resident. He sought a chance to arrange his affairs but was forced to leave Monday morning. The right to expel foreigners was not questioned, but arbitrary action of this sort, it was held, was indefensible. Jaurett claimed loss of $25,000 and asked damages in that amount.

2. The claims of the New York and Bermudez Company,

---

[10] Root to Russell, February 28, 1907, *ibid.*, 1908, p. 774. The detail of the various cases is in "Correspondence relating to wrongs done to American citizens by the Government of Venezuela," *Sen. Doc. No. 413,* 60th Cong., 1st Sess. (Serial 5257).

[11] Secretary of State to Minister Russell, February 28, 1907, *For. Rel.*, 1908, p. 774.

[12] *Ibid.*, 1908, p. 774 *et seq.*

which had been insistently defended by the United States, had involved rights to an asphalt lake near the coast opposite Trinidad acquired under three distinct titles involving a concession of 1883 to exploit the woods and asphalt of the Venezuelan state in which the lake lay, a grant of 1888 giving the right to exploit the asphalt lake for ninety-nine years, and another grant of 1888 giving the company a fee simple title.

The case was complicated by alleged defects in the titles and by a claim that the company had not canalized certain rivers or exploited resources other than asphalt, as Venezuela declared the contracts required. Venezuela on her side had declared that the company had spent at least $130,000 in aiding a revolution. To redress this wrong, the company was to be required to pay $10,000,000 or be sued in court.[13] The Venezuelan Government forbade the company to operate its holdings and later dispossessed it. The United States asked that the case be submitted to an impartial tribunal.

3. The Crichfield case involved an asphalt mine in western Venezuela. The deposit, originally granted to one Guzmán, lay some seventy miles west of the city of Maracaibo. Its original owner sold his rights to Crichfield, who sold out to the United States and Venezuela Company incorporated in New Jersey in 1901. The sale was validated by the Venezuelan Congress the following year. The concession was for fifty years and granted the company free customs entry on machinery for its operations and a low fixed tax rate. On the faith of the contract, about $600,000 had been invested. About 1,000 Venezuelans were employed by the enterprise.

The Castro government, in violation of the contract, increased fourfold the taxes on the property and demanded an export tax of $1.40 per ton on the asphalt. Venezuela pleaded that the foreigner could not ask diplomatic intervention because the contract contained the Calvo clause. The United States would not admit that its citizens could by such agreements barter away the rights attaching to their citizenship and asked that the case be arbitrated.

---

[13] *Ibid.*, 1905, p. 919.

4. The Orinoco Corporation had come to own rights based on a grant of 1883 to one C. C. Fitzgerald to exploit for ninety-nine years certain Venezuelan national lands in the delta of the Orinoco. The grant was reaffirmed in 1895. The Castro government had declared it null in May, 1901. The matter in dispute was submitted to the Mixed Claims Commission of 1903, which declared for the grantees, and their rights were again affirmed by the Venezuelan supreme court in 1906. But, in the latter year, the Government had again granted part of the territory involved to another party. The United States asked that this dispute be referred to the Hague Court unless some other adjustment could be agreed upon.

5. The Orinoco Steamship Company was an American successor to a company earlier incorporated in England which had come to own the rights of two Venezuelan corporations. One of the latter corporations had obtained a grant allowing it to operate for fifteen years a line of steamers from Trinidad up the Orinoco to Ciudad Bolivar over the more accessible mouths of the river except the Boca Grande. This was a monopoly right, for other vessels engaged in foreign trade were prohibited by law from navigating the Orinoco. The other Venezuelan company which had been taken over was the Orinoco Red Star Line, to which the Government owed over $500,000 for services rendered.

In May, 1900, the Government agreed in return for the cancellation of its indebtedness to the latter company to make two annual payments of $19,219 and to extend the concession for Orinoco navigation for six years—to 1915. But in October, 1900, Venezuela repealed the law giving the company a monopoly position in Orinoco navigation, and in December of the next year it annulled the extension of the concession.

Like the one above, this claim was submitted to the Mixed Claims Commission of 1903, where it, like the others before that body, was to be considered "upon a basis of absolute equity, without regard to objections of a technical nature or . . . the provisions of local legislation."

Mr. Harry Barge, the Dutch umpire on the Commission,

had disallowed the claims amounting to $1,209,701 for damages on account of the repeal of the monopoly privileges as well as all other claims of the company except $28,224 in an item of $147,638 covering services to Venezuela and damages suffered by the company in revolutionary periods.

This case the United States now asked to have reheard on the ground that the umpire had not considered the case on the basis on which it had been submitted. He had thrown out some items on account of the Calvo clause in the contracts, which the United States was unwilling to allow could modify its right to protect the interests of its citizens.[14]

Almost exactly a year after the date of this statement by Secretary Root, Castro's government restated its position unchanged.[15] "The cases referred to," it was declared, "cannot be considered as being comprised among those which call for diplomatic action. . . ." The United States was asked to consider the cases closed and the parties were recommended to take their plaints to the local courts if they were still unsatisfied. The minister of foreign affairs hoped that "President Roosevelt would desist from his contentions. . . ."[16]

The United States was now in substantially the same position in which Great Britain had stood as to its "first rank" claims before the setting up of the blockade of 1902–1903. On June 13, 1908, diplomatic relations were severed[17] in view of the persistent refusal "to give redress for the governmental action by which substantially all American interests . . . have been destroyed or confiscated, or to submit the claims . . . for such redress to arbitration. . . ." American interests were turned over to the care of the Brazilian representative.

---

[14] The Castro government had refused to reopen the case on the ground that, having been before the commission of 1903, it was a closed case. The Venezuelan minister of foreign affairs in his report to the Congress in 1904 had taken exactly the opposite position in contesting the awards which the mixed commissions had passed on the cases that had arisen with Belgium and with Mexico.

[15] See *For. Rel.*, 1908, p. 820 (February 29, 1908).

[16] *Ibid.*, p. 823 (June 20, 1908).

[17] *For. Rel.*, 1908, pp. 820–821 (June 13, 1908). Telegram paraphrased.

In this state relations between the two republics continued for a little over six months. Castro found himself in a position of increasing difficulty. Relations with France continued severed. He had temporarily retired in April, 1906, leaving affairs in the hands of First Vice-President Juan Vicente Gómez, whom he reported to be "a very meritorious citizen of well-known civic virtues."[18] But he again took up his presidential duties in July. Foreign relations were still troublesome. The United States had withdrawn its representative and local support of the administration became less enthusiastic. Before the end of 1908 Castro no longer headed the government, and Juan Vicente Gómez, destined to become the "regenerator" of Venezuela, had become its director. With his accession came a quick and complete reversal of the Venezuelan position. The new administration declared for amicable settlement of all the disputes which, as it later stated, its "predecessor had embittered and made difficult."[19] On December 21, 1908, the Brazilian ambassador, at the request of Venezuela, reported this desire to the United States. The United States promptly replied that relations would be re-established if the Brazilian representative should "receive from the Government of President Gómez an explicit statement committing Venezuela to the arbitration of" the claims.[20]

William I. Buchanan shortly afterward received authority to re-establish relations with Venezuela, which now no longer insisted that the Calvo clause controlled in the cases in dispute.[21] The United States had proposed that all five claims be submitted to the Hague Court or to another tribunal of

---

[18] *Ibid.*, 1906, p. 1441. Dispatch from Minister Russell to the Secretary of State, dated April 15, 1906, inclosing a proclamation by Castro dated April 9, 1906.

[19] *Ibid.*, 1911, p. 749 (May 10, 1911).

[20] *Ibid.*, 1909, p. 610 (December 21, 1908).

[21] Later, at the time that relations with France were re-established, this point was specifically covered. A representative was sent to Caracas "on the express conditions that all . . . claims may thereafter be referred, if desire to do so is expressed, to an arbitral tribunal. . . ." *Ibid.*, 1913, p. 531 (August 29). Venezuela accepted this standard September 23, 1912 (*ibid.*, 1913, pp. 532–533), and a protocol incorporated its principles, February 12, 1913 (*ibid.*, 1913, p. 535). Protocol quoted, *ibid.*, pp. 537–538.

three jurists to be created. However, two of the claims were put in course for direct settlement and there was signed on February 13, 1909, a protocol to refer the remaining three claims to The Hague, but with the understanding that in two of them Venezuela was to be free to make settlements otherwise with the claimants.[22] Four of the claims were disposed of as follows:

1. The small Jaurett claim was settled on the day the protocol was signed through payment by Venezuela of an indemnity of $3,000 in gold.[23]

2. The New York and Bermudez Company claim was settled directly between the company and the Government on a compromise basis. No mention of the case is made in the protocol. In sum, the company accepted the sentence of the Venezuelan courts for damages for aiding a rebellion and was to pay about $60,000. It agreed to sell asphalt to the Government at 25 per cent below the current price and to pay an export tax of four bolivars a ton on asphalt shipments. Venezuela recognized certain of the titles to the land involved in the concessions and the right to certain tariff exemptions.[24]

3. The Crichfield case was to be adjusted through negotiations under the auspices of the two governments. It was so settled. The company had claimed damages of $1,500,000, but finally settled for $475,000, to be paid in eight equal annual installments through the Department of State at Washington. In return, the company released to Venezuela all its property in the country.[25]

4. The Orinoco Corporation's claim had been heard by the United States and Venezuela Mixed Claims Commission in 1903 but was now to be given reconsideration. By an agreement signed September 9, 1909, Venezuela agreed to pay $385,000 in eight annual installments under conditions similar to those in the Crichfield adjustment. The corporation

---

[22] *Ibid.*, 1909, pp. 617–622 (text of protocol).

[23] *Ibid.*, pp. 629–630.

[24] *American Journal of International Law*, New York, 1909, Vol. II, pp. 445–446.

[25] Agreement signed at Caracas, August 21, 1909, *For. Rel.*, 1909, pp. 624–625.

in return surrendered title to its holdings and waived all its claims.[26]

There was, therefore, only one of the claims left to be settled at The Hague—that of the Orinoco Steamship Company. This dispute had also been passed upon by the Mixed Claims Commission, but the United States asked reconsideration of the decision of the arbiter. The Hague tribunal found that, though arbitral decisions were ordinarily binding, in this instance both parties admitted that "excessive exercise of jurisdiction and essential error in judgment" might justify review. Against the contention of those representing United States interests, it decided not to review on their merits all items but only those in which error was manifest. The amount which Venezuela was to pay was increased, bringing its total to $64,412.59. The decision disallowed items of large amount claimed by the United States one of which involved over $1,000,000. Though the result was satisfactory to neither party, both accepted it.[27] All issues between them had been peacefully adjusted.

Cipriano Castro, in whose regime the foreign relations of Venezuela had been so turbulent, left for Europe late in 1908 for a "surgical operation," and the headship of the government passed into the hands of Juan Vicente Gómez, the Vice-President, who had been associated with his chief, it is said, since 1892, when Castro after a defeat in one of the revolu-

---

[26] *Ibid.*, 1909, pp. 626–628.

[27] See *For. Rel.*, 1911, p. 749, and Dennis, W. C., "The Orinoco Steamship Company Case Before The Hague Tribunal," in *American Journal of International Law,* Vol. V, pp. 35–64 (January, 1911). Further materials involving the national and international difficulties of Venezuela in this period are found in Rougier, Antoine, "Les Récentes Guerres Civiles de la Colombie et du Vénézuéla," in *Revue Générale de Droit International Public,* Paris, 1904, Vol. II, pp. 225–286; Jules Basdevant, "Le Conflit Franco-Vénézuélan," in *Revue Générale de Droit International Public,* Paris, 1906, Vol. XIII, pp. 509–559; "Protocol Between the Netherlands and Venezuela" (signed April 19, 1909), in *Supplement to the American Journal of International Law, Official Documents,* New York, 1909, Vol. III, pp. 231–233; "The Venezuelan Situation" (editorial comment), in *American Journal of International Law,* New York, 1909, Vol. III, pp. 436–446, and "The Venezuelan Cases," *ibid.*, pp. 985–989; "Executive Decree of Venezuela Concerning Foreign Claims," in *Supplement to the American Journal of International Law, Official Documents,* New York, 1914, Vol. VIII, pp. 174 and 175.

tions of the time had been driven into Colombia and returned to Venezuela with a few tattered soldiers. Gómez was to become one of the outstanding dictators of the first third of the twentieth century in Latin America. Shortly after the President's departure, the Congress suspended Castro from office and started an investigation of his administration. On December 19, 1909, Gómez was made Provisional President. A new constitution was adopted, and on August 27, 1910, Gómez was elected for a four-year term. These actions were only the beginning of manipulations of the fundamental law which since have been characteristic of Venezuela.

In the summer of 1913, Castro, after stormy experiences in Europe and the United States, returned to try to re-establish his control. Gómez, leaving the presidency temporarily, took the field against him and won a victory which brought to an end the political career of his former friend. He resumed the chief magistracy in January, 1914, and called a Congress which framed a new constitution, elected V. Marquez Bustillos Provisional President, and made Gómez Commander in Chief of the Army on April 19, 1914.

Under the new Constitution, re-election was not forbidden, as had been the case in that of 1910. Executive powers were greatly enlarged. The vice-presidency was abolished and the President was given the right to name the person who might substitute for him and wide authority in both civil and religious affairs. The Congress elected under the new Constitution unanimously on May 1, 1915, chose Gómez President for a term now increased to seven years, but he did not assume the office. Under a special clause, the Provisional President and the Commander in Chief of the Army were to continue in office until the constitutional President was sworn in, and Gómez preferred to continue Commander in Chief. He did so until several weeks after he had been re-elected for another seven-year term in 1922, when he finally took the official oath. During this time the Provisional President continued to exercise a shadow authority, carrying out the wishes of the chief of the Army.

On June 19, 1922, there was promulgated another constitution, the fourteenth, which abolished the exceptional clauses referring to the highest civil and military officials and which created two vice-presidents. Gómez then, on June 24, 1922, took over the presidential office. General Juan C. Gómez, a brother of the dictator, was chosen to the first vice-presidency and a son was elected to the second. In 1925 still another constitution was adopted; but, before the term ended, revolutionary activity in which university students played a prominent role broke out and was recklessly suppressed. Nevertheless, when the Congress was again called upon to elect a President, it chose Gómez once more, on May 30, 1929, for still another seven-year term. But Gómez declined the honor, preferring to retire to his estates, though at the urgent solicitation of Congress he again consented to serve his country as generalissimo. Congress then chose Juan Bautista Perez, a close associate of the dictator, President for the term 1929 to 1936. Perez remained in nominal control of the office, however, only a little more than two years. It is reported that the development of unrest caused members of Congress to urge the President to retire, but he continued to refuse to do so until the Legislature made a formal request. His resignation was "unanimously" accepted on June 13, 1931, and on the twentieth the Congress "unanimously" chose General Gómez to fill out the term. On July 13 Gómez "took the oath of office as President amidst scenes of enthusiasm." The term is to end in 1936.

About the man Juan Vicente Gómez, whose history for now more than a quarter of a century has been, in the eyes of the world, to so great a degree the history of his country, highly contrasted opinions have been expressed by both Venezuelans and foreigners.[28] According to his admirers, he is a man of lowly origin and simple habits, a straightforward soldier, practical, conscious of the immaturity of his people, one who feels that the great need of the republic is a strong government which can give it peace and economic development. To the

---

[28] Examples of highly laudatory accounts are found in Clark, Cyrus Norman, *Venezuela and her Progressive Ruler* (pamphlet published by the author), Caracas, 1929.

latter end he has welcomed the entry of foreign capital in large amounts. The ideal sought by him is "freedom and equality of all under the accepted dominance of the recognized Chief."[29] Life and property, it is asserted, are safe, and crimes of violence almost unknown.[30]

On the other hand, by the testimony of his critics, Gómez is an ignorant cowherd able to sign his name only slowly "like a servant," avaricious, ruthless, and intolerant of even the slightest questioning of his authority. Under his rule, freedom of speech and freedom of the press have been crushed out, and even religion is under strict executive supervision. Hundreds of the best citizens have been exiled or have sought safety by fleeing from their native land, and dozens have been tortured and assassinated. Hundreds of university students have been thrown into prison and forced to work on the roads because they have protested against the authority of the dictator. One prominent Venezuelan exile has declared, "Artists, men of letters, soldiers, priests, have been aged, ruined, martyred and killed . . . by the order and will of a single indian. . . . Citizens and foreigners except the blond man, respected and feared, have passed under the yoke and have paid with their deaths only because their faces were displeasing to this corrupted despot."[31]

Public order and economic development in restricted lines have undoubtedly been attained, the former through the army and the latter particularly through the development of the petroleum industry, chiefly by foreign capital. The petroleum resources have been exploited, first around Lake Maracaibo but later also to the eastward. Concessions have been granted over large units of area so that the problems arising where rival companies operate in the same pool have been minimized. Serious exploitation dates from 1912 and there-

---

[29] Laureano Vellenilla Lanz, a Venezuelan journalist quoted in Clark, *op cit.*

[30] Clark, *op. cit.*, p. 3. See also Garcia Naranjo, a Mexican commentator quoted in the *New York Times*, May 8, 1929.

[31] Quoted in Gonzales-Ruano, César, *El Terror en America*, Madrid, Compañía Iberoamericana de Publicaciones, 1930, pp. 5–9. This volume contains a number of comments by leading Latin Americans on the Gómez regime and a detailed account of the abuses charged to the dictator.

fore falls entirely in the Gómez period. Commercial production increased rapidly after 1917, often doubling from year to year and in the late twenties making Venezuela the next largest producer in the world after the United States.[32] The yield in more recent years has fallen because the exploiting companies have preferred to "cap in" wells rather than push them to the limit of production. Government taxes on petroleum have come to be one of the important sources of income for the Treasury. Foreign capital invested in the country totalled at the beginning of the Gómez period only a few million dollars. In current years it is reported as above $200,000,000, a figure which is chiefly represented by petroleum enterprises.

Import and export trade has shown remarkable increase, which is explained by increase of petroleum exports and by the good prices which through most of the Gómez period have obtained for the other chief exports, especially coffee and cacoa. In the period 1906–1910, the average value of foreign trade was $26,428,000; in 1929, the peak year, it rose to $237,-662,000.[33] Public revenue, about one-fourth of which came to be drawn from taxes on mines and petroleum, showed similar satisfactory increase.

These factors plus improvements in administration have enabled Venezuela to put itself in an extraordinarily favorable position in government finance. When the "diplomatic debt" was adjusted in 1905, in the Castro regime, the Government was so weak that the total obligations were sharply scaled down and the interest rate reduced to three per cent. The bonds sold at 50.5 per cent of their face amounts. When Gómez came into control in 1908, the foreign debt totaled 133,059,400 bolivars. Thereafter, the foreign debt was steadily paid off. The three-per cent bonds rose to 98.7 per cent of par in December, 1928, when a value of only 28,445,385 bolivars[34] remained outsanding. Payments began to be

---

[32] Further discussion of the oil yield is in Jones, Chester Lloyd, *Caribbean Backgrounds and Prospects,* New York, D. Appleton and Co., 1931, pp. 146–154. The oil yield rose from 120,000 barrels in 1917 to 141,652,832 in 1930, the peak year.

[33] *Commerce Yearbook,* 1932, Vol. II, p. 493.

[34] Par value of the bolivar, $.193.

made at twice the rate called for in the contracts. Meanwhile, the internal debt had been reduced from sixty-seven to twenty-four million. Yearly budgets showed surpluses, and for several years the cash balances in the Treasury were more than all of the national debt.

Under these circumstances, President Gómez announced in a message to Congress on April 27, 1930 that the Treasury reserves had reached 101,919,251 bolivars while the debt internal and external was only 52,971,296 bolivars. He suggested that on the occasion of the centenary of the death of Bolívar, the liberator, December 17, 1930, Venezuela should stand before the world as "a country free of foreign debt." On May 22, Congress approved the proposal, and before the end of the year the foreign debt account, which had given the republic some of its more precarious moments, was brought to an end. By the end of 1932 the Treasury surplus was more than three times the amount of the outstanding internal debt.[35] The financial position of Venezuela had become unique in the world.

For now more than twenty-six years, the Government of Venezuela has been under the control of the will of one man. He is reported to be seventy-eight years old. Rumors of dissatisfaction with his iron-handed rule drift beyond the national borders, but no serious revolts have appeared on the horizon. The announcement made by the dictator in 1929 might be equally well made in 1935: "The political, financial and economic conditions of Venezuela are splendid. There is complete calm in the country and peace is firm, solid and immovable. . . . There is not a lone bandit perturbing the quiet of the country. . . . It would be ridiculous for any one to attempt to alter the present order. . . . There is no one who would venture to defy the force of public opinion, which is determined to maintain the constitutional normality of the country. In the same manner the Venezuelan army is composed of units well-disciplined and well-organized and armed with modern equipment."[36]

---

[35] At the end of 1933, the internal debt amounted to about 20,000,000 bolivars.

[36] *New York Times,* March 9, 1929.

CHAPTER XII

Colombia and the Panama Revolution

THE Great Colombia which Simón Bolívar succeeded in creating out of the territory now included in the Republics of Colombia, Venezuela, Ecuador, and Panama, had already broken into three states at the time of the liberator's death on December 17, 1830. New Granada (what is now Colombia), like other Latin-American commonwealths, started on its career under great handicaps. It suffered from geographical disunity due to the division of the territory by the northern cordilleras of the Andes into regions among which communication was difficult. It lacked the tradition of unified government, for in later colonial times the administration had been carried on in three divisions independent of each other. In addition, the place which the Catholic Church should occupy in the community became a cause of bitter disputes, and political allegiances were divided between those favoring centralism and the partisans of a federated state.

As happened in the neighboring states, the methods of government adopted by leaders succeeding in getting into power were often harsh, and revolutions were many; but Colombia's governments proved better able to crush local dissent than was the case elsewhere and the political contests turned less on personalities and more on principles, especially the issue of centralism versus federalism. Advocates of the former maintained their control until 1849, by which time remarkable advance had been made under the leadership of "Conservative" presidents. Then came a period of about thirty years in which the "Liberals" were for the greater part of the time in the ascendant. At times the decentralization of authority was carried so far that the "states" had little organic connection with each other beyond common representation abroad.

Out of the unhappy experience of this period sprang a movement for return toward centralism, headed by Rafael Núñez. He became President first in 1880 as a Liberal; but, by 1885, "taught by experience," he was a strong advocate of centralized authority. The "states" became departments and the President practically a dictator. Núñez continued in control till his death in 1894 and was followed by others of the same political faith until 1930, when, through a split in the Conservative party, the Liberals won the presidency.

During this long period under leaders of a single party, the country had again made substantial advance but had by no means enjoyed uninterrupted internal peace. The worst of the many internal conflicts, the worst, indeed, in all Colombian history, was that which broke out in 1899 and lasted to June 1903, thus weakening the position of the government in what proved to be a crucial period in the foreign relations of the Republic.[1]

The chief concerns of Colombian international relations have been negotiations with foreign private companies and foreign governments arising out of projects for an interoceanic canal.

A waterway between the Atlantic and Pacific was a project which had stirred the ambitions of many since the period of discovery; but, until late in the nineteenth century, none of the various plans gave real promise of being carried out. As commerce increased and national ambitions developed for political control or economic development of the former Spanish colonies, foreign countries, especially Great Britain and the United States, showed increasing interest in the Caribbean in general and in the conditions under which any waterway

---

[1] For developments in Colombia, see: James, Herman G., and Martin, Percy A., *The Republics of Latin America,* New York, Harper and Bros., 1923, pp. 283–292; Robertson, William Spence, *History of the Latin-American Nations,* New York, D. Appleton and Co., 1932, pp. 474–506; Williams, Mary Wilhelmine, *The People and Politics of Latin America,* Boston, Ginn and

between the oceans might be built. Out of this concern rose rivalries which, of course, came directly to involve the countries holding isthmian territories.

British interest dated from the early days of the struggle for position in the Caribbean, and that of the United States from the years immediately following its independence. Great Britain sought to insure that no development in the former Spanish colonies should lessen the strength of her own position in the New World—a policy much broader than that concerning canal projects, but one in which these would naturally play a part. She became jealous of the advances which the United States was making in the early 1800's on the north coast of the Gulf of Mexico, and, had it not been for the fact that her freedom of action was limited by developments in Europe which drew her toward alliance with Spain, she might have adopted a much more forward policy in the period of the breakup of the Spanish colonial empire following 1810.

But the chance that the rebellious colonies could be brought back to Spanish allegiance waned. Presently, Great Britain had to face the fact that the United States had sent commercial agents southward and was about to recognize the new states by sending them diplomatic representatives. Control of their trade might follow. Under these conditions, Great Britain, with important trade and investment interests already established in the region, shifted her policy as to recognition to one substantially the same as that of the United States. Thus was laid the groundwork for a keen rivalry between the two Anglo-Saxon countries.

In this contest, Great Britain at first definitely held the lead both in commerce and in political projects in the new states. Time worked, however, for the United States, the rapid growth of which would in the long run turn the balance of influence in the New World; but, throughout the second quarter of the century, the republic found itself in a position far from dominant, and at times there was doubt whether it could keep political developments within such bounds as would insure even equality of opportunity.

The commercial and political rivalry between the two English-speaking nations was reflected in the instructions given their representatives, and in the relations of these to each other in the Caribbean countries in these years furnish some of the most diverting, if not the most dignified, incidents in diplomatic history.

Each country sought to secure in the Caribbean states and Mexico political and commercial advantages from which the other would be excluded. Britain was anxious that the United States should not become the head of an American confederacy. She early put herself forward as an enthusiastic friend of Mexico, delayed the negotiation of a commercial treaty with the United States, and urged Mexico to a strong stand as to its territorial claims to the northward. The British representatives at times seemed to make almost their own the Mexican claims as to the northern boundary. Such coöperation was, of course, highly welcome to those at the head of the Mexican Government. When developments in Texas became acute, the British made it clear that their sympathies were with Mexico. Meanwhile, they secured favorable commercial treaties with a number of other Latin-American states and began to develop political pretentions in Central America. Though actual sovereignty over territories there was not claimed before 1848, rights due to incontinuous activities of British subjects in previous years were asserted in what are now British Honduras and Nicaragua and certain coastal and island districts of Honduras.

American interest in this farther region developed more slowly; but, as the possibilities of conflict with Mexico and of holdings on the Pacific Coast were realized, the isthmian region began to be given more attention. The importance of communications by railway or canal across the isthmus came to be realized. Old ambitions as to any canal which might be constructed were revived and steps were taken to insure that the United States should not be put, in the use of such facilities, in a less favorable position than might be enjoyed by other powers not owners of the territory through which they might pass. To this end, treaties with both Colombia and Nicaragua were sought.

The negotiations with Colombia resulted in a treaty, signed December 12, 1846, and ratified June 12, 1848, in which Colombia, then New Granada, agreed that the citizens, vessels, and merchandise of the United States should enjoy in Colombian ports, including those at Panama, all privileges concerning commerce and navigation which were enjoyed by citizens of Colombia. It was also stipulated "that the right of way or transit across the Isthmus of Panama upon any modes of communication that now exist, or may be hereafter constructed shall be open and free to the government and citizens of the United States" under the same terms as were granted to Colombian citizens. Traffic was not to be subject to import duties and tolls should not be discriminatory.

In return, the United States agreed to "guarantee, positively and efficaciously, to New Granada . . . the perfect neutrality of the . . . isthmus" and "the rights of sovereignty and property which New Granada has and possesses over the said territory." After twenty years the treaty could be terminated by either party on twelve months' notice.[2]

This treaty, which was later to attain a notoriety which could not have been suspected by its negotiators, might insure that the United States would enjoy in any Colombian canal as great privileges as diplomacy could secure for the British.

The United States also put forth efforts to make certain that on no canal to the northward were the British to secure special advantages. British claims there, the United States felt, were tending to crystallize into possession. Alliances with native chiefs on the Mosquito Coast of Nicaragua had led to their support by British arms and to assertion by the British of exclusive rights at San Juan del Norte, the accepted Atlantic terminus for the discussed Nicaragua canal. The United States became convinced that it was the British intention to control any canal which might be built or, at least,

---

[2] Text in Malloy, William M. (compiler), *Treaties, Conventions, International Acts, Protocols and Agreements between the United States of America and Other Powers, 1776–1909*, Washington, United States Government Printing Office, 1910, Vol. I, pp. 302–314, at p. 312.

to prevent the United States from doing so; and agents were sent to Central America to seek treaties to prevent such an outcome. Such treaties they secured; but their terms were so broad that, if ratified, open conflict with Great Britain could not have been avoided, and the Government at Washington therefore did not press for their ratification.[3]

Supplementing these efforts in Latin America were other negotiations undertaken directly with Great Britain, the growing political influence of which in Central America was becoming peculiarly distasteful to American statesmen and to the American public. At the middle of the century expansionist sentiment was widespread in the United States. Great additions to the national territory had recently been made, chiefly at the expense of Mexico. Communications with the Far West by isthmian routes were claiming more attention, especially after the gold rush of 1849; and the desire to insure that British influence in the isthmus and Central America, especially over possible canal routes, should not grow was strong.

In Great Britain the rapid advance of the United States in territorial possessions, population, and commerce had made its impression, and that government in turn was anxious to insure that the United States should not expand into Central America.

Out of these conditions rose the Clayton-Bulwer treaty of April 19, 1850, in which each party felt that it had checked the ambitions of the other. In fact, as the event proved, it did not insure the prompt retirement of Great Britain from her territorial pretentions in the Isthmian region; and, while American political control did not expand southward, the treaty did not check the continued growth of American influence.

The agreement did, however, put limitations about the conditions under which any canal could be built. The governments had engaged "that neither . . . will ever obtain

---

[3] For an account of British and American rivalries in Latin America, see Rippy, J. F., *Latin America in World Politics,* New York, F. S. Crofts and Co., 1928, pp. 54–125.

. . . for itself any exclusive control over" an isthmian canal "or maintain any fortifications commanding the same, or in the vicinity thereof." They agreed to use their influence with the local governments to facilitate canal construction, to encourage private parties offering to undertake the work, and to protect, from any violence whatsoever, parties having the authority of the local governments to build a canal. Though Central American problems had been the occasion of the treaty, a separate clause extended its application to Tehuantepec and Panama.[4] Though that had not been its object, this convention proved for half a century to be an effective barrier to a canal built through funds supplied from public sources.

Both Colombia and Nicaragua continued anxious to promote construction by any means that might be offered. In the former, between 1835 and 1878 there were considered more than a dozen projects of various sorts for waterways by various routes to be constructed by Colombians, or by foreign groups with or without the aid of foreign governments. None resulted in serious attempts at actual construction. In the latter year, the minister of foreign affairs signed a contract with one Lucien N. B. Wyse which was continued for various periods and became the basis of the most serious attempt at canal building on the isthmus during the nineteenth century.[5]

The Wyse concession was later transferred to a company headed by Ferdinand de Lesseps, the famous French engineer who had recently brought to completion the Suez Canal. Work at the isthmus was begun in 1882 and continued until 1889. From the beginning, bad fortune attended the enterprise. Financial mismanagement and corruption cut down what should have been possible with the funds which were

---

[4] Text of the Clayton-Bulwer treaty in Malloy, Vol. I, pp. 659–663. A convenient collection of the canal treaties from the Clayton-Bulwer treaty to that with Panama, with the diplomatic correspondence concerning certain of them, is, "Canal Treaties," *Sen. Doc. No. 456,* 63rd Congress, 2nd Sess., Washington, 1914.

[5] A summary of the various early projects is given in Uribe, Antonio José, *Colombia y los Estados Unidos,* Bogotá, Imprenta Nacional, 1931, pp. 65–67. See also Henderson, John B., *American Diplomatic Questions,* New York, the Macmillan Co., 1901, pp. 65–201, for a review of the earlier canal diplomacy.

raised. The work proved much more costly than had been forecast by the optimistic estimates of the French engineers. Yellow fever and malaria carried off the workmen by thousands. The enthusiasm which marked the beginning of the work gave way to discouragement. No more money could be raised by appeals to the public for subscriptions, and the enterprise passed into bankruptcy. A reorganized company resumed operations in 1894 to keep the concession alive in the hope that the rights and properties acquired might later be sold.

After it became evident that the French canal enterprise was not going to be able to bring the canal to completion, American sentiment in favor of a canal under American control, already strong, steadily increased. Popular and sometimes official statements argued for the modification of the Clayton-Bulwer treaty, on the ground that it did not apply to the Panama route or that it was obsolete, or for its abrogation. True it was, conditions had changed, but the treaty, of course, continued to be a fully binding engagement.

New impetus was given to this feeling by the Spanish-American War. As the probability of the conflict increased, the United States Navy took steps to concentrate forces in the Caribbean. On March 7, 1898, a warship, the *Oregon,* left Puget Sound on the first leg of the long voyage southward to the Straits of Magellan and then north to the West Indies. War broke while the boat was en route, and it was only on May 26 that the vessel reached Key West, where American forces were being assembled. The voyage had been one of 14,700 knots. It was completed in "the nick of time," for a resolution equivalent to a declaration of war was passed by the United States Congress on April 20. On July 1 the *Oregon* was shelling Spanish positions at the east end of Cuba; and two days later, this, the speediest of the American battleships engaged, was in the thick of the naval battle of Santiago.[6] The incident abundantly illustrated the advan-

---

[6] Chadwick, F. E., *The Relations of the United States and Spain, The Spanish American War,* New York, Charles Scribner's Sons, 1911, Vol. I, pp. 12–16; *ibid.,* Vol. II, pp. 99, 135–163.

tages which an isthmian canal, allowing quick mobilization of forces, would have for the American Navy.

Once the war was over, the United States found itself in possession of Puerto Rico in the West Indies and with new responsibilities in Cuba which would make the position of the Navy in the Caribbean of greater importance. A canal which would allow the prompt mobilization of forces in either ocean was evidently highly to be desired.

The newly acquired commercial and military interests in Hawaii and the Philippines enforced the argument, as did also the desire to create easy water communications for the intercoastal trade of the continental United States and the trade of the east coast of the United States to the west coast of South America and, indeed, to all other regions to which a canal would give easier access.

From the British as well as from the American point of view, conditions at the close of the century stood in high contrast to those of fifty years before. The United States had grown from a population of twenty-three millions to one of seventy-six millions. Its economic and political strength had risen in even greater ratio. Its political interests in Caribbean affairs had just been greatly increased. Possible expansion of political control in America no longer attracted the attention of British statesmen. The latter sought, rather, equality of commercial opportunity and the rise of conditions which through creation of greater economic stability would promote trade and investments in the New World. These were ambitions not inconsistent with the American program and would be fostered rather than hindered by the building of an isthmian canal, even if its control were in the hands of the United States.

It is not surprising, therefore, that an American request for modification of the Clayton-Bulwer convention had a favorable reception. Negotiations resulted in the Hay-Pauncefote treaty of November 18, 1901.[7] It was agreed that the canal

---

[7] Text in Malloy, *op. cit.*, Vol. I, pp. 782–784.

might "be constructed under the auspices of the United States, either directly at its own cost" or by any other plan. The United States should "enjoy all the rights incident to such construction as well as the exclusive right of providing for the regulation and management of the canal." Substantially, the rules as to neutralization which applied to the Suez Canal were adopted. The waterway was to be "free and open to the vessels of commerce and of war of all nations . . . on terms of entire equality, so that there [should] be no discrimination . . . in respect of the conditions or charges of traffic, or otherwise."

The way was now clear for construction either directly by the United States or under its auspices, provided the right to dig could be secured from the government owning the land over which the canal would pass. The routes to be seriously considered had narrowed down to the one through Panama, where the French company was still working at a reduced rate, and that through Nicaragua, where a less well-supported American company had attempted construction and had failed. Of the two routes, the latter had long been the more popular with the American public.

Anticipating the removal of the limitations on action in the Clayton-Bulwer treaty, the Congress of the United States had provided for a technical investigation to determine the most practical route across the isthmus and the cost of building a canal there. A commission was created in June, 1899. It later reported that, though the Nicaragua canal would give a shorter sailing distance between the two coasts of the United States, it would cost more to build. The length of the Panama canal would be less, it would involve less curvature, pass ships more quickly, and have better port facilities at both ends than were found in Nicaragua. At Panama, however, the rights of the French company would have to be acquired, and the management did not show itself disposed to sell at a price considered reasonable. Should it later do so, the cost of the canals at the two points would not differ greatly. However, if the French would not sell their concession, which still had several years to run, Colombia could not give the United States as free a hand as could be secured from Nicaragua and Costa Rica.

After warm debate, the Congress of the United States on June 28, 1902, passed the so-called "Spooner Law," which authorized the President to buy the property and rights of the French company for not more than $40,000,000 and to secure from Colombia a perpetual control over a right of way. If these could not be secured within a reasonable time, the President was to seek a right of way on the Nicaraguan route and, on securing it, proceed to construction there.

Whichever route was decided upon, the next step would be to secure the consent of the local interests to undertake the work. Nicaragua and Colombia, it was to be expected, would each be anxious to have the United States build a canal through its territory. "Nicaragua bid eagerly for the privilege." [8] Until about 1900, in fact, the Nicaragua route had been practically the only one widely discussed in the United States,[9] and it still had many advocates. On October 30, 1902, when a hitch in the Colombian negotiations developed, Nicaragua was apparently still anxious to do what she could to secure support of its route. The minister, it is reported, told Secretary Hay that he "was ready to consider any treaty satisfactory to the United States." [10]

Colombia, also, recognized the importance of pushing her case to secure the location in her territory of the canal which for seventy years had been so much desired. She continued to urge somewhat halfheartedly territorial claims to the Central American coast as far north as Cape Gracias a Diós at

---

[8] Roosevelt, Theodore, *Theodore Roosevelt, An Autobiography,* New York, Charles Scribner's Sons, 1921, p. 513.

[9] For efforts made by agents of the French Canal Company to popularize consideration of the Panama route, see Pringle, Henry Fowles, *Theodore Roosevelt, a Biography,* New York, Harcourt, Brace and Co., 1931, pp. 303 *et seq.* The document, United States Congress, "The Story of Panama," *Hearings on the Rainey Resolution before the Committee on Foreign Affairs of the House of Representatives,* Washington, 1913, is the most comprehensive source of information as to the influences surrounding canal development both before and after the Panama revolution. See, on the above points, pp. 70 and 71.

[10] "The Story of Panama," *op. cit.,* p. 189.

the northeastern point of Nicaragua. These claims, if substantiated, would put the canal in her territory whichever route was chosen. But her greatest hopes were for Panama.

Those in charge of the foreign relations of the republic did not fail to see that, while a canal project was now almost certain to be put through, that it would be put through at Panama under conditions satisfactory to Colombia was by no means certain. Nevertheless, the administration did not formulate a plan to which it gave wholehearted support.

A coalition government in Colombia had by a strictly controlled election put in power M. A. Sanclamente, a Nationalist, as President, and J. M. Marroquin, a Conservative, as Vice-President. They became enemies, and early in 1899 a bitter civil war had broken out, in the course of which, on July 31, 1900, the Vice-President seized and imprisoned his aged chief —he was ninety-one years old—at a place some miles out of the capital. Under the Colombian Constitution, the Vice-President acts as chief magistrate in "the temporary absence of the President." This Marroquin proceeded to do until the President died, on March 19, 1902, when by the Constitution Marroquin became President in his own right.[11] By June, 1903, the "revolution" which had torn the country came to an end. It was during the course of these events that the negotiations for a canal treaty were carried on, and the Congress, the first to sit since 1898, which was to pass on its fate was chosen.

It had long been realized that Colombia, as a negotiator, was not in a strong position to meet any demands as to a canal route which the United States might make. In December, 1870, when a canal treaty with the United States had been under discussion, the minister of foreign relations had declared, after conversation with the English diplomatic repre-

---

[11] *For. Rel.*, 1902, p. 292. Discussions of contemporary developments in Colombian politics are found in Robertson, W. S., *History of the Latin-American Nations*, 2nd ed., New York, D. Appleton and Co., 1932, pp. 488–506; Williams, M. W., *The People and Politics of Latin America*, Boston, Ginn and Co., 1930, pp. 506–513; and in Root, Elihu, "The Ethics of the Panama Question," in *The Panama Canal and our Relations with Colombia*, *Sen. Doc. No. 471*, 63rd Congress, 2nd Session, Washington, 1914, pp. 36–53.

sentative, that Colombia should not count on any help from the European maritime powers in opposition to the wishes of the United States. Similar declarations had subsequently been made in articles by prominent Colombians in the local press. Later developments had only emphasized the disparity of the positions of Colombia and the United States.

While the canal question was under discussion in the Congress of the United States, the minister of foreign relations of Colombia sent instructions to his representative in Washington. It was probable, he believed, that the United States would make "extraordinary demands" in the approaching negotiations. The minister at Washington was to keep in close touch by cable with his government both because of the importance of the matters dealt with, on which no promise without previous authorization was to be made, and because thus it might be possible to "quiet the spirit of the inhabitants of the isthmus, [who were] always apprehensive as to what refers to the canal." From the beginning, it thus appears, Colombia was aware that decisions on canal policy might raise embarrassing questions in domestic politics.

Early in 1901, the minister of foreign affairs sought to prepare local public opinion for what might be coming by publishing in the *Anales Diplomáticos de Colombia*[12] an article pointing out the arguments favorable to the Nicaragua route which the technical commission had recently sponsored, the popularity of this route with the American public, and the greater freedom of action which many in the United States felt might be granted by the local governments interested in it. To be sure, construction at Panama necessitated buying out the French company, but the Government had confidence that the president of that company would be able to insure the decision in the favor of Panama, and the Government would loyally co-operate to that end.

Shortly after the publication of the article, the "Spooner Law" was passed, raising the hopes of the advocates of the Panama route. The new minister of foreign relations asked

---

[12] Text quoted in Uribe, *op. cit.*, pp. 55–61.

his predecessor, Antonio José Uribe, best-informed of Colombian men of affairs on canal matters, and certain other leading citizens what they felt should be the course which Colombia should follow in the circumstances.[13] Señor Uribe submitted a detailed memorandum on June 1, 1902, urging that the country should:

1. Treat the canal negotiations as a practical matter, "abandoning the policy dominated by imagination and sentiment which had caused such damage to the republic."

2. Recognize that adoption of the Panama route was of the greatest importance for Colombia itself.

3. Recognize that only by the United States could the canal be built. It had always been interested in the project. Recent developments had accentuated the interest. The new treaty with Great Britain removed former limitations on its freedom of action. Already the Colombian Legation at Washington had sounded out the United States Government as to the demands it would make and the concessions it would give, and other inquiries showed that no European support was to be expected for opposition to the "exorbitant exigencies" on which the United States insisted. The only foreign help to be expected was that found in the neutrality guarantees of the Hay-Pauncefote treaty. Of this there was no doubt and it should be frankly recognized.

4. Bear in mind that, though the Nicaragua canal would cost more, it was favored by American public opinion and by a majority in the Senate, and that a message of the President of Nicaragua had recently announced the signing of a protocol which gave the United States apparently all it asked on that route. The French company had, to advance the case for Panama, now offered to sell its rights for $40,000,000—much less than their cost—and all that remained was for Colombia to arrange with the company to allow transfer of its rights and with the United States as to the conditions under which it should undertake the work. For both of these offices, Colombia should receive compensation. Steps should be taken

---

[13] *Ibid.*, pp. 64–83.

to come to an understanding with the French company, and modifications in the protocol of a treaty with the United States already drawn up emphasizing the sovereignty of Colombia in Panama should be made.

Brief, not free from exaggeration, but showing a keen appreciation of realities had been the reply of Luis M. Isaza, President of the Supreme Court, sent earlier on February 17, 1902. It declared in sum: The United States would construct the canal by one route or the other. World commerce needed the waterway and no power would oppose the American government. If the latter decides for Panama, he declared, "it will not be restrained . . . by opposition which the Colombian government may make." For "that nation neither considerations of foreign sovereignty nor the principles of international law are obstacles when the expansion of its commerce and power are involved. . . . Colombia can not offer resistance and with its acquiescence or without it, the canal will be at Panama, if the Americans wish it so."

> For the rest . . . if the present government of Colombia does not promptly make the concessions which the United States needs, revolution, which as little hesitates before considerations of whatever sort . . . will give it all it wants. The United States will sympathize with the revolution, will aid it, and its triumph with this help will be unquestionable. . . . It is well known that there is strong opinion in Panama in favor of making that territory sovereign and that there is little sympathy with the rest of the country. If, then, the Panamanians persuade themselves . . . that obstacles to the enterprise are being raised by the Colombian government, it will be very difficult to restrain them from separating themselves from the rest of the republic, counting, as they will count, on the support of the United States.[14]

This forecast, it is interesting to note, was made more than a year and a half before the relations between the United States and Colombia came to a crisis.

Though the best-informed leaders realized that national policy might well be directed to securing the best practical terms available under the circumstances, it was far from clear

[14] *Ibid.*, pp. 82–83.

that the Congress, the press, or popular opinion could be brought to accept that standard.

What would be terms acceptable to the United States? In the discussions of a canal treaty which had been going on since early in April, 1901, representatives of the United States had reluctantly consented to consider a money payment to Colombia for the right to dig the canal which it was to undertake at great cost, without prospect of profit, for the use of all nations, and from which Colombia stood greatly to benefit.[15] On May 9, Admiral Walker, President of the Isthmian Canal Commission, presented a draft treaty to the Colombian minister. This was before the Canal Commission had presented its report on November 30, 1901, and before the ratification of the revised Hay-Pauncefote treaty on December 26. There followed a number of interchanges to bring the treaty into line with Colombian demands in the course of which the head of the Colombian Legation, because of political developments in the republic and the stand taken by the minister, was twice changed. On November 29, 1902, negotiations fell into the hands of the Chargé d'Affaires, Tomás Herrán.

Both before and after this occurred, the negotiations involved long-drawn-out controversies on many points, particularly that of the money payments which were to be made. The Colombian representative was careful to refer all major items to his home government for authorization. Its demands were such that the United States many times seemed on the point of terminating the discussions and taking up others with Nicaragua and Costa Rica. A final compromise on money payments was accompanied by an intimation that the terms suggested were all the United States would yield. A treaty was signed on the basis suggested on January 22, 1903, the Colombian representative having received the necessary authority. He did so only after becoming convinced that the

---

[15] Root, Elihu, "The Ethics of the Panama Question," in *The Panama Canal and Our Relations with Colombia, Senate Document No. 471,* 63rd Congress, 2nd Session, Washington, 1914, p. 42.

terms offered were practically an ultimatum which must be accepted unless his government were willing to "abandon all hope that the interoceanic canal [would] . . . be opened through Colombian territory." [16]

By the treaty, Colombia authorized the French company to sell and transfer its property and concessions to the United States. The latter was to have for one hundred years, subject to renewal at its option, the exclusive right to build, exploit, and protect the canal. Colombia conceded, for equal periods, the use of a zone five kilometers wide on each side of the waterway and the right to occupy and use certain islands. The sovereignty over the territory was to remain in Colombia, though the United States was to have extensive police power in the zone and a stipulated control over the terminal ports. Other provisions touched on sanitation, courts, neutrality, and maintenance of order. The United States was to pay to Colombia ten million dollars on the ratification of the treaty and an annuity of $250,000 as long as the convention remained in force.[17]

Action on the treaty by the American Senate was prompt. The day after it was signed, it was submitted to that body by President Roosevelt and after sharp opposition by the minority was ratified on March 17, 1903, by seventy-three votes to five.

The Colombian elections were held shortly before and resulted in the return of many anti-government leaders. It was soon evident that trouble might be expected in securing ratification. On May 11, a Colombian senator in a newspaper article prophesied that the treaty would be unanimously rejected and declared that Herrán deserved hanging for having signed it. The American minister reported that public opinion was strong against the treaty. It would have to receive full support by the Government if it were to pass and even so might fail.[18] But such support it was not to have. In-

[16] "The Story of Panama," *op. cit.*, at p. 315 *et sqq.*, gives the detail of the exchanges. The words quoted are in a letter by Herrán at p. 323.

[17] Text in *Canal Treaties, Senate Document No. 456,* 63rd Congress, 2nd Sess., Washington, 1914, pp. 57–72.

[18] Beaupré to Hay, March 30, 1903, *For. Rel.,* 1903, pp. 133 and 134.

deed, the Government now declared it had "no preconceived wishes for or against the measure" but would leave the decision to Congress. Soon a highly critical press campaign was under way. Shortly before Congress was to convene, the Government informed the representative of the French company that it doubted whether the treaty could be ratified, because the money payment was too small; but if the company would pay $10,000,000, ratification could be secured. Such a proposal would certainly be unacceptable to the United States, which assumed that the authorization to the company to sell and transfer its rights and privileges, spoken of in the treaty, covered that matter finally.

In view of the rising criticism, the United States sent to its minister a cable setting out the position of the United States, the substance of which he reported to the Colombian minister of foreign relations on June 13, 1903. It declared that Colombia apparently did not appreciate the gravity of the situation. Negotiations concerning the canal had been initiated by her, and its construction by the United States had been energetically sought by her for various years. The proposal was finally accepted by the United States, which thus changed its former opinion and decided in favor of the Panama route. "If Colombia should now reject the treaty, or unduly delay its ratification, the friendly understanding between the two countries would be so seriously compromised that action might be taken by the Congress next winter which every friend of Colombia would regret." [19]

The object of the cable was clearly to put pressure on the Government to insure that it would give full support to the treaty, the signature of which it had authorized. What was the import of its closing clauses? Did they refer to the possibility that Congress would feel impelled to shift again to

---

[19] Minister Beaupré reported on October 31 that in Bogotá the people were anxious because of revolutionary activity and reported secession movements in both Panama and Cauca. (*Ibid., For. Rel.,* 1903, pp. 218 and 221.) The feeling in the latter province, the commanding general reported in November, 1903, was such that "the idea about separation is almost unanimous; to crush that opinion not a single batallion could be organized. . . ." Letter quoted in *ibid.,* 1903, p. 317.

favor the Nicaragua route? That to Americans seemed the alternative. To many Colombians it might also hint at the revolution in Panama which it was already forecast might follow defeat of the treaty at Bogotá.[20]

The Congress opened its extraordinary sessions on June 20, 1903. Vice-President José Manuel Marroquin in his message to the legislative bodies favored ratification of the treaty, though he did not make himself its champion. The Government, he said, was confronted by a dilemma. If it accepted the agreement, it would cast a shadow on Colombian sovereignty at Panama and the country would lose the large pecuniary indemnity to which many felt it had a right. Though the "just desires of the inhabitants of [Panama] and those of all Colombians" would be satisfied, the Government would be open to the charge of having failed to defend the national sovereignty and of having sacrificed the interests of the Nation. On the other hand, if the treaty were rejected, the Government would be blamed for losing the canal, "the principal and the condition of our growth." All things considered, "although at the cost of sacrifices, we ought not to put obstacles in the way of so grandiose an enterprise." It would be in itself a great national advantage; and, once opened by the "Americans of the north," Colombia could make closer and broader its relations with the United States, to its incalculable advantage.[21]

The minister of foreign relations was more outspoken. The needs of world commerce and recent political developments made the prompt construction of the canal indispensable. The United States was the only nation actively interested in construction. Negotiations had been undertaken by the United States with Nicaragua and Costa Rica. Opinions in

---

[20] An influential Colombian informed the American minister at Bogotá early in May, 1903, that acceptance of the treaty might prove the only means of preventing secession of the departments of Cauca, Panama, and Bolivar "to constitute of their territories an independent republic." Beaupré to Hay, May 7, 1903, *ibid.*, 1903, pp. 143–144. How serious these threats of revolt really were and the degree to which they were caused by sympathy with Panama on the one hand or local feeling against the Marroquin government on the other are not clear.

[21] *Ibid.*, 1903, pp. 154 and 158–163; Spanish excerpt in Uribe, *op. cit.*, p. 93.

the Congress of the United States favored that route, as did the public, but a special mission to Washington had turned attention to Panama. A treaty which would bring the canal into Colombian territory had now been made. It was presented for ratification in the conviction that it involved the "gravest question . . . for the present and the future of the Republic." [22]

With the debate under way, the American minister again reported on the prospects. Opposition to the treaty, he thought, would be tenacious; but the Government had a "full and ample majority" in each house and it seemed that it could put the measure through.[23]

Technical objections were raised in the debate. It was proposed to return the text to the Vice-President because he had not given it his formal approval by his signature, which was said to be demanded by Colombian customary law. The treaty was no treaty; its title itself declared that it was only a convention. The Government then came to the defense of the form of the proposal through its Cabinet ministers. The members of Congress from Panama arrived early in July and declared that that state would revolt if the treaty were not ratified.[24] Nevertheless, up to July 10, three weeks after the opening of the sessions, the time was taken up by what the minister of public instruction characterized as debates on "questions of mere form," "heated and sterile discussions," giving substance to the belief often voiced in Europe that the people of the Hispanic republics confuse all questions by exaggerated formalism. "When it is known," he declared, "and it already is known in the United States and in Europe that we have employed this debate, so long and warmly sustained, on a question of mere form which over there they cannot understand, will they not say that we are a country not of legists but of shysters?" [25]

---

[22] Text in Uribe, *op. cit.*, pp. 94–95.
[23] Beaupré to Hay, June 20, 1903, *For. Rel.*, 1903, pp. 154 and 155.
[24] Beaupré to Hay, July 5, 1903, *ibid.*, 1903, p. 158.
[25] "Rábulas," speech of the Minister of Public Instruction, July 10, 1903; text in Uribe, *op. cit.*, pp. 95–103, at page 103.

When the substance of the treaty was finally reached various proposals for amendment were offered, chief of them being that the French canal company be asked to make a payment for the privilege of transferring its rights to the United States. Another suggested increasing the payment by the United States to $15,000,000. On July 31, 1903, the United States sought to make it clear that the treaty could not be made to include arrangements of this sort and that any modification would necessitate new action by the United States Senate. It telegraphed its minister:

> Instructions heretofore sent to you show the great danger of amending the treaty. This government has no right or competence to covenant with Colombia to impose new financial obligation upon canal company and the President would not submit to our Senate any amendment in that sense, but would treat it as voiding the negotiation. . . . No additional payment by the United States can hope for approval by United States Senate, while any amendment whatever requiring reconsideration by that body would most certainly imperil its consummation.[26]

This brusque statement was one of fact. Like its predecessor, it was clearly intended to put pressure on Colombia; but that the United States should be drawn into a position in which it would be party to an agreement to force the French company to pay money to Colombia for a privilege already conceded it was felt could not be permitted. That running the gantlet of the Senate a second time would endanger the whole treaty was commonplace to all who were familiar with the fate of treaties in that body.

Whatever the intent of the instructions of July 31, the end sought was not accomplished. On August 4, 1903, the committee to which the treaty had been referred reported it with various amendments. The next day, the minister of the United States sent to the Colombian Ministry of Foreign Affairs a copy of the memorandum of July 31, with supporting commentaries. The United States, he declared, was justified in thinking of "any modification whatever of the terms of the treaty as practically a breach of faith . . . such as may in-

---

[26] Hay to Beaupré, July 31, 1903, *For. Rel.*, 1903, p. 168.

volve the very gravest complications in the friendly relations which have hitherto existed between the two countries." If, he said, "Colombia really desires to maintain the present friendly relations . . . and . . . secure to herself the extraordinary advantages that the construction of the canal in her territory will undoubtedly produce, if backed by so close an alliance of national interests as would supervene with the United States, the pending treaty should be ratified exactly in its present form, without any modifications whatever." [27]

This veiled "demand," Colombians felt, was pressure that came little short of an open threat. Its words were equivocal. From the point of view of the United States, the statements can be interpreted as merely factual, even though they were harsh. The most extreme statement of the repeated instructions of July 31 was, "No additional payment by the United States could receive the approval of the Senate of the United States." In view of the President's control over treaties, this was literally true if the President refused to accept the modification.

The glosses added by the minister in the memorandum of August 5 are less easily defendable. Failure of the treaty through amendment might, it is true, cause ill feeling; but amendment, however inadvisable, was nevertheless clearly the right of Colombia if she cared to exercise it. Exercise of the right to make changes in such situations, indeed, as the Colombian minister of foreign relations promptly pointed out, was in accord with accepted practice in Colombia and in the United States itself. In neither country was such action considered of itself as "practically a breach of faith." [28]

There is no doubt that the American notes aroused a feeling of resentment in Colombia and stiffened the opposition. They were considered an attack on "the sovereignty, dignity and independence of the Republic" and "a formal order . . . to ratify the treaty."

---

[27] Beaupré to Rico, Notes of August 5, 1903, *For. Rel.*, pp. 175–177.

[28] When Beaupré's notes were read in the Colombian Senate, they were "received," he reported, "with loud murmurs of disapproval by the densely packed gallery." (*Ibid.*, p. 182.)

Exactly a week after the sending of the note cited, on August 12, the Colombian Senate voted unanimously against the treaty. Only one senator, Obaldia, who before the session was over was appointed Governor of Panama by the President, had spoken strongly in its favor. He was known to favor revolution if the treaty failed. But, though Colombia clearly did not intend the vote of August 12, 1903, to be a definitive negative to further discussion,[29] events which quickly followed determined that, so far as serious negotiations for a canal under Colombian sovereignty were concerned, an end had been reached.

The American minister asked what the attitude of his government as to the treaty would now be. On August 29 he was informed that the President would be bound by the "Spooner Law." He would wait a "reasonable time" and, if no treaty had been made, "carry into effect the alternative of the statute."

The same day, the Colombian minister of foreign affairs made the same inquiry to his representative in Washington, and Herrán answered that rejection of the treaty had made a bad impression, and a reaction in favor of the treaty was hoped for before September 22; otherwise, probably President Roosevelt would become hostile. Asked what form the hostility would take, Herrán cabled on September 10, "Hostile attitude will consist in favoring indirectly a revolution in Panama,"[30] and in a letter following he made special reference "to the promptness with which the independence of our department of Panama will be recognized." Two days be-

---

[29] Beaupré to Hay, Aug. 15, 1903, *ibid.*, 1903, pp. 180–181. "When action was taken on the 12th instant no one in authority believed that it was final." The day of the defeat of the treaty, General Reyes told the American minister that a prompt reaction in public opinion was expected. He asked that Secretary Hay "before taking other action" should "give two weeks more for the consummation of" a plan to bring up the treaty again before the Senate, where he felt it would be passed "without amendments." To this inquiry the State Department replied that the President would not bind himself, but that it was improbable that any definite action would be taken in two weeks. None was taken, but the change in public opinion did not occur.

[30] Text of the Colombian correspondence is in "The Story of Panama," *op. cit.*, p. 361.

fore, on September 8, 1903, the Colombian administration, still hopeful, sent its minister a cable proposing renewal of negotiations "on bases which it judged acceptable by the congress of the following August."

From these actions it is evident that the door would still have been open to adjustment if Colombia had yielded, although, as is shown below, the Washington administration was already considering alternatives other than those in the "Spooner Law." That such might be the case, indeed, Colombia had learned through its minister; but its administration continued to believe, or appeared to believe, that the case was not one of extreme urgency. The Congress still remained in session after the vote against the treaty, but no definite action developed. The senators from some of the provinces began to go home.

There was then drafted a project of law authorizing the executive to negotiate again for construction of a canal. The committee to which it was referred discussed new negotiations in which should be demanded money payments starting at $20,000,000 and other provisions more restrictive than those of the Hay-Herrán treaty. It reported on October 14, 1903. It suggested that a year's delay in action might find the Government in complete possession of the properties and rights of the French company if the extension of its franchise, the legality of which could be disputed, were found invalid.[31] The canal project was brought up for debate on October 27; but then and in the remaining days of the session no real progress was made, and the Congress adjourned October 31. The next day, the Government again declared it would undertake new canal treaty negotiations.

The newspaper campaigns meanwhile became more virulent, reflecting the discussions in the Congress, and early in September observers reported a wave of nationalistic feeling. The United States had tried to coerce Colombia, which had known how to defend its honor. The treaty should not pass without greater money payment and other modifica-

---

[31] Text of the Report of the Committee, October 14, 1903, is in *For. Rel.*, 1903, pp. 210–213.

tions.[32] Opinions differed as to whether the canal project was unpopular or whether it was being used as a means of opposing a government which itself was increasingly out of favor and which was now anxious to escape responsibility for the proposal which it had submitted.

The real centers of interest had by this time shifted from Bogotá to Panama and Washington and involved possibilities not faced in the routine of diplomatic exchanges. In Panama all interests centered in the canal. Such public opinion as existed among the inhabitants tended to support any means which would bring to completion the work begun by the French. Choice of the Nicaragua route would be disastrous to the province. Defeat of the treaty meant betrayal of its interests.[33] The new Panama Canal Company, whatever its difficulties, was still the greatest economic factor in the region, and its only chance of recovering part of its investment was the sale of its properties to the United States. Under these conditions it was to be expected that it would support the treaty or any other project which would make the sale possible.

What, meanwhile, was coming to be the temper of the administration in Washington and that of the American public? When the chance that the treaty would be ratified declined, President Roosevelt had sent the warnings to Colombia above

[32] Beaupré to Hay, Sept. 5, 1903, *ibid.*, 1903, p. 191.

[33] How widespread the revolutionary movement was at any time has been disputed. In the areas along the proposed route of the canal, which would be directly affected by its creation, it seems fair to assume that there was real concern in its fortunes even among those usually but little interested in public affairs. In the back country, the project doubtless had little attention. President Roosevelt asserted later that independence was declared "by the unanimous action" of the people. James T. Du Bois, later American minister at Bogotá, believed it the work of half a dozen people who would directly profit from it and that not one of the population in a hundred had an idea of what was happening till the revolution occurred. Luis Carlos Rico, minister of foreign relations, in his memorandum of April 12, 1904, speaks of press notices of imminent revolution which Colombia felt safe in disregarding because it relied on the United States to put down disorder as it had done previously under the treaty of 1846. After the revolution, he says, the populace accepted it because certain of their leaders thought it unavoidable. Text in Uribe, *op. cit.*; see especially pp. 152 and 153. See also "The Story of Panama," *op. cit.*, p. 463.

outlined. In August he was already planning what to do if the treaty failed. If Panama remained quiet, there would be, the President felt, two courses open: "either we should drop the Panama Canal project and immediately begin work on the Nicaraguan Canal, or else we should purchase all the rights of the French company and, without further parley with Colombia, enter upon the completion of the canal. . . ." He was ready to recommend the latter course to Congress; but, if it failed to be approved there, he would proceed at Nicaragua.[34] But Panama did not remain quiet.

In the United States, outside the inner circle of the administration, in both official and unofficial groups what should be done to forward the canal project claimed wide attention both before and after the rejection of the treaty. The Nicaragua route had lost in popularity to that at Panama, and it was evident that the administration would act under the alternative outlined in the "Spooner Law" only if circumstances forced it to do so. That extraordinary steps might be taken to secure the canal at Panama was no secret. The Colombian representative had reported to his government as early as December 18, 1902, a movement headed by Senator Shelby M. Cullom in favor of seizing territory at Panama and making an agreement for the canal property directly with the French company if Colombia did not accept the treaty. The minister felt that, in view of the "impetuous and vehement" character of President Roosevelt, it was "to be feared that the proposal of Senator Cullom might not be repugnant to him." [35]

Two days after this dispatch had been sent, Senator Morgan, of Alabama, stanch defender of the Nicaragua route, had moved that, since no treaty had been made with Colombia,

---

[34] The undated draft of this message to Congress is in Roosevelt, Theodore, *Theodore Roosevelt, An Autobiography,* New York, Charles Scribner's Sons, 1921, pp. 530–531. This draft is interesting both for what it states and for what it does not state. Apparently, the President was himself willing to adopt high-handed measures if Congress approved of them, but felt himself bound by the "Spooner Law." The draft does not indicate, as has often been intimated, that he was ready to proceed against Colombia without express authority from Congress.

[35] Text in Uribe, *op. cit.,* p. 116, and "The Story of Panama," *op. cit.,* p. 317.

negotiations with her should be discontinued and steps should be taken under the alternative presented by the Spooner law;[36] but the Panama route continued the general favorite.

As the months passed, a wide variety of proposals reflecting the impatience of public opinion were discussed in the press. One of the more extreme of these appeared on June 14, 1903, in the *New York World* under date of the previous day—thus, a week before the opening session of the Colombian Congress. It was evidently written by someone close to developments in both Panama and the United States and outlined in precise detail the course which events actually took in the five months following.

It declared that the President was determined that the canal should be built at Panama and had no intention of taking up negotiations with Nicaragua. But there was, apparently, strong opposition to the treaty at Bogotá, where it would probably be defeated because national enthusiasm about sovereignty had been aroused to a high pitch. The writer's information, he says, is that Panama "stands ready to secede" and "enter into a canal treaty with the United States." It was known that a plan providing that Panama should secede if the treaty failed had been suggested to representatives of the administration. A republic could be organized easily, since there were not more than 100 Colombian soldiers in Panama. The new state would make a treaty with the United States giving it the equivalent of absolute sovereignty over the canal zone, and the agreement would involve no increase in money payments over those stipulated in the Hay-Herrán treaty. The President would recognize the new state promptly and at once appoint a minister. Data for the treaty were all ready. Roosevelt was "said to strongly favor this plan if the treaty is rejected." The Cabinet was known to favor the proposal if it became necessary to act on it, and leading Senators had encouraged the President concerning it. If nothing was done by Colombia within a reasonable time, the plan would be put into operation.[37]

---

[36] *Ibid.*, pp. 317–319.
[37] *Ibid.*, p. 345.

A large part of the statements in this article, it seems clear, must have been shrewd political prophecy rather than fact at the time of its publication; but, between its appearance and the early days of November, events were remarkably to follow its outline and cause the disappearance of Colombia from direct connection with the canal.

Most active *provocateurs* of a revolution at Panama in the United States were the representatives of the French company, William Nelson Cromwell, its counsel, and Philippe Bunau-Varilla, its engineer. Whether Cromwell or Bunau-Varilla was the moving spirit back of the revolution has been disputed. Cromwell claimed to have been the more active in official circles in Washington, in early agreements with the Panamanian conspirators, and in stimulating the American press campaign,[38] but he later withdrew all support of a revolution or at least became more circumspect in his support, apparently as the result of a letter from Herrán warning that aid given to a revolution might be made a reason for forfeiting the rights and properties of the French company.[39] During the active planning of the revolt, Cromwell was absent from the United States.

In visualizing the possibilities of a revolution and how it might be used, and in dealings with the revolutionists in the period just preceding the outbreak, Bunau-Varilla, it seems clear, played the major part.[40] He had long been active as an engineer and promoter of the Panama enterprise but, after operations were reduced to a low level, had been living in

---

[38] See Uribe, *op. cit.*, p. 117, and "The Story of Panama," *op. cit.*, pp. 6–8 and 344–361, for Cromwell's activities in Washington and his alleged connections with conspirators in Panama. The greater part of "The Story of Panama" is based on material collected by Cromwell in the support of a claim for $800,000 he later urged against the French company.

[39] "The Story of Panama," *op. cit.*, p. 362.

[40] In Philippe Bunau-Varilla's *Panama; The Creation, Destruction, and Resurrection,* New York, Robert M. McBride and Co., 1914, and in his *The Great Adventure of Panama,* New York, Doubleday, Page and Co., 1920, this author gives a history of the Panama Canal enterprise and of his connection with it and the revolution. The steps taken, as outlined in the paragraphs which follow, are as reported in these volumes and in "The Story of Panama," *op. cit., passim.* See also a long statement by Bunau-Varilla published in "The Story of Panama," *op. cit.*, pp. 10–44.

Paris. From 1900 on he had sought by his writings and by speeches in the United States to turn American preference to the Panama route. Through his influence, the French company was induced to make its offer to sell its properties to the United States for $40,000,000.

When Colombia hesitated to sign a treaty along the lines of the later Hay-Herrán agreement, he had cabled President Marroquin on November 23, 1902, warning him that an intransigent policy might cause the canal to be made "against Colombia instead of being made with her, amicably,"[41] and he later urged that the money payment by the United States be limited to the amounts finally stipulated in the treaty.

When the agreement was about to be debated by the Colombian Congress, Bunau-Varilla was disturbed by the highly nationalist opposition which was developing, and, wishing to strengthen Marroquin's stand, cabled him his belief that failure to ratify the treaty meant either adoption of the Nicaragua route or "construction of Panama Canal after secession and declaration of independence of the Isthmus of Panama under protection of the United States. . . ."[42]

This was a prophecy made long before it was clear that the treaty would be defeated and a veiled forecast of future activities by representatives of the French company. But it did not check the rise of the opposition in Bogotá. Bunau-Varilla himself became increasingly active as Colombian resistance crystallized. On August 17, 1903, he telegraphed the leader of the opposition insisting that "terrible and immediate consequences" would follow rejection of the treaty.

But he did not wait for the adjournment of the Congress before starting to prepare the "terrible and immediate consequences." On September 2 he published in *Le Matin,* of Paris, where the main offices of the French company were located, an article intimating that President Roosevelt, to whom he sent a copy, was now confronted by the alternative

---

[41] Speaking of this message, Bunau-Varilla later wrote, "If the conception of the Panama revolution can be found anywhere, it is in this telegram sent one year minus 20 days before it burst out." *Ibid.,* p. 41.

[42] Telegram of June 13, 1903.

of waiting till Panama revolted and then making a treaty with the new state or forcing Colombia to give over control of the territory necessary for the canal.[43] Shortly after, Bunau-Varilla sailed for New York, where he arrived on September 22. There he found that Amador-Guerrero, one of the Panamanian leaders, was already on the ground but in despair because he could not raise the $6,000,000 which his friends declared essential for a revolution.[44] This amount the Frenchman regarded as fantastic, but the plot for revolution he could use. He at first hoped that Roosevelt might coerce Colombia, but dismissed the idea in favor of encouraging a revolution on which, he learned by indirect inquiries, the President was not disposed to frown. For some time he was unable to get into touch with Washington officials, but finally he met the Assistant Secretary of State and the President. They were both noncommittal, but when he left the President's office on October 9, 1903, Bunau-Varilla thought he was "finally in possession of all the elements necessary for action."

The "revolution," he now felt, should be confined to a small area in Panama—the canal zone. Such a revolt could be financed on $100,000, which, if needed, he would advance from his own funds. If it could be sprung before fresh Colombian troops arrived, no real opposition was to be expected, for the garrison was disaffected. Once the revolution was a fact, the United States would be forced to prevent fighting to keep

---

[43] Uribe, *op. cit.*, p. 119. Senator Henry Cabot Lodge wrote Roosevelt from Paris, September 13, 1903, "I do hope we shall not go to Nicaragua. . . . I am in strong hopes that either under the treaty of 1846 or by the secession of the Province of Panama we can get control of what is undoubtedly the best route." *Selections from the Correspondence of Theodore Roosevelt and Henry Cabot Ladge, 1884–1918,* New York, Charles Scribner's Sons, 1925, Vol. II, p. 54. Roosevelt himself, it seems clear, was entertaining similar "hopes." He wrote to Albert Shaw, editor of the *Review of Reviews,* on October 10, 1903, that he would be "delighted if Panama were an independent state or if it made itself so at this moment."

[44] Uribe, *op. cit.*, p. 119, says that an employee of the Panama Railway had already made a trip to New York and had been promised by William Nelson Cromwell funds and military assistance. Bunau-Varilla says that such assurances had been given by an unnamed person, but that after Amador-Guerrero's arrival they had been withdrawn. See "The Story of Panama," *op. cit., passim,* for the early moves in the conspiracy.

traffic open. But the revolution must occur before Bunau-Varilla would advance funds. Amador was with difficulty brought to assent to a plan of this sort. Bunau-Varilla next contrived a meeting with Secretary Hay, who, like his colleagues, was silent as to American plans, although his visitor became convinced that a revolution was expected and that military precautions had been taken.

Amador now went back to Panama on October 20, with a declaration of independence and other documents and instructions which Bunau-Varilla had prepared, including one for appointment of himself as diplomatic agent of the state still to be created. Bunau-Varilla would have $100,000 ready for use after the revolution and assured the Panamanian that United States forces would police the new republic forty-eight hours after its creation. Amador would reach Panama on October 27—before the adjournment of the Congress at Bogotá, as it developed—and the revolution was to occur not later than November 3.

The French engineer now went in search of funds, which on October 22 he secured in two lots of $50,000 each on loan from two European banks on his own credit.[45] By cable the amount was transferred to Heidelbach, Ickelheimer and Company, of New York.

Arrived at Colon, Amador lost courage, as did his associates. They expected him to return with promise of help by the United States; instead they had only an assurance by Bunau-Varilla. They cabled him on the 29th in code, "Colombian troops arriving Atlantic five days more than 200 urge steamer Colon."

The Colombian troops, Bunau-Varilla felt, were imaginary; but evidently the conspirators wanted proof that American aid was coming. He found that the *Nashville* had been sent somewhere, jumped to the conclusion that Colon was its destination, and cabled his associates that within two days a vessel would arrive. This cable he was able to support by others in the days following based on the press reports of

---

[45] *Ibid.*, pp. 38–39.

the movements of American war vessels. Looking back on the measures taken, Mr. Bunau-Varilla later declared, "I built all this subtle diplomatic structure as a bridge is built: that is, by calculating its various elements, and not by trying to obtain direct information, which it would have been impossible to obtain." [46]

That a revolt was shortly to be expected had now become common knowledge. Colombia had already taken steps to have forces on the ground, but their actual sailing for Panama had been delayed, though on the night of November 2 they were on their way to Colon.

The United States also had taken precautions against an outbreak which might find it unprepared to act promptly in any emergency that might arise on either coast. On November 2, officials of the United States Navy telegraphed to the officer in charge of its forces of five vessels at Acapulco, Mexico, and San Juan del Sur, Nicaragua, to proceed "with all possible dispatch to Panama." His instructions were to "maintain free and uninterrupted transit. If interruption is threatened by armed force occupy the line of railroad. Prevent landing of any armed force, either government or insurgent, within fifty miles of Panama. . . . Government force reported approaching the Isthmus. . . . Prevent their landing if in your judgment landing would precipitate a conflict."

The *Nashville* had already been ordered to Colon, as were other vessels later. It arrived at 5:30 on the afternoon of November 2. All was quiet. Talk of an independence proclamation was current, but no action had been taken. During the night, the Colombian gunboat *Cartagena* arrived with between 400 and 500 troops for the garrison at Panama. No instructions as to landing of Colombian troops having been received by the commander of the *Nashville,* he allowed them to disembark at 8:30. Two hours later, he received a cable instructing him to make every effort to prevent Colombian

---

[46] Bunau-Varilla, *The Great Adventure of Panama,* New York, Doubleday, Page and Co., 1920, p. 240. The naval movements reported were, in fact, not the first showing intent to have forces at Panama. The first orders for ships to go to the region of the isthmus were given on October 16.

troops from proceeding from Colon to Panama and to keep open transit and order. The Colombian officers crossed to Panama to make arrangements for their troops there. Late in the day, steps were taken to insure that the troops of neither party should be transported by the railroad, when it was learned that at Panama revolutionists had seized the Colombian officers who had gone over.

At last the distrustful conspirators had summoned courage to make the break. The "revolution" was started—indeed, it was also almost over, for it was a momentary affair without bloodshed by either party.[47] But for the moment let us continue to follow developments at Colon.

The next morning—the fourth of November—the revolution in Panama became known in Colon. Representatives of the new government sought to induce Colonel Torres, who had been left in charge of the Colombian troops, to re-embark his forces and return them to Cartagena on the boat on which they had come. He refused and through the prefect of Colon informed the American officials that, if the officers who had been arrested at Panama were not freed by two o'clock that afternoon, he would "open fire on the town of Colon and kill every American citizen in the place." [48]

The commander of the *Nashville* thereupon landed 42 men and occupied a stone shed of the Panama railroad, into which the men among the United States citizens of the town were summoned while the women and children were put on boats in the harbor. The Colombian troops surrounded the building, apparently intending to provoke an attack. Meanwhile the *Cartagena,* on which they had come, had left the port, to the disgust of the Colombian officials.

---

[47] Promptly after it was over, on November 9, 1903, the United States House of Representatives requested the President to submit to it "all correspondence and other official documents'" relating to the uprising, and the request was complied with by the various departments. A few dispatches not then submitted are found in "The Story of Panama," *op. cit.* For the American dispatches, see Richardson, *op. cit.,* Vol. X, pp. 565–589, 636–675, 678–709. Uribe, *op. cit., passim,* quotes the Colombian documents. On these statements and those concerning the Colombian movements later issued, the following paragraphs are based.

[48] "The Story of Panama," *op. cit.,* p. 442.

Later Colonel Torres asked for a train to be sent to Panama so that the ranking Colombian officer held there might be asked to direct discontinuance of the show of force. The train was provided. Next the Colombians suggested that they would retire outside the town if the Americans re-embarked.

The following day, November 5, the Colombians had not retired to the point decided upon and the Colombian general at Panama had declined to give orders to Colonel Torres. Colombian troops reoccupied Colon and American forces were again landed. The American officer had declared to Colonel Torres that he had no interest in the affairs of either party, but that troops of neither party should be transported on the railroad. He would, however, protect threatened lives and property of American citizens. During the afternoon of November 5, representatives of the new government persuaded Colonel Torres to embark his troops on the *Orinoco,* a British steamer, and, to the number of 474, they sailed for Cartagena at 7:35 P.M.[49] In this arrangement the representatives of the United States had no part. So far as operations on the Atlantic side were concerned, the revolution was over, though

---

[49] The arguments used by the revolutionary agents to induce Colonel Torres to re-embark his troops are apparently not a matter of record. It seems that the action was taken without authority from his commanding officer, General Tobar. The latter declared in a report he made to the Minister of War on November 20, 1903, that Amador Guerrero visited him in prison on November 8, that the revolution, Amador Guerrero had assured him, had been the result of "a well matured plan, largely discussed in Panama and Washington and executed under the protection and guarantee of the government of the United States, with which he himself had come to an understanding and from which he had received two and a half million dollars for the first expenses of the new Republic, that there were already several American ships in Colon to protect the revolutionary movement; therefore any resistance was useless, and the said general ought, in a spirit of humanity, to order that (the troops) re-embark." Amador Guerrero later denied Tobar's statement. (Uribe, *op. cit.* p. 151.)

Such arguments may have been used by the revolutionists. The correctness of the statements is another matter. That arguments of this sort were used in the above case seems extraordinary, since the troops in question sailed for Cartagena three days before the interview.

"The Story of Panama," *op. cit.,* at p. 456, narrates that Torres finally took a bribe of $8,000 to leave, the money being promised by the revolutionary junta and paid by the Colon manager of the Panama railroad. The volume contains the available evidence on money payments to various groups in the revolution.

on November 9 the Americans prevented the landing of a body of revolutionists at Colon.

The "revolution" on the Pacific coast, at Panama City, also was a summary affair. It was planned for eight in the evening of November 3, 1903; but everything was ready at six, and at that time it occurred. Shortly before, the Colombian general, who continued loyal, sensed the complot and rushed to the barracks to stop it. Arrived there, he was arrested, as were the Colombian officers who had come over from Colon. General Huertas, the "universally beloved," second in the local Colombian command, had gone over to the revolution, as had all his troops.

The *Bogotá*, a Colombian warship at Panama, at 8 P.M. sent a message that it would bombard the town if the captive officers were not released, and two hours later did fire several shells, which were answered from the fort. One of the shells killed a Chinese in his house. This was the only casualty of the revolution.[50] The *Bogoá* then steamed away. The next afternoon the other Colombian gunboat, which had remained in the harbor, went over to the revolution. On the afternoon of the fourth, also, independence was proclaimed at Panama under an executive board of three.[51] On the fifth, with a British man-of-war, the *Amphion*, temporarily protecting American interests, the United States Navy Department ordered the American forces on the Pacific, then on the way to the scene, to prevent recurrence of naval bombardment; but none, as it proved, was attempted. On the sixth it was reported that all was quiet, that there was no soldier of Colombia known to be on Panamanian soil, and that the Republic of Panama had been proclaimed at Colon at 10 o'clock in the morning by the local governor. Bunau-Varilla was appointed minister to Washington on the same day.

The promptness with which the "revolution" arose and

---

[50] This is as reported in the American official despatches. The *Star and Herald* [Panama], on November 5, 1903, reported the deaths of two Chinese. (*For. Rel.*, 1903, pp. 256–257.)

[51] *Ibid.*, pp. 252–259. These documents include the Panamanian Declaration of Independence.

came to an end was almost equalled by that with which relations with the United States Government were cemented. Bunau-Varilla on the seventh notified the Secretary of State at Washington of his appointment, presented his credentials to the President on the thirteenth, and signed with Secretary Hay the treaty which guarantees the independence of Panama on the eighteenth.[52]

Abrupt as these steps were, recognition of the new state by foreign powers followed promptly. France led the way on November 16. Before the end of the year, she had been joined by all the states of western Europe except the Netherlands, Spain, and Portugal. Russia, Japan, and China had followed the lead, as had also Nicaragua, Peru, Cuba, and Costa Rica.

---

[52] Text in Malloy, *op. cit.*, Vol. II, pp. 1349–1357.

CHAPTER XIII

Colombia and the Apology Controversy

ONCE the revolution was a fact, Colombia promptly sought to find means to recoup the position which she had formerly held. Herrán, the Colombian representative at Washington, was informed on November 6 by the Department of State, through a copy of a telegram sent to the American minister at Bogotá, that the United States had "entered into relations" with Panama and that the United States recommended that Colombia and Panama settle all questions between them peaceably and amicably.[1] Herrán at once protested, as did shortly after the minister of foreign relations in three notes to the American minister.

As soon as the news of the recognition of Panama reached Bogotá, a session of the Council of Ministers was called. It considered declaring war on the United States for its alleged complicity in the revolution, as popular opinion demanded. The diplomatic corps presented itself in a body to counsel against such action, and the Government decided to rely on diplomacy.

On the sixth and seventh of November, General Rafael Reyes, who was influential with the chief of state but not informed of the rapidity with which the revolution had come to an end, proposed to the American minister that, if the United States would meanwhile maintain Colombian sovereignty, Colombia would "declare martial law, and by virtue of vested constitutional authority, when public order is dis-

---

[1] Texts in Richardson, James D., *A Compilation of the Messages of the Presidents, 1789–1907,* Washington, Bureau of National Literature and Art, 1897–1907, Vol. X, pp. 576 and 579.

turbed, [would] approve by decree the ratification of the canal treaty as signed; or, if the Government of the United States [preferred, would] call extra session of Congress with new and friendly members next May to approve the treaty." He would leave promptly for Panama with full powers and had already telegraphed the isthmian chiefs, but wished assurance that the American commander would co-operate to arrange peace and the approval of the canal treaty.[2]

Confirmation of this proposal, however, the minister of foreign affairs refused to give. He confined his inquiries to whether Colombia would be allowed to send troops to fight at the ports and on the railway line, and whether "in accordance with Article 35 [of the] treaty of 1846" the United States would maintain Colombian sovereignty if Colombia proved "entirely unable to suppress the secession movement." To these inquiries Secretary Hay replied that instructions had been sent to the consul-general at Panama "to secure for General Reyes a courteous reception and considerate hearing," but that landing of troops was not desirable since it would disturb the peace and interfere with "the free transit which we [were] pledged to protect." [3] Reyes promptly went to Panama, but could get no satisfaction from the local officials. Thence he went to Washington, hoping to be more fortunate with the Panamanian officers there—but again to no purpose.[4]

In spite of these discouragements, Colombia still hoped that an adjustment saving her sovereignty on the isthmus could be made. General Reyes next presented himself under an appointment on special mission to Washington. He assured the Washington Government that Colombia was ready to reopen the interrupted negotiations. On December 8 and several times thereafter he raised the question as to the attitude of the United States in case Colombian troops attempted reconquest. The responses were unsatisfactory. Panama had been recognized by many governments, and the United States had made with the new state a treaty which, though unratified,

---

[2] *For. Rel.*, 1903, pp. 225–226.
[3] Texts in Richardson, *op. cit.*, Vol. X, pp. 577–579.
[4] See dispatches in "The Story of Panama," *op. cit.*, p. 486.

bound it to maintain its independence. An invasion would cause bloodshed and disorder, and, in the opinion of the President, the time had come to close the chapter of civil war in Panama.[5]

On December 23, 1903, General Reyes filed with the Secretary of State a detailed memorial of grievances proposing arbitration of claims before the Hague Court. Secretary Hay replied that the Panama affair was one of accomplished facts, the Republic was a member of the family of nations, and the questions involved were political and thus not such as even the most advanced nations considered arbitrable.[6]

Renewed attempts to open the question of Colombian recovery of Panama by force also brought disappointment. The American officials replied that an invasion of Panama would create a "painful impression" in the United States. What the position of the United States would be if one were undertaken would depend on circumstances. Evidently, military moves did not promise a solution, and they ceased to be proposed. Arbitration or direct settlement would have to be relied upon. As a basis for future claims, on April 12, 1904, the Minister of Foreign Relations Luis Carlos Rico addressed to the Chargé d'Affaires ad interim a long note setting out historically the Colombian case. This for the time closed the discussions.[7]

The actions of the United States and Colombia immediately preceding and following the Panama revolution formed the basis of a long-drawn-out controversy. They became the most discussed issue in Latin-American relations and continue to be the cause of sharp differences of opinion both within the United States and elsewhere.

That both governments were aware of the impending revolt

---

[5] Texts in Richardson, *op. cit.*, Vol. X, pp. 704–707, and see dispatches in "The Story of Panama," *op. cit.*, p. 486.

[6] Uribe, *op. cit.*, p. 127, and *For. Rel.*, 1903, pp. 284–314.

[7] Spanish text in Uribe, *op. cit.*, pp. 133–166; English text in *For. Rel.*, 1904, pp. 206–224. A detailed correspondence, which did little more than go over the arguments already stated, followed a demand for arbitration by the Colombian minister on October 21, 1905. See *For. Rel.*, 1906, Part I, pp. 412–419 and 421–434.

for a fairly long period before it occurred is clear. In Colombia there had been received the warnings of Bunau-Varilla and Herrán. The newspapers had discussed local disaffection. The senator from Panama, Obaldia, had made it clear in the Colombian Congress that a revolution might come and that he would be in sympathy with such a move if the Hay-Herrán treaty were defeated. Before the end of the sessions, he had been appointed governor of the province. Troops were started toward Panama, but only at a late date and their movement once started was delayed, but that a revolution was brewing was assuredly no secret.

In the United States, the coming revolution in Panama had been discussed for months. In June, 1903, the press had given a detailed forecast as to what would occur. By August, newspapers began to report rising dissatisfaction almost daily. The moves of representatives of the canal company encouraging the revolt were given in detail. The attitude of the local governor, the disaffection of the Government troops, the Colombian plans to send loyal forces, and the smuggling of large quantities of arms into Panama had become common knowledge.

The United States Government had at the beginning of the negotiations shown willingness to meet what were considered reasonable demands of Colombia. The demands, however, became more exigent as negotiations proceeded, and, especially after the signing of the treaty, there were indications that the American administration recognized the strong position in which it stood to put pressure on the other party to the agreement. The President's preference for the Panama route, the rise of public opinion supporting it, the reactions in the United States to proposals for modification of the treaty which were made in the Colombian Congress, and the reports from Panama all contributed to stiffen the American attitude as time passed. According to his own statement, President Roosevelt was willing to propose extraordinary measures to Congress if Colombia did not yield, but events rendered these unnecessary. As he later said, through the revolution, Bunau-Varilla was able to present Panama on a silver platter.

It is clear that the military measures taken by the United States created a condition which made the presentation easier. On the other hand, assertions, frequently made after the revolt, that the United States Government encouraged and supported the conspirators in their plans lack substantiation.

There has never been offered evidence proving untrue the assertion of President Roosevelt on January 4, 1904, "that no one connected with this government [the United States] had any part in preparing, inciting, or encouraging the late revolution on the Isthmus of Panama, and that save from the reports of our military and naval officers . . . no one connected with this government had any previous knowledge of the revolution except such as was accessible to any person of ordinary intelligence who read the newspapers." [8]

The propriety of the actions taken by the United States during and immediately after the uprising have been even more widely questioned by Colombians and others. The chief points discussed have been the following:

1. Did the United States fail to fulfill its obligation to Colombia under the treaty of 1846, by the thirty-fifth article of which it undertook to "guarantee, positively and efficaciously to New Granada . . ., the perfect neutrality of the . . . isthmus with the view that the free transit from the one to the other sea may not be interrupted . . . and, in consequence, the United States also guarantee . . . the rights of sovereignty and property which New Granada has and possesses over the said territory"? [9]

The conflict of opinion here turns upon whether the guarantee given applied only in case a foreign power attacked Colombia, or whether it extended also to any attack rising out of civil war between parties within the republic. Colombia interpreted the guarantee as one "against all aggression" by any enemy, internal or external. This article of the treaty

---

[8] Special Message, Jan. 4, 1904, in Richardson, *op. cit.*, Vol. X, pp. 679–704, at p. 697. A collection of documents including excerpts from the Presidential messages showing the position taken by the United States is *The Panama Canal and Our Relations with Colombia, Sen. Doc. No. 471*, 63rd Congress, 2nd Session, Washington, 1914.

[9] Text in Malloy, *op. cit.*, Vol. I, pp. 302–314.

was cited during the debate over the Hay-Herrán treaty, when rumors of revolt were afloat, as an "impregnable defense" against disruption by revolution.[10]

The United States claimed that long-standing interpretation showed that such wide responsibilities were not assumed. In 1865, for example, Secretary Seward had said, "The United States have taken and will take no interest in any question of internal revolution . . . but will maintain a perfect neutrality in connection with such domestic altercations. The United States will . . . protect the transit trade across the Isthmus against invasion of either domestic or foreign disturbers of the peace of the State of Panama. . . . The purpose of the stipulation was to guarantee the Isthmus against seizure or invasion by a foreign power only." [11]

It seems clear, though it was not frankly admitted by either government, that the clauses concerning the protection of traffic, maintenance of order, and the guarantee of sovereignty did create an exceptional relation which might work well as long as the interests of the two governments coincided but which laid the ground for unavoidable misunderstandings once these interests became divergent. If the traffic was to be kept open and order maintained, interference with local disturbance of order could not be avoided, and such interference would favor one side or the other.

In fact, displacement of the usual degree of local governmental control had, during the life of the treaty, occurred repeatedly through action by the United States. The landings of American forces in at least four cases had been at the request of Colombia, but in five other instances had occurred

---

[10] Uribe, *op. cit.*, p. 143, in note of Luis Carlos Rico. The quotations from American authorities given by Rico should be compared with those cited below. (See Uribe, *op. cit.*, p. 125.) See also quotations in "The Story of Panama," *op. cit.*, pp. 55–56, which indicate lack of uniformity in American interpretations.

[11] Richardson, *op. cit.*, Vol. X, p. 660. Quotations from Colombian and American sources showing that the treaty, when negotiated, was understood to protect Colombia against foreign powers only are found in Root, Elihu, "The Ethics of the Panama Question," in *The Panama Canal and Our Relations with Colombia, Sen. Doc. No. 471,* 63rd Congress, 2nd Session, Washington, 1914, p. 39 *et sqq.* See also *For. Rel.*, 1903, p. 227.

independently of such suggestion.[12] In effect, these landings had, as a rule, substantially protected Colombia against local subversive movements and gave color to the Colombian assertion that the treaty guaranteed its possession of the isthmus against enemies within the country. But it could be argued that protection in these cases was undertaken merely in fulfillment of the duty to keep traffic open, and that the treaty had not intended to guarantee Colombia against a division of sovereignty and territory resulting from a civil war.

Whether the clash which came in the first days of November, 1903, was a civil war and hence not comparable to previous outbreaks was, to say the least, not clear. Nevertheless, sending vessels to the coast towns as soon as disorder threatened was in accord with previous practice under the treaty, and, indeed, followed the custom of the United States and other powers in all disturbed areas. The order that no landing of Colombian troops be allowed within fifty miles of Panama, on the other hand, was certainly far beyond what could be necessary for keeping open traffic, but exercise of authority of that extent did not actually occur, and, hence, that part of the instructions has less significance than has often been given it. Prohibiting landing of troops appears to have been without precedent; but, as the order was ineffective, it also, therefore, cannot be cited as an overt act of the United States. Forbidding the passage of troops of either party over the railroad did have precedent[13] and such passage, it may be granted, would

---

[12] Richardson, *op. cit.*, Vol. X, p. 664.

[13] Recent actions of the sort cited by President Roosevelt were the order of July 25, 1900, protesting against a threatened bombardment of Panama by Colombian forces; that of November 20, 1901, instructing that "all parties molesting or interfering with free transit" be notified that "such interference must cease" and authorizing the landing of marines if necessary; and that of September 12, 1902, declaring that "any transportation of troops" which "might convert the line of transit into [a] theater of hostility" should be prevented. (Richardson, *op. cit.*, Vol. X, p. 688.) In refutation, Colombia has asserted that the United States "had never, in disturbances, impeded the disembarking of the troops of the Colombian government nor their transit by the railroad." The United States had insisted that the soldiers be carried in one train and the arms in another, a practice against which Colombia had complained. (Luis Carlos Rico, in Uribe, *op. cit.*, at pp. 148–149.) Obviously, such an arrangement would have been unacceptable to the United States in November, 1903.

have caused interference with the open traffic which the United States was bound to protect. But, again, that action did make it impossible for Colombia to defend her right to territory of which she was the acknowledged sovereign and it prevented her setting on foot any military action worthy of the name.

2. Did the United States violate the rules of international law through the prompt recognition of the independence of Panama, followed by discouragement of Colombian proposals to attempt to re-establish her control and by the making of a treaty through which the United States undertook to guarantee the independence of the new state?

During the Civil War, when the United States Government had sought to influence European states not to recognize the Confederacy, it had sent instructions setting out the doctrine of recognition. "We freely admit," wrote Secretary of State Seward, "that a nation may, and even ought, to recognize a new state which has absolutely and beyond question effected its independence and permanently established its sovereignty. . . . On the other hand, we insist that a nation that recognizes a revolutionary state, with a view to aid its effecting its sovereignty and independence, commits a great wrong against the nation whose integrity is thus invaded, and makes itself responsible for a just and ample redress." [14] Was it not clear that the United States had, by recognizing Panama, done so "with a view to aid its effecting its sovereignty and independence" and was it not obligated to make "just and ample redress"?

Colombia maintained that the American actions had been clearly contrary to accepted international standards. President Roosevelt admitted that, if justifiable, the steps taken must rest on the unusual circumstances to be faced. "I have not denied . . .," he asserted in explaining his position to Congress, "either the validity or the propriety of the general rule that a new state should not be recognized as independent till it has shown its ability to maintain its independence.

---

[14] Instructions of April 10, 1861, by Secretary of State Seward to Charles Francis Adams, quoted in "The Story of Panama," *op. cit.*, p. 470.

This rule is derived from the principle of nonintervention. . . . But, like the principle from which it is deduced, the rule is subject to exceptions; and there are in my opinion clear and imperative reasons why a departure from it was justified and even required in the present instance."[15]

The exception to the rule, he declared, was justified on three grounds:

(1) The treaty of 1846, by which the United States undertook to keep traffic open and to maintain order in communications on the isthmus, implied, though it did not specifically state, that Colombia would grant concessions for the creation of communications on reasonable terms. "Only because it was not imagined that such concessions would ever be withheld" was explicit statement omitted.[16]

(2) "Considerations of our national interests and safety" demanded that the canal be built.[17] Always important for us, it had by recent events been rendered essential.

(3) The recognition of the Republic of Panama was an act justified by the interests of collective civilization.[18] The world had long demanded a canal. Great Britain had modified her treaty with the United States to permit its construction. The Pan-American Congress at Mexico had applauded the project in January, 1902, and the prompt recognition of Panama by other governments all showed that the position of the United States was that of "the mandatory of civilization."

---

[15] Presidential Message, January 4, 1904, in Richardson, *op. cit.,* Vol. X, pp. 697–704 at p. 697.

[16] *Ibid.,* p. 698.

[17] *Ibid.,* p. 699.

[18] *Ibid.,* p. 701. A detailed criticism of President Roosevelt's arguments is in Uribe, *op. cit.,* pp. 128–132. In pages 133–166 is the text of the memorandum by Luis Carlos Rico, Minister of Foreign Relations, of April 12, 1904, presenting the Colombian case. American criticisms are Du Bois, James T., *Colombia's Claims and Rights,* Halstead, Pa. (pamphlet), 1914; Taylor, Hannis, *Why the Pending Treaty with Colombia Should be Ratified* (pamphlet), Washington, 1914; and Chamberlain, Leander T., "A Chapter of National Dishonor," in the *North American Review,* February, 1912, pp. 145–174. For a recent tart survey, see Pringle, Henry Fowles, *Theodore Roosevelt, A Biography,* New York, Harcourt, Brace and Co., 1931, pp. 301–338. A well-documented discussion of the Panama developments is Hill, Howard Copeland, *Roosevelt and the Caribbean,* Chicago, University of Chicago Press, 1927, pp. 30–68.

Responsibility for the position he had taken under the circumstances President Roosevelt shared with no one else. He later declared, "I did not consult Hay, or Root, or any one else as to what I did, because a council of war does not fight; and I intended to do the job once for all."[19]

The propriety of Roosevelt's acts was later unqualifiedly defended by those who had been most closely associated with him. Secretary of State John Hay wrote shortly after the event, "The action of the President in the Panama matter is not only in the strictest accordance with the principles of justice and equity, and in line with all the best precedents of our public policy, but it was the only course he could have taken in compliance with our treaty rights and obligations."[20]

After her many endeavors to persuade the United States to re-establish Colombian sovereignty at Panama or to secure assurance that she would be allowed to attempt to do so herself, and after the refusal of her proposals to arbitrate the differences which had arisen, Colombia decided to seek reparation for her alleged wrongs through direct negotiations.

General Rafael Reyes was declared elected as the next Colombian President on July 4, 1904. He announced support of a conciliatory policy. War between the two countries, he felt, was out of the question and arbitration had been declined. Therefore, a peaceful settlement by negotiation was the only practical method of ending the disagreement.

Whatever the merits of the controversy, desires to restore the former friendly relations promptly made themselves evident on both sides. Elihu Root, Secretary of State from 1905 to 1909—all but a short period in the second Roosevelt admin-

---

[19] In a letter to W. R. Thayer, of June 2, 1915, in Thayer, W. R., *The Life of John Hay,* Boston, Houghton, Mifflin Co., 1915, Vol. II, p. 328.

[20] Quoted in Theodore Roosevelt, "The Monroe Doctrine and the Panama Canal," in the *Outlook,* December 6, 1913, pp. 745–754, at p. 753. Further expressions of Hay's opinion are quoted in Maxey, Edwin, "The Pending Treaty with Colombia," *Review of Reviews,* February, 1916, pp. 191–196. The most detailed and forceful statement of the American position by one prominent in the Roosevelt administration is that by Elihu Root, in "The Ethics of the Panama Question" in *The Panama Canal and Our Relations with Colombia, Sen. Doc. No. 471,* 63rd Congress, 2nd Session, Washington, 1914, pp. 36–53.

istration—visited several of the Latin-American nations at the time of the Third Pan-American Conference in 1906 and set forth the desire of the United States to maintain friendly relations with its neighbors on the basis of mutual respect for sovereignty.

President Reyes outlined a program of adjustment with the American minister and asked Mr. Root to call at Cartagena on his return voyage there to discuss outstanding differences with the minister of foreign affairs. At the meeting on September 24, 1906, Secretary Root voiced the desire that "all questions pending between" the republics should be settled in the spirit of friendship and in accordance with honor.[21] The minister of foreign affairs presented the Colombian proposal, which later became the basis for a formal protocol signed August 17, 1907.[22] Panamanian demands as to the Colombian boundary for a time held up progress; but the United States, after a special investigation, supported the Colombian claims in the region. On January 9, 1909, a treaty between the United States and Colombia and related treaties between the United States and Panama and Panama and Colombia were signed.

Colombia was to recognize the independence of her former province within stipulated boundaries, to renounce in favor of the United States the rights she had held in the canal and railway, and to receive specially favored treatment in the use of the canal. Panama was not to be under obligation to assume a part of the Colombian public debt—though she had previously offered to do so—but was to agree to transfer to Colombia the first ten annuities of $250,000 which she was to receive from the United States under the treaty made promptly after the recognition of her independence.[23]

These treaties, the result of long negotiations, represented the mature efforts of the Roosevelt administration to re-estab-

[21] *For. Rel.*, 1907, Part I, p. 286, quoted from the message of President Reyes to the Colombian Congress, April 1, 1907.

[22] Exposition by the Colombian Minister of Foreign Affairs, in *For. Rel.* 1910, pp. 367–376, at p. 369.

[23] The texts are in *For. Rel.*, 1909, pp. 223–233.

lish the interrupted friendly relations. They had had the support of successive Colombian ministers of foreign relations and were presented for ratification by the President, General Rafael Reyes.[24] Everything, at first, appeared to insure unanimous acceptance. Opposition soon developed, however, though the American minister telegraphed on March 1, 1909, "Ratification is certain unless Reyes weakens."[25] Shortly, inflammatory attacks on the treaty appeared in the press, and student demonstrations broke out in the capital and in the provinces, motivated not only by the treaty but by other alleged abuses of the Reyes administration. These protests had their effect on the members of Congress and on the President, and the latter resigned on March 13. Mobs attacked the houses of Government officers. Reyes reassumed the presidency and declared a state of siege. He would put the treaties through. But threats against those who might vote for the treaty continuing, he again changed his mind, withdrew the agreement from consideration, and later left the country. In the following election, the Government passed into the control of Carlos E. Restrepo, an avowed enemy of a conciliatory settlement.[26]

In the next administration in the United States—that of Mr. Taft—his Secretary of State, Mr. Knox, sought to end the controversy. The minister appointed to Bogotá in the latter half of 1910, James T. Du Bois, was ardently in sympathy with the Colombian point of view.[27] He reported to his chief, on December 30, 1912, that President Roosevelt's refusal to allow Colombia to land troops to defend her sovereignty, guar-

---

[24] See "Message of President Reyes" and "Exposition of the Minister of Foreign Affairs" in *For. Rel.*, 1910, p. 366.

[25] *Ibid.*, p. 376.

[26] The agreement between the United States and Panama had been ratified by Panama, January 27, 1909, and by the United States, March 3, 1909. That between the United States and Colombia was ratified by the former on February 24, 1909, and that between Panama and Colombia by the former on January 30, 1909. Since the agreements were not ratified by Colombia, all remained inoperative.

[27] President Restrepo, in a message to the Colombian Congress in 1914, remarked, "Unfortunately his good will was far superior to the instructions which he had received from his government. . . ." (*Ibid.*, 1914, p. 142.)

anteed by an international treaty, had broken the long-standing friendship of the two countries, awakened the indignation of all Colombians and of millions of other Latin-Americans, and created a situation which urgently called for redress.

On February 15, 1913, Du Bois presented to the Colombian minister of foreign relations an informal proposal of agreement which went much farther than the previous discussions.[28] The United States, it was said, "honestly regret anything should ever have occurred" to interrupt the international friendship and wished to remove the ill feeling which had arisen. It would pay $10,000,000 to Colombia for an option on a canal route via the Atrato River and for the privilege of establishing coaling stations in two Colombian islands. It would lend its good offices to settle disputes with Panama, arbitrate claims of Colombia concerning the Panama railway, and give special preferential treatment to Colombia for canal traffic.[29]

But even such a proposal was inacceptable to the Colombian government then in power. It was rejected because it did not meet the demands of public opinion, fell short of "a just reparation . . . moral and material" measured by the damages Colombia had suffered,[30] and "on the fourth of March following was to begin the presidency of the illustrious statesman Mr. Woodrow Wilson, Apostle of justice and the law, who would give satisfaction to Colombia." [31] He would grant, it was confidently believed, either "the arbitration of the whole Panama question or a direct proposition . . . to compensate . . . for all the moral, physical and financial losses sustained by" Colombia.[32] In his message to the Congress on July 20, 1913, President Restrepo announced that the "advent of the new administration in the United States . . . caused

[28] Text is in *For. Rel.*, 1913, pp. 289–294.

[29] A preliminary proposal, made January 20, to review the Root-Cortés-Arosemena treaties of the Roosevelt administration as a part of the proposed agreement had been refused by President Restrepo.

[30] Uribe, *op. cit.*, pp. 213–214.

[31] *Ibid.*, p. 184. See also Secretary of State Knox to President Taft, *For. Rel.*, 1913, pp. 297–308.

[32] This is a statement of the minister of foreign relations. (See *For. Rel.*, 1913, p. 307.)

the Colombian people to conceive great hopes" of "complete compensatory justice."[33]

The Wilson administration sent as its minister Thadeus A. Thompson, with instructions which recognized that Colombia had suffered moral and material damages and stated the desire of the United States to end the differences that had arisen therefrom. On October 1, 1913, Thompson offered $20,000,000 to end all differences including all claims. In the negotiations which followed, he made an "earnest endeavor to keep the Colombian demands within reasonable bounds."[34] This proved difficult of accomplishment, for the Colombian government now felt that the day had come when far more might be secured than had ever before been possible.

Against the judgment of the American representative as to what was likely to be granted, the Colombian minister of foreign relations asked that the treaty include (1) an expression of the sincere regret of the Government and people of the United States for the events which interrupted friendship, (2) a grant of the right to Colombian citizens, goods, and ships to pass through the canal at all times without payment of any kind, (3) entry of certain goods into the canal zone on the same terms as goods of the United States, (4) special rates on the isthmian railway, (5) an agreement that Panama yield certain territory which by the law of 1855 had been within the province, and (6) a payment of $50,000,000 by the United States. Of special importance was considered the expression of the "regrets" of the United States. The proposals of the Taft administration for coaling stations and options on a canal route were to be definitely dropped.

So far as this the Wilson administration was not willing to go, but it was ready to grant more than its Republican predecessors to meet the Colombian desires. From the Department of State there was sent to the American representative, on December 19, 1913, a counterproposal which used the expression "sincere regret" but cut down the special privileges greater than would be enjoyed by United States citizens, which

[33] Text is in *For. Rel.*, 1913, p. 317.
[34] The exchanges used in this summary are in *For. Rel.*, 1913, p. 321 *et sqq.*

Colombia had asked, kept the boundary of Panama practically as defined by the law of 1855, and reduced the money payment to $20,000,000. From this draft, after minor modifications, came the agreement of April 6, 1914.

In its original form, the treaty [35] declared that the United States "wishing to put at rest all controversies and differences with . . . Colombia arising out of the events from which the present situation on the Isthmus of Panama resulted, expresses . . . sincere regret that anything should have occurred to interrupt or to mar the relations of cordial friendship that had so long subsisted between the two nations."

Colombia on its part accepted the "declaration in the full assurance that every obstacle to the restoration of complete harmony between the two countries will thus disappear." There followed guarantees that Colombia could use the canal for war purposes free of any charges. Colombian goods and mails should pay on the canal only the same rates as goods and mails of the United States. Certain Colombian products should enter the canal zone on the same terms as United States products. Special rights for military use of the railroad were granted, and likewise equality with the United States in commercial use except for certain Colombian products which were given exceptionally favored treatment.

The United States further agreed to pay to Colombia within six months after exchange of ratifications $25,000,000 in gold. Colombia recognized the independence of Panama, with stated boundaries, and relations with Panama, including adjustment of claims, were to be established with the cooperation of the United States.

After debate for some forty days, the measure was approved by Colombia on June 9, 1914.[36] Its constitutionality was promptly questioned in a case before the supreme court, which refused to take jurisdiction.

The previous proposals had failed through opposition by

---

[35] *Ibid.*, 1914, p. 163.

[36] Speeches made in defense of the treaty before the Colombian Congress are in Uribe, *op. cit.*, at pp. 186–203. A detailed report at pp. 206–246 summarizes the Colombian viewpoint.

Colombia. Could this one pass the United States Senate? There it was to meet many amendments and long delays due to Republican defense of the actions of President Roosevelt and the national preoccupation with the World War.

The treaty did not come up for consideration in the Senate in 1914 or the next year. The Colombian officials continued to urge action and the American Secretaries of State to explain the delay. In February, 1916, the Foreign Relations Committee reported the measure by a vote of 8 to 7 with amendments reducing the indemnity to $15,000,000 and making the expression of regret mutual. The proposal to reduce the payment made a bad impression in Colombia, and its government urged that President Wilson come to the support of the treaty by a special message to Congress. No comment was made as to the acceptability of a "mutual regret" clause, and the American minister felt that the financial necessities of Colombia might make her willing to accept whatever was offered.

On the other hand, demands that Colombia withdraw ratification and suggestions of possible German military activity looking toward the Panama Canal began to appear in the Colombian press. The treaty might again become the prey of local party divisions. Meanwhile, it had become evident that the United States would be dragged into the World War. President Wilson in March, 1917, urged action in a letter to the Chairman of the Senate Committee on Foreign Relations. "We need now," he wrote, "and it is possible shall need very much more in the immediate future all the friends that we can attach to us in Central America [*sic*] where so many of our most critical interests center." [37]

The Washington administration urged that Colombia be calm and gave assurance that one of the reasons for calling the special session of the Senate for March 5, 1917, was the Colombian treaty. But again action was postponed. Wilson returned to the treaty in his famous message of December 2, 1918, but Congress still refused to act.

The chance that the treaty would be ratified as signed had

---

[37] *For. Rel.*, 1917, p. 296.

from the beginning not appeared great. The "sincere regret" clause was sure to be bitterly opposed. As early as November, 1914, it had been suggested that the money payment be made in annuities of $5,000,000. Less important objections were made to other clauses. There rose in Colombia apprehension that ratification by the United States would prove impossible, while at the same time the financial needs of the Government increased and made greater the desire for such indemnity as might be securable. Facing realities, the Colombian minister reported in February, 1919, that ratification could be counted upon if the "apology clause" were dropped and some minor modifications conceded.[38] On the twenty-seventh, the Colombian administration accepted the changes asked. The fact that there remained but three working days of the session of the American Senate and that in the new one there might develop greater opposition to the treaty were alleged as reasons for the desire to secure prompt action.[39] But the sessions closed with the treaty still unratified.

The change in the Colombian position at the close of the first half of the second Wilson administration, it seemed, ought greatly to increase the chance that the treaty might pass, for it took away the chief ground for opposition by the friends of ex-President Roosevelt, who had died shortly before on January 6, 1919.

In the new session, the treaty for a time seemed well on the way to approval. It had been unanimously recommended for passage with eleven amendments by the Committee on Foreign Relations on July 29; but Senator Lodge on August 7, 1919, raised the question as to whether a Colombian decree of June 20 concerning petroleum lands might not prove confiscatory of American properties and asked that the treaty be returned to the Committee. There occurred another delay of almost two years, which saw the end of the Wilson administration.

---

[38] Chief among these was the payment of the $25,000,000 in installments. This had been discussed since 1914. The reasons for the change are set out in Uribe, *op. cit.*, pp. 263–264.

[39] Minutes of the Council of Ministers of February 27, 1919. (Uribe, *op. cit.*, pp. 222–223.)

President Harding, head of the new Republican regime, had as Senator been opposed to the treaty as originally submitted, but he had approved it in the form recommended for passage in July, 1919. On March 9, 1921, five days after entering office, he urged its prompt ratification. Early in the new Congress—in April, 1921—it was agreed to discuss it in public session. Congress seized the opportunity to review the history of the canal policy of the United States and to air the historic charges and countercharges to which it had given rise.

The widest variety of opinion influenced the voting. Some looked upon the treaty as an open avowal of wrongdoing for which reparation was to be made and favored its passage to right a wrong. Some of the harshest Republican critics of the treaty now reversed their positions. The apology clause having been withdrawn, there was for them no further reason for antagonism.[40] It now no longer reflected, they argued, on the action of President Roosevelt and the policy of his administration. Others argued that new conditions demanded that the United States draw closer to the Latin-American nations. The treaty would bind together the United States and Colombia and open up opportunities for development of commerce and for investments in Colombian enterprise, especially in the development of petroleum resources. In addition, a commercial treaty which would give the United States greater advantages might also be forecast. A minority continued their opposition to any treaty which involved payment of money to Colombia even if the "apology clause" were dropped, on the ground that any payment carried an implied reflection on the policy the Government had followed.[41]

The vote came on April 20, 1921. Ratification with amendments was recommended by 69 to 19. The convention was approved by Colombia as amended on March 1, 1922, and ratifications were exchanged the same day.

---

[40] The debate in the United States Senate is found in *Congressional Record,* Vol. 61, 67th Congress, Special Session, March 4–March 15, 1921; 1st Session, April 11–May 4, 1921, pp. 75–491.

[41] The influence of economic motives in securing the adoption of the treaty is analyzed at length in Rippy, J. Fred, *The Capitalists and Colombia,* New York, Vanguard Press, 1931, especially in Chaps. VI and VII.

The treaty for the settlement of differences,[42] as it became law in 1922, though it is still the treaty of April 6, 1914, the date of its signing, differs much from the original text. In the latter, the United States, desirous of terminating all controversies and differences, had expressed in its own name and in the name of its people its "sincere regret" for whatever had happened at Panama to interrupt the long-standing friendship, and Colombia had accepted the declaration. The new treaty declared in its preamble that both countries were desirous to remove misunderstandings arising from the events in Panama and for this reason engaged themselves in the treaty. The "apology clause" which had originally been a part of the treaty proper and which Colombia had considered an essential factor had been dropped. On its face, the agreement was one of mutual concessions. Colombia recognized the title to the interoceanic canal and the Panama railway to be vested entirely and absolutely in the United States without any incumbrances or indemnities whatever, thus quieting previous demands to submit to arbitration the annuities of $250,000 and reversionary rights of Colombia to the railway. Concession of these rights had been one of the factors in increasing the cash payment from the $10,000,000 formerly proposed to the $25,000,000 which the United States on its part now undertook to pay.[43] In addition, Colombia received the stipulated privileges, outlined above, in the canal zone and in the use of the canal.

Thus, the long-disputed treaty of 1914 to adjust the differences arising from the Panama revolution had become law. In appraisals of the acts of both parties, in this the greatest controversy which has arisen between the United States and the nations of South America, partisan opinion has been much

---

[42] Text in *Treaties, Conventions, International Acts, Protocols and Agreements between the United States of America and other Powers, 1910–1923*, Washington, 1923, Vol. III, pp. 2538–2541.

[43] See Report of the Committee on Foreign Relations of the Colombian Senate in Uribe, *op. cit.*, pp. 206–246 at pp. 230–231. Colombia had originally asked $50,000,000 for yielding these claims. See Uribe, *op. cit.*, pp. 259–262.

more prominent than frank consideration of facts. Both the events which led up to the Panama revolution and the efforts made to quiet the rancors which grew out of it, when viewed in long perspective, include actions which leave the student with qualified conclusions.

The Colombian contention that Panama was its "richest province" is hollow. It was a long-neglected area. The larger part of it was, at the opening of the century, in the same condition as in the period of discovery. The governments of Bogotá valued it for the income which could be pressed out of it, not for its natural resources. Rich it was only in what it could contribute to Colombia and the world at large by the communications which could be developed through its narrowest part. Rather than raise barriers to construction of a canal, Colombia might well have adopted the policy of turning over the right of way as a free gift to any who would undertake the work. The national advantage which would be reaped by any money payment was negligible compared to the larger benefits which would come to both Colombia and the world from the existence of the canal.

The attitude of the various Colombian governments cannot be understood without appreciation of the political trials through which the Government had passed and which continued to hamper normal action when the treaties negotiated were under discussion. Party struggles discolored policy. Quick reversals of position under the influence of romantic nationalistic enthusiasm and prejudice made calm discussion impossible. Such developments are common in weak states and not unknown elsewhere.

Whatever may have been the motives of the more responsible leaders, there can be no doubt that at times a powerful group were actuated by the desire to get the most possible out of an asset which Colombia alone could not bring into use but which could be made of great advantage to the world at large. Finally, the adjustment reached was agreed to, at least in part, because the Colombian leaders became convinced that no larger payment would be forthcoming and because the Government was badly in need of money. The apology which was long announced as the main issue for which Colombia contended finds no place in the treaty.

At a number of points, clouds appear also in the policy pursued by the United States. The best that can be said concerning the earlier developments was aptly stated by John Hay, the Secretary of State at the time. In a private letter, he wrote, January 20, 1904:

> Some of our greatest scholars, in their criticisms of public life, suffer from the defect of arguing from pure reason, and taking no account of circumstances. While I agree that no circumstances can ever justify a Government in doing wrong, the question as to whether the Government has acted rightly or wrongly can never be justly judged without the circumstances being considered. I am sure that if the President had acted differently when, the 3d of November, he was confronted by a critical situation which might easily have turned to disaster, the attacks which are now made on him would have been ten times more virulent and more effective. He must have done exactly as he did, or the only alternative would have been an indefinite duration of bloodshed and devastation through the whole extent of the Isthmus. It was a time to act and not to theorize, and my judgment at least is clear that he acted rightly.[44]

This amounts substantially to declaring that President Roosevelt was forced to choose between bad alternatives. While the general rule "Of two evils choose—neither" applies in both public and private life, those in public affairs do not always have the easy means of escape suggested. It is clear from his explicit statements that President Roosevelt believed that the canal should be dug at Panama, that he was disposed to take extraordinary steps to bring that about and willing to justify such steps by the exceptional circumstances which he felt had developed. Whether Congress would have followed the plan he at one time considered is highly doubtful, and whether, if further delay had been permitted, there might have come into power in Colombia a government momentarily able to put through an agreement in nominal observance of normal standards may well be argued. When it became evi-

---

[44] Thayer, W. R., *The Life of John Hay,* New York, Houghton, Mifflin Co., 1915, Vol. II, p. 323. Letter to G. P. Fisher, January 20, 1904.

dent that Panama would revolt, he discarded the plan he was debating and then chose to wait for events. They could hardly have failed to create a situation similar to that which arose early in November, 1903. They led to concentration of naval force at Panama, the restraint of free action by Colombian troops, the recognition of Panama, and frowning on Colombian proposals to re-establish her sovereignty.

The later action by the United States on the proposed treaties for adjustment of claims is not free from the influence of partisan feeling in certain groups; the desire to quiet criticism, just or unjust, by money payments; the wish to assure friendship because of problems in Europe which had no connection with the Panama dispute; and the hope that the treaty, if adopted, might be to the advantage of commercial and financial interests in the United States.

All in all, the Panama problem and its solution are illustrations of the fact that, in international as in private affairs, mixed motives and compromise in the face of circumstances often affect the outcome and blur the observance of standards of action which under more normal conditions would control.

The misunderstanding between Colombia and the United States was curiously coincident with the beginning of profound changes in the national life of the southern republic. To observers of the time, there was little reason to believe that a period of greater calm in domestic political life was at hand; but such proved to be the case. Among the advantages which Colombians had argued would come to them from the canal treaty were a great stimulus to the development of national resources, the rise of foreign investment in the country, increase in domestic and foreign trade, and, especially, close economic relations with the United States. All these have come, since 1903, in spite of the fact that the failure of the canal treaty resulted in the passing of the waterway out of Colombian control.

Some of these changes would doubtless have come even if the canal had not been built; some were, indeed, already under way and became pronounced before its completion. Some have been stimulated by the creation of the waterway.

Only small amounts of foreign capital sought investment in local developments in Colombia until recent years. United States citizens held properties valued at only some two million dollars in 1912, and other countries had hardly more. In 1920, the total American investment had risen to 30 million. It was about to be rapidly and not in all cases conservatively increased. At the beginning of 1929, estimates of American holdings ranged between 250 and 300 million. They represented chiefly loans to the central and local governments and the properties of petroleum and fruit interests.

Foreign trade showed an equally spectacular rise, but with great fluctuations in value from year to year. In 1905, the imports and exports were worth somewhat less than 24 million dollars; by the time the canal was opened, the value was over 51 million; and in 1928, the peak year in Colombian foreign commerce, over 175 million. Exports normally exceed imports, thus providing the credits to carry the much-increased public debt service, which in turn bears heavily upon the foreign exchange market—as was shown in the period of crisis following 1929, when the value of total foreign trade fell to 76 million in 1933.

The increase in economic co-operation with foreign countries has been chiefly with the United States. As is indicated above, the great flow began in 1920 practically coincident with the final adjustment of the dispute concerning Panama, though the effect of the one on the other is easily exaggerated. Trade with the United States has increased with the growth of general imports and exports, though at a more rapid rate. It was rising long before the political adjustment of differences occurred. In 1905, United States trade with Colombia reached $10,000,000, or 42 per cent of the total ($24,000,000). In 1913, as the canal was approaching completion, it was $21,115,000, or 34 per cent of the total ($60,000,000); in 1929, $148,000,000, or 60 per cent of the total ($244,000,000). In the foreign trade of Colombia, the United States was more important than all the rest of the world. Of the imports, 46 per cent came from the United States and 75 per cent of the exports were sold there. In the reduced trade of Colombia in the depression period, the share taken by the United States sank to about two-thirds.

The great foreign trade increase has a number of causes. New communications by sea, partly created by the existence of the canal, facilitated interchange. Domestic transportation, still backward, was better than in previous periods. Prices for coffee averaged high. The locally produced grades found increasing popularity in the United States, the world's greatest coffee market. Finally, the United States was, for Colombian products, practically a free trade market. In some years, less than one per cent of the shipments to the northern neighbor paid any import duty.

The public debt of Colombia has risen sharply in recent years, chiefly through expenditures for public works. It totalled 124,292,688 pesos at the end of 1933, of which about 79,000,000 pesos represented external long- and short-term debts. There is, in addition, an internal floating debt of about 19,000,000 pesos. The world-wide depression caused at first partial and, early in 1934, a complete suspension of interest payments on the national debt.

The circumstances surrounding the life of the Colombian people in the period since 1903 have brought a remarkably rapid increase in the population, an increase very little influenced by immigration. In the thirty-four years preceding 1905, the total rose by less than 1,200,000. In the twenty-six years following that date, the population is estimated to have increased by more than 4,200,000. It doubled in the period, reaching an estimated total of 8,380,000 in 1931. Here, as in Brazil, population figures are rising at an unprecedented rate, which up to the present time, with the greater exploitation of the national resources, does not show signs of falling.

These rapid advances in Colombia since the opening of the century have made the country one of the most promising of the Caribbean. It has far outstripped any of its neighbors in population. It has now more than double the number of people found in any other Caribbean republic. Its economic advance indicates that at last its long-locked resources are coming into exploitation. The progress made and the directions which that progress has taken make Colombian relations of particular interest to the United States. The fortunes of the two, already closely allied, promise to become still more closely associated through the further growth of common economic and political interests.

CHAPTER XIV

Panama

PANAMA is the youngest of the New World republics. Except for Salvador and Costa Rica, it is the smallest continental state of the New World, having a territory of 28,575 square miles. In population it stands at the foot of the list of American states. With 467,459 inhabitants in 1930, it ranks with the small West Indian possessions of France. In the decade ending in 1930, the increase in population was only 21,361.

The back country is very sparsely settled, little exploited, and in some districts practically unexplored. Panama, as the world thinks of the republic, is the area close to the Panama Canal, and that is, in fact, the only portion now of significance in world affairs. In two cities of this area, Panama and Colon, live one-fourth of the inhabitants of the republic. Five other towns have populations of from 2,500 to 5,000. All of these are in the region west of the Canal. To the east there is no town with 2,000 inhabitants. Roads, except for a strip about fifty miles east of Panama City, are little better than they were in the period of the conquest.

The strategic position of the republic, which lies on both sides of one of the world's great crossroads, gives it an importance in commercial and military affairs far out of proportion to its resources and their development. It is an area which has been coveted by the great maritime nations almost since the discovery of the New World.

Settlers early reached the west coat of Central America across the isthmus, and eastward across this neck of land, for generations, the precious metals trade passed on its way from

Peru to Spain. Only in our own day, through the building of the Panama Canal, has the isthmian region become one through which has passed a far more valuable trade serving the world at large. Present-day traffic bears a strong contrast to the traffic in the days of the silver fleets. It is now overwhelmingly of bulky goods of small unit value. Its destination is no longer a single country but widely scattered areas under many flags. In greater part, the shipments are no longer between the New World and the Old, but between American ports—to a high degree, those of the United States. In 1929, the peak year up to the present time, 30,663,006 tons passed through the Canal, over two-thirds of which went from the Pacific to the Atlantic. About a third of the total was intercoastal trade of the United States. About a fifth was trade between Europe, the United States, and Canada. Almost another fifth involved trade of the United States with the west coast of South America and the Far East. In the years following 1929, the tons of cargo declined, owing to the world crisis, to a total of only 18,177,728 in 1933.[1]

The Canal has become a vital factor in the national defense policy of the United States. Unrestricted passage from one ocean to the other through the waterway is essential for the naval protection of the widely separated coasts of the republic. With international relations such as they are in our time, it is argued that the strength of the United States Navy, but for the Canal, would have to be practically doubled.

These two elements—world commerce, affecting particularly the United States, and the naval policy of the United States—give to Panama its major role in international affairs. Inevitably they exercise a far-reaching influence on the politics and prosperity of the little republic and make its relations with the United States of capital consideration. In comparison, its connections with its neighboring republics are of secondary importance and those with other foreign states of almost incidental significance.

To understand political developments within Panama, it is

[1] The *Annual Report of the Governor of the Panama Canal,* Washington gives a detailed analysis of canal operations and traffic.

necessary to bear in mind the treaty of November 18, 1903, which set out the relations between the Republic and the United States.[2] The promptness with which this agreement followed the revolt against Colombian authority has already been discussed. By its chief clauses, the United States guaranteed the independence of Panama. Panama granted to the United States "in perpetuity the use, occupation and control of a zone . . . of the width of ten miles . . . for the construction, maintenance, operation, sanitation and protection" of a canal and the right to take other lands essential for such purposes. Within the lands taken, the United States was to have power and authority such as it "would possess and exercise if it were the sovereign of the territory. . . ."

Other provisions gave to the United States (1) extensive rights over sanitation and policing in the cities of Panama and Colon, which were not included within "the Zone," and (2) Panama's rights in the Panama railroad. For the concessions made by Panama, the United States agreed to pay $10,000,000 at once and $250,000 annually during the life of the treaty, beginning nine years after ratification.

With these agreements should be considered Article 136 of the Constitution of Panama, of 1904, which declares that the "Government of the United States of America may intervene in any part of the Republic of Panama to reëstablish public peace and constitutional order in the event of their being disturbed." It is clear that, under the rules set up, the United States might wield great influence in both the domestic and international affairs of the republic, and such influence has, in fact, been exercised.

One of the recurring problems has been the part which the United States should play in the maintenance of public order. At a number of times, action has been taken under the policing powers given by the treaty to send forces for short periods into Panama City and Colon. Crises have been raised by such incidents as action by a mob denouncing the local government, an election dispute, and rent riots. "Intervention"

---

[2] Text in Malloy, *op. cit.*, Vol. II, pp. 1349–1357.

has occurred at times without any request on the part of the local government, and at other times in response to more or less formal appeal.[3]

The policing provisions of the treaty, under which the United States may assume authority for maintaining order in Panama City and Colon and territories adjacent in case Panama "should not be, in the judgment of the United States, able to maintain such order," have been a matter of continuing disagreement. Panama insists that intervention under these clauses can occur only after disorder has occurred, while the United States holds that they justify taking preventive measures.

The degree to which the United States has the right or the duty under existing arrangements to take a hand in the internal affairs of Panama involves, indeed, not merely the clauses concerning policing of the two chief cities, but also the meaning of the general guarantee of independence and the provision of the Panama Constitution above cited. Upon the degree of authority to act, representatives of the United States themselves have not held a uniform opinion. In 1905 the party out of power in Panama raised the question of whether the United States would support a dictatorship against a revolution. Secretary of State Root felt that the action of the United States would depend upon (1) whether the revolution imperiled independence, (2) whether it disturbed public order in the two cities, and (3) whether Panama could handle the crisis. Landing troops to enforce American rights without consent of the local government would be an act of war, but Panama had given such a right to the United States in Article 136 of its Constitution.[4] In sum, a revolution might or might not be opposed by the United States, according to circumstances. Secretary of War Taft agreed that, while action might be delayed till it was

[3] Cases cited in Buell, R. L., "Panama and the United States," in *Foreign Policy Reports,* New York, Foreign Policy Association, 1932, Vol. VII, No. 23, pp. 409–426.

[4] *For. Rel.,* 1906, Part 2, p. 1205. Compare Root's interpretation of the Platt Amendment in Cuba.

clear that Panama could not handle a revolt, still "insurrection in any part of the Republic would disturb the order in Panama and Colon and adjacent territory," and hence the United States might "properly . . . suppress any insurrection in any part of the Republic." [5]

Later, in 1918, when order was disturbed in the Chiriqui region, American forces were landed to protect American life and property, the guarantee of independence in the treaty and Article 136 of the Panama Constitution being relied upon. Panama protested that the first guarantee referred to foreign invasion and that the constitutional clause merely authorized the Government of Panama to ask American intervention.[6]

Still later, in 1928, Secretary of State Kellogg intimated that, if the local elections were followed by revolution, the United States would maintain order if Panama proved unable to do so. On January 2, 1931, there occurred, however, a revolution in which the United States did not act.[7]

Overnight a dissentient group seized the government, against which charges of corruption and dictatorship had been current, set up a provisional administration, and sought recognition from the United States. There was no disorder after the *coup d'état*. The revolutionary junta called to the presidency R. J. Alfaro, who had been for eight years Panamanian minister to Washington. On January 15, the United States Department of State instructed its minister to attend the inauguration of the new President and stated that a new act of recognition was not necessary. The relation of the United States to developments involving disturbance of domestic peace in Panama, as these incidents show, continues to be ill-defined.

Problems comparable to those involving public order have arisen in connection with Panamanian elections. The oppo-

---

[5] *Ibid.*, 1906, Part 2, p. 1207.

[6] Buell, "Panama and the United States," *op. cit.*, p. 414, and authorities there cited.

[7] See *New York Times*, January 3, 1931, p. 1:1; *ibid.*, Jan. 4, 1931, p. 19:1; *ibid.*, Jan. 11, 1931, Section I, p. 14:5; and *ibid*, Jan. 16, 1931, p. 3:2, for accounts of the revolution.

sition party in 1905 demanded that the United States supervise the voting,[8] arguing that the guarantee of order implied the obligation to guarantee "an absolutely lawful system of government." The conclusion would obviously be justified only by an interpretation of the treaty obligations which would include "preventive" action of a far-reaching sort. The United States was indisposed to assume such duties. Nevertheless, on the request of the Panamanian Government, apparently pressed to act by the opposition, there was appointed in 1908 a commission to co-operate with a similar Panamanian body in carrying out the election which was then approaching. A somewhat similar procedure was followed in the presidential election of 1912, again at the request of the Panamanian administration, which in this case justified its action under Article 136 of the Constitution.[9] The practice did not fail, however, to arouse bitter criticism.

In 1916 the opposition demanded supervision, but the United States Department of State refused to grant it unless the Panamanian Government made a formal request, which it did not do. As a result, the opposition stayed away from the polls, and the party in power "imposed" its candidate. In the municipal and assembly elections of 1918, supervision was again asked by the Government and was granted, but dissatisfaction with the result was so great that it was necessary for the American arbitral commission to pass on contested elections before the results would be accepted by the population.

The complications arising in this and previous contests appear to have convinced the United States Department of State that further supervision of elections should be avoided if possible. It had been widely argued in Panama that demands of the party out of power for "observers" implied that those in power intended to "control" the choice, and that yielding to the demand by the party in power gave the charge added color. The "observers" had in some cases been charged with unfairness, and the conclusiveness of any supervised

[8] *For. Rel.*, 1905, pp. 717–719.
[9] *Ibid.*, 1912, pp. 1139–1141.

election was dimmed when, as had happened at different times in both the opposition and government parties, those anticipating defeat refused to go to the polls. The election of 1918 was the last one "supervised" by the United States.

In 1928 Secretary Kellogg, in reply to a renewed request for intervention to guarantee a free election, refused to authorize it. The United States, he declared, had the right and authority to maintain order, but he felt that the facts submitted did not call for intervention. The primary obligation to hold free elections rested on Panama, and the United States would do nothing to help either party to the contest. If, as the opposition stated, failure to intervene should bring revolution, the United States would then decide what course to take.[10]

Public finance in weak states not infrequently comes to be a subject lying on the boundary of domestic and foreign affairs. The currency system and domestic borrowing are both, on their face, matters for internal arrangement; but, if either falls into confusion in any country, the domestic order may be affected and it may become more difficult for the country to fulfill its international obligations. Borrowing abroad may further upset the balance of payments, raise questions concerning the good faith of the borrower in fulfillment of the loan contracts, and cause pressure by foreign governments to induce the local government to fulfill its obligations. While

---

[10] *New York Times,* July 28, 1928, p. 12:8. Other instances in which the United States has successfully maintained its right under the treaty to control domestic developments in Panama involve requests by the United States for a monopoly on radio communication—considered necessary to the guarantee of independence and the operation and defense of the Canal—and for the right to pass upon certain sorts of concessions, especially those involving railway and port facilities. Extensive concessions for mining, chiefly for gold, have been granted by Panama to British interests. The question whether concessions for developing oil resources would pass without protest has not been raised; but, presumably, such grants to foreigners would be opposed by the United States, as they have been when applying to Costa Rican and Colombian territories where the opposition does not rest on treaty rights. Some of the concessions granted in Panama to other than American citizens appear to involve water power and telephone and telegraph lines which might be held to have relation to the Canal and its defense. See "Why Britishers in Panama?" by H. K. Norton in *World's Work,* November, 1930, pp. 29–32.

proposals to collect public debts by force now seem, because of the Hague agreements of 1907, less likely to disturb international relations than has sometimes threatened to be the case, it is clear that sound national financial policies still contribute to the ability of all countries to play their roles in the world's affairs and help to assure their political and economic independence.

No provisions in the treaty between Panama and the United States expressly refer to public finance. Nevertheless, the close association of the two states has given the United States a keen interest in the budget and public debts of Panama and a far-reaching control over its financial policy.

Out of the treaty of 1903 arose two extraordinary sources of income, the payment of $10,000,000 and the annuity of $250,000. Panama started its existence, therefore, not only without debt but "with money in the bank." The Department of State of the United States has exercised a degree of supervision over the use made of these funds through the assumption that the treaty payments were intended to help assure income which would contribute to the maintenance of stable government. Of the first item, $6,000,000 was invested in the United States in the so-called "constitutional fund," and from it Panama continues to receive revenue. In the two-year period from July 1, 1930, to June 30, 1932, the annual average payment was $307,249, or somewhat more than five per cent. The estimated receipts for 1932–1933 were $270,000. A proposal to pledge the income from this fund to promote the building of railways was abandoned after objection by the United States, though a later plan was approved on the acceptance by Panama of certain modifications.

Supplementing the income from the constitutional and the annuity funds, Panama has developed revenues which contrast favorably with those of many Caribbean countries of greater extent and resources. Nevertheless, budget deficits have been frequent and have been followed by their conversion into internal and foreign loans. Other obligations have been assumed to finance public works which could not be paid for out of current receipts, so that Panama, like all other Caribbean republics with the exception of Venezuela, now carries a public debt the service of which is normally an important item in the budget.

Five major foreign loans have been floated. For the service of the first, that of 1914, the annual annuity payments from the United States were pledged. That of the loan of 1926 was made a claim on the income from the constitutional fund and, if that were not sufficient, the annuity payments were to be drawn upon. For two smaller loans of 1926 for various purposes, especially roads and railroads, the incomes from the Chiriqui railroad and certain taxes were pledged. In 1928 an external consolidation loan of $12,000,000 was floated with American bankers. In addition, the Government has guaranteed loans made by certain semipublic undertakings, and there is an internal debt of uncertain total.

Evidently, such control as the United States has exercised over Panamanian public finance has not prevented the accumulation of a debt of relatively high total. Neither has it assured conservative management of Government finances. In 1929, when financial problems were already threatening, a commission of American experts made recommendations for improving the administration of public finances which resulted in the adoption of an improved accounting and an economy program.

The total debt of Panama is variously reported. The figure given by the Minister of Finance as of June 30, 1932, was $18,980,943, including the external and internal commitments. This statement does not include several small items, the National Mortgage Bank bonds, or the Chiriqui railroad loans guaranteed by the Government. These three classes total about $3,500,000.

In the distress period following 1929, the decline in economic activity affected Panama as it did other states. Treasury receipts fell off and the debt service could not be wholly maintained. The loans secured by the constitutional fund and the canal annuity depended on income which the Government did not directly control, but the consolidation loan of 1928 went into default on May 15, 1933. This was the first blot on the debt record of the Republic.

The foreign affairs of Panama, like those domestic, are intimately connected with the position created by the treaty relations to the United States. Every major development in the relations with other governments has come to involve action by the latter. Two have involved boundary questions with the neighboring republics and one the relation of Panama and the United States in the Canal Zone, from which arose also a question involving the duties of Panama as a member of the League of Nations.

Any special rights which the United States has to being consulted in incidents touching the foreign relations of Panama rise from the clauses of the treaty between the two countries, especially the promise that the United States "will maintain the independence of Panama." In disputes over the boundaries of Panama, evidently the United States may be called upon to decide what is the Panama whose independence is guaranteed.

In 1908, territories along the Colombian border having been occupied by Colombian troops and Panama having asked the assistance of the United States, the latter made it plain that it did not consider itself bound to support all territorial claims which Panama might make, but would form its own judgment as to whether the rights which it had promised to guarantee had been violated.[11] The next year, it was asserted that the United States might nevertheless take steps to restrain Panama from doing acts which "might eventually require the United States to take part in the controversy and support Panama."[12]

By the treaty of 1914, ratified in 1922, between Colombia and the United States, the former agreed to recognize Panama "as an independent nation taking as a basis the Colom-

---

[11] *Memoria, Relaciones Exteriores,* Panama, Imprenta Nacional, 1908, p. iv, quoted in Buell, "Panama and the United States," *op. cit.,* p. 410.

[12] *For. Rel.,* 1909, p. 469.

bian Law of June 9, 1855," and the United States undertook to forward a treaty of peace and friendship [13] and the adjustment of financial claims between Panama and Colombia. On January 13, 1932, there was reached an agreement to proceed to the actual survey of the Colombian boundary line; but on November 1, at the request of Panama, the work was postponed to "a more favorable moment." [14]

A more acrimonious controversy with Costa Rica arose over the boundary on the west. This dispute dated from the colonial period and had continued after the continental holdings of Spain had established their independence. Colombia, then owning the province of Panama, had insisted, even in the opening years of the twentieth century, that her possessions extended on the Atlantic coast as far north as Cape Gracias a Diós at the northeastern point of Nicaragua. While this claim was not strongly urged, the boundary between Costa Rica and the province of Panama had been long in dispute and never satisfactorily settled.[15]

In 1836, territory near Bocas del Toro claimed by Costa Rica had been seized by Colombia. Treaties looking toward adjustment of the dispute had been signed in 1856, 1863, and 1873 but had failed of ratification. The matter had been later referred, in 1880 and 1886, to the King of Spain for decision, but no settlements had been reached. In 1896, a new agreement had turned the case over to President Loubet of France, who handed down a decision, on September 11, 1900, not based on an actual study of the land in dispute. It gave to Colombia land not included in the controversy and

---

[13] Spanish text in Uribe, *op. cit.*, pp. 246–249.

[14] *Informe del Ministro de Relaciones Exteriores al Congreso de 1933*, Bogotá, 1933, pp. 90–91.

[15] A treaty intended to settle these and other claims was signed by representatives of Nicaragua and Colombia on March 24, 1928. By it the latter recognized Nicaragua's sovereignty over the Mosquito Coast between Cape Gracias a Diós and the San Juan River and Great Corn and Little Corn Islands. Nicaragua recognized Colombia's sovereignty over Providence, Santa Catalina, San Andrés, and other small islands of the Archipelago of San Andrés. (Mimeographed *Press Releases* of the United States Department of State, September 21, 1928.)

through deficiency in the maps employed did not fit the geography of the region to be divided. Thus matters stood when Panama became independent in 1903.

A new treaty between Panama and Costa Rica in 1910 accepted the boundary on the Pacific as Loubet had defined it and submitted the Atlantic boundary to the arbitration of Chief Justice E. D. White, of the United States Supreme Court, who handed down his decision on September 12, 1914. On the whole, it supported the Costa Rican contentions. Thereafter, a commission of engineers definitely surveyed the line between the two republics. Panama, however, continued dissatisfied. In 1921, there broke out a "war" with Costa Rica in which the territories assigned to both countries were invaded.

In March, 1921, the United States insisted that the guarantee of independence given Panama was conditioned on its observance of its international obligations, and urged acceptance of the White award. Panama appealed to the chief South American republics, protested that the arbitrator had exceeded his powers and that the United States was setting itself up as an "international Executive Power compelling other sovereignties to carry out arbitration awards." Finally, Panama yielded, but only after the United States had sent a battleship and 400 marines to the isthmus.[16]

Two other problems in Panamanian foreign relations were brought to a head by developments in 1926. They concern the rights of the United States in the Canal Zone and the relations of the two countries in time of war.

The treaty of 1903 granted to the United States in the area within which the canal was to be constructed "all the rights, power and authority" which it would possess "if it were the sovereign of the territory." [17] Though these words seem to be explicit, they have been variously interpreted. The Gov-

---

[16] This summary is based on Guardia, Ricardo Fernández, *Cartilla Historica de Costa Rica,* San José, Costa Rica, Librería Lehmann, 1927, *passim;* Waddell, A. S., *Unsettled Boundary Disputes in Latin America,* Foreign Policy Association, Information Service, March 5, 1930, p. 494; and Buell, "Panama and the United States," *op. cit.,* pp. 410–411.

[17] Article III.

ernment of the Canal Zone allowed foreign merchants to establish themselves in the territory, and Panama protested that competition with merchants in Panama was thus created. The authority of the United States in the Zone, it was argued, was that necessary for carrying out the purpose of the grant—the building of a canal. In December, 1904,[18] there was made the so-called Taft agreement, by which, among other provisions, it was agreed that private trading in the canal should be eliminated. Abuses, it was alleged, continued, especially when the Government commissaries undertook to trade in a wide variety of goods not essential to canal construction and to supply these not only to United States employees but, it was charged, to any others who sought to buy. This and a large number of other causes of misunderstanding were from time to time covered by executive orders, issued by the President of the United States and approved by Panama, looking toward confining retail sales to canal employees. The agreements were restated in the Panama Canal Act of August 24, 1912, but did not bring a satisfactory understanding. Commercial disputes continued to be the major cause of ill will. Various rules to restrict sales within the theoretical limits were alleged to be generally evaded.

In 1922 the United States abrogated the Taft agreement. Causes of dispute had come to include certain lands, harbor rights, road building, and control over telegraphs, telephones, and radio in the republic. A new treaty, modifying that of 1903 and intended to settle the matters in controversy, was signed at Washington, July 28, 1926, but has failed of ratification.[19]

In this agreement was included a clause concerning the military co-operation of Panama and the United States which was perhaps the main reason for the failure of the measure. Its most important provision declared, "Panama agrees to

---

[18] *Treaties, Conventions, International Acts, Protocols, and Agreements between the United States and other Powers, 1910–1923,* Washington, 1923, Vol. III, pp. 2758–2761.

[19] Text in *Congressional Record,* 69th Congress, Second Session, January 18, 1927, Vol. 68, Part 2, pp. 1848–1852.

cooperate with the United States in the protection and defense of the Panama Canal. Consequently the Republic of Panama will consider herself in a state of war in case of any war in which the United States should be a belligerent . . . ," and on request will give to the United States during hostilities the control of wireless and radio communication, aircraft, airports, and aerial navigation.

Opposition arose in Panama not only because of the alleged effect of these clauses on the national sovereignty but because they put the Government in an equivocal position as to certain specific international obligations. Panama had become a member of the League of Nations. Under Article XII of the covenant, Panama was bound to submit all disputes which might lead her into war to an inquiry or arbitration, and was obliged not to resort to war until three months after a decision had been reached. This and other articles of the League agreement were already binding international engagements. Ratification of the proposed treaty would violate them. On the other hand, it could be pointed out that, as a consequence of the relations with the United States created by the treaty of 1903 and the close association of the two governments in the canal enterprise, Panama could hardly avoid being promptly drawn into any war in which the United States might be engaged. As a consequence, the actual position of the Republic would be substantially that contemplated by the proposal of 1926, whatever might be its legal obligations under its membership in the League of Nations.

CHAPTER XV

Costa Rica

AMONG Caribbean states none has developed greater individuality than Costa Rica. Its affairs show what a small tropical country can accomplish under domestic, social, economic, and political circumstances by no means uniformly favorable. In its international relations it has had peculiar responsibilities, because of the weaknesses of its immediate neighbors, and equally perplexing problems in its relations with the United States. The regional political interests of the latter have so steadily increased during the past generation that they have directly and indirectly had a continuing influence on Costa Rican affairs. In addition, capital of citizens of the United States has been heavily invested in the fruit industry and public utilities, and has more recently financed a large part of the loans floated by the Government.[1]

The early settlers of Costa Rica, like their descendants, found the coastal districts less attractive than the small central plateau in which the moderate elevation tempered the tropical climate and in which lay the more easily worked agricultural lands. On the plateau was established the center of Spanish control, which by 1565 had at least nominally been extended to practically all the land now claimed by the Republic.

Geographically and in the character of its population, native and European, this southern projection of what later was

---

[1] A detailed study of economic, political, and social development in Costa Rica is found in Jones, Chester Lloyd, "Costa Rica and Civilization in the Caribbean," *University of Wisconsin Studies in the Social Sciences and History,* No. 23, Madison, Wis., 1935.

the Captaincy General of Guatemala had features which from the beginning of the Spanish colonial period set it in contrast to the other divisions of Central America. It was isolated from the other provinces by lands either of little value or rendered difficult of access by mountain barriers. As a consequence, it did not attract large numbers of Spanish adventurers, but continued backward in its economic development and neglected by the representatives of the mother country. Later, when Costa Rica became independent, this physical separation from its neighbors contributed both to its development of local nationalism and to its comparative freedom from the intraregional dissensions which made the history of the neighboring republics turbulent.

The indigenous civilization was sharply differentiated from that of the northern states. In the latter states lived Indians with a developed tribal organization and a more advanced agriculture and local industry, all of which facilitated imposition of the typical encomienda system elsewhere found in the better-favored regions in which Spanish control came to be established. The colonial system came to rest on grants of Indian villages to the conquerors, who collected tribute from their subject serfs and in course of time developed the large landholdings typical of most of the Spanish-American colonies.

But in Costa Rica the Indian population was sparse, little organized, and of relatively low culture. Efforts were made to enslave the aborigines with but little success. The native population to a large degree disappeared, and, while it is still evident to a larger degree than in the regions northward settled by north Europeans, it has not become in Costa Rica an important or dominant ethnic factor, as has occurred elsewhere in Central America and Mexico.

In contrast to the neighboring republics, Costa Rica is distinctively a white race community. The racial divisions reported are: 82.20 per cent white, 14.40 per cent mixed, and 5.40 per cent colored. There is only a small number of Negroes in the country, all but a small fraction of whom are comparatively recent arrivals living in the banana-producing districts.[2]

Costa Rica differs also from the other divisions of Central America in the character of its Spanish population. Elsewhere the conquerors and those who followed them are reported to have come largely from Andalusia, but Costa Ricans are said to have come largely from northwestern Spain and to show the qualities of frugality and industry for which the people of that region are noted.[3] As Indian labor disappeared, the settlers fell more and more under the necessity of working their lands themselves.

Access to European markets in the colonial era and until late in the nineteenth century was by the roundabout Pacific route, causing an isolation from the rest of the world which kept the purchase of imported goods at a low level, and restricted the goods which could be sold abroad. The chief items in the export trade of the present day are recent developments. Coffee was introduced only toward the end of the colonial regime. When bananas and plantains became a staple crop for local consumption is not clear, but their cultivation appears to have been well established by at least the early 1840's.[4]

A large part of the land in colonial times was held in common by the villages. These areas, in the second half of the

---

[2] The racial factors in the Caribbean region are discussed in Jones, Chester Lloyd, *Caribbean Backgrounds and Prospects,* New York, D. Appleton and Co., 1931, pp. 14–42.

[3] Recent Costa Rican researches seem to indicate, however, that the immigration came from more scattered areas than this, the traditional statement indicates.

[4] Bananas were brought from the Canary Islands to Santo Domingo in 1516 by Fray Tomás de Berlanga and gradually found their way to all countries of the Caribbean. Berlanga later became bishop of Panama and may have introduced the fruit there, whence the cultivation may have spread westward and northward to what is now Costa Rica. The fruit is alleged to have been introduced into Mexico in 1531. For a long period after the conquest, it does not appear to have been a staple article of Costa Rican diet. It is unmentioned in the Governor's reports to the King, which not infrequently go into detail as to the local crops. An agent of President Van Buren found plantains and bananas generally cultivated in the plateau region in the early 1840's, and it is not unlikely, therefore, that the banana was introduced at a considerably earlier period.

nineteenth century, were largely divided into small farms which became private property and, contrary to the experience in Mexico in the Diaz regime, continued to be held by small owners. Thus there grew up a class of small landholders which has been and continues to be a steadying influence in Costa Rican life. Indeed, until the later part of the nineteenth century, when unoccupied areas were also disposed of liberally by the Government, large estates were decidedly the exception.[5]

This small, compact, homogeneous population, predominantly European in inheritance, without the marked distinctions found in many Latin-American countries, and comparatively free from entanglements with its neighbors, has had a political development of a distinct character that is not surprising. The early history of independent Costa Rica, however, does not show as sharp a contrast to that of the other Central American republics as might be expected. The population was overwhelmingly illiterate—it was often a problem to find men who could read and write to fill the public offices —and the great majority of the population showed no interest in public affairs. Neighborhood jealousies were often highly developed, and national consciousness, even as to internal affairs, had yet to be aroused.

As a consequence, the government fell into the hands of the chief families, possessed of greater wealth, education, and social prestige. Control of the army, as elsewhere in Central America, was also an important factor in political developments. This condition, indeed, though now less marked than formerly, continues in large degree to be the case even to the present time. The dominance of the "first families" was broken in 1870, when Tomás Guardia, leader of an almost bloodless revolution, established himself in control, which he continued to hold until his death in 1882. Since his dictatorship, the older aristocracy has never been able to regain its former position. Associates of Guardia and their relatives continued at the helm until 1899, when the first "compara-

[5] For a more detailed statement, see Munro, Dana G., *The Five Republics of Central America*, New York, Oxford University Press, 1918, p. 138 *et sqq.*

tively free and popular election which the Republic had ever known" [6] was held.

While the standards of political action in Costa Rica during the first three-quarters of a century of its independent existence were by no means such as are prevalent in the most advanced republics, it is clear that those who controlled the country's public affairs brought to it, as the years passed, substantial improvements in its position and governmental practices similar to those obtaining in republics popularly governed. The creation of a middle class of small landowners in itself established a basis for national life which worked toward the elimination of government by *caudillos,* or military leaders. Government contests came to be confined largely to contests between various groups in the capital and did not plunge the people into civil wars, as they did in neighboring communities.[7]

The economic development of the country was later stimulated by legislation favoring the development of coffee and banana culture. Public finances were, in the long run, put on a sounder basis. Free and compulsory popular education was established in the late eighties. As a result, illiteracy fell steadily. It stood at 68.59 per cent in 1892, but at only 23.6 per cent in 1927. This is the best record in the Caribbean.[8]

Popular influence in elections and observance of constitutional standards have increased markedly in Costa Rica since the turn of the century. With the exception of an upset in 1917, discussed below, Costa Rica has in this period enjoyed almost uninterrupted internal peace. Elections have been held regularly and popular participation in them has been general.

In spite of the notable advance achieved, Costa Rica still furnishes strong contrasts to the best-developed democracies, and some of the evident shortcomings are not soon to be eliminated. The economic foundation of the republic's na-

[6] Munro, *op. cit.,* p. 147.

[7] This condition is, however, one which reflected also the popular apathy toward public affairs which has only recently shown signs of lessening.

[8] See Jones, Chester Lloyd, *Caribbean Backgrounds and Prospects, op. cit.,* pp. 58–76.

tional life is still narrow. Coffee and bananas are the chief crops, and the fortunes of the markets for these two products determine the prosperity of the country. Local industry is poorly developed and can hardly become greatly diversified in view of the limited natural resources. Communication facilities, though praiseworthy efforts for their improvement have been made, are still inadequate. Under these conditions the standard of life of the people, though it compares favorably with that in other tropic communities, is not such as to leave a satisfactory social surplus beyond the minimum of subsistence, a fact which accounts in part for the limitations on popular interest in public affairs and the backwardness of public improvements.

Political life has continued interest only for a small group, chiefly in the capital. Parties of impermanent character center around personalities rather than issues, and, as is perhaps natural in a small community in which families are large, their action is greatly influenced by consanguinary ties. The discussion of public issues in the press, which in contrast to the rest of Central America here enjoys a freedom bordering on license, seldom turns on fundamentals. Election periods are by no means free from vote buying and similar abuses.

Though the army is no longer as important a factor in Costa Rican affairs as was formerly the case, the executive continues to exercise a far-reaching influence on the choice of his successor—so great an influence, in fact, that rarely does a candidate actively opposed by the outgoing administration succeed to power.[9]

But, in spite of all these limitations, Costa Rica stands out as the most successful of Central American attempts at popular government, and the development toward constitutional standards promises to continue. The abuses still prevalent tend to become less, and those who are disposed to discount what can be done in tropical countries in achieving good standards of self-government will do well to remember the conditions prevailing, for example, in many American com-

[9] An excellent analysis of the Costa Rican attitude toward public affairs is found in Munro, *op. cit.*, pp. 148–163.

munities a generation ago and even in some of the larger municipalities of the United States in our own time.

The only forcible overthrow of government in Costa Rica since the beginning of the century occurred in the Tinoco *coup d'état* of 1917. It merits special attention since it reflects the conditions in Costa Rican local politics, illustrates the degree to which even in this, the strongest of the Central American states, domestic affairs become dependent upon the attitude taken toward the government by foreign powers, particularly by the United States, and because it shows the difficulties which the Isthmian republics meet in trying to live up to their desires to promote peaceful methods of government within their own borders and in neighboring states.

In the desire to normalize their political development, the five Central American republics had engaged, in one of the treaties signed at Washington in 1907, not to recognize any government which might come into power in any one of them "as a consequence of a *coup d'état,* or of a revolution against the recognized Government," until the freely elected representatives of the people should have "constitutionally reorganized the country." To the agreement Mexico and the United States were not signatories, though they had, to a degree, sponsored the calling together of the Central American delegates, and though, on invitation of the latter, representatives of the two larger republics had been present at all the deliberations. If the engagement entered could be carried out, it would bring a marked change in previous practice and a distinct advance.

In 1914 Alfredo Gonzales Flores became President of Costa Rica by Congressional action after an election in which no candidate had received a majority in the popular vote. As the end of his administration approached, it was charged that he wished to succeed himself. Re-election was prohibited by the Constitution; but the President held that, having been chosen by the Congress, he had never been "elected" in the sense contemplated by the constitutional provision, and that therefore the prohibition did not apply to him. Popular opinion was reported as strongly opposed to such a strained interpretation of the fundamental law. In addition, the President had lost the support of a number of influential leaders through his advocacy of property and income taxes and a land policy which would affect adversely the wealthy classes. Nevertheless, it was generally feared that through exercise of the executive power he might be able to carry the election.

Under these conditions the Tinoco brothers arranged a barracks revolt. Federico Tinoco, Minister of War, replaced many army officers by his partisans. His brother, Joaquin Tinoco, seized the barracks on January 27, 1917. Federico Tinoco then set himself up as military dictator. He issued a proclamation that he had "taken control to save the country." [10] The deposed President and his associates sought refuge in the American Legation and requested "the protection of the United States to sustain legal government." [11] They later left under safe-conduct for the United States.

The new government set up a cabinet representing all factions and called a popular election, to be held early in April, to elect a President and delegates to a constitutional convention to assemble on May 1. A general amnesty was declared. The new regime appeared to have the support of the majority of the people, who preferred peace to the possibility of further disturbance. Later, five ex-Presidents declared their support of the new regime, and the *coup d'état* "almost ceased to be discussed."

The United States was thus confronted by a dilemma. If it refused to recognize the new government, it would discountenance an administration which apparently was at least accepted by the local population. If it recognized the new regime, it would turn its back on the 1907 treaty which it had sponsored and would lay itself open to the charge of discouraging the efforts which the Central American governments had undertaken to improve their political practices.

The decision as to the course of action was taken promptly.

---

[10] The opposing Costa Rican versions of the revolt are found in *For. Rel.*, 1917, pp. 309–320.

[11] *Ibid.*, 1917, p. 301.

On January 30 the American minister was instructed to "take no action which might be construed as recognition of any new government unless instructed by the Department." [12] This was followed by a declaration that the United States viewed the "overthrow of the established Government in Costa Rica with the gravest concern," and "in view of its policy in regard to the assumption of power through illegal methods" would not "give recognition or support to any Government" not "elected by legal and constitutional means." No government set up by Tinoco would be recognized, even if he were chosen by election, and any claims later made by United States citizens because of financial aid given Tinoco would be denied diplomatic support.[13]

The Tinoco administration went ahead, nevertheless, and at the voting on April 2 Tinoco was chosen President without opposition in an election reported to be accompanied by little enthusiasm and much corruption. The situation which developed did not lack in amusing features. The United States declared war against Germany on April 6, 1917. On April 9, Tinoco announced that Costa Rica considered it the duty of all American republics to support, at least morally, the noble attitude assumed by the United States in defense of the highest ideals of law, of right and justice, and of democracy. Costa Rica, it was declared, regretted that it could not more substantially co-operate with the United States, but was glad to offer "the use of its waters and ports for war needs by the American Navy." [14]

On April 11, Tinoco in a letter to President Wilson announced that he had taken over the Presidency to which he had "been called by the free and manifest will" of the people and protested his "devoted and sincere sympathy" [15] with the United States in the existing crisis. But the welcome declaration of the Costa Rican position in the war produced no change in the attitude of the American administration.

---

[12] *Ibid.*, 1917, p. 304.
[13] *Ibid.*, p. 306.
[14] *Ibid.*, 1917, pp. 321–322.
[15] *Ibid.*, p. 322.

Already, by May, there were rumors of revolt, and Joaquin Tinoco, now Secretary of War, was inquiring whether objection would be made to his entry into the United States as a private citizen. Press censorship, a widespread spy system, and forced recruiting were turning public opinion against the *de facto* government.[16] In June the President asked the American representative to inform President Wilson that he sought recognition but could dispense with it. Right, he said, was on his side, and to retire at the bidding of a foreign power would be treason. Contemporaneously, the representatives of the ousted government were praising the nonrecognition stand taken by the United States Department of State.

Soon Tinoco was in need of money. Congress voted him authority to issue paper not redeemable for four years. He still hoped for recognition, and meanwhile increased his military control of the country. Further to align himself with the United States, he severed diplomatic relations with Germany on September 21.[17]

What attitude would the countries signatory to the treaties of 1907 adopt toward the revolutionary government? Would they follow the interpretation of its intent which had been given by the United States? Honduras recognized Tinoco on June 11, 1917, after his letter declaring that he had been constitutionally elected.[18] In July it was reported that he had received ammunition from Guatemala,[19] and recognition was later reported.[20] In September, the United States had taken steps to influence Nicaragua by letting it be known that recognition of Tinoco would not be regarded "as evidence of a friendly feeling toward the United States."[21]

If it were to be accepted as settled that the United States would not recognize Tinoco, how far would it go in encouraging or acquiescing in forcible opposition to the Tinoco regime by Costa Ricans? The answer to this question was unequiv-

---

[16] *Ibid.*, pp. 323 and 326.
[17] *Ibid.*, 1918, pp. 233–238.
[18] *Ibid.*, 1917, pp. 345–347.
[19] *Ibid.*, p. 340.
[20] *Ibid.*, 1918, p. 252.
[21] *Ibid.*, 1917, pp. 343–344

ocal. Revolutions in favor of partisans of the old government were discouraged as early as June, 1917.[22] A proposal by a certain Volio and others that they be allowed to start a movement against Tinoco from Nicaraguan territory gained importance toward the end of the year. Nicaragua was, apparently, willing for the plan to go through if the United States would consent; but the latter discountenanced armed activity and insisted that moral force was the only means through which a constitutional government could be established.[23] Permission for revolutionaries to proceed to Nicaragua from Panama was not forthcoming.[24]

By the opening months of 1918, the position of Tinoco was desperate. His actions in domestic affairs became more and more highhanded. He tried to induce the ex-Presidents to reaffirm their support, but they refused and now told him that the country was almost unanimously against him.[25] In a revolution against Tinoco, the opposition was forced to surrender by putting the two daughters of the Minister of Finance in the Gonzales Flores regime in front of the Government troops.[26]

Hopes of recognition had faded away by April, 1918. Both the President and his brother Joaquin now pleaded that public reaffirmation of the position of the United States should be avoided. If it should occur, they declared, they would be assassinated within twenty-four hours.[27] Volio had by this time succeeded in reaching Nicaragua, which caused the brothers added anxiety. They would welcome an opportunity to leave the country in some official capacity,[28] and on May 24, 1918, once more tried to secure American favor by declaring war against Germany. But no modification of American attitude occurred, and the *de facto* government held on because it did not dare to let go.

---

[22] *Ibid.*, p. 332.
[23] *Ibid.*, pp. 348–349; *ibid.*, 1918, p. 229.
[24] *Ibid.*, 1918, pp. 229–230.
[25] *Ibid.*, 1918, p. 238.
[26] *Ibid.*, p. 242.
[27] *Ibid.*, pp. 257–259.
[28] *Ibid.*, pp. 258–259.

Public opinion against the usurpers was now definitely crystallizing. Economic conditions were upset by the interference of the European war with established markets and by the disastrous financial measures of the Government. Public opinion was swinging to open support of the position taken by the United States. A crowd gathered before the American Legation to cheer the United States and President Wilson, but was dispersed by the police. This and other acts of the Tinocos brought the closing of the American ministry. Armed opposition to the government steadily increased and reached the capital by the middle of June, 1918. The end was evidently at hand. In August the revolutionists were demanding that constitutional government, as it existed under Gonzales, should be re-established, and the next month brought reports that the President was in flight to Kingston, Jamaica, and his brother assassinated.[29] Julio Acosta was nominated Provisional President and chosen President at the following election.

The Tinoco regime brought into high relief the weaknesses of the treaty of 1907. Even in Costa Rica the standards espoused represented ideals sought but not achieved. Had recognition by the United States been granted, possibly the new government would have been able to maintain itself and it might not have resorted to the extreme measures to which it was forced by non-recognition. On the other hand, recognition by the United States would have meant support of a government set up in defiance of treaties entered into by the Central American states with the solemn desire to avoid the difficulties arising from their self-recognized weaknesses. To be sure, not even the refusal by the United States to recognize the *coup d'état* brought loyal support by the Central American republics of the treaty they had ratified. But, had the opposite course been taken, the United States could and perhaps would have been charged with abetting the discard of principles for which all the Central American states

---

[29] *Current History,* Vol. X, Part II, pp. 417–418; and *ibid.,* Vol. XI, Part I, p. 64.

had declared themselves and to which it had itself given its support at the time when the treaty was made.

Following the period of the Tinoco regime, Costa Rican political affairs returned to their normal course. The laws on voting were recast by adoption of a literacy test [30] and by other political reforms. The Republic entered the League of Nations.[31] Efforts were made to settle the Panama and Nicaraguan boundary problems, elsewhere discussed, to promote foreign trade, to increase transportation facilities, and to establish cable, radio, and air mail communication with foreign countries. Sustained support was given to popular education. New treaties to guarantee Central American peace were consummated in 1923. Conservative management characterized public finances. Government control of electric power development, insurance, and banking was extended.

Two issues, domestic in character but involving foreign interests, merit special consideration.[32] As a result of the financial irregularities of the Tinoco regime, claims for damages arose. Concessions of certain lands alleged to contain petroleum deposits had been granted by Tinoco to British interests. They were repudiated by the Costa Rican Congress in 1921.[33] Other claims were for damages to British subjects. These were settled by arbitration before Chief Justice Taft of the United States Supreme Court.

Another controversy which has claimed wide attention in Costa Rica is that involved in the policy to be adopted toward the fruit industry, the exports of which are now second in importance in the foreign trade of the republic. Though the banana was long before introduced into Costa Rica and estab-

---

[30] *Ibid.,* XIII (October, 1920), Part I, p. 107.

[31] *New York Times,* December 17, 1920, 2:4; entry as of December 16, 1920. Costa Rica withdrew from the League of Nations on January 1, 1925, effective January 1, 1927, apparently because of questions raised by non-payment of dues to the League. (*Current History,* Vol. XXI (March, 1925), p. 930.) Steps looking toward re-entry were taken by the Congress in 1930. (*Current History,* Vol. XXXII (September, 1930), p. 1200.)

[32] The boundary disputes of Costa Rica with neighbors are discussed in the chapters on Panama and Nicaragua.

[33] *New York Times,* October 13, 1922, p. 27:2; *ibid.,* Nov. 2, 1922, p. 24:2; *ibid.,* March 8, 1923, p. 9:2.

lished as a subsistence crop, it began to be cultivated for export there, as in other Caribbean regions, only in the last quarter of the nineteenth century, the first sizable shipments dating from 1883, when 110,803 bunches were exported. Shipments reached 1,034,765 bunches in 1890 and 11,170,812 in 1913, the record year.[34] At that time, about 800 square miles were under cultivation for this fruit. Meanwhile, the Panama disease had made its appearance in the plantations and had spread with alarming rapidity. The exports fell off after 1913, and in 1932 were only 4,251,016 bunches, the lowest figure since 1903.[35] The chief producing area has been in the east near Port Limon, where American interests have developed extensive holdings and practically monopolize the export business, though independent producers raise about three-fourths of the crop on land owned by them or rented from the fruit interests.[36] In the industry as a whole, about fifty per cent of the laborers are native Costa Ricans, the balance being West Indian Negroes who have not the prejudice felt by many Costa Ricans against work in the hot lowlands. The transportation facilities to the east coast have also come to be operated by the fruit interests.

Under these circumstances, the Costa Rican Government has had conflicting impulses in the development of its policy toward the fruit industry. Like the governments of competing areas, it has not felt free to demand as high taxes on the export of fruit as it would like to ask because high taxes would tend to discourage production and drive the industry elsewhere. The predominance of foreign initiative and the size of foreign capital in the business create local jealousies and the belief that the "extractive industry" should contribute more than it now does to the support of the country.

In addition, the influx of West Indians is looked upon with disfavor because those who do not become permanent resi-

---

[34] *Commerce Reports,* 1916 (Washington, 1916), Vol. I, p. 665.

[35] The figure for 1932 is as reported by the United States Department of Commerce. In 1933, banana exports were 4,341,565 bunches.

[36] Letter from Thomas J. Maleady, American Vice Consul in Port Limon, December 12, 1930.

dents are held "to take money out of the country," and because those who decide to remain contribute an unwelcome racial factor to the population.

The critical attitude is not removed by realization of the benefits which the fruit industry has brought to the republic. The industry has used land formerly almost without value, and has made possible the creation of railway and steamship facilities which would otherwise not have come into existence. It has created towns in which health conditions are exceptional for the tropics where formerly there were only malarial ports commonly referred to as "white men's graves." The health campaign carried on has been continuous and of recognized success. The fruit interests have provided the country with its best hospital facilities. They have strengthened the economic position of the republic by bringing large amounts of money into the country through wage payments and capital expenditures and by diversifying its export crops.

In the tax adjustments which have been reached, the Republic has entered with the foreign interests producing fruit a number of contracts by which it has sought to protect and encourage independent planters and to assure the national Treasury increased "banana income." The agreements and the legislation affecting the fruit industry, as is to be expected, have never given full satisfaction to the nationalist desires. On the other hand, foreign interests have complained of what has been considered ill-advised restrictive legislation and arbitrary acts on the part of the administration. The situation, moreover, has not been made easier by the fact that the transportation and marketing of the product are controlled in all but insignificant degree by a single company.

The controversies concerning banana export which have arisen have involved the contracts with the interests operating the railroads, wharf charges on exports, which the Legislature has at times sought to differentiate from export taxes, export taxes as such, freight rates on bananas to be charged on the railways, the minimum prices to be paid per bunch to independent producers, and various special undertakings by the concessionaires. The export taxes have long been an issue of importance and were the center of the recent controversy and adjustment.

As early as 1892, there was passed a law putting a tax of two and a half cents per bunch on banana exports.[37] In 1900 the Republic made a contract, which later came to be owned by the United Fruit Company, under which the export of bananas was to be kept free from taxes for a period of ten years. Attempts by the Congress to evade this agreement were vetoed by the President in 1907. In the same year, the Republic entered into two new contracts by which, in return for services to be done by the company, Costa Rica, among other engagements, agreed that for ten years after 1910 the export tax on bananas should not exceed one cent, to the exclusion of all other charges on exports of the fruit. In 1909 there were made further adjustments by which the export tax on bananas was fixed at one cent per bunch up to July 7, 1930.[38]

As this period, in turn, came to a close, the question of a new contract again became a matter of primary concern. The fruit interests slackened their new plantings because the conditions under which the crops from fresh areas could be marketed had become uncertain. The ultranationalists made proposals to have the export tax greatly increased and formulated far-reaching plans for nationalizing the fruit industry and the public utilities. After long-drawn-out negotiations and congressional discussions, there was signed in July 1930, a new contract by which the fruit interests agreed that the export tax on bananas should be increased from one cent to

[37] The following paragraph is based on the facts stated in a veto to a law of 1907 held by the President to be violative of the rights of the fruit interests. It is found in Saenz, Alfredo, *Contratos y Actuaciones de las Compañias del Ferrocarril de Costa Rica, la Northern Railway Co. y La United Fruit Co., en Costa Rica,* San José, Imprenta "La Tribuna," 1929, p. 83 *et sqq*. This publication and *Trabajos y Opiniones sobre las Cuestiones Agraria y Ferrocarrilera en relación con los Concessionarios Extranjeros en Costa Rica,* published by the Cooperative Bananera Costarricense, San José, 1928, give a comprehensive review of Costa Rican relations with the chief foreign concessionary interests. The documentary material is followed by a collection of articles highly critical of the foreign interests.

[38] Saenz, *op. cit.,* p. 257.

two cents per bunch. The minimum price per bunch to be paid to independent planters was increased and special arrangements to apply to all fruit which was rejected were made. New company plantations of not less than 4,000 acres were to be set out within five years. In return, the fruit interests received a guarantee that the export tax should be the only one to which they should be subject and should not be changed until 1950. They were also granted the right to import certain railway materials free of taxes.

The relations with the fruit producers, the railway companies—to a degree, representing the same interests—and the power companies, all of which are largely in the hands of foreign capital, are an almost constant subject of discussion by the Costa Rican Congress and the press. The charges made on one side and the other are typical of those found elsewhere in Latin America. They show the same perfervid rhetoric and extravagance in assertion which appear in arguments concerning purely domestic affairs. That the extreme assertions are always without some foundation is not to be presumed here any more than in countries where discussions of public affairs are carried on in more measured terms. Instances of flagrant abuse are found in all countries. The more serious statements made by those in responsible positions, and the contracts entered show that the actual standards of action established are at least much less subject to criticism than the declarations of their critics indicate.

In general, it is to be borne in mind that all enterprises in undeveloped countries must of necessity assume economic risks not found elsewhere, and that, among these, the political risk is not to be overlooked. In common with domestic enterprises, they are disposed to seek to protect themselves by special clauses in their contracts with public authorities. Local governments, realizing their weakness, may seek to include terms intended to protect their own interests—demands which would not elsewhere be suggested. Witness, for example, the appearance—even in Costa Rican contracts—of clauses by which the concessionaire is required explicitly to renounce the right to appeal for diplomatic protection. That items of exceptional character of both sorts are found in Latin-American public contracts is no discovery for anyone generally familiar with the terms of such contracts and the conditions under which they are made. That items restrictive of local freedom of action are seized upon by local politicians and capitalized in appeals to an impressionable and often poorly informed public is by no means characteristic only of Costa Rica or less stable Latin-American republics.

Costa Rican public finance in the years following independence had a history similar to that of public finance in other Central American states. In 1827 the debt of the then already disintegrating Central American Federation was divided among the five component states, Costa Rica's share being fixed at one-twelfth, or £13,000. This obligation promptly fell into default, but was canceled in 1840 by an adjustment with the bondholders. Negotiations for loans to construct a railway to the Atlantic were later undertaken, but they met repeated defeat. In 1871 and 1872, two loans were at last floated in Great Britain under conditions which proved to be unfortunate for both the Republic and those who bought its securities. Default again became chronic. A new series of adjustments was negotiated in the period 1883–1885; and from the latter date to 1895, interest payments were made punctually. Then they fell into arrears again until a refunding in 1910, when the Republic entered a new arrangement involving a loan in 1911, service on which was met punctually even during the years of the World War. Meanwhile, internal debts accumulated, to be refinanced by a loan in France.

After the war, prices for Costa Rican products rose and the condition of the Treasury permitted cutting down the debt—to a large extent by making possible a settlement of French claims in 1925 on a compromise basis made possible by the depreciation of the franc. The prosperous conditions of the time led to confidence in "the new era" and to fresh borrowings, this time in the United States. The total of the public debt thus became 101,433,588 colones ($68,341,190) on December 31, 1930. From 1911 to 1932, the Republic made a good record in meeting its foreign debt obligations, but the world-wide depression forced suspension of payments, in the latter year, on the British loan of 1911 and the American issues of 1926 and 1927. In order to avoid complete suspension, it was announced on December 15, 1932, and February 17, 1933, that the obligations on stated issues would be met partly in cash and partly in new securities during periods ending in 1935 and 1936, after which it was planned to resume the full service of the debts.[39]

The more extreme nationalist partisans in Costa Rica, as in other republics southward, look upon foreign capital and foreign initiative as influences always malign. They would exclude all but domestic enterprise, or at least all but that which covenants to place itself exclusively under the control of the local authorities. Such a position disregards the lessons given by the advantages which have been reaped by other countries until recently undeveloped, such as the United States, Canada, and the stabler commonwealths of South America, through the encouragement of foreign participation in the development of the national resources.

The more responsible elements in Costa Rica are fully aware of the advantages of closer connection with the economic forces which have conditioned progress elsewhere. They are anxious to stimulate immigration of European stocks and the co-operation of foreign entrepreneurs and foreign capital. Better schools, better communication facilities, and a higher standard of life, they recognize, have come to them and will come to them in the future in still greater measure through the stimulation of trade interchange with foreigners and through the development of the national wealth which would be denied or at least greatly delayed if local initiative were depended upon solely.

---

[39] Costa Rican public finances are analyzed in greater detail in *Fifty-Fifth Annual Report of the Council of the Corporation of Foreign Bondholders of the year 1932,* London, no date, pp. 170–185; Jones, Chester Lloyd, *Caribbean Backgrounds and Prospects, op. cit.,* pp. 276–278; *Bulletins of A. Iselin and Co.,* New York, February 9, 1931, and September 2, 1932; and Güell, Tomás Soley, *Historia Monetaria de Costa Rica,* San José, Trejos Hermanos, 1926.

This constructive point of view receives frequent support from the spokesmen of the more serious classes of Costa Rica. Ex-President Ricardo Jimenez, in a report on the 1930 banana contract, declared "that foreign capital should have assurance that plans founded on reasonable calculations will not be altered by unexpected changes in the fiscal policies of the government." Another Costa Rican leader, in commenting upon the radical point of view, declares,[40] "We suffer from anti-foreignism carried to dangerous extremes. Everything with a tint of the foreign creates ill-feeling and although it may be for our benefit our first impulse is to reject it. . . . Foreign capital horrifies us although we need it. . . . We should be more harmonious and . . . examine business matters . . . without ruinous sentimentalism. Business has no nationality. Commercial exchange is indispensable. The more business we have, the more our industries and agriculture are developed, the greater will Costa Rica become."

On the other hand, the forward-looking classes in the Costa Rican public are not content to become a reflection in miniature of any other civilization. They are anxious that Costa Rica shall continue to develop a distinctive nationality. They are disposed neither to ally themselves closely with their more turbulent neighbors nor to accept an indefinite increase of the Americanization which they feel threatens them. Co-operation they welcome, but absorption into any other larger unit has few partisans and will have still fewer with the development of an already active national consciousness.

---

[40] Montejo, Manuel, in *Diario de Costa Rica,* quoted in *New York Times,* February 22, 1931, Section III, p. 8:6,7,8.

CHAPTER XVI

Political Developments in Nicaragua

NICARAGUA, with an area of approximately 49,500 square miles, slightly more than that of the State of New York, is the largest state of Central America. Unfortunately for the development of a strong sense of nationalism, the territory lies in two sharply contrasted physical areas which make it to a large degree a country "divided against itself." The separation into a thinly inhabited northern region and a better-settled southern region found in Honduras is here replaced by one showing a thinly populated east and a more densely occupied west. The east, in general, is a region of heavy rainfall, the precipitation reaching 251 inches per year at San Juan del Norte, while the average in the west is 61.5 inches—roughly twice that of Rome, Amsterdam, or Minneapolis. Although the west has an average temperature at the coast slightly higher than that on the east coast, its climate is more attractive. The east has heavily wooded lands and, near the coast, low-lying districts with some rivers which in the rainy periods permit navigation far into the country; while the west, with its two large lakes, is a well-drained, rolling plateau with a narrow coast belt and better-defined dry and rainy seasons.

Seven-eighths of the population lives in the more attractive western region. There lies, comparatively, the largest portion of the national wealth, there centers political and cultural life, and there the bulk of public income is expended.

The east is an orphan area, badly neglected, valuable, if the practice of the Government be taken as an indication, chiefly for the revenue it can contribute to the Treasury and a section with little claim on the Government for money for development of its unexploited resources.

A large part of the land in Nicaragua is not actively used. Of the practically thirty million acres, about one-third is waste land and another third is in merchantable timber but little exploited. Perhaps five per cent is under crops, three per cent in pasture, and the rest is cultivable but not exploited. Raw land is cheap; but the expense of clearing, the lack of good roads and railroads, the insecurity of life and property, a poor system of education, and the lack of initiative on the part of the greater part of the population have retarded development which might otherwise have occurred.

As in Honduras, the population is relatively sparse. No accurate census has ever been taken. In 1880 the total was estimated at 350,000 souls. Fifteen years later, it was put at 420,000—slightly greater than that of the neighbor republic; but in 1929 the number was estimated at 750,000—a relative decline, as compared to Honduras.[1] The reported ethnic division of the population is also little more than an estimate. The portion most affected by European immigration is found in the west and in the towns, though immediately east of the lakes there are some distinctly Indian communities. Practically purely Indian districts are also found in the low-lying districts east of the mountain region. Of the total population, seventeen per cent are of reputed European ancestry, about ten per cen are Negroes who live chiefly in the east coast regions, and the balance—of more than two-thirds—are at least predominantly Indian though "wild Indians" are not found in large numbers.

The social structure of the republic is simple. There are few persons of great wealth. Landholdings of a wide variety of sizes are found—some of the largest being held by foreign companies exploiting the east coast. Racial lines do not sharply divide the people in their social relations. Family connections here, as in all Spanish civilizations, play a prominent part in both economic and political affairs. The average income, calculated on a money basis, is almost unbelievably low. One careful estimate puts the cash income at "some-

---

[1] The population of Honduras was reported as 859,761 in the 1930 census. (*Commerce Yearbook,* 1932, Vol. II, p. 439.)

what less than $40 per capita per annum." [2] That life can be maintained on such an income means that the average Nicaraguan has to be satisfied with the simplest of clothing and household equipment and that his food must be confined to the products available in the local market—chiefly corn, rice, beans, bananas, cheese, and meat. When primary wants are satisfied, there is little money left. There is but little of the national income on which the Government can draw for taxes. Educational facilities and other services dependent on the public treasury remain at a low level. The census reported almost three-fourths of the total population in 1920 as illiterate.

In spite of this rather discouraging background, the average Nicaraguan, though not of great initiative, is of distinctly attractive mental quality, independent and democratic in spirit, familiar in address, kindly in his personal relations with his associates, and interested in public affairs. These are qualities which, once the limitations under which the country has lived for generations are modified, should allow the Republic to make consistent advance.

Long after the skirting of the east coast by Columbus in 1502, Nicaragua was a source of international controversy but a region of backward social and economic development. The first explorations and settlements were in the west coast region. Granada was founded in 1524. After other experiments had been tried, Spain put the region under Guatemala in 1570, but progress of all sorts was slow. Hawkins and Drake attacked the east coast shortly after, and other English, Dutch, and French "pirates" followed their example in the sixteen hundreds. In 1687 the Governor of Jamaica set up a protectorate over the territory of the east coast tribes, then

---

[2] Cumberland, W. W., *Nicaragua, An Economic and Financial Survey,* Washington, Government Printing Office, 1928, p. 17. Calculation of per capita incomes is always difficult, and estimates have fairly high variations. A recent compilation of gross per capita income less taxes shows the following contrasts as of 1929: United States, $657; United Kingdom, $329; Argentina, $216; Germany, $189; France, $173; Uruguay, $159; Spain, $135; Cuba, $88; Puerto Rico, $81; Costa Rica, $60; Venezuela, $51; Colombia, $47; Peru, $45; Salvador, $41; Guatemala, $32. (Crowther, Samuel, *America Self-Contained,* Garden City, Doubleday, Doran and Co., 1933, p. 291.)

known as the Misskitos. Thus began a long-contested British activity in this region. There the British flag was formally hoisted in 1740, and there a young sea captain, later Lord Nelson, in 1780 seized and held for a time a port on the San Juan River. In 1786 England by treaty recognized the region as Spanish, though she continued to have influence there until well into the nineteenth century.[3] In the long run, Spain, as the colonial period advanced, gradually strengthened its hold—especially in the west, where by 1750 cacao production for the Mexican and South American market had become an important industry. Coffee, never so important here as in the republics to the south and northwest, was not an important export in the Spanish period.

By the end of the 1700's, the colonial period was drawing to a close, and, when the other divisions of the old captaincy general of Guatemala broke away from the mother country, Nicaragua went with them. Spain made no effort at reconquest.

A division of opinion promptly arose among the inhabitants over the annexation to Mexico forced on Central America by Iturbide. Conservative Granada favored it; Liberal Leon, then and now the largest city, did not. Thus, at least so tradition has it, arose the political division which has ever since added to the problems of this much divided republic.

Shortly after the end of the brief Mexican conquest, Nicaragua joined the Central American Federation; but it seceded in 1838 under the lead of the Leon faction, which made their city the capital. For two decades there followed practically continuous civil war. By 1855 the Granada group was in the lead and shifted the capital to their own stronghold. The Liberals, to strengthen the opposition, accepted the help of an American soldier of fortune, William Walker, who, arriving in

[3] The record of British operations in Nicaragua is a complicated chapter too little known. It extends long beyond the period of the colonial regime. "England seized the port of San Juan del Norte, on the Atlantic, in 1848; took possession of Tigre Island, in the Gulf of Fonseca, in 1849; and claimed the whole of the eastern coast as a protectorate, this latter pretension not being given up until 1894, during the Cleveland administration." (Weitzel, George T., "American Policy in Nicaragua," *Sen. Doc. No. 334,* 64th Cong., 1st Sess., Washington, 1916, p. 6.)

June, 1855, soon got possession of the San Juan region, which had had increased importance since the gold rush to California, and the use of the "transcontinental" route across Nicaragua used to reach the Far West. Before the end of the year, Walker made himself practically a dictator over the nominal chief of state and was called by his partisans "the Guardian Angel of Nicaragua." Later, though unrecognized by the United States and already facing armed opposition from other Central American countries, he convened a controlled Congress which elected him President, an office which he assumed on June 12, 1856. The opposition, however, steadily increased in strength, and after reverses the adventurer was forced to leave the country in May, 1857.[4]

After these painful experiences with asking the help of foreigners in settling their affairs, the Conservatives and Liberals agreed on a compromise capital at Managua in 1858. There followed from 1863 to 1893 the period still known in Nicaragua as "The Thirty Years." A group of Conservatives handed on the presidency from one to another of its members, kept down disorder, and gave the country the most constructive period of its history.

But even the best run of oligarchies have contests among their own members, and in 1893 the Conservative party became divided against itself and a young Liberal, José Santos Zelaya, seized control of the government.[5] He was to become a notable figure in Central American politics. At the end of his first term, he forced his re-election, and, now firmly established, continued to dictate in Nicaraguan affairs until 1909. During his seventeen years, he made an irregular record, favorable in its first part but more and more unfortunate thereafter.

Arbitrary government, the grant of indefensible favors to

---

[4] Walker later headed two other expeditions to Central America, but was finally captured and shot outside the fort at Trujillo, Honduras, on September 12, 1860.

[5] The best surveys of recent Nicaraguan developments are: Cox, Isaac Joslin, "Nicaragua and the United States, 1909–1927," *World Peace Foundation Pamphlets,* Vol. X, No. 7, Boston, 1927; and Stimson, H. L., *American Policy in Nicaragua,* New York, Charles Scribner's Sons, 1927.

his friends—resulting in a "curse of concessions"—heavy taxation, inflation of the currency, and large military expenses for repressing civil disturbances and forwarding Zelaya's ambition to dominate in the politics of neighboring states brought the country into lamentable economic conditions. The dictator had openly violated the terms of the treaties of 1907, to which his government had been a party. Against such action Costa Rica, Salvador, and Guatemala all protested to the United States. A revolution under Conservative leadership broke out on the east coast in 1909. Largely as the result of the actions of Zelaya, during the summer six American and two Mexican gunboats "patrolled the Atlantic and Pacific coasts of Central America in an effort to intercept filibustering expeditions and to preserve some semblance of order." [6]

In November, two Americans who had served in the revolutionary army were summarily tried and shot by Zelaya's forces after, it was alleged, having been cruelly tortured.[7] On reviewing the situation, the United States broke off relations with Zelaya, who promptly but unsuccessfully sought a reconciliation. Upon the failure of his efforts, he resigned and ultimately fled to Mexico on a Mexican gunboat. Juan J. Estrada, leader of the revolution, took control of the government on August 21, 1910.

The United States now made a forward move to try to bring about normal conditions. The treaties of 1907 had not fulfilled their promise. A suggestion to Mexico that the two powers guarantee the neutrality of Honduras and compel observance of the conventions had been declined by President Diaz, who said that the interest of his country was confined to the border state of Guatemala, but that anything the United States might do to the southward would be endorsed in advance.[8]

The latter country next sent to Nicaragua Mr. Thomas C. Dawson, its minister to Panama, to report on conditions and to present its views. The position then taken has been the

---

[6] Weitzel, *op. cit.*, p. 4.
[7] *For. Rel.*, 1909, pp. 455 and 456.
[8] Weitzel, *op. cit.*, p. 4.

background of the subsequent American policy in the Republic. The principal proposals made by the minister were: (1) that a constitutional government be re-established and a President promptly chosen at a free election; (2) that there be adopted a liberal constitution with guarantees for the rights of foreigners and prohibition of commercial monopolies; (3) that an impartial commission pass on the claims against the Government; (4) that the national finances be stabilized —a move which might necessitate the making of a loan, in negotiating which the United States would lend its good offices. The so-called "Dawson Agreements," embodying these principles, were signed in October, 1910. Not all the items of this program were subsequently carried through, and new ones, especially those looking toward guarantee of public order, have since developed.

The next two years, in fact, indicated anything but the dying down of party animosities and the coming of peace. An election not entirely free was held in November, 1910. A light vote—totalling some 30,000—was cast and resulted in a Conservative victory. General Estrada was inaugurated President on January 1, 1911. But disorder did not end. The Zelaya party continued to cause trouble locally and fostered attacks from the neighboring republics. The Conservatives were divided among themselves; indeed, some of their leaders were active influences in preventing the reconstruction program from getting under way.

As a result of the continued political rivalries, Estrada resigned in favor of Adolfo Diaz, the Vice-President, who in turn was unable to deal with the Liberals or to bring co-operation among the factions of his own party. He threatened to resign, but later proposed that the United States be given, in the Constitution, the right to intervene to keep the peace under an arrangement similar to that in force in Cuba. The United States did not support the suggestion.

By August of 1912, disorder had become so serious that the United States felt justified in adopting exceptional measures which, with those rendered necessary by the first steps taken, marked a second and long forward step in its relations with

Nicaragua. A Legation guard of 100 men was sent to the capital by the Navy. American forces were in the republic practically continuously thereafter for twenty years. Revolutionary activities at first increased. Property of foreigners, including Americans, Italians, British, and others, was seized. An additional force of 360 marines was sent to guard the Legation, and another was put ashore at Bluefields to protect American and foreign interests there. The United States authorities requested President Diaz to assure protection of American lives and property. He replied that he could not, and asked that United States forces protect American property and "all the inhabitants of the Republic." Step by step, the northern republic became committed to a policy involving guarding the Legation, keeping open communications, protecting American life and property, and seeking by appropriate means to restore order and the resumption of its functions by the Nicaraguan Government.

Such a task proved by no means simple. The continuing revolutionary activities were marked by broken armistices, maltreatment of messengers, torturing of noncombatants to force contributions, bombardment of the capital, and slaughter of defenseless bodies of enemies. American forces were engaged in active warfare against three revolutionary groups until October, 1912, when the war was brought to an end by the capture of Leon. The total of the American military reached, at its height, about 2,700.

On November 2, 1912, President Diaz was re-elected. The following four years, though not without local disturbances, were relatively peaceful. As elections again approached, the United States offered its help to assure that they would be free, but Diaz declined, though he gave verbal assurance that proper standards would be observed. Emiliano Chamorro, a Conservative, was chosen, having obtained 50,000 votes. This term also passed without serious disturbance of the peace. As the next election approached, the United States Department of State again suggested that reforms in the electoral laws be made, but the President of Nicaragua considered the time inopportune and the existing law assurance of free elections.

This opinion events did not justify. In an election characterized by irregularities, Diego Chamorro, uncle of the retiring President, was chosen by 58,000 votes to 32,000 cast for the candidate of the Liberals. The election over, the Nicaraguan President accepted American assistance in drafting a new electoral law, which was adopted by the Congress in 1923.

The elections of 1924 brought three interesting developments. One of the Liberal chiefs made inquiry as to whether he would be acceptable to the United States as a candidate. The Department of State replied that it would not choose among rivals for the presidency. Its policy was to co-operate to promote stability, constitutional government, and fair elections. This position was reiterated during the campaign. Efforts to quiet party dissensions brought about a coalition ticket, supported generally by the Liberals and a portion of the Conservatives but not by the faction of Emiliano Chamorro, which proceeded to run him on a separate ticket. Carlos Solorzano, Conservative, headed the coalition ticket, while Juan Sacasa, Liberal, was candidate for Vice-President. The third factor was the announcement on November 14, 1923, by the Government of the United States that it desired to withdraw the marines.

In varying numbers, American forces had been in Nicaragua continuously since their entry had been requested by President Diaz in 1912. The Legation guard, which it was now proposed to withdraw, had taken no active part in keeping order, but its presence had acted as a stabilizing influence. The enactment of a fair electoral law, the United States declared, was a first step toward free elections and constitutional government; and other constructive measures, it was confident, would be adopted. Therefore, it was proposed to evacuate the American forces as soon as the Government to be chosen at the approaching election was installed in January, 1925. Indeed, the marines were to remain in the country during the electoral period only if Nicaragua felt that their doing so would assist in insuring free elections.

In addition, the United States was willing to co-operate in bringing stable government if the Nicaraguan Government desired. It stood ready to suggest assistants who would help in putting the still untried electoral law into effect and would be glad to help in the organization and training of an efficient constabulary which would assure maintenance of peace after the withdrawal of the marines.

The Government of Nicaragua hesitated to accept the proffered aid. Arrangements for assistance at the elections fell through. The vote was held without major disturbance and resulted in victory for the coalition ticket by 48,072 votes to 28,760 for Chamorro in a total vote of about 84,000. Patent frauds had occurred in the voting, but the United States, after some hesitation, recognized the new Government.

With the election past, the new President Solorzano declared for strict observance of the new electoral law, for full freedom in the elections to be held at the end of his term in 1928, and for close co-operation with the United States, the assistance of which, he declared, had in all ways been to the advantage of his country.

The date for withdrawal of the marines, as proposed after the inauguration, was now at hand; but in January, 1925, President Solorzano declared that he wished to establish a constabulary of the sort proposed, and, after setting out the bad results which would follow prompt withdrawal, asked that the marines be left in the country until the constabulary under American officers could be set up.

To this was made the reply that the intent to withdraw the Legation guard had been expressed fourteen months previously. No steps had been taken in that time to create the constabulary. In view of the statements made by Nicaragua, the guard would be allowed to remain for such period as was absolutely necessary to organize the new force if steps to organize it should be undertaken "immediately and energetically." If satisfactory progress were made, the guard would be maintained in the republic to September 1, 1925. Though the Nicaraguan Government had agreed to proceed to organize its constabulary, once the assurance that the marines would stay temporarily was given, it neglected to do so. In these circumstances the Legation guard sailed from Corinto on August 4, 1925.

The recall of the United States military forces merits comment as to the success of the policy which had caused their entry and as to the wisdom of leaving the country to its own resources at the time that the forces were withdrawn. The marines had entered on invitation from the Nicaraguan Government and had stayed at the expressed wish of the local authorities. This point may easily be overstressed, for it is often a question whether the government in power in weak states actually represents the people of the territory over which it exercises nominal sovereignty. It is fairly clear that the Diaz regime of 1912 would have had great difficulty in maintaining public order. Once the armed forces of the United States were established in the country, the Conservative governments showed a tendency to be satisfied with the *status quo*—a willingness not to bestir themselves to develop a local force and to assume that the presence of American forces might be indefinitely prolonged.

Such a standard was unacceptable to the United States, since it was inconsistent with its announced intent to act only in a temporary role looking toward the creation of conditions and institutions which would allow the discharge of normal duties by a responsible local government. Indefinite maintenance of United States troops to keep the peace in a foreign country was also not acceptable to public opinion in the United States, in which, to a greater extent than is justified by the facts, all "republics" are considered to be "governments of the people, by the people and for the people." Further, other New World states, under misapprehensions of local conditions, resented what to them appeared to be the imperialistic policy of the "Norte-Americanos." Finally, though the foreign armed forces might, and to a great degree did, keep the peace by their mere presence, it was natural that such local opinion as existed in Nicaragua, outside the government party, should look upon them as interlopers whose stay, if it must be accepted, should be made of as short duration as possible.

All these considerations argued for withdrawing the American forces in 1925. Nevertheless, judged by the events which followed, the action was of doubtful wisdom. The entry into the country had been undertaken to restore public order. The long stay had been made with the avowed intent to assure order for the future. But the hopes that, in spite of longstanding political habits promotive of unsettled conditions, it would still be possible to set the Nicaraguan people on the road to real popular and constitutional government within a relatively short time were sanguine indeed, and the efforts to bring them to set themselves to the task had not been successful. The government which was at the time in power did not have strong or united leadership. It was a coalition of antagonistic elements and almost certain to suffer from the limitations of "coalition" governments.

Judgment in retrospect is always easy, but it is hard to believe that those in charge of American policy at the time were without grave doubts as to the probable result of withdrawal. Though there was clearly the chance that, if the troops were not withdrawn, their stay might be indefinite if the local government continued its policy of inaction, it was equally evident that withdrawal at the moment might precipitate a period of disorder.

The United States had, months before, informed the defeated factions that it would look with disapproval on revolution against the established government. With the military forces gone, however, this moral influence was far from sufficient to restrain the malcontents, especially the faction of the defeated Conservative candidate, Chamorro. Disturbance spread rapidly, and in September, 1925, American naval vessels were again at Corinto and Bluefields. The Conservative-Liberal coalition promptly broke up. Solorzano appointed Chamorro, his fellow Conservative, General in Chief. The Liberal Vice-President Sacasa fled the country in November, alleging threats against his life. In the next month, through Chamorro's influence, opposition members of the Congress were expelled and his own faction put in control by the seating of other men.

Throughout this period, the United States had taken the position that, if Chamorro were made President, he could not be recognized because he would have obtained power by *coup d'état,* in violation of the terms of the treaties of 1923,[9] to which Chamorro, as the representative of Nicaragua, had himself affixed his signature.

With Congress now in his control, however, Chamorro was in a position to force his own election under a plan which he could argue was technically legal—if the legality of the individual steps in the program were not questioned. The Constitution of Nicaragua provides that in case of the absence, temporary or permanent, of the President, the Vice-President shall act. If both be absent, the office passes in turn to officers chosen by Congress. Of these there are two, the First and Second Designates.

Chamorro now developed his plan. He had himself elected to Congress, and shortly Congress chose him First Designate. On January 12, 1926, the Congress impeached Vice-President Sacasa, who was already a fugitive, and four days later President Solorzano, who had offered to resign, was instead given an indefinite leave of absence. He was kept for a time under surveillance for fear that he, also, would flee the country. Chamorro, First Designate, was now in line for the presidency. He took over the chief magistracy on January 17, 1926. Not until March 14 was the "resignation" of Solorzano finally accepted. The procedure throughout was the merest sham observance of constitutional standards.

The United States Department of State continued to insist that Chamorro was ineligible because of the provisions of the treaty of 1923 and refused to recognize his government. So did all the neighboring states of Central America. No government in the world, indeed, recognized the Chamorro regime.

As the year progressed, the new government showed itself even less able to dominate the situation than its predecessor has been. Revolution spread in the east. From July to the

[9] See pp. 424–429.

end of the year, various vessels were carrying men and munitions from Mexico to Nicaragua for the revolutionists. In August, American naval vessels were on both coasts. Sacasa, the nominal leader, was busy promoting the opposition, though he never took the active lead of forces in the field. He left the United States, where he had taken refuge in June, for Mexico City, whence he proceeded to Guatemala City, and late in November returned to Nicaragua to be nominal head of the revolutionary forces. He returned, thus, only after Chamorro, as will be seen, had been forced out and Adolfo Diaz had again been chosen President.

The United States attempted in the fall of 1926 to bring peace by a conference of the leaders of the various factions, though its representatives were warned to be careful not to assume any responsibility for carrying out agreements which might be reached by the factions.

A suspension of hostilities was agreed to and a meeting at Corinto, to which representatives of Sacasa—Sacasa himself declined to attend—were taken to the west coast by a United States war vessel, in the absence of commercial shipping, was arranged. At the request of both parties, marines established a neutral zone at Corinto during the sessions. The meetings occurred on board the U.S.S. *Denver,* the first being held on October 16, 1926. Various compromises were suggested, but, the Liberals having suddenly taken an uncompromising attitude, the sessions came to an end on October 24. The attempt at mediation had proved a failure.

Hostilities began again, but shortly another solution seemed to be at hand. Many of his Conservative supporters were deserting Chamorro, against whom in other Central American states hostile sentiment had developed. He continued for a time to declare that he would hold out to the end against all Nicaraguans, but quixotically stated that he would welcome American intervention to settle the political difficulties. Finding this position untenable, he later resigned in favor of one of his own party, who, like Chamorro and for the same reasons as Chamorro, was denied recognition by foreign countries. The Conservatives then turned again to support Adolfo Diaz, whom the Congress chose First Designate and, on November 11, 1926, President. He assumed the office on November 14, 1926, and was recognized by the United States on November 17.[10]

Whether this election was one which observed the terms of the treaty of 1923 and whether it was carried on under observance of the requirements of the Nicaraguan Constitution is by no means clear. It will probably always remain subject to dispute. Constitutional government had been so thoroughly upset and partisan feeling ran so high both before and after the election that it is impossible to dispel doubts as to what the facts were. The Congress was hurriedly summoned. The members who had been expelled, 18 in all, were recalled, but only nine were there when the body organized.

The President of the United States, in his message to Congress on January 10, 1927, declared:

> This Congress, whose acts may be considered as constitutional, designated Señor Adolfo Diaz as first designate. At this session . . . 53 members were present out of a total membership of 67, of whom 44 voted for Diaz and 2 for Solorzano. The balance abstained from voting. . . . As President Solorzano had resigned and was then residing in California and as the Vice President, Doctor Sacasa, was in Guatemala, having been out of the country since November 1925, the action of Congress in designating Señor Diaz was perfectly legal and in accordance with the Constitution. Therefore the United States Government on November 17 extended recognition to Señor Diaz.[11]

It has been explicitly stated, "At no time did the Department of State, as has frequently been charged, put forth any

---

[10] The Department of State, *Latin American Series, No. 6,* "The United States and Nicaragua, A Survey of the Relations from 1909 to 1932," Washington, 1932, p. 64. Chamorro on December 15, 1926, temporarily took himself out of local politics by becoming diplomatic representative of Nicaragua in Europe.

[11] Excerpt from quotation in *A Brief History of the Relations between the United States and Nicaragua, 1909–1928,* Government Printing Office, 1928, p. 36. The order of political events as here outlined follows that given in this pamphlet. The positions taken by various leaders and the Central American governments as to the Diaz government are discussed in Cox, Isaac Joslin, "Nicaragua and the United States, 1909–1927," *op. cit.,* p. 789 *et sqq.*

effort to force the election or designation of Diaz upon the Republic or the Conservative Party." [12]

On December 28, 1926, the United States representative in Nicaragua was authorized to inform Diaz that, while it accorded him recognition, it assumed no obligation to protect his government against the revolutionists. It would give him the "moral encouragement" ordinarily granted to "constitutional governments" but "was not prepared to go further." [13]

Had the Conservatives, constitutionally or unconstitutionally found the way to peace, and would the Liberals now be willing to let the issue of control of the Government go over till the elections of 1928? It was soon evident that both questions must be answered in the negative.

No one, evidently, was more aware that this was the case than President Diaz, for on the day after his inauguration, in an appeal to the United States, he declared that Mexico was acting "in open hostility to Nicaragua" and that therefore he could not make headway against the revolution. He could not protect "the interests of American citizens and other foreigners." Would the United States help "to reach a solution in the present crisis"? He would approve the American action "whatever . . . the means chosen."

By the end of the year, conditions had become intolerable. Mexico continued to look complacently upon the operations of Sacasa, whose revolt, started on December 1, continued to spread from the east coast. The representative of the United States renewed his efforts to bring the factional leaders to an agreement. President Diaz offered peace, payment of salaries in cash, and a share in the government for the followers of Moncada—the general in command of Sacasa's forces—in addition to a diplomatic post for Moncada himself, but the latter refused to negotiate without consulting Sacasa.

As disorder spread through the country, the possibility that other nations would feel that they must take steps to protect their citizens appeared on the horizon. In February, 1927, Great Britain, through her ambassador, drew "the attention

[12] *A Brief History, op. cit.*, p. 37.
[13] Quotations from summary in *ibid.*, p. 40.

of the United States . . . to the menace to British lives and property arising from the . . . disturbances in Nicaragua." The ambassador was "instructed to remind the United States Government that His Majesty's Government looks to them to extend to British subjects . . . the same measure of protection as they afford to United States citizens in the districts now threatened by revolutionary disturbances."[14] Shortly after, a British war vessel was sent to Corinto to serve as "a base of refuge for British subjects," though, it was declared, "it is of course not intended to land forces." Great Britain would "continue to rely on" the United States for assistance. The next day, the United States Secretary of State assured the British ambassador "that the American armed forces which have been landed in Nicaragua for the protection of American and foreign lives and property will be pleased to extend to British subjects such protection as may be possible and proper. . . ." The Belgian, Chinese, and Italian Governments also formally requested protection for their nationals.

Diaz was now thoroughly convinced that the situation which he faced demanded the closest co-operation with the United States as the only way to avoid the development of general anarchy. On February 24, 1927, the same day that the American Secretary of State had given assurance that the American armed forces would extend protection to British subjects, Diaz proposed a close alliance with the United States. Nicaragua, he said, had wanted such a treaty "for some time past." Its early negotiation had been proposed to the Department of State on February 20. By it the United States would assure Nicaraguan sovereignty and independence and "the maintenance of a government adequate for the protection of life, property and individual liberty."[15] To this end it would have the right to intervene "whenever it might be necessary." This would mean the end of *coups d'état* and remove the "uncertain" features of intervention without

---

[14] Department of State, *Press Releases,* Nos. 197 and 200, Feb. 24 and 26, 1927.

[15] These words are a paraphrase of a clause in the permanent treaty between Cuba and the United States then in force.

treaty. The United States would thus better assure their rights to build a canal and to maintain a naval base. Nicaragua would welcome, also, aid in economic rehabilitation through acceptance of a financial adviser and a receiver-general. It would be grateful for assistance in improving health conditions and in establishing an efficient national constabulary.[16]

The Congress of Nicaragua favored the proposed alliance by 45 votes to 10. Certain Liberal leaders also were reported to approve its principles. The United States, however, at once instructed its representatives that the plan should not be encouraged.[17] The separate features of his program Diaz proceeded to develop as he found the United States receptive to suggestion.

The constabulary plan had been put forward by Nicaragua as early as 1911, and the following year the United States had recommended an American to carry it out; but the upset conditions which soon developed brought abandonment of the effort. In 1923, negotiations on the subject were revived, and in June, 1925, the United States authorities again helped in setting up a "non-military and non-political constabulary." [18] Shortly after assuming office, Diaz proposed an American mission to train the army, but for the moment, the country being in revolution, the United States Department of State thought the suggestion inopportune. Diaz now, on May 15, 1927, returned to this project as a part of his program for free elections. A more explicit arrangement for a constabulary to be set up with the assistance of the American Navy and Marine Corps was signed on December 22, 1927.

Meanwhile there made its appearance another proposal involving extensive supervision by the United States of the elections to be held in 1928. Since this proposal came later to have an important part in bringing the Sacasa revolution to an end, it is necessary to review the developments which had been taking place in the conflict. In the closing months

---

[16] Text in *New York Times,* February 26, 1927, p. 2.
[17] "The United States and Nicaragua," *op. cit.,* p. 68.
[18] *A Brief History, op. cit.,* p. 38.

of 1926, though President Diaz continued to try to come to terms with the revolutionists, the latter declared that they would not submit so long as active intervention by the United States was not in prospect. This stand they maintained, though they were repeatedly told that, even if the government were overthrown by revolution, Sacasa would not be recognized. The leaders of both parties shortly declared for American supervision of the elections of 1928, but Sacasa insisted on the withdrawal of President Diaz in the interim.

As the revolution had progressed, disorder had become so widespread that the activities of American armed forces tended to increase. "Neutral zones" had been established on various occasions, especially on the east coast. On January 8, 1927, a Legation guard of 175 men was established in the capital. In February, United States naval forces were protecting the railroad from the capital to the coast. At President Diaz' request, American troops occupied the fort commanding the capital. In March, an additional force of marines was placed in an outlying neutral zone. By this time 2,000 from the naval forces were ashore. Conditions in the country were growing steadily worse and efforts to secure adjustment were at a deadlock.

Under these circumstances President Coolidge sent General Henry L. Stimson, nominally as his special representative, to report the President's views to the American officials and to report to the President the information received from them. In fact, his mission assumed much wider scope. General Stimson arrived in Nicaragua on April 17, 1927. He held conferences not only with the American officials but with leaders of both the contending parties. All agreed that supervision of elections in 1928 was essential if the choice were to be free, that otherwise the party in power would perpetuate its control, as in the past, by dominating the elections. Since revolution, the recourse of those not in power, was contrary to the principles of the treaties of 1907 and 1923, supervision by outside agencies was, for the time, essential.

President Diaz proposed that an electoral commission be nominated by the United States, that the constabulary plan be perfected, and that, pending the time when it could be put into effective control, a naval force sufficient to assure peace be left in the country. Both of the warring factions should surrender their arms into the hands of the Americans, a general amnesty should be declared, and the Liberals should at once have a share of the Cabinet and local offices.

There was suggested a conference at which Sacasa or his representatives should discuss these terms with General Stimson and representatives of President Diaz. Sacasa refused to come to such a meeting, but men representing him were brought to the west coast by an American vessel. At the resulting conference, the latter accepted certain items but wished to refer definite commitment to Sacasa and General Moncada, his representative in the field. Subsequently, under a truce, a conference was held with Moncada at Tipitapa.

Both Sacasa's representatives, who had been brought from the east coast, and Moncada approved the plan for a supervised election, but to the last continued to demand that Diaz retire immediately. General Stimson came to believe that no impartial Nicaraguan who could take the interim presidency could be found, and that an attempt to have Congress elect such a man would result only in further conflict. He informed Moncada that the retention of Diaz till the time of elections was essential and that the United States would accede to the request of the Government that it supervise the elections of 1928. Moncada admitted that, if the United States supported Diaz, he would not oppose the American troops. The other Sacasa representatives took a similar position. Agreement seemed, thus, assured; but, since groups of armed men unconnected with either the Government or the revolution were roaming the country, at the request of President Diaz and Moncada 800 additional marines were landed.

The program for supervision of elections was then advanced. The military chiefs of the revolution agreed to deliver their arms to the American authorities. The Government forces took similar action.[19] President Diaz issued the formal re-

[19] By May 26, 1927, the disarmament of both sides had put 11,600 rifles, 303 machine guns, and 5,500,000 cartridges in the hands of the American forces.

quest for supervision of the elections and for help in training "an impartial and non-partisan force of constabulary." At the same time, he submitted a schedule outlining the standards that he felt desirable in the drafting of a new electoral law and the provision for public order during the election.

Sacasa, though he declined to accept office under Diaz for the period before the election, agreed that his party would co-operate in the voting. By the end of June, the country was at peace except for operations by Augusto C. Sandino, who, after promising General Moncada to do so, refused to lay down his arms and with a few men betook himself northward toward the Honduras border. His force was insignificant and, it was alleged, representative of no political group, but his operations in the inaccessible northern regions were to prove a serious problem for the Nicaraguan Government and, indirectly, for the American forces in Nicaragua.[20]

Attention now turned to the forthcoming elections and the attitude which the United States would assume toward the candidates. General Chamorro, returning from his European mission, went to Washington to interview the Secretary of State. He was informed that the United States was "not supporting or opposing any political candidate" but that clearly General Chamorro was ineligible under Article 104 of the Nicaraguan Constitution and Article 2 of the treaty of February 7, 1923. General Moncada also made a trip north. The Secretary of State informed him likewise that the United States did not intend to "use its influence for the election of any particular person. The United States is going to do its best to see that there is a fair, open, and free election where everybody who is entitled to vote has an opportunity to do so."[21]

The choice was called for November 4, 1928. Before that date, an acceptable electoral law was adopted and registration under the supervision of American representatives was pro-

[20] *A Brief History, op. cit.*, at pp. 54–55 and 58 gives the text of the letter from Sandino to Moncada concerning laying down arms and a summary of his subsequent actions. See also, for a similar review, "The United States and Nicaragua," *op. cit.*, pp. 103–107.

[21] *A Brief History, op. cit.*, pp. 56 and 57.

vided. In this work 352 enlisted marines took part as precinct chairmen. Each was assisted by two Nicaraguan colleagues representing the two chief parties. About 145,000 voters were inscribed, or some 35,000 more than in the election of 1924.[22] After the registration, Moncada suggested to Bernard, who, as Chamorro had withdrawn, had become the Conservative candidate, that "we who desire an era of peace and of industry for Nicaragua . . . agree to accept this same supervision for one or several periods more of constitutional government." Bernard replied, "Your proposition is . . . definitely accepted" and outlined a program of continued economic co-operation in addition.[23]

The election was held without disturbance. To prevent repeating, a chemical stain was used to mark the finger of each voter. President Diaz set the example by voting early and by himself dipping his fingers in the stain.[24] The total reported vote was announced on November 13 as 133,663, with a Liberal majority of about 19,500.[25] The leaders of both parties and the local newspapers joined in testimony that the voting was orderly and fair.[26] It was the first election in Nicaraguan history not dictated by the party in power.

Expressions of good will toward the United States were general. When President-elect Hoover shortly made a visit to Nicaragua on his trip to visit Latin America, at a banquet in his honor President Diaz—soon to retire—President-elect Moncada, and ex-President Chamorro were guests. It was an occasion heralded as unprecedented and symbolic of a new era in Nicaraguan affairs. Early in the following year, Mr. Juan B. Sacasa, former head of the revolution, presented his credentials as minister of the new Liberal government to the United States, declaring the desire of Nicaragua "that the bonds of cordial friendship existing between both nations be augmented without impairment of any kind." [27]

Hopes aroused by adjustments of political conflicts are sel-

---

22 Department of State, *Press Releases,* Oct. 12, 1928.
23 Department of State, *Press Releases,* Oct. 24, 1928.
24 *Ibid.,* Nov. 4, 1928.
25 *Ibid.,* Nov. 13, 1928, and Dec. 17, 1928.
26 *Ibid.,* Nov. 6, 1928, and Nov. 14, 1928.
27 *Ibid.,* April 15, 1929.

dom fully realized, but the arrangements of 1927 were at least followed by greater internal tranquillity and by economic recovery. Sandino, throughout the Moncada administration, remained a source of disturbance to the administration and to the American forces which continued to be kept in the country. Under an agreement of December 22, 1927, the constabulary, now called the "Guardia Nacional," was organized, chiefly under American officers. It undertook both police and military functions. As its organization was perfected, the marines were withdrawn. In 1932, the marines serving with the Guardia Nacional were relieved from duty at country posts, thus leaving native officers in complete charge, and late in the year plans were developed for their complete retirement from the republic, which occurred in the opening days of 1933.

Political developments also became of more normal character after 1928. Juan B. Sacasa, who had become minister to Washington, commended the action of the United States in the republic, particularly its efforts to assure fair elections. When the choice of a President again came up in 1932, the voting was again under American supervision; but such supervision the United States indicated would not thereafter be continued. Sacasa was the Liberal candidate and won by a majority of some 19,000 votes. On February 3, 1933, the new government signed a "peace pact" with Sandino by which the latter, in return for amnesty and land for his soldiers, agreed that with the exception of 100 they should be disarmed.

Later Sandino agreed to leave the question of disarming this group in the hands of President Sacasa, as had been demanded by the Nicaraguan leader of the Guardia Nacional, who had recently announced himself a candidate for the presidency in 1936. Shortly after, on February 21, 1934, the "rebel leader" was killed in cold blood by members of the Guardia Nacional acting, it was declared, without orders from the Sacasa government. That there were no political influences back of the assassination was nevertheless not clear, and the degree to which the forces which were to keep public order could be relied upon to be "impartial" in electoral contests was at least open to question.

CHAPTER XVII

International Relations and Economic Developments in Nicaragua

TWO outstanding features of the recent history of Nicaragua remain to be discussed: the advance in public finance and the Bryan-Chamorro canal treaty. The first is primarily an economic development, but one with far-reaching political consequences. The latter, though its importance at the time of its ratification to many appeared to rest in the emergency relief given to the Nicaraguan Treasury, greatly disturbed Central American politics and may play a prominent role in the Central American policy of the United States.

Like all the other Central American countries, in its financial history, Nicaragua has gone through periods characterized by long-continued defaults and the pledging of specified revenues to the services of foreign loans. In 1827, it assumed two-twelfths of the old debt of £163,000 contracted by the Central American Federation, but made no payment on its obligations till 1874, when the creditors agreed to a heavy reduction of their claims. Other loans were made later and were followed by defaults and "settlements" with results which to the end of the century were of little satisfaction to either the creditors or the debtors.

The more recent financial trials of the Republic date from the closing years of the Zelaya regime, when issues of irredeemable paper money flooded the country. This currency made business speculative and the meeting of foreign obligations difficult—indeed, in the long run, impossible. In 1895, there were 3,000,000 paper pesos in circulation. Beginning in 1901, there were successive issues the total amount of which the Government itself did not know, or, at least, did not reveal. By 1910, there were reported to be 30,950,000 pesos out, and in 1911 some 48,758,000. The exchange value of the peso fell from par—fifty cents, American gold—to about five cents.[1] Reform of the currency had become a crying necessity.

Meanwhile, other features of the national finances had become equally disturbed. In 1909 there had been floated in London and Paris the Ethelburga bond issue for £1,250,000, for which the entire customs income and other properties were pledged. The loan went into default on July 1, 1911. There were also large outstanding claims against the Government; and internal trade, upon which the discharge of the national debts depended, was at a low ebb.

To remedy the difficulties which had already arisen, one of the clauses of the Dawson agreements of August 27, 1910, had contemplated negotiating a refunding loan through the good offices of the United States, to be secured by a certain percentage of the customs. The Nicaraguan Congress voted to borrow $20,000,000 in the United States, and the Knox-Castrillo convention of June 6, 1911, designed to carry out the Dawson plan, was signed. The arrangement as to the national debt had many features similar to those in the Dominican treaty already operating. The new convention would establish a basis for sound economic progress through creating a stable currency, refunding the foreign debt, and pledging the customs for the loan service. It was hoped that it would remove one of the incentives to revolution, since the control of the customhouses would no longer be one of the prizes of victory. In addition, since the loan was to be floated in the United States and would take up outstanding issues, it would remove the possibility of forward British action to protect the rights of European investors. A number of bank-

---

[1] Detailed tables are found in Playter, Harold, and McConnico, Andrew J., *Nicaragua, United States Bureau of Foreign and Domestic Commerce, Trade Promotion Series, No. 54,* Washington, 1927, p. 80.

ing groups in the United States were interested in the project, which it was agreed, as negotiations progressed, should involve borrowing $15,000,000.

If the aid sought was to be effective, prompt action was essential. Nicaragua was already in dire financial straits, and the foreign debt went into default less than a month after the Knox-Castrillo agreement was signed. Nicaragua had ratified the convention on June 14, 1911, by a vote of 30 to 6, but action in the United States Senate was delayed and efforts to have it reported by the Committee on Foreign Relations failed by its tie vote on May 9, 1912.[2] With this check and the outbreak of a new revolution, the refunding loan plan was definitely abandoned by the banking interests. Contrary to what came to be a widely held popular opinion as to what would follow, no treaty for collection of customs in Nicaragua was ratified, nor was any loan of the size contemplated made then or later.

Before the failure of the treaty, however, in anticipation that it would be ratified, Nicaragua and the bankers had taken steps to meet the most pressing needs of the Government and had in effect set up an "unofficial" customs control. With supplementary measures later adopted, the regulation of local finance came to have an extent in some respects even wider than the treaty itself had contemplated.

It had been agreed in September, 1911, that the bankers would lend Nicaragua $1,500,000, would set up a customs collection agency, substantially on the Dominican model, would aid in composing differences with the Ethelburga syndicate, and would study the reform of the currency. Nicaragua was not to alter the customs while the loan was outstanding without the agreement of the bankers, and she was to set up a national bank, on 51 per cent of the stock of which the bankers were given an option. Presently the loan contract for $15,000,000 was signed and was shortly ratified by the Nicaraguan Congress. Meanwhile, an American, Mr. Clifford D. Ham, had been "nominated" for the proposed cus-

[2] Texts of the Dawson and Knox-Castrillo agreements are in "The United States and Nicaragua," *op. cit.*, pp. 125–128.

toms-collectorship by the intending lenders. He was "approved" by the United States Secretary of State on November 11, was appointed by the President of Nicaragua on November 23, and assumed his duties on December 6, 1911. Thus, when the treaty failed to be ratified in May of the following year, a small loan had been made, there was already a customs-collectorship in operation under a private contract, and other steps similar to those contemplated in the treaty had been taken under the same auspices—but the project for a refunding loan had failed. In June, 1912, an adjustment of the British bond claims was secured by the bankers and the bond service for the Ethelburga loan was brought under the collectorship. These arrangements, later still further enlarged, are still in force. Mr. Ham continued in office until June, 1928, when he was succeeded by Mr. Irving A. Lindberg, Deputy Collector since 1912.

In the same year (1912), a new monetary law was passed establishing the *cordoba,* equal in value to the United States dollar, which was to replace the depreciated paper currency. To effect the conversion, United States banking groups made loans amounting to $780,000 and $500,000. In all, some 49,000,000 paper pesos were presented for redemption. They were paid for at rates varying from 16 to 1 to 12½ to 1, and paper pesos were no longer accepted as legal tender after November 1, 1915. Nicaragua now had a stable currency.

But financial difficulties were not at an end; indeed, in 1912 the country was entering upon its darkest period. The expenses caused by the revolution then under way were still heavy, many damage claims were unpaid, and the possibility of the $15,000,000 loan had disappeared. In October, 1913, there were arranged for new resources totalling $2,000,000, secured by a secondary lien on the customs and a direct lien on the state holdings in the National bank and railway not pledged to previous creditors. Again, in 1914, Nicaragua sought to borrow fresh money, but the bankers felt that the limit of credit had been reached.

The financial horizon was indeed anything but bright. The European war was cutting down foreign trade. President

Diaz considered, but was induced to abandon, plans for a new bond issue and inflation. He did declare a moratorium, and the European and American creditors agreed to allow temporary suspensions of payments due and to make other emergency financial adjustments. These were subject to change if the Bryan-Chamorro treaty—which was then under consideration and which is described below—should become law; for, if that occurred, it was argued, Nicaragua would be in possession of cash upon which the emergency loans she had received should be a claim.[3] Nevertheless, in spite of these concessions and in spite of the fact that Nicaraguan finances were being better administered than ever before, the situation of the Treasury was highly precarious and promised to continue to be so until domestic peace was better assured and until the bad conditions created by the European war should cease. No new loans were granted after those of October, 1913, pending the adoption of the canal treaty, which seemed the only way in which extraordinary assistance might be secured.[4]

The failure of the Knox-Castrillo treaty had turned attention to an alternative agreement which might give relief to the Nicaraguan Treasury. This was the sale of an option on Nicaragua's rights on a canal route passing through the San Juan River to the Pacific. Negotiations were begun in February, 1913, and an agreement known as the "Bryan-Chamorro" treaty was ratified, with amendments proposed by the United States Senate, by Nicaragua on April 16, 1916, and by the President of the United States on June 19, 1916.[5] For the concessions which Nicaragua was to grant, the United States was to pay $3,000,000. This amount was not sufficient to meet all claims but would at least tide over the crisis.[6]

---

[3] This arrangement had received the approval of Secretary Bryan. (See *For. Rel.*, 1916, pp. 898–917.)

[4] The political features of the Bryan-Chamorro treaty are discussed below.

[5] *For Rel.*, 1916, pp. 849–898.

[6] The Nicaraguan Legation summarized the state obligations as follows:

The Ethelburga loan contracted by Zelaya in 1909 at 75, bearing 6 per cent interest, secured by a first lien on the customs receipts. The original amount was £1,250,000. About £629,000, after adjustments, remained unpaid in 1912.

The financial experience of Nicaragua from 1910 to 1916 illustrates both the sort of problems which confront the public treasuries of countries politically and economically weak and the unforeseeable circumstances which confront those who loan them money. The Republic had, since 1893, had a government which was inefficient or disturbed. It had destroyed its local credit and was faced with heavy claims for damage arising out of the revolution. It could not borrow at home, and the "security" it could offer to foreign lenders was not unquestionable. It might have to mortgage the national assets to an extraordinary degree, and even then the lender would feel that his risk was heavy with incalculables.

In the years following the establishment of the customs-collectorship, at times it seemed to many foreign observers that all the pledgeable assets of the Government were falling into the control of foreign financial interests. The customs, the national bank, the Pacific Railway, and liquor and tobacco taxes all seemed at times definitely to be passing out of national control.

After 1917, however, the national finances improved. The internal debt was refunded. When payments under the Bryan-Chamorro treaty were being arranged in 1918, there was taken a step, little commented upon at the time, by which it was sought to stabilize finances by setting up substantially a financial adviser with a degree of authority over both revenues and expenditures. This was done by the creation of a high commission of two members, one Nicaraguan and one

---

American bankers, acting on behalf of Nicaragua, had secured a reduction in the interest rate to 5 per cent.

The loan of March 26, 1912, of $755,000 at 6 per cent by American bankers, secured by the balance of the customs receipts, due October 15, 1913, plus the balance of sums aggregating $2,655,000 advanced since January, 1912, at par.

A floating debt of $1,500,000.

Other claims against the Government arising out of revolutions and bad government of a nominal total of $10,000,000, which could probably be reduced to $3,000,000 or less.

The above paragraphs are summarized from *For. Rel.*, 1913, pp. 1043–1044, and *A Brief History, op. cit.*, p. 13.

The Fifty-Eighth Annual Report of the Council of Foreign Bondholders for the year 1931, London, 1932, states that the Ethelburga bonds were "offered at London at 92" and "in Paris at 93½."

American, the latter appointed by the Secretary of State of the United States. If disagreements as to policy arose between these two, an arbiter was to be appointed by the Secretary of State of the United States.[7] The Commission has done much to assure conservative management of the budget. The World War raised the prices for Nicaraguan products. Public finance reflected the more favorable development in trade, and on June 30, 1920, the last of the deferred charges on the old debts was paid off. In spite of new revolutionary troubles in 1924, the Government was able to start a policy of regaining control of national enterprises, parts of which had been pledged or sold to secure emergency funds. The national bank was repurchased, as was later the Pacific Railway. In July, 1924, all amounts owing to New York bankers were repaid and they "completely retired from their connection with Nicaraguan finance." [8]

These were the circumstances when the United States was urging on the Nicaraguan Government that the marine forces be withdrawn and when the election which finally resulted in the election of Solorzano was in course. The hostilities arising in the subsequent conflict with Chamorro and in the Sacasa revolution again made finance a serious national problem and resulted in various loan proposals in the Diaz presidency. In 1927 a loan was contracted in New York for $1,000,000, at 6 per cent, for which the stocks of the bank and of the railway were given as security. The last repayment on this obligation took place on April 21, 1928. Other minor borrowings have characterized later years.

The world crisis beginning in 1929 brought further difficulties in Nicaraguan finance which were increased by the earthquake which destroyed the capital on March 31, 1931, and by the withdrawal of United States marines, whose expenditures had favorably affected the balance of payments. Foreign trade also fell off sharply. Payments on the foreign debts

---

[7] *For. Rel.*, 1917, p. 1119. The high commission had its origin in provisions of the 1912 contracts.

[8] *A Brief History*, *op. cit.*, p. 21. In 1929, the Corinto wharf was bought from the concessionaire.

were kept up with increasing difficulty to the end of 1931. Then a request was made to the bondholders that amortization at a reduced rate be accepted, interest payments being continued. The request was granted in view of the good record made since 1911 and because of the credit standing of the Republic, which caused Nicaraguan bonds to be "quoted higher than any other known Latin American issues." [9]

What Nicaragua had done to justify its credit position may be thus summarized. The Ethelburga loan of 1909 had totaled £1,250,000, or about $6,000,000. Of this issue there were outstanding on February 28, 1935, bonds representing $2,276,938. The guaranteed customs bonds of 1918, the only other major debt outstanding, had been reduced from $3,744,150 to $955,000.[10] Amortization payments in 1932 were five years ahead of schedule on the first and seventeen years ahead on the latter of these loans. There were no outstanding obligations to American bankers.[11]

American investments in Nicaragua and the policy toward them adopted by the Government have been so widely criticized that they merit some summary comments. The public loans of Nicaragua have been in greater part British, not American. The United States loans, with the exception of the guaranteed customs bonds, issued to pay off claims against the Government, have been small and have all been paid off. The total of public and private investments by foreigners in the republic has grown steadily, especially since the time of the customs control agreement of 1912. At the end of 1928, they were estimated at about $24,000,000, of which American holdings comprised $17,000,000 and British investments $6,000,000. Far the greater part of the foreign money which has gone into Nicaragua has entered, therefore, in private undertakings. The increase in American investments in later years has been rapid. In 1912, they were estimated at about $2,-

---

[9] *Nicaragua, Report of the Collector-General of Customs and High Commission for 1932,* Managua, Nicaragua, 1923, p. 3.

[10] *Nicaragua, Memoria del Recaudador General de Aduanas y Alta Comisión por 1934,* Managua, Nicaragua, 1935, p. 9.

[11] Statement of Irving A. Lindberg, Collector-General of Customs, in *New York Times,* February 21, 1932, Section II, p. 8:5.

500,000. About $13,002,000 of the American holdings were reported in 1928 as representing direct investments in business enterprises, chiefly in fruit production and mining.

Though the increase of American holdings has been marked and has carried them far above those of the citizens of any other foreign country, the total is little more than half as great as that in any other Central American republic and is less than in any Latin-American country except Paraguay.[12] It seems fair to conclude that the policy of the United States in Nicaragua has been determined only in minor degree by financial considerations. On the other hand, the influence of financial arrangements on the domestic development of Nicaragua and thus, indirectly, on the position it has occupied in relation to other countries has been and continues to be far-reaching. Between the close of the Zelaya regime and the end of 1930, in spite of recurring additions to national obligations arising out of revolutions, an inflated currency was retired, the country was firmly established on a stable monetary basis, and there was set up an efficient customs administration which brought in increasing revenue and, with minor exceptions, assured the regular service of the foreign debt. National credit was strengthened, claims against the Government were adjusted, and national obligations, foreign and domestic, were reduced. The Pacific Railway and the national bank, which in the ebb of financial fortunes had passed out of the control of the Government, were bought back. Improvements in health conditions were made possible and there occurred some advance in giving the country a transportation system. There can be no doubt that the economic stability of the country increased during the period, to the advantage of both private enterprise and the public treasury. These are very definite and concrete advantages.

The Bryan-Chamorro treaty of 1916, the other leading feature in recent Nicaraguan international relations, also has

---

[12] For tables on which these statements are based, see Dickens, Paul D., *American Direct Investments in Foreign Countries, United States Department of Commerce Trade Information Bulletin No. 731,* Washington, 1930, pp. 18–19.

had both economic and political results.[13] It is the last of seven conventions looking toward the construction of a canal through the republic which Nicaragua and the United States have negotiated. Discussions concerning a waterway were resumed in the Taft administration. At one time, agreements with American bankers involved the grant of an option on a canal route to them. Later the plan came to involve the grant of the option to the United States, which was also to assume wide functions in maintaining public order throughout the republic.

In December, 1911, President Diaz made a suggestion that the United States establish by treaty with Nicaragua a protectorate "like that which resulted so well in Cuba" to assure domestic peace and freedom from interference from the neighboring republics. Secretary Knox thanked Diaz for the confidence in the United States Government which his proposal indicated but gave the plan no encouragement.[14] Representatives of both countries continued to favor an agreement, especially in view of the failure of the Knox-Castrillo convention and the financial distress of Nicaragua. Diaz was anxious to establish a close political alliance to supplement the relations which a canal treaty would create. On February 4, 1914, he expressed his satisfaction that the Secretary of State, Mr. Bryan, who had succeeded Secretary Knox with the advent of the Wilson administration, had approved the terms of the modified treaty including an option on a canal route then under negotiation, and reported that he had cabled President Wilson asking "that said convention be made to embody the substance of the Platt Amendment, so that my countrymen may see Nicaragua's credit improved, her natural resources developed and peace assured throughout the land." [15] Mr. Bryan favored the amendment; but Senate opposition made itself evident, and the treaty he signed on August 5, 1914, with Mr. Emiliano Chamorro—then Nicaraguan min-

---

[13] The negotiations leading up to the treaty are discussed in detail in an excellent study by Isaac Joslin Cox, "Nicaragua and the United States, 1909–1927," *op. cit.*, pp. 722–728.

[14] *Ibid.*, pp. 670–671.

[15] *Ibid.*, pp. 953–954.

ister in the United States—omitted it. In revised form it passed the Senate, with further amendments, and was ratified by President Wilson on June 19, 1916. Nicaragua had ratified it on April 13. It was proclaimed on June 24, 1916.

The treaty was to strengthen the "ancient and cordial friendship" of the parties "by the most sincere co-operation for all purposes of their mutual advantage and interest and to provide for the possible future construction of an interoceanic ship canal . . . whenever the construction of such canal" should "be deemed by the government of the United States conducive to the interests of both countries."

To this end Nicaragua granted, in perpetuity and free from all public charges, the exclusive property rights necessary and convenient for canal purposes. To enable the United States to protect the Panama Canal and the rights granted to it in the treaty, Nicaragua leased Great Corn Island and Little Corn Island in the Caribbean and granted it the right to construct a naval base on the Gulf of Fonseca. These grants were for 99 years with an option of renewal for a similar period. During this time, the territory needed for the canal, if it were constructed, was to be exclusively under the sovereign authority of the United States. On its side, the United States undertook, as is indicated above, to pay Nicaragua $3,000,000.[16]

The convention had not been adopted without vigorous protest by Costa Rica and Salvador. While it was still in draft form, Costa Rica called attention to the "Platt Amendment" provisions then included, which, it was maintained, "would implicitly establish a protectorate" and, "considering the special nature of the relations between the states of Central America, . . . would seriously affect the autonomy of the Republic of Costa Rica" and overthrow the treaties of 1907, which were created to strengthen relations among the Central American states.[17] Salvador joined its protest to that of Costa Rica, and objected also to the provisions in the draft

---

[16] The text of the treaty is found in *For. Rel.*, 1916, pp. 849–852.

[17] The Minister of Costa Rica to the Secretary of State, July 7, 1914, and July 18, 1914. (*Ibid.*, 1914, pp. 959–961.)

treaty referring to the naval base on the Gulf of Fonseca.[18] Honduras also later became involved in the discussions.

The correspondence which followed, in the endeavor to meet the Central American position, shows a desire on the part of the United States to make adjustments which would satisfy the protesters, though it was not admitted that the terms of the treaty involved any violation of their rights. Among those in authority in the Central American states there was apparently a divergence of opinion as to what would be a satisfactory compromise.

Secretary of State Bryan maintained that no rights of the Central American states had been disregarded, that the treaty, as it was to be presented to the Senate, did not involve a "Platt Amendment" clause such as Costa Rica had feared, and that the United States would safeguard Costa Rica from injury in case a canal were built along the San Juan River. The United States would stand willing to purchase an option from Costa Rica "on terms as favorable as those given to Nicaragua." The United States would be willing to purchase a naval base from Costa Rica, but the Republic had indicated it did not wish such an arrangement.

For a time during the negotiations, it seemed as if Costa Rican objections were to be satisfied. The United States minister reported the impression that the chief grievance of Costa Rica was that she had not been consulted as her treaty with Nicaragua of 1858 provided, and that her "national pride had been touched."[19] Early in 1915, Secretary Bryan believed that "all misunderstandings" had been removed, and was discussing with the minister of Costa Rica a treaty with an option "similar to that with Nicaragua."

The objections of Salvador, to which Honduras also gave support, Mr. Bryan proposed to solve in a similar manner. The naval base purchased from Nicaragua was sufficient for

---

[18] The Chargé d'Affaires of Salvador to the Secretary of State, July 8, 1914, and July 21, 1914. (*Ibid.,* 1914, pp. 960, 962–963.) See, for detailed discussion of the case of the canal treaty, Moreno, Landelino, *Historia de las Relaciones Interstatuales de Centroamerica,* Madrid, Compañía Iberoamericana de publicaciones, 1928, pp. 220–244.

[19] *For. Rel.,* 1914, p. 967.

the purposes of the United States; but, to show its "desire to treat all nations alike," it was "perfectly willing to purchase a naval base from Salvador and also Honduras if they desire to sell," though the initiative should come from the latter.

Early in 1915 the objections of Salvador also seemed in course of solution. The President of El Salvador appeared to prefer in return for the naval station which the Government would grant, not a money payment, but American co-operation in stabilizing finance and developing educational and transportation facilities. He was in favor of a naval station conference at an early date to be attended by representatives of all the countries of Central America and the United States.[20] But before the treaty was ratified, in the three republics opinion against it crystallized.

Salvador led the arguments opposed to granting a naval base on the Gulf of Fonseca. They were based on the claim that there was a condominium over the gulf and that rights over it could not be granted without a plebiscite in Salvador, Honduras, and Nicaragua. The United States cited action by them which in its opinion showed that joint ownership did not exist, but the opposite conclusion was drawn from the same evidence by the Central Americans. They also alleged, among other contentions, that a powerful naval station on the gulf could not fail to influence their domestic and foreign relations.

The latter contention is doubtless correct, but it is also clear that the Central American states had in the past acted as if they were free agents in matters relating to naval bases on their coasts. On September 28, 1849, Honduras had signed a treaty with Mr. Squier, the minister of the United States, granting land for a naval station on an island in the Gulf of Fonseca and for fortifying the adjacent coast. Later, in 1885, Honduras had made a formal proposal to grant to the United States the right to maintain coaling and naval stations on both coasts, including one on the Gulf of Fonseca.

---

[20] *Ibid.*, 1915, pp. 1115–1116.

In May, 1883, the President, the foreign office, and leading men of Salvador had approved a proposal for a canal across Nicaragua to be owned and operated by the United States, and even sought to influence Nicaragua to sign the Frelinghuysen-Zavala canal treaty with the United States then under discussion. Two commissioners were sent to Washington with a petition for annexation of Salvador to the United States—a proposal of much wider significance for the Republic than the grant of a naval base on the gulf such as Nicaragua now proposed.

Guatemala in 1881 had proposed to cede Ocos Bay, on its Pacific coast, to the United States for a coaling station, and her foreign minister later enthusiastically endorsed the Frelinghuysen treaty.

Costa Rica also at an earlier time had not made objection to proposals for a canal treaty and arrangements for coaling stations. It had urged the construction of the Nicaraguan canal on Secretary Frelinghuysen on the ground of "fraternity and joint interests"; in December, 1901, it had entered negotiation to lease Port Elena for 200 years, and in April, 1906, had offered to sell Cocos Island, some 200 miles off the Pacific coast, for a naval or wireless station.[21]

The Costa Rican objection based on her treaty with Nicaragua had, at least prima facie, greater force. A boundary dispute between Costa Rica and Nicaragua had arisen in the period when the American filibuster, William Walker, was a figure in Central American affairs. It was nominally settled by the Canas-Jerez treaty of April 15, 1858, Article VIII of which bound Nicaragua not to make any grants for canal purposes "without first hearing the opinion . . . of Costa Rica as to the disadvantages which the transaction might occasion the two countries." If Nicaragua declared the case urgent, the opinion was to be delivered in thirty days; and, if the

[21] For these cases and earlier Central American action favoring the construction of a canal, see Weitzel, George T., "American Policy in Nicaragua," *Sen. Doc. No. 334,* 64th Cong., 1st Sess., Washington, 1916, pp. 24–25, and *For. Rel.,* 1915, p. 1104.

proposed action did not "injure the natural rights of Costa Rica, the vote asked for [should] be only advisory." [22]

In later negotiations concerning the canal, Costa Rica had demanded that it be consulted. Both parties agreed in 1886 to submit to the President of the United States the question of whether or not the treaty was still valid. President Cleveland gave an interpretation of affirmative character on March 22, 1888.[23] By another convention, the boundary line was to be surveyed with the co-operation of an engineer named by the President of the United States. The survey was declared completed September 30, 1927, and was accepted by the Republic.[24]

The rights of Costa Rica in relation to the canal route are thus based, primarily, on the Canas-Jerez treaty and its interpretation by President Cleveland. His statement set out that Nicaragua could not "make any grants for canal purposes across her territory without first asking the opinion of Costa Rica." The "natural rights" of Costa Rica were defined as rights which she possessed, by virtue of the treaty, in the soil "recognized as belonging exclusively to her; the rights which she possesses in the harbors of San Juan del Norte and Salinas Bay," certain rights in a stipulated portion of the San Juan River, "and perhaps other rights not here particularly specified." These rights were spoken of as being subject to injury in case the Costa Rican territory were occupied or flooded, or in case the harbors were encroached upon, or if the San Juan River were obstructed or its navigation impaired at a point where Costa Rica was entitled to navigate it.[25]

The treaty, so the decision held, did not give "Costa Rica the right to be a party to grants which Nicaragua" might make; but "where the construction of the canal . . . [would]

[22] The excerpts above are as quoted in *The United States and the Nicaraguan Canal,* New York, Foreign Policy Association Information Service, May 25, 1928, p. 115. See also *For. Rel.,* 1916, pp. 811–898; *ibid.,* 1917, pp. 1100–1112; and *ibid.,* 1916, p. 875 *et sqq.*

[23] *Ibid.,* 1888, Part I, p. 456.

[24] Summarized from a more detailed discussion in Howland, Charles P., ed., *Survey of American Foreign Relations, 1929,* New Haven, Yale University Press, 1929, pp. 221–223.

[25] *For. Rel.,* 1916, p. 875 *et seq.*

involve an injury to the natural rights of Costa Rica her opinion or advice . . . should be more than 'advisory' or 'consultative.' It would seem in such cases that her consent is necessary, and that she may thereupon demand compensation for the concessions she is asked to make; but she is not entitled as a right to share in the profits that . . . Nicaragua may reserve for herself as a compensation for such favors and privileges as she, in her turn, may concede."

Had the Bryan-Chamorro convention violated Costa Rican rights? This was a nice question allowing various arguments as to the intent of the parties and the rules for the interpretation of treaties. Was the canal treaty one demanding that "the opinion of Costa Rica" be sought before it could be properly brought to conclusion? Did the fact that Costa Rica and Nicaragua had in 1900 entered separate protocols with the United States engaging each to settle with the United States the details "found necessary to accomplish the ownership and control" [26] of a canal have any bearing? Was the agreement one involving a "grant for canal purposes" such as was contemplated in the Canas-Jerez treaty and President Cleveland's decision, or was it an option on rights exclusively Nicaraguan such as any sovereign government could grant? Did Costa Rican rights continue to run against Nicaragua or against the purchaser of the option or against both parties? President Cleveland's interpretation of the Canas-Jerez treaty spoke of "cases where the construction of the canal will involve an injury to the natural rights of Costa Rica" and stated that "it would seem in such cases that her consent is necessary." Could it be pleaded that the Bryan-Chamorro treaty merely granted "the exclusive proprietary rights necessary and convenient for the construction, operation and maintenance" of the canal, and that, therefore, "cases where the construction of the canal" might "involve an injury" to Costa Rica could not yet have arisen? These and many similar questions were promptly raised.

Before the final acceptance of the treaty by the Senate of

[26] *Ibid.*, p. 820. Costa Rica claimed that the protocol she had signed had not been validated.

the United States, a proviso was added in an endeavor to meet the objections which had been raised. It set out, "That, whereas, Costa Rica, Salvador and Honduras have protested against the ratification of the said Convention in the fear or belief that said Convention might in some respect impair existing rights . . . therefore, it is declared by the Senate, that in advising and consenting to the ratification of said Convention . . . [it] be expressed as a part of the instrument of ratification, that nothing in said Convention is intended to affect any existing right of any of the said named States." [27]

With this amendment the treaty was ratified by the parties. The change did not meet approval by the protesting states, and on March 27, 1916, in the interval between action by the Senate and ratification of the treaty by President Wilson, Costa Rica informed the Department of State that it had brought suit against Nicaragua in the Central American Court of Justice to enjoin Nicaragua from carrying out the treaty.

The case of Costa Rica against Nicaragua was promptly considered by the tribunal, and a decision was handed down on September 30, 1916. The representatives of all the Central American states except Nicaragua concurred in the opinion that Nicaragua had violated the Canas-Jerez treaty, the Cleveland Award, and the Treaty of Peace and Amity of December 20, 1907. It rejected the Nicaraguan contention that the treaty granted merely an option. It held that property rights had been alienated "in perpetuity and without any limitation." The amendment added before ratification by the United States was held "ineffective" because, as to the rights of Costa Rica, it did not restore the "legal status." Since the court had no jurisdiction over one of the parties—the United States—it declined to declare the treaty void. The suit brought against Nicaragua by Salvador resulted in a similar decision on March 2, 1917.[28]

Nominally, these cases in the Central American Court of

---

[27] Text in *ibid.*, p. 851.
[28] *Ibid.*, 1917, pp. 1100–1104.

Justice[29] involved only disputes among Central American states. As such, the court clearly had jurisdiction, though, as must have been seen before the decisions were actually given, they could not be given practical effect if they were against Nicaragua unless both Nicaragua and the United States agreed to revoke the Bryan-Chamorro treaty. Neither then nor subsequently has either made any move toward doing so.

The decision had no effect on the Bryan-Chamorro treaty, but it forecast the dissolution of the tribunal which gave it. It may be argued that the court itself never rested on a well-thought-out basis. The political foundations of both the court itself and the member states were, as history shows, of the frailest sort. Controversies between the members had regularly been determined by political and military rather than judicial standards. Though the tribunal was set up with only the most altruistic intent, it was hardly to be supposed that such an institution could at once dominate long-established custom. The court might be expected to deal with minor issues with a good measure of success. On major issues, particularly those involving political matters, representatives of the various states could hardly fail to act, to a degree, as parties in interest. Its record measured with these standards. The respect paid its decisions by the countries which had appeared before it was not such as to justify considering it a body with prestige and influence. When an issue involving deep-seated political feelings was brought before it for consideration, it crumbled.

Though all this is true, it is highly unfortunate that a case

---

[29] Subsequent efforts to make the canal treaty and its implications acceptable to Central American states have not been successful. Signature of a protocol at San José, Costa Rica, in June, 1921, looking toward cession to the United States of rights in the San Juan River, which the proposed canal would follow, did not result in a treaty. (Howland, *op. cit.*, p. 224.) During the negotiations of the Washington treaties of 1923, the Costa Rican representative signed with the American Secretary of State a protocol providing that, if the United States should exercise the option of the Bryan-Chamorro treaty, it would negotiate with Costa Rica to satisfy any rights which Costa Rica possessed. This protocol is not reported as having been ratified by the parties. (*The United States and the Nicaraguan Canal, op. cit.; For. Rel.*, 1917, p. 1100.)

like that involving the canal treaty should have brought the occasion for the practical abandonment of the tribunal. It had been set up with the blessing of the United States, though the United States was not a party to the treaty establishing it. Public opinion throughout the New World had expected much from it—too much. But, however problematical its success might otherwise have been, it was greatly to be regretted that the case which gave the *coup de grace* to its efforts should have been one involving the United States.

Looking back on the events which led up to the decision, it seems lamentable that some means could not have been found at least to delay the ratification of the Bryan-Chamorro treaty. The Nicaraguan canal, if it comes to be built, will be an asset not only to Nicaragua but to all the Central American states. They have expressed themselves repeatedly in favor of its construction; and the United States, as was abundantly shown during the negotiations for the ill-starred convention, was willing to go far to make financial adjustments acceptable to the republics whose fortunes a canal would most greatly affect.

Not all the factors to be considered are financial, it is true, and it is not to be denied that building great fortifications for the defense of an isthmian canal, if they be built, cannot fail to have an influence on Central American domestic and international affairs. The contention of the republics that such fortifications would be a point of attack against them in case the United States itself became involved in a major conflict also has weight. But, if these are circumstances inacceptable, are the alternatives more to be welcomed? That the United States should have a special interest in their affairs and in their orderly development is almost axiomatic in view of the growing interdependence, commercial and financial, between it and them. In international relations, anything that compromises the position of the Central American republics in relation to non-American nations has its repercussion on the United States and all other New World nations. In any war of wide extent and long duration, an attack on the United States could hardly fail to involve Central America and the

Caribbean region generally. Standards which limit the possibility of successful defense in such cases are to the advantage of neither the United States nor its neighbors southward.

It is hard to conceive a serious questioning of the authority of the New World states in the Caribbean which would not promptly bring the closest co-operation by the republics of Central America and the United States. Even in the European war, fought thousands of miles from American shores, Panama and all of the Central American states except Salvador promptly ranged themselves with the United States when the latter entered the conflict. Costa Rica did so in spite of the fact that the United States did not recognize the government then in power. Salvador, though technically a neutral, expressed its sympathy with the United States at various times and offered to let the United States use its ports without condition. Should similar circumstances again arise, similar action could hardly fail to be taken.[30]

No country with a history as troubled as that of Nicaragua has been during the past generation shows satisfactory domestic development. But economic advance has occurred, and more steadily than might be expected. The character of local enterprise has not changed. The raising of live stock and corn, beans, sugar cane, rice, and tobacco for the local markets still comprises the characteristic national activities. Coffee,

---

[30] Martin, Percy Alvin, *Latin America and the War,* Boston, World Peace Foundation, 1919, Vol. II, pp. 261–262. The international relations of Nicaragua with countries other than its immediate neighbors and the United States have been, in the current century, of minor importance. British interests in public loans have already been discussed in connection with the general development of Nicaraguan finance. British political relations with Nicaragua have become less active than formerly. The troubled and sometimes amusing history of British activities at San Juan del Norte and on the Mosquito Coast dates from long before the end of the colonial period and extends to 1894. (See Henderson, John B., Jr., *American Diplomatic Questions,* New York, the Macmillan Co., 1901, pp. 65–289.)

Colombia set up, in 1880, a claim based on rights, dating from the colonial period, to all the Atlantic coast of Central America up to Cape Gracias a Diós. In the Cleveland administration, American naval forces were sent to keep the peace between the local authorities and Colombian forces which were being made ready to seize Great Corn Island. ("American Policy in Nicaragua," *op. cit.,* p. 7.)

bananas, cabinet woods, and some silver are exported and, with the exception of coffee, are largely produced by foreign enterprises. Manufacturing industries are of little importance. On the whole, the country is distinctively agricultural and promises to continue to be so.

As is true in other Caribbean countries, Nicaragua's foreign trade has a far-reaching effect on its prosperity, for the crops marketed abroad determine to a large degree the available surplus over the minimum of subsistence which is supplied by local economic activities. Upon the revenue derived directly and indirectly from foreign trade the Government is largely dependent for financing its functions.

Foreign trade, though it continues highly irregular, has had an encouraging growth.[31] The values of imports and exports in 1928 were almost five times as great as in 1900. The share of the export trade going to the United States and the share of the import trade originating in the United States are each now well above half.

Along with the growth of foreign trade and foreign investment has gone an encouraging rise of public income, though this item also, since it depends so largely on the return from customs duties, shows great differences from year to year. As late as 1915 it was equal only to $2,145,402, but it rose fairly steadily to $6,553,094 in 1929, after which it declined in the

---

[31] NICARAGUAN IMPORTS AND EXPORTS IN CERTAIN YEARS *

In Thousands of Dollars or Cordobas (Equal at Par to the United States Dollar)

	Imports	*Exports*
1901–1905 av.	2,709	3,197
1913	5,770	7,712
1915	3,159	4,567
1920	13,864	10,787
1922	5,124	7,903
1928	13,350	11,693
1932	3,479	4,541
1934	4,610	5,230

* Compiled from *Commerce Yearbook, 1930, Foreign Countries*, Washington, 1931, Vol. II, p. 429; *Nicaragua, Report of the Collector-General of Customs and High Commission for 1932*, Managua, Nicaragua, 1933, p. 118; and *Nicaragua, Memoria del Recaudador General de Aduanas y Alta Comisión por 1934*, Managua, Nicaragua, 1935, p. 19.

world economic crisis to $2,770,574 in 1932. It rose to $3,124,792 in 1934.[32]

A comparison of the outlook in 1900 with that at the present day gives reasonable ground for satisfaction with what has been accomplished and a basis for the hope that the Republic may continue to develop toward a fair degree of political stability on an unfortunately limited economic foundation.

---

[32] *Nicaragua, Memoria del Recaudador General de Aduanas y Alta Comisión por 1934,* Managua, Nicaragua, 1935, p. 87.

CHAPTER XVIII

Honduras

HONDURAS holds a key position among Central American states, with Guatemala and Salvador on one side of it and Nicaragua and Costa Rica on the other. Its borders touch those of all the other nations of the group except Costa Rica. This central location has brought weakness, rather than strength, to the country. The Republic has been powerless to stabilize conditions within its borders, powerless to defend its own sovereignty. It has been dragged into the quarrels of the neighboring areas and has been made the recruiting ground on which forces for revolutions against them have been assembled. In no part of Central America has the desire for peace which shall sink localism and bring all five of the republics under a single government been more ardently advocated, and no part has suffered more from its lack.

Honduras has not been richly endowed with natural resources. The regions back of the short coastline on the Gulf of Fonseca, which gives it its only outlook on the Pacific, are broken by mountain chains and are not highly fertile. The advantage of volcanic soils, which the neighboring republics east and south enjoy, Honduras lacks. The northern section facing the Caribbean, also, is not of unusual promise, though the low-lying plains along the coast have in more recent years proved especially suited to the production of tropical fruits, especially bananas. Here American fruit companies have established themselves and have made what was formerly commercially an almost valueless region by far the most active in the republic.

Physical division into a north section and a south section has its reflection in political life. The south continues to dominate politics. Its leading families have little interest in the north except as it can be made a source of public revenue. The politically active, the "principal families," living chiefly in the south, are usually more nearly of Spanish stock than the common people and the people of the north. Of the latter, only a small proportion "pass for white." By far the majority are of mixed blood or Indian inheritance. On the north coast there are, also, large numbers of Negroes. The national censuses make no attempt at racial differentiations. Throughout the country educational standards are low. The census of 1927 reported seventy-four per cent of the total population to be illiterate.[1]

Modern communication facilities which might break down sectionalism in the country do not exist, and even the capital, located in rugged country back from the Gulf of Fonseca, is still without the service of a railroad. Railway mileage in the country is nominally greater than in any of the neighboring republics, but the lines are local services running back from the northern coast to the plantations of the fruit companies. No railway line effectively opens up the back country and none crosses to the Pacific. Passengers and freight in the hinterland must still travel in crude carts or on the backs of animals—more frequently, the latter.

The political history of Honduras since it became independent of Spain has been characterized by "permanent instability." When a federal union was attempted in 1830, Francisco Morazán, a Honduranean leader, became its most prominent figure and remained so to its dissolution. Thereafter, normal political life was made impossible by the personalistic ambitions of the leaders of family groups, barrack revolts, civil wars, and "international" wars into which the local factions pushed the Republic or into which it was dragged by force or persuasion from its neighbors. Even in more recent years, progress toward political stability has been slow, halting, and at times nonexistent.

---

[1] *Censo general de población, 1927,* Tegucigalpa, Tipografia Nacional, 1927, p. 118.

In 1907, with the help of an army supplied by Zelaya, of Nicaragua, Miguel R. Davila made himself President. In 1910, Manuel Bonilla headed a revolution from the north coast. Mediation by the United States brought all parties to accept Dr. Francisco Bertrand as Provisional President.[2] At the following election, Bonilla was elected.[3] He died in 1913, and Bertrand, the Vice-President, succeeded him. Bertrand won again in 1913. Revolution broke out as the next elections approached, Bertrand fled the country, and the revolutionists, under General Lopez Gutiérrez, seized control. At the following election, Gutiérrez was overwhelmingly "elected" and the regime was "legitimized." [4] The dictatorship which the President established was recognized by the United States in 1920.[5] Between February 1 of that year and August, 1923, some thirty-three revolutions against the government were reported.[6] The United States again sought, but without success, to promote a compromise between the factions before the elections of 1923.[7] At the voting on November 1, no presidential candidate received a majority. The election then

---

[2] Efforts to end the differences of the parties in Honduras in 1911 are discussed in *For. Rel.*, 1911, pp. 297–305. In the course of the conversations, the American commissioner indicated his belief that Dr. Francisco Bertrand was the best of the proposed candidates for the office of Provisional President and Bertrand was then accepted by all parties. His subsequent entry into the capital to assume his duties is thus described in a report of the American minister to the Secretary of State, March 25, 1911: "I have the honor to report that this afternoon the diplomatic and consular corps rode out some three miles to meet the President Designate. Dr. Bertrand was accompanied by about 300 persons, including the members of the peace conference, friends, delegations from Congress, the Executive and the Supreme Court, and some 50 armed men. As we approached the city, the cavalcade increased in numbers. First rode a small troop of cavalry. Next came Dr. Bertrand on a white mule. I rode on his right, the Mexican Minister on his left, and heads of delegations on either side. The streets were filled with people. An expression of relief, of satisfaction, and almost of joy was seen on every face. Perfect order prevailed.

"All political factions cooperated to bring about the first peaceful entrance of a new executive that the capital of Honduras has seen in many years." *Ibid.*, 1911, p. 305.

[3] *Ibid.*, p. 307.

[4] *New York Times*, October 31, 1919, p. 12:7.

[5] *New York Times*, August 14, 1920, p. 6:7.

[6] Hackett, Charles N., "The Background of the Revolution in Honduras," in *Review of Reviews*, Vol. I, pp. 69, 390–396, April, 1924.

[7] *New York Times*, October 2, 1923, p. 6:6.

devolved on the Congress, which failed to make a choice commanding general support.

Through the year 1924, the republic was in an anarchic condition. At one time, ten candidates were competing for the presidency. United States vessels were sent to the coasts, troops were landed to protect foreign interests, and an embargo was put on shipments of arms to Honduras, while "provisional presidents" exercised fleeting control. Salvador, Guatemala, Nicaragua, Costa Rica, and the United States sought to adjust the party differences, and peace conferences were held on American vessels, but with only momentary results. Finally, on December 30, the "National Party" at a new election chose Paz Barahona President, "complete order prevailing." The new magistrate, in spite of recognition by the United States and its sale to him of arms and ammunition, was promptly called upon to put down fresh revolutionary activities and kept order on the north coast only with the aid of American forces landed at his request. By August, 1925, however, peace was "completely restored." [8]

The next elections, held on October 28, 1928, brought Vicente Mejia Colindres to the presidency on February 1, 1929. Revolutionary movements were again under way in April, 1931, and continued well into the summer. American warships were again dispatched to the north coast and were not withdrawn until July.[9] The following year, it was declared that the next presidential campaign would be marked by absolute freedom of speech. The contest at once developed fever heat, which promptly brought revolutionary activities. In November there was held an "orderly election" in which again the Conservative candidate, Carias Andino, was victor. Liberal revolt continued. A German merchant

---

[8] Summarized from dispatches through the year in the *New York Times*.

[9] Department of State, *Press Releases,* April 25, 1931, p. 311; *ibid.,* May 2, 1931, p. 363. The character of the conflict in some of these revolutions is indicated by the report to the Department of State that on May 1, 1931, the revolutionary general, Ferrara, attacked with 350 troops Santa Rosa de Copán. The Government troops, numbering 100, surrendered when their ammunition was exhausted. Fifty persons who were unable to escape were massacred by the insurgents. (*Ibid.,* May 9, 1931, p. 378.)

ship, at the request of the German consul, evacuated citizens of that country from Amapala, the chief Pacific port, and not until the end of the year was the country again nominally "pacified." [10]

The fact is that popular government has never existed in Honduras and that the government is more often than not a military dictatorship. Honduras has been a *republic,* so far as that word reflects a relation between government and citizens, only by a stretch of the imagination.[11] It has remained "independent," not through its internal strength of organization, but by virtue of the weaknesses of its neighbors and because of their jealousies. It has been a "sovereignty" willing and capable to fulfill the duties of a state under international law only, at most, intermittently. Honduras, weak in resources, divided against itself economically and politically, with no real boundaries—physical, ethnic, or historic—separating it from its neighbor states, is an example of a country for which independence has been a highly expensive luxury, and one in which arguments for union with adjoining areas to cut down the overhead expense of government should have strong appeal.

Realization of the national handicaps has, indeed, not been lacking, nor has there been a lack of enthusiasm for federation with the other Central American republics. Leaders in all the five states have dreamed of Central American union since the first days of independence—sometimes, it is true, as a means by which they might themselves become dictators on a larger scale.

After the failure of the first federation, efforts to establish a new one were repeatedly made, the more important instances being in 1842, 1849, 1895, 1898, 1907, and 1921. None of these ripened into a real union, though the developments in the later cases deserve study because of their special interest to Honduras and because of the attitude adopted toward them by nations outside of Central America itself.

[10] *New York Times,* December 28, 1932, p. 6:4, and Jan. 5, 1933, p. 5:4.

[11] A vivid picture of Honduranean politics and the part played therein by the picturesque American filibuster Lee Christmas is found in Deutsch, Hermann B., *The Incredible Yanqui,* New York, Longmans, Green and Co., 1931.

In 1895, two years after he had become President of Nicaragua, Zelaya induced Honduras and Salvador to join Nicaragua to form the "Greater Republic of Central America." The union was given qualified recognition by the United States, but soon disintegrated.

Three years later, in 1898, the star of another dictator, Manuel Estrada Cabrera, appeared on the other side of Honduras, and both he and Zelaya were seeking allies. For years all the countries of Central America suffered from the rivalries of these two men. In 1902 another federation agreement was signed by all the republics except Guatemala. It was a loose engagement to establish compulsory arbitration and a "Central American Arbitral Tribunal." Sectional rivalries continued, and in 1906 Salvador and Honduras invaded Guatemala, apparently supported also by Zelaya.

The interest of the United States in Central American affairs had by this time increased. The United States was already constructing the Panama Canal, and any general Central American war would be embarrassing, especially if it carried the possibility of action by European powers to protect the rights of resident citizens. President Theodore Roosevelt under these circumstances sought the co-operation of Mexico to bring peace in Central America.[12] It was granted, and an offer of mediation was sent to the belligerents and accepted by them. Representatives of Guatemala, Salvador, and Honduras met off Corinto on the deck of the U.S.S. *Marblehead* with mediators from the United States and Mexico, joined later by representatives of Nicaragua and Costa Rica. The belligerents agreed, among other things, to prevent their territories from being used for revolutionary activities against neighbor states and to submit misunderstandings which might arise to arbitration by the Presidents of the United States and Mexico.[13] This looked like a step toward acceptance by Central America of guidance by the strongest Anglo-Saxon

[12] *For. Rel.*, 1906, Part I, p. 836.

[13] See *ibid.*, pp. 836–855, for a discussion of these developments. At the instance of the Argentine delegation, the Third Pan-American Conference approved by acclamation the successful mediation of the United States and Mexico. (P. 855.)

nation and the strongest Latin-American nation of North America. Following the *Marblehead* agreement, all the Central American states except Nicaragua in September, 1906, signed a treaty of peace and amity at San José looking toward closer association and peaceful settlement of their misunderstandings. The contemplated arbitral tribunal had not finished organizing when cases involving alleged attack by Honduras on Nicaragua came before it, and, after a dispute over its functions, the court dissolved.

The effort for peaceful union under international patronage had failed like its predecessors. Nicaragua now refused to be bound by the *Marblehead* treaties, and by the end of March, 1907, Zelaya, backing his Liberal friends in Honduras, had overthrown the government and was apparently ready to attack Salvador. Again Mexico and the United States acted as mediators and it was agreed that a new conference should be called—this time by Nicaragua—looking toward a treaty for settling international differences by arbitration. Once more local political rivalries upset the plan and it soon appeared that a general Central American war was on the horizon.[14]

On August 28, 1907, therefore, President Roosevelt and President Porfirio Diaz suggested a peace conference outside of Central America. Nicaragua had proposed that it be at Mexico City; but the other states preferred Washington, and there it was agreed that it should be held.[15]

The regular sessions of the conference began November 15, 1907, and resulted, before their adjournment on December 20, in eight agreements, the most important provisions of which were an amplification of the San José peace treaty of the previous year. All five states agreed to settle every difference arising among them "of whatsoever nature it may be by means of a Central American Court of Justice." Honduras was to

---

[14] *For. Rel.,* 1907, Part II, pp. 606–635.

[15] The long correspondence involved in the conference is in *For. Rel.,* 1907, Part II, pp. 636–727. The report is at pp. 665–680. More detailed discussions of the steps leading up to the conference are found in Buell, Raymond Leslie, "The United States and Central American Stability," *Foreign Policy Reports,* July, 1931, pp. 165–166; and in Munro, D. G., *The Five Republics of Central America,* New York, Oxford University Press, 1918, pp. 204–226.

be considered neutral territory. Leaders of foreign political factions were not to be allowed to reside near the national frontiers, and those provoking revolutionary movements were to be promptly tried. No government was to be recognized which came into power "as a consequence of a coup d'état or of a revolution . . . so long as the freely elected representatives of the people [had] not constitutionally reorganized the country." No government was to intervene in civil war in the country of another of the group. Other steps intended to "prepare for the fusion of the Central American peoples into one single nationality" were outlined. To carry out the judicial work contemplated by the treaties, a "Central American Court of Justice," with jurisdiction over interstate disputes and claims of individuals against governments, was created. The agreements were to be binding for ten years.

The court opened its sessions auspiciously; but, since the cases which would be brought before it were highly political in nature, its course could not be expected to be smooth. From the beginning, the votes of its judges seemed influenced by their national interests, and its chance of gradually accumulating prestige was destroyed by the continued interference of Zelaya, of Nicaragua, in the affairs of the neighboring states.

The United States had, meanwhile, been drawn into an effort to bring Nicaragua to observe the peace treaties. The court had sought to act as intermediary in the civil war going on in Nicaragua, though such action was beyond its jurisdiction. At the same time, the United States undertook active intervention, landing troops and otherwise influencing internal developments in the republic. These steps were taken, it was announced, to promote peace in Central America "under the moral mandate of the Washington conventions," [16] though the United States had not been a party to the agreement. The United States continued to act independently to carry out its interpretation of its "moral" duties as sponsor of the treaties,

---

[16] *For. Rel.*, 1912, p. 1042. The actions taken in Nicaragua are discussed in greater detail in the chapters on that republic.

though doing so was protested against by Central American authorities as contrary to the intent of the agreements.

Before the ten-year period for which the court had been created came to an end, a case involving the Bryan-Chamorro treaty was submitted for its judgment. The issue once more illustrated the political character of the body and brought the practical abandonment of its activities.

The cause of "constitutionalism" in Central America continued, however, to have support both in the republics and in the United States. President Wilson early announced it as a policy of his administration in all Latin America. He had declared: "Disorder, personal intrigues, and defiance of constitutional rights weaken and discredit government. . . . We can have no sympathy with those who seek to seize the power of government to advance their own personal interests or ambition. . . . We shall prefer those who . . . respect the restraints of constitutional provision. . . ." [17]

Statement of these principles, it was soon evident, was easier than their application under the conditions of Central American politics. The standards announced in the peace treaties of 1907 were such that interpretation of the clauses on recognition forced outside governments to pass on the meaning of the clauses of the local constitutions. Under such circumstances, there was no assurance that all the parties to the treaties and the governments which had sponsored them would interpret them in the same way. Even the decisions of a single government in different cases might not be clearly consistent. Difficulties of this sort did not fail to appear when the United States faced the problem of recognition in the Tinoco case in Costa Rica in 1917, in a revolution in Honduras in 1919, and in the Estrada Cabrera case in 1920.[18]

The practical breakdown of the treaties of 1907 after the decision on the Bryan-Chamorro treaty had been followed by proposals of new efforts for Central American co-operation.

---

[17] *Ibid.*, 1913, p. 7.

[18] The discussion in Buell, "The United States and Central American Stability," *op. cit.*, pp. 177–186, shows the difficulty of applying the standard of "constitutionalism" in Central America.

They resulted in a "union" of Nicaragua, Salvador, and Guatemala in 1921 which dissolved within the year.[19] In 1922 representatives of Nicaragua, Salvador, and Honduras met representatives of the United States on the U.S.S. *Tacoma* in the Gulf of Fonseca, declared the treaty of 1907 still in force, and made plans for a new conference "to promote union 'in a practical way.'"[20]

Under a modified program, representatives of the five republics again met at Washington late in 1922 and concluded, on February 7, 1923, a new series of agreements. The provision as to the neutrality of Honduras included in the treaties of 1907 was dropped. The principle that none of the group should interfere in civil war in territory of its neighbors was reaffirmed, as was that concerning the use of border areas for fostering revolutions. Governments arising from *coups d'état* could be recognized if the "freely elected representatives of the people had constitutionally reorganized the country"; but, even in such cases, leaders of the revolution or those closely related to such leaders by blood or marriage could not be elected to the highest offices. Disqualified, also, were persons who had held certain high offices, civil or military, during the revolution or within six months preceding it. All the states promised, in addition, that they would not recognize any person coming into power in violation of the rules as to eligibility laid down by the local constitutions. To replace the Central American court, there was created a panel of jurists from which were to be chosen judge-arbitrators to settle disputes submitted to them. At the same time, Honduras sought to raise again the question of a more definite Central American union, but without success.

Opinion as to whether the treaties strengthened or weakened the cause of peace differed in the republics. The delegates left Washington enthusiastic in their praise. Nevertheless, the conventions met sharp criticism within and out-

---

[19] This movement and those similar which followed it are discussed in Buell, Raymond Leslie, "The United States and Central American Revolutions," *Foreign Policy Reports,* Vol. VII, No. 10, July 22, 1931, *passim.*
[20] *Ibid.,* p. 189.

side of the local Congresses. Some considered the treaties backward steps, especially since they might accentuate the activity of the United States in Central America; but the major engagements were in the long run ratified.

Though the United States was not a signatory of the treaties of 1923, as it also had not been to the treaties of 1907, its policy as to recognition in Central America was conformed to them. Even more than in the treaties of 1907, the application of the theory to facts proved difficult.

The ink on the agreements was hardly dry before question of their application arose in Honduras in a hotly disputed election. The United States offered its good offices and announced its intent, in reference to recognizing any new governments in Central America, to follow a policy in accord with the provisions of the recently made treaties. Shortly after the election of October, 1923, in Honduras, revolutionary activity became general, a dictatorship was set up with which the United States broke off relations, and, in the confusion that followed, American cruisers were sent to Honduranean ports on both coasts and marines landed on the Atlantic and later, apparently at the suggestion of the diplomatic corps, on the Pacific.[21] At times it seemed that, even though the actions

---

[21] Department of State, *Press Releases,* April 25, 1931, p. 312. The details of the developments above described and the difficulties met in applying the treaties of 1923 in other states of Central America are given in Buell, "The United States and Central American Revolutions," *op. cit.* Action by the United States in the affairs of Honduras has occurred at numerous times not listed above. A partial list of recent "interventions" or acts approaching intervention follows:

1. The United States and French consuls seek to check fighting between Government and revolutionary troops. (*For. Rel.,* 1908, p. 456.)
2. Honduras asks the United States for "decisive cooperation" in putting down revolution. (*Ibid.,* 1911, pp. 292–293.)
3. The President of Honduras asks the United States to arbitrate dispute over the presidency or to name a candidate. (*Ibid.,* p. 297.)
4. United States representative sent to arbitrate differences of political parties. (*Ibid.,* p. 299.)
5. The United States representative recommends a candidate for the presidency. (*Ibid.,* pp. 302–305.)
6. American naval force landed at Puerto Cortez. (*New York Times,* Sept. 12, 1919, p. 17:3.)
7. An American "landing force" enters Tegucigalpa, the capital. (*Ibid.,* March 21, 1924, p. 12:1.)

of all the countries pledged to conform to the policies announced in the treaties of 1907 and 1923 were not consistent, on the whole they promoted the cause of peace. Later opinion has swung in the opposite direction, particularly after the Martinez revolution in Salvador in 1931, though unrecognized, proved able to maintain itself. Thereafter Costa Rica and Salvador denounced the treaty of 1923. Nicaragua, Honduras, and Guatemala recognized the new regime on January 25, 1934, by which date Costa Rica had already done so. Under these circumstances, the United States took a similar step on January 27.[22] Whether another effort would be made to promote "constitutionalism" in Central America through international engagements was for the moment in doubt.

Public finance in Honduras has a record as irregular as the politics of the Republic. It is not surprising, in a country in which the economic development is still so backward, to find that the revenues have always been low with budgets, as a rule, showing deficits. In a state the political history of which has been so troubled, it is to be expected, also, that a large proportion of the resources of the Treasury must be spent in financing the efforts to keep public order or in paying for past civil wars. But the most striking features of the financial record of the Republic lie in neither of these fields but in the history of its foreign loans.

Like its sister states, Honduras assumed a share of the debt of the Central American Federation upon its disintegration in 1827. The service on this obligation, one-sixth of the old debt of £163,000, did not become a burden to the budget, for no interest was paid. No attempt at an adjustment with the bondholders was made until 1867, when a loan for £90,000, to take up the old debt and other liabilities which then totaled, with interest, some £120,450, was negotiated.

---

8. An American cruiser sent to the north coast. (*Ibid.,* August 16, 1924, p. 3:2.)
9. American forces landed at Ceiba, on the north coast. (*Ibid.,* April 21, 1925, p. 1:4.)
10. The *Memphis* visits the north coast to safeguard American interests. (Department of State, *Press Releases,* April 25, 1931, p. 311.)
11. Two other United States vessels on the north coast. (*Ibid.*)

[22] *New York Times,* Jan. 26, 1934, p. 11:5, and Jan. 27, 1934, p. 14:4.

This was the beginning of an experience in international finance which is so fantastic that it has few, if any, parallels. Three firms which became notorious in Latin-American affairs, in the years from 1867 to 1870 sponsored for Honduras bond issues which are perhaps unprecedented in the degree to which the representations made to the investing public were false and in the extent to which they involved the carrying on of sharp practices against the borrowing nation. It is proper to state that the negotiations were also not free from irregularities on the part of Honduranean representatives. Also to be borne in mind is the fact that in the long run the contracts did not have the disastrous effect upon Honduras which they would have had if their terms had actually been enforced. The loans stand, in any case, as shining examples of the shaky bases on which some of the foreign issues of the period rested.

The financing was nominally intended to promote construction of an interoceanic railway, which Honduras hoped might bring its products into the reach of more advanced nations and thus increase its economic strength. All told, the four issues totaled £6,080,108 at their face value. The larger series were put out at 75 and 80. The largest bore interest at 10 per cent and called for 3 per cent for the sinking fund; another called for an annual payment of £140,000, then far above the entire revenue of the Government, in addition to half the profits of the railway for a period of fifteen years. A British parliamentary committee which investigated the transactions in 1875 reported that the buyers of the bonds had acted in profound ignorance of what they were buying. The prospectus was made up with "exaggerated statements," the guarantee for the bonds was "absolutely inadequate," the methods used in handling them were "flagrantly fraudulent," and the operations as a whole merited "much censure." [23] Part of the money received by the houses issuing the securities was taken to manipulate the market and part was used

---

[23] *Parliamentary Blue Book Select Committee Report (1875)* quoted by Samuel MacClintock in "Refunding the Foreign Debt of Honduras," *Journal of Political Economy,* Vol. 19 (1911), pp. 216–228, at p. 222.

to pay interest to the bondholders until 1872–1873, when all four issues went into default.

A Spanish authority estimated that the money actually received by Honduras reached $11,699,259. A representative of Honduras sent to London to make an adjustment in 1904 declared that the only material benefit which the Republic received was fifty-three miles of easily constructed railroad, payment of the old Federal debt, and a quantity of arms, ammunition, and nickel coin, of a total value of £312,000.[24] This was the result of borrowing by a nation which is referred to by one author as made up at the time of "two hundred thousand half-naked indians." Few if any of the scandalous deals which have been perpetrated upon too trustful bond buyers and equally simple borrowers show an equal degree of rascality.

The obligations which Honduras had undertaken were far beyond its ability to pay, and no payments from the Republic were made. The loans, for which practically all of the national resources had been specifically pledged, continued, however, to be at least nominally a first claim upon its resources and probably did prevent further borrowing for purposes which might have been more productive. Unpaid service charges continued to pile up through long years of default. After 1887, various projects to bring about an adjustment, at an amount much less than that nominally due, were launched by British and American interests. These efforts continued without success for almost forty years.

Greater prospects of success seemed to be offered through an adjustment between the President of Honduras and the British minister in March, 1909. The Taft administration, however, preferred to forward a plan which would make American instead of British financial interests the creditors of the Republic. It proposed to establish, in both Nicaragua and Honduras, customs controls similar to the one already operating in the Dominican Republic.[25] The Morgan and other

---

[24] MacClintock, *op. cit.*, pp. 223–225.

[25] An editorial on the "Proposed Loan Conventions Between the United

groups were to buy the Honduras bonds of the old debt at fifteen per cent of their face amount, all interest being disregarded, provided a customs control had been previously agreed upon by treaty between Honduras and the United States.

The old debts were by this time calculated to total some $26,000,000 principal and $124,000,000 interest. The proposed American loan would be of $10,000,000, bearing five per cent interest and to be sold at 88, from the yield of which $4,512,000 was to be set aside to cancel the old debt, the balance to be available for other purposes.[26] In January, 1911, however, the Congress of Honduras rejected the plan. The following year, the Morgan interests announced their withdrawal from the agreement with the representatives of the British bondholders, and the debts therefore continued in default.[27]

Adjustment of the debt was again taken up by the British with the Government of Honduras in 1922, and, after long discussions, an agreement was approved by the Congress in March, 1926. Accumulated interest charges amounting to some £25,000,000 were abandoned. It was agreed that the principal, reported as £5,398,570, should be canceled by the payment of £1,200,000 in sixty half-yearly installments of £20,000 beginning in January, 1927.

This agreement is now in operation. Money for the payments is secured through an unusual arrangement. Exporters of goods to Honduras are required to affix to all invoices for shipments certain stamps in amounts equal to three per cent of the value of the shipments. The stamps are sold exclu-

---

States and Honduras and the United States and Nicaragua" in *American Journal of International Law,* Vol. V, pp. 1044–1051 (1911), analyzes the proposals and compares them to the Dominican convention. The text of the Honduras Convention is in *ibid.,* Vol. V (Supplement), pp. 274–276.

[26] The President of Honduras, Miguel R. Davila, was a supporter of the loan project and would have welcomed the "valuable intervention" of the United States to quell the hostility of revolutionists who apparently opposed it. See his telegram to the President of the United States in *For. Rel.,* 1911, p. 297.

[27] *Fifty-Ninth Annual Report of the Council of the Corporation of Foreign Bondholders,* London, 1932, p. 268. See also *For. Rel.,* 1912, pp. 561 and 588, and 1913, p. **557** ***et seq.***

sively by the National City Bank of New York. If this "Consular Service Tax" is insufficient to meet the agreed-upon payments, other consular revenues are to be drawn upon for the balance. The bank, with the funds collected, makes the payments in cancellation of the old bond issue. This adjustment has thus far enabled the Republic to maintain its debt service.[28]

Though Honduras is not endowed with a wide variety of natural resources, and though irregularity has characterized its financial and political history, in more recent years and especially since the end of the first decade of the century, there has occurred an encouraging rise in foreign commerce—based chiefly on the development of the tropical fruit industry on the north coast.

Banana growing, introduced into the West Indies as early as 1516, spread throughout the American tropics; but, until the last quarter of the nineteenth century, though the fruit had become a widespread article of local diet, it did not figure in international trade.[29] In Honduras the first commercial exports seem to have been from the Bay Islands in 1878. In the eighties, the fruit companies began to develop regular shipments to the United States, which thereafter furnished a steady and widening market for all Caribbean banana producers. After the World War, cargo shipments to Europe, which had just begun before the outbreak of the conflict, were re-established and increased markedly.

The share of Honduras in this commerce rose sharply after 1911, when the larger American fruit companies became actively interested in the long-neglected north coast. Banana exports—the only exports of importance in the district—rose from 6,246,000 bunches in 1913[30] to 29,084,000 in 1929.[31]

---

[28] A new loan of $1,500,000, repayable in monthly installments of $25,000, for which the customhouse receipts of three north coast ports were pledged, was made in February, 1928.

[29] For a description of the influence of the banana industry on the Caribbean, see Jones, Chester Lloyd, *Caribbean Backgrounds and Prospects*, New York, D. Appleton and Co., 1931, pp. 127–144.

[30] *Commerce Yearbook*, 1924, p. 575.

[31] *Ibid.*, 1931, Vol. II, p. 437.

Honduras and Jamaica now compete for first position in supplying the banana trade of the world.

A large part of the fruit exports is produced [32] and almost all of it is marketed by firms financed by foreign capital. Foreign companies have heavy investments in the local lands, railroads, and docks and in the steamship lines serving the trade. Through the fruit industry, the north coast has come to have much greater importance as a source of national wealth and as a factor in both local politics and international relations. In many years, as much as from seventy-five to eighty per cent of the exports of the country are now bananas.

In the period since 1911, chiefly as a result of the expanding fruit industry, the foreign trade totals have shown remarkable increase. From 1906 to 1910, the exports averaged a value of only $2,241,000; but from 1921 to 1925, they were worth $8,142,000 and in the boom period of 1926–1930, $20,977,000. The peak in exports was reached in 1930 with shipments worth $26,171,000.

The peculiar character of the banana trade, carried on and financed as it so largely is by foreign capital, causes the trade balance to show a heavy excess of exports. In many years, indeed, exports are almost twice as great as imports. The actual influence on the balance of payments is not so favorable as these figures seem to indicate, however, because a large part of the profits of the banana operations goes abroad to the stockholders of the fruit companies. On the other hand, the market created for fruit raised by local interests, the wages paid laborers in Honduras which are spent within the country, the customs and other taxes paid by the fruit companies and others on the increased imports which the industry makes possible, and the investment of new capital in the development of the fruit and other ventures contribute materially to the economic strength of both the north coast and the Republic as a whole. There can be no doubt that the development of the fruit industry has not put the country in as strong an economic position as it would have held had equally

[32] In Honduras and Guatemala, as much as half of the fruit exported is grown by the large fruit companies.

vigorous enterprises developed with local capital. But there is also no doubt that, but for foreign capital, industries such as now exist on the north coast would not have come into existence.

The benefits brought through the advance in the fruit industry are reflected also in the steady growth of imports and in the increase of the public revenue. Imports in 1906–1910 had an average value of $2,602,000, but in 1926–1930 they were worth $12,782,500.[33] The actual net revenues in 1913–1914 were 5,895,194 pesos, but reached, at the peak in 1929–1930, 14,314,299 pesos.[34] Since imports in the long run depend, in all countries, upon the exports, and since public revenues in countries like Honduras are drawn primarily from consumption taxes, these figures make it clear that the fruit industry has very materially aided in strengthening the economic position.

The history of the Republic, even in recent years, is so full of incidents disturbing public order that it is not to be expected that others will not occur. The development of popular government is a long process of trials and errors. Concluding a statement concerning the struggles for better government which the Republic has made, the minister of Honduras on presenting his letters of credence at Washington on August 22, 1929, declared: "Honduras has gone through . . . tests and suffered the consequences of its mistakes; and through a long term of unsettled life which for a time stopped its development and consumed part of its vitality, it has at last found the way to its own resurrection in the practice of political systems which harmonize, in one common aspiration, all the factors that determine national progress. . . . In brief, we have done away with the policy of violence and set the Republic on solid foundations of progress, civilization and culture." [35] Such a statement, as events since 1929 have shown, is one of hopes rather than of accomplishment, though there

---

[33] *Ibid.*, 1932, Vol. II, p. 441.

[34] *Fifty-Ninth Annual Report of the Council of the Corporation of Foreign Bondholders for the year 1932,* London, 1933, p. 274.

[35] Department of State, *Press Releases* (mimeographed), August 22, 1929.

are few students of Central American affairs who do not believe that Honduras and the other states of the Isthmus are making real, if limited, progress toward more stable government.

CHAPTER XIX

Salvador

LEAST in area, Salvador is the most densely settled and, next to Guatemala, the greatest of the Central American states in population. Its political and economic advance in the twentieth century has been marked. Like the other Central American areas facing the Pacific—Salvador alone has no Atlantic coast—its development during the colonial period was retarded by difficulty of access. Immigration was by a roundabout route and never reached great volume. The shipment of local products always entailed high costs, and the natural resources of the country did not yield large quantities of exportable goods which because of high value per unit of weight could bear such charges.

The population has in general the same ethnic characteristics as that of Nicaragua and Honduras. What the racial divisions are is not indicated in the census, but the Director of the Statistical Office reports eighty per cent as "mestizos and white" and the rest as Indians. Far the majority are of mixed blood. The ruling classes are of pure or nearly pure Spanish ancestry—a condition caused, it appears, by a group consciousness based on family prestige and ability rather than any discrimination against those of other inheritance, for race prejudice against aboriginal blood plays no important role in the social life.[1] The Indians are less active than the other classes in public affairs and in economic develop-

[1] This tolerance is not, however, shown toward all races. In 1925 the Congress approved a motion forbidding the entry into Salvador of members of the "colored races." (*New York Times,* May 4, 1925, p. 6:3.) Similar action was taken in 1929 against Chinese and Arabs, whatever their citizenship. (*Ibid.,* March 31, 1929, Sec. III, p. 6:2.)

ment. They have been more generally affected by Spanish civilization here than in Guatemala, Honduras, and Nicaragua. There are few Indian communities which do not speak Spanish and few which continue to live under tribal conditions.

For a country of agricultural character, the density of settlement is surprising. The population has increased almost tenfold since 1778, and growth has been especially rapid since the third quarter of the last century, when coffee culture became a popular industry. As late as 1878, the republic counted only 554,785 citizens. In 1930, the census reported 1,437,365, or over 109 to the square mile as compared to 18 in Honduras and 15 in Nicaragua. In spite of its nonindustrial character, Salvador is more thickly populated than the East North Central States of the United States.

For more than half a century after the winning of its independence, Salvador was torn by internal dissensions and by the quasi-foreign contentions which embittered its relations with surrounding countries. This is a period which, though it has contributed to make Salvador what it is today, shows in the detail of its contests no clear-cut path of national progress. The personalism which characterized most of the military leaders and the bitterness which developed in the feeling between rival sections held back the growth of a true national spirit. On the other hand, the conflicts with the neighboring states did emphasize nationalistic feeling, though they by no means stifled the enthusiasm for a larger Central Americanism, of which Salvador has been an ardent though not always a consistent champion.

Salvador promptly supported the movement for the first Central American Federation, and there arose the first organized opposition to the annexation to the Mexican Empire of Iturbide. In the period when the Honduranean leader Morazán was the champion of the union cause, the Federal capital was moved to San Salvador, and Salvadorean troops thereafter were frequently defenders of federalism against secessionist movements in other states. Salvador was the last of the republics to admit that the first union was a failure.[2]

From 1840 to practically the end of the century, control alternated between Liberals and Conservatives, the latter during the first part of the period generally imposed on the country by the Guatemalan dictator Carrera, or at least ruling with his support. Though some of the Salvadorean leaders were men of undoubted ability, they were not able to lay the foundations of an orderly political advance based on popular suffrage and continued to rely heavily on the army for control of the government. Republican institutions of advanced character have never had a virile existence.

Many of the external quarrels in which Salvador became embroiled before the beginning of the current century, like a large part of those arising within her borders, were conflicts into which she was drawn by interference on the part of her neighbors. The struggles of Liberals and Conservatives in the period of the Federation extended across the boundaries of the member states; and, after the Union was dissolved, they continued to do so. Thus, in Salvador, as in the other states, the laudable ambition to achieve Central American union has been accompanied by external partisan alliances which have been disturbing factors in local politics. Parties in power in Salvador did not hesitate to ask help from those in neighboring states to maintain themselves, and neighboring governments did not scruple about interfering in Salvador.

A number of influences tended to change these conditions in the years before and after the close of the nineteenth century. The political chieftains of the Federation period and the era immediately following were passing out of the scene, and the party animosities which they had aroused became less marked. The basis of the economic life of Central America was changing, and especially was this true in Salvador.

Coffee had become the great contributor to national wealth. The propertied elements in the country—a small proportion

[2] See Munro, D. G., *The Five Republics of Central America, op. cit.*, pp. 101–103, for a more detailed statement of local political developments.

of the population, but the one which had furnished the initiative for the previous conflicts—came to realize that peace and security offered greater returns for them than the irregular gains coming with control of public affairs. The growth of population and national wealth in Salvador, particularly as compared to that of its neighbors, Nicaragua and Honduras, made interference by them in the affairs of the Republic less likely to be successful. As the new century progressed, greater imports and exports emphasized the better living standards—at least for the better-to-do—attendant upon peace and steadier economic conditions.

After the negotiation of the treaties of 1907 and those of 1923 among the Central American republics, international conflicts and internal hostilities were discouraged. How great the influence of these engagements was it is not possible to estimate. It is clear that they did not accomplish all that their makers had hoped, and it seems more than probable that what was acomplished was due at least as much to the influence of the United States, which was not a party to them, as to the efforts of the signatories. In any case, it is fair to say that the diplomatic pressure put upon the Central American states by the United States did contribute to making wars among them less frequent. That it had a definite influence, favorable or unfavorable, on the development of institutions of self-government among them is not so clear.

It is not too much to say that the political and economic advance which has occurred in Salvador in the past generation is greater than that in all its previous history. From 1898 to 1932, no President was overthrown by revolution—though revolts of minor character occurred. "International wars" have arisen—notably the wars provoked by the Nicaraguan dictator Zelaya resulting in threat by the United States to use force to bring hostilities to an end.[3]

Political development has not meant the rise of democracy

---

[3] A similar case involving threatened aggressions on Salvador by Cabrera of Guatemala is discussed in *For. Rel.*, 1912, pp. 1310–1328. The United States asserted that the republics should follow the procedure for peaceful settlement outlined in the Washington treaties of 1907.

in the Republic. Public affairs continue to be controlled by a small upper class, chiefly of Spanish inheritance, which keeps the more important public offices rather strictly within its own membership. This group is often referred to locally as the "forty families." They are in great part large landowners, including the "coffee aristocracy," which has been assuming increasing importance in the economic activities of the country since the late seventies.[4] Party divisions of the traditional sort have now much less influence than they had formerly, and the divisions among the ruling oligarchy tend to be determined by personal allegiances and family connections rather than by public policies, real or fancied. In later years, a group of younger men active in the economic affairs of the country has become active in movements for cleaner public administration.

In recent elections, the powerful Melendez family has played a prominent role. Carlos Melendez became President on the assassination of Manuel Araujo and remained in power from 1913 to 1919, when the chief magistracy was handed over to his brother Jorge—the Constitution does not allow a President to succeed himself.[5] In 1923, at the end of his term, Alfonso Quinonez, a brother-in-law, was made head of the government. He wished to remain in office another term but in 1927 backed Romero Bosque in the election, while he had himself chosen First Designate, or Vice-President, intending, it is alleged, later to force the resignation of the President and thus "constitutionally" come into the chief magistracy again. Romero Bosque, however, developed greater strength than many had expected, and Quinonez went into voluntary exile in Europe.

Romero Bosque, though not a "strong man," gave to Sal-

---

[4] Landholding in Salvador is, however, less concentrated than in many Latin-American countries, though there cannot be said to be a landholding middle class.

[5] The political moves in these years are outlined in *For. Rel.*, 1913, pp. 1304–1308, and 1914, pp. 1077–1080. Melendez, as First Designate, became President on Araujo's death. He resigned August 29, 1914, so that under the Constitution he could become a candidate for the term beginning March 1, 1915.

vador a liberal administration. He brought an end to the period of martial law instituted in the Melendez regime, removed restrictions on the press—which promptly began to criticize alleged financial irregularities of former Presidents—and promised "a free election" at the end of his term. These measures were not acceptable to the Army, which felt its prestige to be threatened, nor to certain influential groups in the oligarchy. Revolutionary movements and plots to assassinate the President had, therefore, to be suppressed. At the end of his term, there was an orderly election at which, from a field of five candidates, Arturo Araujo was chosen President for the period ending March 1, 1935.[6]

On December 2, 1931, the record established for orderly political development was broken by a military *coup d'état* led by the former Secretary of War, M. H. Martinez.[7] Following its usual practice, the United States refused to recognize the new government because of the Central American treaty of 1923. Mexico, however, did so. Shortly the new government faced a so-called communist revolt. The lives of foreigners were endangered. The Italian representative asked that the United States protect the lives and properties of Italians.[8] American vessels were promptly sent to safeguard "American and foreign lives." British and Canadian ships were also sent to the Salvadorian coast.[9] The new government succeeded in repressing the revolt against it, but recognition continued to be refused.

Formal notification of this position was given to the Martinez government by the United States, Guatemala, Honduras, and Costa Rica.[10] The next year, however, Costa Rica changed its attitude and approached Guatemala with a pro-

---

[6] *New York Times,* December 15, 1927, p. 60:2; February 5, 1928, Section III, p. 1:3; April 17, 1929, p. 30:2; January 6, 1930, p. 4:4; January 13, 1931, p. 34:1; February 13, 1931, p. 9:4; Department of State, *Press Releases,* February 14, 1931, p. 78. Araujo had been the Liberal candidate in 1919 and later led an unsuccessful revolution. (*New York Times,* May 16, 1920, p. 4:2.)

[7] *Press Releases,* Department of State, December 5, 1931, pp. 510–511.

[8] *Ibid.,* January 30, 1932, pp. 91–93.

[9] *Ibid.,* and comment in *New York Times,* January 4, 1932, Section I, p. 1.

[10] *New York Times,* December 24, 1931, p. 8:3.

posal to abrogate the peace treaties of 1923.[11] Later Guatemala and Honduras became more favorably disposed toward the Martinez government, and Costa Rica proposed its recognition.[12]

Martinez, unlike Tinoco in an earlier period in Costa Rica, proved to be able to get along without United States recognition. He denounced the treaties of 1923, and, after he had kept himself in power for two years, Costa Rica took similar action and recognized the revolutionary government on January 1, 1934, as Nicaragua, Honduras, and Guatemala also did before the end of the month. In view of this unanimous position taken by the Central American states, the United States extended recognition to Martinez on January 26.

In its international relations outside Central America, Salvador has had few serious problems to solve. In the earlier years, the lack of an Atlantic coast, the handicaps to communication with the outside world, the small contribution to international trade, and the limited foreign interests in the territory contributed to that result. Later, the increase of domestic stability has had a similar influence.

Adjustments of controveries other than those with the Central American states have as a rule been accomplished either through the direct negotiations of private groups with the Government or with only the co-operation of diplomatic agencies.[13]

Most important of the settlements with foreign interests which Salvador has made during the past generation are those involving her public finance. These are not, strictly speaking, a part of her foreign relations, though the engagements have involved a secondary relation to foreign governments. The contracts are, however, of the first importance because

[11] *Ibid.*, November 30, 1932, p. 4:3.

[12] *Ibid.*, September 29, 1933, p. 3.

[13] An example of the latter sort is the adjustment obtained by the Salvador Commercial Corporation, which operated a harbor concession. (See *For. Rel.*, 1902, pp. 838–873, and 1904, pp. 533–541.) The part which Salvador has played in efforts to establish Central American union is discussed in the chapter on Guatemala. The opposition to the Bryan-Chamorro canal treaty, one of the chief issues in recent Salvadorian international relations, is discussed in the chapter on the international relations of Nicaragua.

of their bearing on domestic credit, the extension of public works, the increase of the general economic strength of the country, and, thus, the whole range of its relations with other states.

The developments in Salvadorian finance in the twentieth century are an excellent illustration of the difficulties into which states which have not fully attained political stability may come, as well as of the steps which may be taken both with and without foreign assistance to normalize the position of both the budget and the public debt. The conditions to be met and the steps taken to meet them are discussed in some detail, not because the case of Salvador involves extreme circumstances, for a number of other Caribbean countries have fallen into less favorable economic conditions. They are outlined because the measures adopted embody some of the more advanced expedients by which it is sought to guarantee the interests of both lenders and borrowers. Further, the experience during the world-wide economic crisis following 1929 shows some of the difficulties which may hinder the carrying out of even the most carefully planned loan controls.

Up to 1923, the public debt of Salvador had a history similar to that of the debts of the other Central American republics. In 1827, one-sixth (£27,200) of the debt of the old Central American Federation had been taken over, but interest payments upon it had promptly lapsed. In 1860, an adjustment was made for ninety per cent in cash. In 1889, the first of a series of loans made in Great Britain was floated. These loans were intended primarily to make railway construction possible. For the service of the debts created, taxes on imports and, in the later loans, on exports were pledged. The payments undertaken were met with fair regularity; but, in the thirteen years ending in 1923, the budget was balanced only twice. The postwar conditions brought new problems which made a general readjustment in public finance advisable. An effort to this end began to take shape in 1921 with discussions for a bank of issue to stabilize the currency and for a loan for general refunding of the public obligations, internal and external, railway extensions, and certain public improvements.[14] In September, 1923, an agreement was made with United States capitalists for a series of loans for these purposes. Three issues totalling about $21,500,000 were contracted. They were guaranteed by mortgages on seventy per cent of the national customs returns, which in the years 1910–1920, the latest years for which information was available, would have been almost twice the amount necessary to carry the debt service. The customs rates, it was agreed, would not be changed so as to reduce the gross return while any of the bonds remained outstanding and unpaid. The lenders agreed to establish in Salvador a fiscal representative whose agents should have the right to take part in inspection of merchandise and to inspect the customhouse accounts. Customs receipts reserved for the loan service were to be paid directly to the fiscal representative, who would transmit them monthly to New York. If a delay of thirty days occurred in the loan service, the first lien, on demand of the representative of the lenders, was to be extended over all customs revenues and their administration was to be turned over to a collector general appointed by Salvador from persons selected by the fiscal agent in concurrence with the Secretary of State of the United States.

While the United States was not a party to this agreement, the two governments exchanged formal diplomatic notes by which they took cognizance of the contract. Salvador promised its co-operation with the United States and the bankers in carrying it out. Another provision stated that "any disagreement, question or difference of any nature whatever" concerning the contract should be referred through the Secretary of State to the Chief Justice of the Supreme Court of the United States, or, if he did not act, to some other member of the Federal judiciary, for decision. His judgment thereon should be accepted by the parties as "final and conclusive."[15]

---

[14] *New York Times,* June 26, 1921, Section I, p. 23:3, and July 14, 1922, p. 18:2; and *Fifty-Sixth Annual Report of the Council of the Corporation of Foreign Bondholders,* 1929, p. 314.

[15] The text of the agreement is in *Diario oficial, San Salvador, viernes, 21 de Julio de 1922, num. 163.* This and other loan agreements involving unofficial controls over public finance in the Caribbean region are discussed

Under the contract the lenders set up their local representation,[16] which, with the co-operation of the local authorities, improved the customs administration. The seventy per cent of the customs proved more than sufficient to meet the debt services; in fact, in the most prosperous years, this percentage of receipts for only a few months was sufficient. The regular service of the loan, however, was interrupted after the *coup d'état* of December, 1931.[17] In January, 1932, the Martinez administration took possession of the customs administration, and on February 27, by executive decree, suspended customs collection under the loan contract. It declared, however, that this action did not indicate an intention to repudiate the national obligations, but that, because of the world depression in progress, the Government was forced to this step to meet the expenses of maintaining itself. Steps were not taken to establish an agency for the collection of customs under the conditions outlined in the loan contracts, but on May 16, 1933, the Congress of Salvador approved an agreement with representatives of the bondholders by which amortization payments were to be suspended and future interest payments were to be met partly in cash and partly in certificates.[18]

---

in Jones, Chester Lloyd, *Caribbean Backgrounds and Prospects, op. cit.*, pp. 237–289.

[16] Originally, the fiscal agent was the Chatham Phoenix National Bank and Trust Company of New York. Subsequently, it became the Manufacturers' Trust Company.

[17] At this period, the three series of bonds of the loan of 1923 had been reduced from about $21,750,000 to about $17,346,950. A. Iselin & Company, *Bulletin on Foreign Securities,* New York, April 30, 1932.

[18] The public debt of Salvador was reported to total on December 31, 1933, 46,934,094 colones (par, $.50). Of this amount, 34,176,900 colones represented the capital of the external debt.

CHAPTER XX

Guatemala

AMONG Central American states, Guatemala ranks next after Nicaragua and Honduras in size. Its area is approximately 42,364 square miles, a little less than that of Pennsylvania, a little more than that of Ohio. Like most of its neighbor states of the group, it is divided into a mountainous portion and low-lying areas, one of which on the Pacific coast is a comparatively narrow fringe while that draining into the Atlantic, chiefly from north of the plateau, is much larger and is in extended districts sparsely inhabited and little exploited.

In population, Guatemala occupies a much more important position among the Central American republics than its area indicates. According to the official estimates, there were 2,219,000 persons in the republic in 1931,[1] or about as many as in Costa Rica, Honduras, and Nicaragua combined. Except for Salvador, Guatemala is by far the most densely populated of the republics, the greater part of the inhabitants living in the higher regions locally designated as temperate and cold.

On the whole, the people are not of high standard of life or initiative. The greater proportion, almost two-thirds, are of unmixed Indian blood. All but a small percentage of the balance are mestizos.[2] There were only some 15,470 persons of European ancestry reported at the time of the census of 1921, and, of these, all but a negligible proportion lived in the

[1] *Commerce Yearbook,* 1932, Vol. II, p. 424.

[2] *Censo de poblacion de la republica levantado el 28 de agosto de 1924,* 4° Censo, Parte 1, Guatemala, p. 139.

department of the capital city.[3] Less than fourteen in a hundred of those over seven years of age can read and write. Taking the population as a whole, Guatemalans are distinctively agriculturists living a simple life and but little touched by developments outside the country. The per capita imports and exports, as a result, are only about one-fourth those in Costa Rica.

Under these circumstances, only a small portion of the population has had any influence in shaping public policies. Public opinion is poorly developed and real self-government has never had a chance to develop.

Since Central America had been governed as a unit in the colonial period, it might have been expected that it would remain a single state when the authority of Spain was overthrown and that Guatemala City would continue to be the capital. Efforts to create a Central American nation promptly appeared, and the idea has continued to have appeal for Central American leaders, particularly those of Guatemala.

The first attempts to bring Central America under a single government were not, however, under Guatemalan leadership. After the break with Spain in 1821, there occurred a short-lived union with Mexico, followed, as has been shown above, by an endeavor to effect a "Federation" of the Central American provinces among themselves. Sectional rivalries appeared from the beginning. Feeling against Guatemala, the former center of Spanish administration, was marked. A constitutional Congress dominated by the Liberal factions set up in 1825 a government which was overthrown in 1829 by dissatisfied Liberals under the leadership of a Honduranean general, Francisco Morazán, who ruled affairs from Guatemala and later from Salvador. His power, however, gradually decreased, and the Federal Congress in 1838 bid the states to govern themselves. The following year, the Federation passed out of existence.

---

[3] From an unpublished study based on the census of 1921 in the files of the Dirección general del Censo at Guatemala City. The proportion of persons of white blood in the total population is there reported as .77 of one per cent.

The return to localism gave an opportunity for the Conservatives, including the partisans of the Church, to reassert themselves in Guatemala. They had been subject to constant persecution in the previous period, but, under the leadership of Rafael Carrera, called by the Indians "The Son of God," and with the support of the Indian and mestizo population, completely defeated their enemies in 1840.

Through about half of the subsequent history of the Republic, it has been under the control of dictators who, sometimes giving formal observance to constitutional standards, have made their own wills the law of the land. Through long periods they have kept both the Indian population and the mestizos in voiceless subjection and, relying on the relatively large population of the country to give them military advantages, have at times developed ambitions to play a leading role in Central American affairs and even to bring it again under a single government controlled from Guatemala.

Carrera became the first of the line of Guatemalan caudillos. A mestizo of the humblest origin, he was the outstanding Guatemalan from 1840 to 1865. After 1844, except for two short periods, he held the presidential office—after 1854, as President for life. The large landowners and the clerical faction controlled the government, and the more progressive elements left the country or were forced into silence.

Guatemala for the time became the center of opposition to any plans for federation. The better-to-do felt that the country had suffered during the period of the Federation from the weakness of the other states, especially Honduras, Nicaragua, and Salvador. At times, it is true, the influential showed willingness to join a new union, but as a rule they opposed it—on some occasions by force of arms.

With the fall of Carrera in 1865, the Liberal hopes revived. They won control of the government in 1871, and in 1873 Justo Rufino Barrios, a Liberal of progressive tendencies, became President. He is one of the national heroes of the Republic. Now the propertied classes and the Church had a term of persecution. Many Conservatives were exiled, ecclesiastical property was confiscated, the Church was disestablished, and some steps were taken toward educating the overwhelmingly ignorant mass of the population.

A part of Barrios' energies was devoted to an attempt to revive the Liberal projects for federation. Failing to bring it about peacefully, he sought to force it on the other states—among which Nicaragua and Costa Rica were now in the opposition. They were later joined by Salvador, which had become suspicious of the ambition of the Guatemalan leader. War broke out between the factions, and Barrios fell in battle against Salvador on April 2, 1885.

Another Liberal leader, Barillas, who held what is characterized as "the only comparatively free election in the history of the Republic," [4] was followed by José María Reino Barrios, nephew of the former President. Both he and his predecessor were guilty of extravagant public expenditures. Together they brought the country into a serious economic plight, and, on the assassination of Barrios on February 8, 1898, the office passed into the control of Manuel Estrada Cabrera, who shares with Zelaya of Nicaragua the reputation of being the greatest Central American tyrant of the current century. He was regularly "elected" President in September, 1898. The Constitution then prohibited a chief magistrate from succeeding himself. In 1903 Cabrera had this limitation removed, and he was thereafter chosen President successively for six-year terms ending in 1911, 1917, and 1923.

The government was a despotism which, through control of the army, made the elections farcical. The polling of votes was seriously carried on under constitutional forms, but the voters were herded to the elections by Government troops and there allowed to cast their ballots freely, provided they voted for Cabrera, who was the only candidate. So "free" was the voting, in fact, that the returns in some elections are reported to have shown that all the qualified voters or even a greater number voted.

During the Cabrera dictatorship, freedom of the press vanished. Discussion of public affairs was discountenanced even

---

[4] Munro, *op. cit.*, p. 52.

in private meetings. Suspected individuals disappeared mysteriously or were summarily executed.[5] The better-educated classes fell into political apathy. A large portion of both foreigners and influential natives came, indeed, to look upon such a condition with a degree of complacency so long as, on the surface, the country had a semblance of economic prosperity, for they felt that the only alternative to dictatorship was even less acceptable open civil strife.

But steady debasement of the currency, distress caused by earthquakes in 1917 and 1918, which the Government did little to relieve, and the general economic depression, which in the long run affected all lines of activity, finally brought a successful revolt in April, 1920.[6]

Nominally, the issue was a projected revival of the old plan of Central American union, which, though a member of the "Liberal" party, Cabrera had opposed. The President surrendered on the sixteenth. His successor, Carlos Herrera, in his manifesto declared in favor of a four-year term for the President and for adopting a constitutional prohibition of re-election, in order that never again might one man remain in power indefinitely.

But, in less than a year and a half, the revolutionary wheel went around again,[7] and José María Orellana, Chief of Staff of the Guatemalan Army, became Provisional President. In February, 1922, he was regularly "elected" by an overwhelming majority. After an extended investigation by special representatives sent for the purpose, he was recognized by the United States on April 15, 1922. Orellana showed his leadership by putting the country on a gold standard, by establishing the quetzal—equal in value to the American dollar—and by adopting measures for improving education and the roads system. He died suddenly on September 26, 1926, and was succeeded by a personal friend, the First Designate, an ob-

[5] On April 20, 1908, an attempt was made to assassinate the President. "The following day martial law was declared . . . and three days later the president announced that eighteen men, implicated in the plot . . . had been executed." (*New International Yearbook*, 1908, p. 325.)

[6] Previous revolts were reported in October, 1915, and January, 1916.

[7] *New York Times*, December 8, 1921, p. 2:3.

scure colonel, Lazaro Chacón, who in due course was "very peacefully" chosen President at the ensuing election by a large majority. Chacón continued the work of Orellana with fair success until stricken by cerebral hemorrhage in December, 1930, necessitating first a temporary and later permanent resignation.

The choice of his successor vividly illustrates the difficulty which in practice attached to the application of what appeared to many the simple rules which the Central American countries, and in principle the United States, had set up for themselves in the Washington treaties of 1923.

The First Designate, De Leon, had in a recent reorganization of the Cabinet become the Secretary of War. That position made him ineligible, and he joined in approving the choice of the Second Designate, Palma. Three days later, Manuel Orellana, a cousin of the former President, headed a military junta which unseated Palma on the ground that De Leon and the Army supported the "usurpers." In the street fighting which accompanied the upset, De Leon was killed. Palma resigned and the National Assembly in special session appointed Orellana Provisional President. The new government declared its intent to return the power to Chacón should he recover. The United States held, however, that Orellana was ineligible under the treaties of 1923, and under this pressure he resigned.[8] The Assembly then proceeded once more to accept the resignation of Palma and the Third Designate. It chose a new set of designates, Reina Andrade being first on the list and then approved the definite resignation of Chacón, which had meanwhile been given; thereupon, Reina Andrade assumed the provisional presidency on January 2, 1931. The United States recognized the new government on January 8. In the popular elections subsequently called, General Jorge Ubico was chosen "Constitutional President of Guatemala."[9]

---

[8] Orellana was not recognized by any Central American republic. Stimson, H. L., "The United States and the Other American Republics," *Publications of the Department of State, Latin American Series, No. 4,* Washington, 1931, p. 10.

[9] Summarized from the contemporary issues of the *New York Times* and the *Press Releases* of the United States Department of State.

Evidently the engagement in the treaty of 1923 to recognize only constitutional governments was far from an easily followed standard. It forced the recognizing government to pass judgment as to whether the principles set out in the local constitution had actually been observed. To do so in situations such as those which arise in Guatemalan politics was by no means as easy as to follow the usual international practice of recognizing governments which exercise *de facto* control and seem capable of maintaining order and protecting life and property.

Under the conditions which still exist in Guatemala, popular government in the broad sense and the uniform observance of the standards set up in the Constitution cannot be expected to arise soon. The population lives on a low standard of life. It is made up of communities which have little contact with each other or with the outside world. They include groups among whom there is even now no common language and which are little touched by even domestic legislation and less concerned with the standards it sets. The people, as a whole, are overwhelmingly illiterate [10] and are still dominated by a small, politically active minority sharply divided against itself. Such a population still has before it the task of winning its place politically among the more advanced communities of the world.

As in its sister republics, the better-settled plateau sections of Guatemala are nearer the Pacific than the Atlantic and find their natural outlet to the sea on the west. This fact, coupled with the low standard of life of her people, the slight development of her natural resources, and the comparative insignificance, until recently, of her exportable products, has made Guatemala's contact with countries other than her immediate neighbors of minor importance.

The isolated condition of the country has in the twentieth century been modified by the opening of the railroad from the Atlantic to the capital in 1908 and by the opening in 1914 of the Panama Canal, which placed the west coast in a better

---

[10] *The Censo de la poblacion de la republica levantado el 28 de agosto de 1921* (Guatemala, 1924), 4 Censo, Parte 1, p. 67, reports that 86.82 per cent of the population over 7 years of age at that time could not read or write.

position as to markets in Europe and on the east coast of the United States.

Even before these facilities became available, the economic production of the country had begun to be of greater international importance through the rise of coffee exports. The berry was introduced, so the report runs, about the middle of the eighteenth century, but intensive cultivation did not start until about 1875. The crop is of high grade, and in recent years the exports vie with Venezuela and Salvador for second place among New World shipments of mild coffee.[11] Since 1900, too, fruit shipments from the east coast have had a rapid increase, banana shipments reaching, in the best years, over six million bunches. This trade has strengthened the economic position of the country. Cultivation of tropical fruit for export has also started on the Pacific coast. These changes have brought Guatemala, in the twentieth century, into much more intimate relations with the other countries.

The problems in international affairs have involved chiefly controversies over foreign loans, relations to the neighbor republics, already sketched, and boundary disputes with them.

Guatemala has not been an exception to the rule that public finance in Central America has involved the republics in unfortunate experiences. The first public financing occurred in 1825, when Guatemala was a part of the Central American Federation. When the Federation was breaking up in 1827, Guatemala assumed five-twelfths of the obligations, the total of which was £163,000. They promptly went into default the next year, and, except for three intervals aggregating twenty years, the Republic was continuously in default up to 1913. This did not prevent the negotiation of a number of new loans and of adjustments on loans the service of which had gone into arrears. Various special guarantees were given for the fulfillment of these contracts, including the customs duties, the maritime revenue, arrangements that importers should

[11] Coffees are classified as "hard coffees"—those from Brazil—and "mild coffees." The latter include some similar in quality to those from Brazil, but the typical "milds" are full-bodied, of fine aroma, and in general demand for blending. They bring a price appreciably higher than Brazilian coffees.

pay certain revenues only to representatives of the creditors, special taxes on coffee, "irrevocably" to be paid to agents of the bondholders, other agreements by which the governments of the bondholders were to take note of the contracts, and still others guaranteeing the right of the bondholders to ask for the protection of a foreign government in case the agreement was not met. In spite of these exceptional provisions, the Republic on a number of occasions was not able to meet its obligations, or at least felt itself forced to break the contracts.

Various adjustments looking toward the establishment of special and far-reaching guarantees that the loan contracts would be carried out were attempted in the opening years of the century, but they repeatedly failed of ratification by Guatemala. In the attempted settlements Germany, France, and Great Britain were involved. The pressure put upon Guatemala by the last-named resulted, in 1902, in a popular outbreak, followed by the landing of two parties of armed British sailors at San José. Under this compulsion settlement was then made with the three powers. The United States had declined to join with the other powers in this coercive action, but declared that it would reserve for its citizens all rights secured for foreigners by the actions of the other powers.[12]

A similar later controversy furnishes an excellent example of the sorts of guarantees which had been given by the Government in securing loans and of the difficulties which may arise from such understandings. In 1895, British financiers made an arrangement for refinancing certain external and internal debts the interest on which had fallen into arrears. For the service of the new debt, Guatemala pledged the income from an export tax on coffee. This levy was fixed "irrevocably for 10 years from 1st July, 1895, at $1½ gold (six shillings) per quintal of coffee exported, to be paid to the Agent of the Bondholders at Guatemala."

In the same year, however, the Government negotiated

---

[12] *For. Rel.*, 1902, p. 569.

another loan with German financiers for building the Northern Railway, and pledged the coffee tax in a way which the British felt affected their prior claim. This matter was hardly arranged when, in 1897, a new contract with German interests still further complicated the question of claims on the coffee tax. Next, Guatemala reduced the "irrevocably fixed" coffee tax, in 1898, to one dollar silver per quintal and, in 1899, to one dollar paper—which was later increased to two dollars paper. Cabrera meanwhile authorized new issues of paper money, so that the gold yield of the tax fell. Later, Guatemala twice changed the bank to which payment of the yield of the coffee tax was to be paid and in other ways violated the terms of the contracts accepted by the British. New changes were made in the rate of the coffee tax. Still later, a contract by which the coffee export duty was to be turned over to an American syndicate was entered.[13]

In 1912, at about the middle of the Cabrera regime, Guatemalan finance had become highly confused and the holders of the external debt became insistent that the Government should meet the loan contracts. The bonds had been in default since 1899. The British adopted a firm position at the beginning of the year and the Guatemalan attitude toward the foreign debt was called to the attention of the United States. The United States Department of State in May informed Guatemala that, if the measures for rehabilitating the finances of the country, which the President had promised, did not materialize promptly, the United States might find it impossible further to dissuade Great Britain from adopting such measures for enforcing its claims as under the circumstances might be justifiable. Guatemala pleaded for a delay of sixty days, in which it hoped to be able to arrange matters through negotiations with American bankers.

No settlement was forthcoming by August, when Great Britain declared it had exhausted all means to secure a settlement and asked the good offices of the United States in induc-

---

[13] The details of the transactions summarized above are reported in the *Fifty-Seventh Annual Report of the Council of the Corporation of Foreign Bondholders for the year 1930,* London, 1930.

ing the debtor country to submit the affair to arbitration—a course proposed at the same time to Guatemala. The United States again urged upon Guatemala the necessity of settlement and called its attention to the Hague convention of 1907 concerning the use of force in the collection of contract debts.

On Guatemala's request, the United States secured another postponement of action by Great Britain. Alternative plans for settlement suggested by the United States did not meet the approval of the British, who continued to insist that Guatemala should live up to her contract by resuming payment to the bondholders of the revenues pledged.[14] No agreement for arbitration or other adjustment acceptable being forthcoming, Great Britain in May, 1913, sent a cruiser to Puerto Barrios, the chief Guatemalan Atlantic port, and shortly after an agreement for paying the bond service from the coffee export tax at its original rate was accepted by the local government.[15]

From this time to the world economic crisis of 1929, financial relations of the Republic became less contentious. Better returns for the coffee industry made meeting the public debt services less burdensome. On the other hand, the easy money conditions of the 1920's made it possible to contract new public loans, and the Republic undertook borrowing rather than the more conservative policy of repayment of outstanding obligations in a period of prosperity.[16] Six times between 1924 and 1931, new loans were contracted abroad, raising the public debt, as reported on March 1 of that year, to £1,632,783 plus 7,167,110 quetzales in the beginning of a period of world-wide hard times.[17] For the debt services new

[14] *For. Rel.*, 1912, pp. 500–512.

[15] *New York Times*, May 15, 1913, p. 8:3, and *Fifty-Seventh Annual Report of the Council of the Corporation of Foreign Bondholders for the year 1930*, London, 1930, pp. 229–235. The resumption of sinking fund payments under the agreement of 1913 was to occur in 1917. It was not fulfilled until October, 1919. Arrears of interest were settled in 1927. *Annual Report . . . for the year 1932*, p. 259.

[16] The actual budget operations from 1920–1921 to 1929–1930 showed, except for one year, either negligible deficits or sizable surpluses.

[17] *Fifty-Eighth Annual Report of the Council of the Corporation of Foreign Bondholders for the year 1931*, p. 265.

"guarantees" pledging the coffee export tax, a tax on sugar, consular invoice taxes, liquor taxes, railway and hydroelectric profits, and the real estate tax had been given. Inasmuch as the monies borrowed had to a large extent gone into enterprises of doubtful productivity, it was by no means clear that the better position brought by the prosperous 1920's had been used to strengthen the national position.

Because of increasing budget difficulties, Guatemala was forced to ask suspension of amortization payments on part of her foreign obligations early in 1932; and, by the end of that year, three annual installments on a subsidy to the International Railways of Central America were unpaid.[18]

The chief incidents in Guatemalan foreign affairs in the nineteenth and twentieth centuries, besides those involving its general Central American relations and its public loans, were those arising with its neighbors, Mexico and Honduras. From the colonial regime, Mexico has had a special interest in the territory beyond its southern boundary. As has already been pointed out, for a short time it succeeded in at least nominally extending its political control over all of Central America.

When Iturbide declared the Captaincy General of Guatemala annexed, his troops occupied Chiapas and from there invaded the south. When his power failed, the military forces withdrew to Chiapas, previously an *intendencia* of Guatemala. The Central American Constitutional Convention, which was convened, feared that Chiapas, through Mexican influence, might not join with the other states in the new union and contented itself with declaring that Chiapas would be admitted whenever it should freely declare that it wished to do so, "because, although it had always belonged to the old kingdom of Guatemala, since the empire had disappeared, the question remained open as to which of the two republics it would join." [19]

---

[18] The public debt of Guatemala on December 31, 1933, totaled 22,733,125 quetzales (par $1), of which 14,174,708 quetzales represented the external funded debt.

[19] Villacorta C., J. Antonio, *Curso de Historia de la America Central,* Guatemala, Tipografia Sanchez and de Guise, 1928, pp. 154–155.

Chiapas has remained a part of Mexico. The boundary between it and its southern neighbor is an artificial one. The two regions are, to a degree, an economic unit. Their products are similar and the coffee region of Chiapas extends into Guatemala. These circumstances have made the boundary region one which has on a number of occasions given rise to international incidents.[20] Mexican interest in Central American affairs has been declared to be primarily in Guatemala.[21]

Eastward from Chiapas lies the Peten region, partly in Guatemala and partly in Mexico. The latter at one time, it appears, supported claims to all the district, which, if enforced, would have taken roughly the northern half of the territory of Guatemala. A part of the sparsely settled territory, some 10,000 square kilometers, was forcibly seized by Mexico "about 1881" and has since been held by her. Further advance, it is reported, was abandoned in deference to "a slight pressure on the part of the United States." [22]

The Honduras boundary of Guatemala has also given rise to strained international relations. The long-standing dis-

---

[20] These have seldom taken on serious proportions, for the trade between the districts is limited and the two republics have not been able to make an arrangement by which connections may be established by the railroad systems which reach the boundary. Many of the minor controversies turn on alleged mistreatment of nationals in the border areas. Among the more recent of these were those involving alleged arbitrary treatment of Mexicans, which caused the breaking off of diplomatic relations and the massing of Mexican troops on the border in 1907 (*New International Yearbook,* 1907, p. 352), and similar troubles in 1908 (*ibid.,* 1908, p. 325) and in 1916 (*ibid.,* 1916, p. 304).

[21] In the administration of Theodore Roosevelt, an attempt was made to associate Mexico and the United States in efforts to solve Central American problems. The Central American treaties of 1907 were drawn up under the joint auspices of the two republics, and later, in 1909, two Mexican and six United States gunboats, on the request of the several Central American powers, patrolled the Atlantic and Pacific coasts to prevent filibustering expeditions. When in the Taft administration it was proposed that Mexico and the United States co-operate to compel observance of the treaties, "Mexico replied that it was unwilling to go so far, as it had no interest, commercial or political, to justify interference, except in the bordering state of Guatemala." President Diaz did not wish to embarrass his friend Zelaya, President of Nicaragua, "but he gave in advance an endorsement of whatever the United States might see fit to do south of Guatemala." (Weitzel, *op. cit.,* p. 4.)

[22] Sapper, Karl, "A Modern Boundary Question," in *Geopolitik,* Berlin, November, 1928, pp. 5–8.

pute involved a region along the Motagua River southeast of Lake Izabal. Various attempts at settlement had been made but without result. The area, about 4,000 square miles in extent, was but little developed, sparsely inhabited, and, until the spread of the fruit industry into the region, little valued by either of the disputants. In 1917 the dispute became more serious because the republics had granted conflicting concessions, Honduras to the Cuyamel Fruit Company and Guatemala to the United Fruit Company. The United States extended its good offices for the peaceful settlement of the question. They were accepted by both parties and a temporary neutral zone was set up in the disputed territory.[23] Settlement continued to drag, however, until 1928, when the United States was asked to act as mediator.

The Secretary of State recommended that the question be referred unreservedly to arbitration before the International Central American Tribunal under the convention of 1923. Guatemala accepted the proposal but Honduras demurred, because, among other reasons, it was alleged that the court did not offer an adequate panel of judges from which those to decide the case could be drawn. Preference was expressed for arbitration by "the President of the United States of America, the Chief Justice of the Supreme Court of the United States or any other tribunal established in regular and permanent form. . . ."[24] The Department of State again urged submission to the Central American court, but, on renewed refusal by Honduras, both republics accepted an invitation of the United States to a conference at Washington in January, 1930. In July the delegates signed a convention submitting the question to arbitration and providing for marking the boundary when the decision should have been made. Chief Justice Hughes agreed to act as presiding officer at the arbitration.[25] On January 23, 1933, the arbitrators signed a

---

23 *For. Rel.*, 1917, pp. 760–801.

24 Department of State, *Press Releases*, August 1, 1928.

25 *For. Rel.*, 1917, pp. 760–801; *New York Times*, March 21, 1928, p. 14:3; *ibid.*, June 7, 1928, p. 26:8; *ibid.*, August 2, 1928, p. 24:2; *ibid.*, August 26, 1928, p. 5:2; *ibid.*, Dec. 29, 1929, Section II, p. 2:5; *New International Yearbook*, New York, 1928, p. 330; State Department, *Press Releases* (mimeo-

lengthy award marking the boundary in detail,[26] substantially on the basis of actual occupation.[27] The following spring, engineers proceeded to the definitive survey.[28]

Like the other states of Central America, Guatemala promptly declared its sympathy with the cause of the Allies in the World War. On April 9, 1917, in consequence of disturbances of alleged German origin on the northern frontier, martial law was declared.[29] Diplomatic relations were broken with Germany on the 27th and it was declared that the government would co-operate with the United States and adhere to its policy. Use of her territorial waters, ports, railways and other facilities was offered to the United States.[30] Ultimately a formal declaration of war was issued.[31] Like her neighbor states Guatemala took no active part in the conflict but the prompt alignment with the position of the United States reflected not only the great influence which that country has in the Caribbean but a realization of common interests. Only on November 25, 1924, was a new commercial treaty with Germany negotiated.[32]

---

graphed), August 1, 1928; *ibid.,* August 8, 1928; *ibid.,* August 22, 1929; *ibid.,* Jan. 18, 1930, p. 20; *ibid.,* July 19, 1930, p. 37; *ibid.,* February 28, 1931, p. 145; *ibid.,* March 7, 1931, p. 160.

[26] On this controversy, see:

Guatemala-Honduras Boundary Arbitration, Brief on Behalf of Guatemala, Washington, 1931.

Guatemala-Honduras Boundary Arbitration, Reply of Guatemala to the Counter Case of Honduras, Washington, 1933.

Guatemala-Honduras Boundary Arbitration, The Case of Guatemala, Washington, 1932, and a supplementary volume of "Annexes."

Guatemala-Honduras, Special Boundary Tribunal, Opinion and Award, Washington, 1933.

[27] *New York Times,* January 24, 1933, p. 11:1.

[28] *Ibid.,* April 13, 1933, p. 10:3, and May 21, 1933, Section IV, p. 2:7.

[29] *Ibid.,* April 11, 1917, p. 6.

[30] *Ibid.,* April 29, 1917, Section I, p. 1:6, and Kelchner, Warren H., "Latin American Relations with the League of Nations," *World Peace Foundation Pamphlets, No. 206,* Boston, 1929, pp. 37–38.

[31] Martin, Percy Alvin, *Latin America and the War,* Boston, 1925, pp. 1–2.

[32] *New International Yearbook,* New York, 1924, p. 319.

CHAPTER XXI

Independence or Interdependence

IN THE first years of the twentieth century, students of tropical areas turned their attention to reviews of the political and economic changes which had occurred within these areas in decades then recently past and tried to forecast probable developments in those ahead. European writers pointed to the disappearance of the independent states of Africa and the threatened dismemberment of China—then for the moment checked by the open-door policy supported by the United States—as indications of what might be expected to happen in the disturbed and undeveloped areas of the New World. The United States itself had recently been involved in a war with Spain which left it in control of a tropical area in the Far East, in possession of Puerto Rico, and with a special position in relation to Cuba. Would not the political "control of the tropics" continue to slip into the hands of the great industrial and maritime powers? That seemed the natural and almost inevitable course to most European observers, and it was the opinion also of many in the United States.[1] But the third of a century which has since passed has seen no such development in the Americas.

Appraisal of the position of the tropical states of the New World in relation to the world at large and, particularly, to the United States continues to bring out wide differences of opinion. The years since the Spanish-American War have

[1] See Kidd, Benjamin, *The Control of the Tropics,* New York, the Macmillan Co., 1898, pp. 41–43, 50–53; and Baring, Evelyn, The Earl of Cromer, *Ancient and Modern Imperialism,* London, J. Murray, 1910, *passim;* and Dilke, Sir Charles Wentworth, *Problems of Greater Britain,* 2 vols., London, the Macmillan Co., 1890, Vol. II, p. 582.

shown the difficulties of discharging the duties which come with taking up "the white man's burden." In the Old World, there have arisen strong demands for greater local autonomy in areas the independence of which had long disappeared. In the New, the weaker states have advanced to a point which indicates that the establishment of extranational political control to assure that order may be maintained, that life and property may be given adequate protection, and that natural resources may be developed is less necessary than it formerly seemed. In the United States—the power looked upon as the most likely to extend its political boundaries through absorption of the weaker tropical states of the New World—there has been gained a keener realization of the problems which annexation would raise in its domestic affairs, political and economic, and in its foreign relations.

Public opinion in the strongest of the American states seldom crystallizes more than momentarily about any feature of foreign policy, for the great majority of its citizens confine their attention almost exclusively to domestic affairs. Gradually, however, as the mastery of national resources has advanced, a minority of increasing numbers in the United States has come to realize that more rapid communications, increasing industrialization, greater touch with other countries through rising imports and exports, greater international flow of capital, and wider participation in world affairs give vital significance to the foreign relations of the United States and particularly to its relations with its neighbors southward.

Two points of view divide those with an active interest in our foreign relations, particularly those whose attention is attracted to the Caribbean. One group emphasizes its belief in the equality of all nations and the rights of sovereign states to complete independence in the management of their affairs. The other views the relations of states more objectively. While it accepts the doctrine of the equality of nations, it emphasizes the opinion that membership in the family of nations carries with its duties as well as rights, and that nations can enjoy the greatest real liberty only if their rights are exercised in a way which recognizes the rights of others.

This group points out that the rights of sovereignty which states enjoy carry with them not only duties in formal relations with other states, but duties touching the rights of life and property of citizens of foreign states within their territories.

The more extreme of the latter group would maintain that, though states are equal in international law, in actual international relations they are in practically all respects unequal. Size, population, natural resources, and degree of advancement—social, political, and economic—all differentiate them to such a degree that the weaker units stand, from an objective point of view, not in the position of independent states with rights recognized and duties performed in a uniform manner, but in that of nations struggling to exercise the functions which fully developed countries perform as a matter of course.

Whichever of these points of view we as individuals may adopt in judging international affairs and in contributing to the development of public opinion upon them, it must be evident to us that the independence which was formerly possible in interstate relations no longer exists for either the strong or the weak. In fact, if not in theory, the independence which a nation had when international relations were incidental is no longer possible, and rights and duties tend increasingly to overflow national frontiers. In neither political nor economic relations does any nation stand alone in our day. Interdependence in both has displaced the old independence and will do so increasingly in the future.

In no region of the world is this relationship more strikingly illustrated than it is in the Americas, in the obligations which have arisen between the United States and the eleven republics of the Caribbean area. In no part of the world have such obligations been more accentuated by the changes which have come in the past generation.

In the first third of the twentieth century, the Caribbean has become increasingly dependent politically upon the United States. The withdrawal of the British West Indian fleet in the early years of the century showed a recognition of a change in international positions in the American area which had been going on for half a century. American influences were replacing those of the greatest power in Europe. "The whole naval strategic situation", declared a British statesman, "has undergone a complete revolution . . . that revolution is the birth of the United States navy." [2] The next year, the white garrisons were ordered withdrawn from St. Lucia, Barbados, and Jamaica. In current years, a small force is maintained in Jamaica, though proposals have been made for the abandonment of even the antiquated fortifications which still exist in the island. France maintains only negligible forces in the Caribbean. Both countries have organized their naval forces for defense of their interests elsewhere.

The strengthening of its position by the United States has gone steadily on since the beginning of the century. Then Key West and Puerto Rico were the southward outposts of its influence. In 1903, by treaty, Cuba engaged never to allow a foreign power to obtain "lodgment in or control over any portion of the island" and later leased Guantánamo, on the Windward Passage, for the use of the United States Navy. By treaty of the same year, there were secured in Panama extensive political rights which later, on the completion of the Panama Canal, "doubled the strength of the United States Navy." The agreements with the Dominican Republic set up in 1905–1907 and replaced by new engagements in 1924, established special relations with that republic. Nicaragua, by the treaty of 1914, granted an option on a canal route, leased Great Corn and Little Corn Islands, and gave to the United States the right to establish a naval station on the Gulf of Fonseca. By the treaty of 1915, Haiti has agreed not to alienate by "sale, lease or otherwise" any of its territory to a foreign power. In 1917, the Virgin Islands were purchased from Denmark, and in 1928 an agreement with Colombia confirmed the right of the United States to use three groups of outlying islands in the Caribbean for naval and

---

[2] The Earl of Selborne in the House of Commons, March 22, 1904, quoted in Aspinall, A. E., *The British West Indies,* London, Pitman and Sons, Ltd., 1912, p. 396.

aerial purposes. Though, except for the Danish West Indies, no territory has been added to the holdings of the United States in the Caribbean during the twentieth century, an unquestioned dominant position in Caribbean waters has been secured by it.

This broadened influence does doubtless strengthen the position of the United States, not only against possible attack from outside the New World, but also in relation to the states of the Caribbean itself. On the other hand, the possibility of conflict between these nearer nations and the United States is remote; and, should conflict occur, the outcome could hardly be determined by the advantages which the leading American power has secured. It is hard to imagine a major conflict with a nation outside the Americas in which the Caribbean nations would not find themselves ranged on the side of the United States. They might be made points of attack against the republic, but their alliance with non-American powers in opposition to it is little short of inconceivable. It is not too much to say, indeed, that the steps which have increased the ability of the United States to defend its own interests have strengthened both it and the Caribbean states for the preservation of their common interests. The relations that have come to exist between these neighbor nations and the United States in these respects only emphasize the unavoidable interdependence of them all. If it is true that their defense against non-American powers depends upon the United States, it is also true that effective defense of the latter depends upon their co-operation and friendship.

The peculiar interrelationship which binds the group together in political interests is paralleled by an equally intimate economic interrelationship. The Caribbean states find to the northward their nearest and greatest industrialized market, one to which access is easy through well-established shipping lines and in which all but one of their major products—sugar—enter either free of all tariff charges or on payment of low rates. In many years, the export trade of some of the more important areas enters the United States paying tariff on less than one per cent of its value.

Conversely, the United States is economically dependent on the Caribbean region. From the latter come practically all of its heavy imports of sugar and tropical fruits. From it and through the waters off its eastern borders come all but a small fraction of its coffee supplies. Through it arrive heavy shipments of minerals, vegetable fibers, wool, and hides for its industries. Through the Panama Canal passes the great trade between the east and west coasts of the United States, making up roughly half of the movement through the waterway. This commerce has reached such importance that it is no exaggeration to describe the Canal as one of the great arteries of its national economic life. The ocean-going ships engaged in the increased coastwise movement made possible by the Canal are also a valuable addition to that part of the merchant marine available as auxiliaries for the Navy.

Supplementing the commercial flow connecting the areas, there has arisen, especially since the World War, a great international flow of capital, chiefly from the north to the south, which has financed exceptional public expenditures in the Latin states and has entered to a much greater degree into developmental enterprises for the exploitation of local resources. These ventures represent the savings of large numbers of people scattered over all the States of the Union. They bring with them a new community of interest, for, like the interchanges in international trade, they can prosper only when the countries into which the capital has flowed prosper. Citizens of highly contrasted states thus come to stand, to a degree, in the relation of stockholders in the same firm.[3]

The connections of the United States and the Caribbean have now become so intimate that only in a technical sense can they be spoken of as "foreign relations." No major development, political or economic, in the Caribbean can be without its reflection upon the United States, and none in the United States lacks its effect on the countries southward.

Though interdependence is steadily growing and becoming

---

[3] An analysis of the trade and capital flow between the United States and the Caribbean republics is found in Jones, Chester Lloyd, *Caribbean Backgrounds and Prospects,* New York, D. Appleton and Co., 1931, pp. 197–310.

a recognized normal relationship, it is not necessarily an influence which will lessen the contrasts, social, political, and economic, which exist among the various states. Whether or not these differences tend to disappear depends on what is happening in the particular states considered. All the units, it may be assumed, are advancing; but each may advance at a different pace, with the result that at the end of a stated period some may be farther apart than at its beginning. In not a few of the Caribbean units, that seems, indeed, to be what has occurred in the last generation.

As a consequence, in spite of increasingly intimate relations emphasizing common interests, there may at the same time be accentuation of the problems of public policy which call for attention. An area in which public order is disturbed and economic development retarded may be progressing, but at a rate so slow that greater contact with foreign groups through travel, trade, and investment may increase rather than lessen its international responsibilities. The converse is also true. Social, political, and economic advance may be so marked that problems in international relationships which were formerly troublesome may disappear. Both of these circumstances may be present in the countries of the Caribbean.

For the United States, the interests of which in the broader affairs of the region are greater than those of any other single country, the variance in the degrees of local advance may accentuate in some cases and in other cases lessen the responsibilities which it may be forced to assume in that broad field of public policy lying close to, but not regulated in detail by, the rules of international law.

In the field of economics, obviously the policy adopted by any nation which plays so outstanding a role as that of the United States in Caribbean trade and financing will have a far-reaching effect whatever that policy may be. The program as to import trade may favor one region above another, as the reciprocity treaty between the United States and Cuba did in the early years of the century and as the new commercial treaty in lesser degree continues to do. A policy of economic nationalism looking toward domestic production of greater supplies of a commodity imported may cut down the prosperity of a region from which the supplies come and even reduce it to a condition in which public finances are upset and public order made difficult to maintain. Such a policy as to sugar has already seriously embarrassed Cuba, and manipulation of the American tariff on products from the other monoculture areas might grievously affect their export outlook, cut down their buying power, and upset their balance of payments.

Continuation of a liberal customs policy toward them may, on the other hand, support their progress toward economic stability, political advance, greater contribution to world trade, and normal international relationships. It is intended at this point not to argue what is, in any particular case, the policy which the United States should adopt, but to emphasize the fact that, whatever action it takes, even though it be nominally within the field of domestic affairs, may have a far-reaching influence upon the fortunes of its southern neighbors or upon those of certain of them. Fortunately for both the Caribbean republics and the United States, their typical products are to such a degree supplementary that mutual advantage certainly lies, in the great majority of cases, in the development of economic interchange rather than in attempts at national self-sufficiency.

As far as the United States is concerned, a strong position in this growing export market and assurance of satisfactory supplies of the basic raw materials and foodstuffs which the region can furnish are clearly a greater national advantage than the "independence" which might come from artificially stimulating domestic industries in the ambition to make the country "self-sustained."

Further, and this is a consideration generally overlooked, upon the liberality of the trade policy which the United States adopts depends very largely the degree to which the Caribbean states can develop not only economic but political stability. Any trade policy which cuts down economic advance in the neighbor states undermines the foreign trade and renders insecure the investments of citizens of both the United States and other countries. It disturbs the basis for local economic development and weakens the forces working for public order, which it is a primary interest of the United States to strengthen. The adoption by the United States of a liberal economic policy toward the neighbor republics may promote stability. The adoption by it of an illiberal one may destroy stability, and, through the local disorder it creates, may raise political questions involving the rights of both the United States and non-American nations.

In the political field, there is no clear-cut standard marking the line of national or international advantage which can be applied to individual cases, and, as a consequence, probably to a greater extent than where general economic policy is involved, decisions will rest on the circumstances of each case. Since action will often have to be taken without knowledge of all the facts, the course will not always be consistent with precedent and it will be subject to the charge that it is determined by a short-sighted opportunism.

In political decisions which are made by the United States in its Caribbean policy, it will be quite as true as in those on economic matters that, whether the choice fall this way or that, the influence exerted will be far-reaching. The interdependence of the members of the group of Caribbean powers is so intimate that there is no escaping responsibility. When, for example, it must be decided whether or not to recognize a government which has newly established itself in power, the decision by the United States, unquestionably a matter in its discretion, may determine whether or not the regime will be able to maintain itself. Whether other nations grant recognition or not may be of small importance, but recognition by the United States may be of capital concern.

Similarly, the action which the United States may adopt as to allowing shipments of arms and ammunition to a country where a revolution threatens or is in progress cannot fail to have influence on the outcome. Since it is the only source from which military and other supplies can come quickly, it may, in effect, dry up all shipments, or allow them to one faction only, or, by inaction, allow all parties to buy. Decision on the policy to be followed lies clearly with the United States, but no policy adoptable can keep it free from influencing the result.

Still other examples of the unavoidable interrelations which exist between the United States and the Caribbean nations are found in the problems arising when conditions prompt foreign powers to displace local authority by force, that is, when intervention becomes an issue.

As in the case of recognition and in that of shipment of arms, there exist in textbooks rules recognized in the practice of nations setting out the conditions under which intervention may occur, but the decision as to when action shall be taken and what action shall be taken must rest on the circumstances of each case. In any event, intervention lies in a narrowing twilight zone between matters of policy and international law. The field shrinks as nations advance in the ability to protect life and property, but there is no ground for believing that it will soon disappear under conditions such as still exist in the Caribbean.

There, through the position which the United States has adopted in defense of the "America for Americans" policy, intervention, as a rule, occurs only by the United States. Other American nations often overlook the fact that otherwise intervention almost certainly would raise broader international questions. Were it not for the policy of the United States, the problems which the weaker states might have to face on occasion might be much more acute. Though an apparent paradox, it is true that, far from being a threat to their independence, as they have often believed it to be, for some of the weak states the practice of intervention may have helped to maintain their independence. Had no such right been exercised, it is quite possible that the "America for Americans" policy would have been more seriously questioned and its maintenance might have proved impossible.

Both for their own interests and for those of the United States, the Caribbean republics' achievement of stability which will minimize or remove conditions prompting intervention is of major concern. The end to be sought, if policy is to be constructive, is the creation of conditions which will automatically decrease the causes of intervention or the excuses for it, rather than a denial that conditions which make it unavoidable at times exist.

Encouraging advance in this direction has been made in the generation now coming to its end. The declarations at The Hague in 1907, rising indirectly from the Venezuelan imbroglio of the opening years of the century, have minimized the chance of intervention for the collection of public debts. To be sure, but few of the Latin-American states have ratified this agreement; but its general acceptance by the powers whose citizens are most prominent in financing bond issues of foreign governments lessens the chance of resort to force for collection of public obligations in the future. To the same end, at least in the New World, the well-established policy of the United States as to the use of force for the collection of pecuniary claims contributes. More important than these influences, however, is the advance toward better maintenance of public order which has occurred in Latin-American states. The right of intervention in the stronger of these has now become little more than theoretical. While that is still not the case in the weaker Caribbean communities, occasions for its exercise are declining.

There are those who believe that conditions have now changed to such an extent that intervention, whatever may once have been its justification, should now be abandoned, and that the United States as the champion of the "America for Americans" policy should take the stand that under no circumstances will it itself intervene in the affairs of American states nor allow non-American powers to do so. If this position were taken, it is argued, the weaker states would be freed from the danger of intervention but would still be anxious to respect the rights of citizens of other states, since failure to do so would discourage entrance of foreigners, foreign capital, and foreign enterprise. Abolition of intervention would therefore not reduce their efforts to reach political maturity nor their desire to discharge the responsibilities that attach to independence. It would eliminate a source of international friction and, especially, lead to better relations between the United States and Latin-American powers.

The opposing argument points out that the United States itself may well question whether it is ready to promise never to resort to intervention in defense of the interests of its own citizens. This is especially true as to the Caribbean region, where American holdings have an estimated value of well over $2,000,000,000.

Even if the United States were willing to adopt for itself a policy of no intervention in any circumstances in the Caribbean or in Latin America, it is, to say the least, far from clear that it could impose that policy upon the rest of the world. Even in current years, in spite of the position which the United States holds in the New World and in spite of the preoccupation of other powers with affairs elsewhere, there is no reason for believing that the announcement of such a policy would escape vigorous opposition. No single nation or group of nations can assume the right to change the rules of international law. The right to demand just treatment of its citizens in foreign countries is one which will be stoutly maintained by most of the advanced states. Certain of the European powers, moreover, have by no means given up hope of colonial expansion and would not freely close one of the doors through which such expansion has frequently occurred in the past.

Even if the announcement of the new policy did not at once provoke a break with non-American powers, it might well be that the added friendliness which it is assumed would arise among American states would be more than counterbalanced by ill will aroused in non-American nations. Then, too, it is to be remembered that if, at a later time, the halfway measure of intervention no longer being permitted to the United States, a war between a weak American state and a non-American power were declared, the defense of the "America for Americans" principle would fall overwhelmingly upon the United States and not upon the republics of Latin America.

It may even be questioned whether, if all states could be

brought to abolish the practice of intervention, the result would be of unqualified benefit to the weaker American nations. They might secure a nominal advantage in greater political independence of action; but, if foreigners engaging in commerce and industry felt that they must indeed "take their own chances," their willingness to assume such risks as attend investments in the weaker nations might be cut down. They might not devote their energies to develop local resources—a result which almost all weak states would consider unfortunate. The retarding of local developments might continue indefinitely the weaknesses which the less well-established states seek to outgrow.

Out of this complex of economic and political interrelationships among the nations of the New World there should arise a policy resting on a broader base than that suggested by purely nationalistic interests. Such a policy should seek to promote normal conditions for the development of all the nations of America and, indeed, for the development of all the nations of the world. All such far-reaching plans must be lacking in definiteness. They will be, at least at the beginning, warped and twisted by national interests and prejudices which will yield only as a sense of international social responsibility develops. The adjustments will be difficult because of the contrasts, as sharp in America as in any other part of the world, between the theoretical equality and actual inequality of the nations. Their nominal isolation as "sovereignties" will stand over against the fact of group association, and their technical "independence" over against their actual "interdependence." Programs which overlook these contrasts and fail to make policy conform to them are unreal.

May not the constructive approach to the problems to be solved be one similar to that adopted in the regulation of the relation of classes and individuals of civil society? Legislation of all modern nations recognizes inequalities among their citizens, without its being assumed that such recognition is in contradiction to the accepted doctrine that all have equal rights before the law. The laws making differentiations are felt to be justified as recognizing inequalities which have arisen from special circumstances and as measures restoring the equality of opportunity which such special conditions have upset. Modern legislation on hours of labor, minimum wages, the working conditions of women and children, employers' liability, and bankruptcy illustrates the viewpoint which stresses a larger social responsibility undertaken in the belief that, for the individual and for society as a whole, better circumstances of life can be created than would follow a rigid observance of *laissez faire.*

Less of this point of view has carried over into policies adopted in international relations, though the inequalities among "sovereign powers" are quite as great as those among individuals. To insist that all states are equal, that their "rights" presuppose that any limitations upon their freedom and independence are necessarily contrary to their long-time interest and that of the world at large, seems only as logical as to hold that all regulation of activities of individuals is objectionable. May it be that the weaker states stand in a position comparable to the position of immature individuals in relation to those with fully developed abilities? Though their "equality" with stronger states is recognized, may they slip, fall, damage themselves and others, act irrationally at times, and create situations in which their freedom of action may properly be restrained for the common good? When any control is attempted, it is, of course, true that possibilities of abuse of the weak by the strong exist, whether the cases involve individuals or states; but such possibilities exist in any attempt to regularize conditions by government action.

In the differences in attitude toward efforts at social control in the case of persons and in the case of nations, a curious contrast appears. In shaping conditions modifying the practice of *laissez faire* within national boundaries, the liberal elements in the community have regularly been sanguine as to what can be accomplished through public action. The conservatives have been least attracted by the proposed modification of "personal rights," the "freedom of contract," and similar traditional doctrines. In international affairs, the division runs on opposite lines—the liberals have been the defenders of "sovereign rights" and "independence" against the establishment of any control agencies. The latter cause, on the whole, has been supported by those who in domestic affairs have usually been characterized as conservatives.

Which in the long run is the truly constructive attitude will doubtless long continue to divide public opinion. True it is that up to the present any control exercised in the Caribbean region has tended to be supported by the United States alone. It is to be admitted also that the efforts undertaken have not always met with unquestioned success—though that is true in all human efforts to shape the course of events, whether the basis be national or international.

Lack of development of public opinion based on appreciation of the actualities of economic and political life in the Caribbean in part explains the uncertainty which has at times characterized the action of the United States in creating or supporting control agencies. Liberals have too frequently acted on the assumption that conditions in the Caribbean are in all ways comparable to those in the communities in which they live. They have been too confident as to what the communities can work out on their own initiative. Conservatives have at times been oversanguine as to what can be accomplished through such assistance as can be given. They have not appreciated the economic and human limitations which surround all efforts to improve conditions in the American tropics and have expected returns from the controls which have been set up to come more promptly than there is ground to expect.

Beginnings have been made toward broadening the base on which any measures of control shall rest so that they may be less subject to the suspicion that they are shaped in the interest of a single nation—the United States. Advance in that direction may become easier as some of the stronger states of Latin America reach the point where recognition of the need of assured public order in the Americas overbalances the feeling of distrust they have had toward any forward action by the United States alone. Realization that control may be beneficent was reflected in the efforts of the United States and

Mexico in the first decade of the century, later abandoned, to shape developments in Central America to promote peace. Later, President Wilson on two occasions welcomed the co-operation of groups of Latin-American powers in endeavors to bring peace between warring factions in Mexico.

In 1933, President Franklin D. Roosevelt encouraged Latin-American co-operation in considering the serious conditions of unrest in Cuba resulting from the Machado regime, and the Government of Mexico again showed interest in promoting Latin-American co-operation. At a meeting of the Woodrow Wilson Foundation, President Roosevelt reaffirmed that the United States had no desire to annex territory by conquest. It was, he felt, easy to understand that "a citizen of some other American republic" might in a political campaign be "strongly tempted to play upon the fears of . . . that republic by charging the United States of North America [sic] with some form of imperialistic desire for selfish aggrandizement. . . . In particular . . .", he continued, "I might have found it hard to approve of the occupation of other republics, even as a temporary measure." The policy of the United States in the future would be, he felt, "opposed to armed intervention."

This was not a guarantee that no intervention would occur if conditions again rendered it unavoidable, though, if that should happen, Mr. Roosevelt felt that the action taken might well be on joint responsibility. "The maintenance of constitutional government in other nations is not, after all, a sacred obligation devolving upon the United States alone. The maintenance of law and the orderly processes of government in this hemisphere is the concern of each individual nation within its own borders first of all. It is only if and when the failure of orderly processes affects the other nations of the continent that it becomes their concern; and the point to stress is that in such an event it becomes the joint concern of the whole continent in which we are all neighbors." [4]

---

[4] Speech at the dinner of the Woodrow Wilson Foundation, Washington, December 28, 1933 (pamphlet), no publisher or date given.

Comprehension of this point of view by the American states in the crises which from time to time arise in the Caribbean area would do much to lessen the suspicions which now hamper the development of a basis of cordial co-operation. It would emphasize the interrelationships which should be as real in political as they are in economic activities. Attainment of the common point of view need not necessarily mean joint action by practically all or even the majority of the American states, nor, indeed, action by more than one. Joint action might be halting, whereas in some cases promptness of decision would be essential.

The development of a sense of joint responsibility for the maintenance of an acceptable minimum of public order and respect for life and property on the part of all the American states cannot be expected within any short period. Individually they are too diverse in development for that to be possible and the urgency of a crisis may appear in very different light to one country close to the area of disturbance and another distant from it. Joint action by all in the average case is not a realizable ideal. On the other hand, more objective approach by all nations of the New World in reaching opinions as to the facts prompting intervention may not only lessen their apprehension concerning it but, through support of the objects sought, give substantial increase of authority to those seeking to restore normal conditions. It may also act as a restraint against extreme measures to which the intervening authorities might otherwise lend themselves.

The economic relationships of the states of America, particularly those of the United States and the republics of the Caribbean, which have become so remarkably interlocked must be supplemented by an equally far-reaching co-operation in political affairs. Without it the full advantages of their interdependence cannot be reaped and without it each nation stands in a weaker position. In some of the weaker members which have not yet reached that stage of self-control which would enable them at all times to meet their international obligations fully, at least occasional exercise of short-time extranational control seems unavoidable; but the occasions when it will be so may already be disappearing.

In some of the units, more than occasional functions in maintenance of public order have been assumed by the United States under pressure of circumstances threatening non-American intervention and in furtherance of what have been assumed to be the interests of the United States and the communities controlled. The status of such activities, always looked upon with anxiety by Latin-American nations, has at times aroused harsh criticism both in Latin America and in the United States. Their history has by no means been uniformly happy, though it is not clear that alternative courses would have brought better results.

Whether such activities shall be continued or expanded may continue to be one of the fields in which wide degrees of difference of opinion may develop. If the decision is affirmative, it is greatly to be desired, whether the actual control be by a single power or other means, that a better understanding as to the purpose sought be reached, that the controls established have a broader basis of support through international sharing of responsibility, and that the task, once undertaken, shall not be limited in its chance of success by the hesitation which has at times characterized the execution of policy.

Diverse influences will continue to shape the relations of the American nations. Differences in race, natural resources, availability of local capital, aptitudes for industrialization, intimacy of communication, commercial policies, nationalistic programs, and a long list of less evident items will determine the degree to which common interests will develop. Some of these will have exceptional significance in shaping the relations to each other of countries with Caribbean holdings, particularly the relations of the weaker republics to the United States. None can effectively check a growing realization of common needs. Political co-operation will continue to lag behind economic relationship; but, as public order becomes better established and as public opinion in all the units comes to rest upon broader understanding of the facts which condition policy, there will be laid the foundation for greater emphasis of public policies promotive of that interdependence among the members of the group which is the basis of their prosperity and safety.

A Brief Bibliography of the Caribbean

THE books listed below include representative works dealing with the development of the Caribbean. Most of them have been published since 1910. They vary widely in character and include propaganda materials listed to show partisan points of view, popular discussions, authoritative studies, and Government manuals.

General Works

Adams, Frederick Upham, *The Conquest of the Tropics,* New York, Doubleday, Page and Co., 1914.

Austin, O. P., *Trading with Our Neighbors in the Caribbean,* New York, National City Bank, 1920.

Bayo, Ciro, *Historia Moderna de la America Española,* Madrid, Caro Raggio, 1930.

Beals, Carleton, *Banana Gold,* Philadelphia, J. B. Lippincott Co., 1932.

Bigelow, John, *American Policy,* New York, Charles Scribner's Sons, 1914.

Blakeslee, George Hubbard, ed., *Latin America* (Clark University Addresses, 1913), New York, G. E. Stechert and Co., 1914.

————, ed., *Mexico and the Caribbean,* New York, G. E. Stechert and Co., 1920.

Bonsal, Stephen, *The American Mediterranean,* New York, Moffat Yard and Co., 1912.

Bynum, M. L., *International Trade in Coffee, United States Department of Commerce, Bureau of Foreign and Domestic Commerce, Trade Promotion Series, No. 37,* Washington, 1926.

Calderón, F. García, *Latin America: Its Rise and Progress,* New York, Charles Scribner's Sons, 1913.

Chandler, Charles L., *Inter-American Acquaintances,* Sewanee, Tennessee, University Press, 1917.

Colmo, Alfredo, *La Revolución en la America Latina,* Buenos Aires, Nosotros, 1933.

Commerce Yearbook, United States Department of Commerce, Bureau of Foreign and Domestic Commerce, Washington, Vol. II. (Annual)

Coolidge, Archibald C., *The United States as a World Power,* New York, the Macmillan Co., 1908.

Corlett, W. T., *The American Tropics,* Cleveland, Burrow Bros. Co., 1908.

Corliss, James C., *Latin American Budgets, Trade Information Bulletin No. 524,* Washington, January, 1928.

Corporation of Foreign Bondholders, Annual Reports, London, England.

Crichfield, G. W., *American Supremacy,* New York, Brentano's, 1908.

Crokaert, Jacques, *La Méditerranée américaine,* Paris, Payot, 1927.

Crowther, Samuel, *The Romance and Rise of the American Tropics,* Garden City, N. Y., Doubleday, Doran and Co., 1929.

Dunn, R. W., *American Foreign Investments,* New York, Viking Press, 1926.

Enock, C. R., *Republics of Central and South America,* New York, Charles Scribner's Sons, 1913.

Filsinger, E. B., *Commercial Traveler's Guide to Latin America, United States Department of Commerce, Bureau of Foreign and Domestic Commerce, Miscellaneous Series, No. 89,* Washington, 1926.

Franck, H. A., *Roaming Through the West Indies,* New York, Century Co., 1920.

Froude, J. A., *The English in the West Indies,* New York, Charles Scribner's Sons, 1888.

González-Ruano, César, *El terror en América de Gómez a Leguía pasando por Machado,* Madrid, Compañía Iberoamericana, 1930.

Great Britain, Department of Overseas Trade, *Reports of the British Commercial Diplomatic and Consular Service.* (Annual)

Halsey, Frederic M., *Investments in Latin America and the British West Indies, United States Department of Commerce, Bureau of Foreign and Domestic Commerce, Special Agents Series, No. 169,* Washington, 1918.

Haring, Clarence H., *South America Looks at the United States,* New York, the Macmillan Co., 1928.

————, *The Buccaneers in the West Indies in the Seventeenth Century,* New York, E. P. Dutton and Co., 1910.

Harris, Garrard, *The West Indies as an Export Field, United States Department of Commerce, Bureau of Foreign and Domestic Commerce, Special Agents Series, No. 141,* Washington, 1917.

Hart, A. B., *The Monroe Doctrine: An Interpretation,* Boston, Little, Brown and Co., 1917.

Hearn, Lafcadio, *Two Years in the French West Indies,* New York, Harper and Brothers, 1923.

Hill, Howard C., *Roosevelt and the Caribbean,* Chicago, University of Chicago Press, 1927.

Hoskins, H. L., *Guide to Latin-American History,* Boston, D. C. Heath and Co., 1922.

Howland, Charles P., *Survey of American Foreign Relations,* New York, Council on Foreign Relations, 1929. (Annual)

Hughes, Charles Evans, *Our Relations to the Nations of the Western Hemisphere,* Princeton, Princeton University Press, 1928.

Inman, S. G., *Problems in Pan-Americanism,* Garden City, N. Y., Doubleday, Doran and Co., 1925.

James, Herman G., and Martin, Percy A., *The Republics of Latin America,* New York, Harper and Brothers, 1923.

Jones, Chester Lloyd, *Caribbean Backgrounds and Prospects,* New York, D. Appleton and Co., 1931.

———, *Caribbean Interests of the United States,* New York, D. Appleton and Co., 1916.

———, *Costa Rica and Civilization in the Caribbean,* Madison, Wis., University of Wisconsin, 1935.

———, Norton, H. K., and Moon, P. T., *The United States and the Caribbean,* Chicago, University of Chicago Press, 1929.

Jones, Clarence F., *Commerce of South America,* Boston, Ginn and Co., 1928.

———, *South America,* New York, Henry Holt and Co., 1930.

Kelchner, Warren H., *Latin American Relations with the League of Nations,* Boston, World Peace Foundation, 1930.

Keller, A. G., *Colonization,* Boston, Ginn and Co. 1908.

Klein, Julius, *Frontiers of Trade,* New York, Century Co., 1929, pp. 119–142.

Koebel, W. H., *South America: An Industrial and Commercial Field,* London, Fisher Unwin, 1923.

Lahee, A. W., *Our Competitors and Markets,* New York, Henry Holt and Co., 1924.

Latané, J. H., *A History of American Foreign Policy*, Garden City, N. Y., Doubleday, Doran and Co., 1927.

———, *America as a World Power (1897–1907),* New York, Harper and Brothers, 1907.

———, *Diplomatic Relations of the United States and Spanish America,* Baltimore, Johns Hopkins Press, 1900.

———, *The United States and Latin America,* Garden City, N. Y., Doubleday, Doran and Co., 1920.

Lufft, Hermann, *Lateinamerika,* Leipzig, Bibliografisches Institut, A. G., 1930.

Manington, George, *The West Indies with British Guiana and British Honduras,* New York, Charles Scribner's Sons, 1925.

Mann, W., *Volk und Kultur Lateinamerikas,* Hamburg, Verlagsbuchhandlung Broschek, 1927.

Martin, P. A., *Latin America and the War,* Baltimore, Johns Hopkins Press, 1925.

Masefield, John, *On the Spanish Main,* New York, the Macmillan Co., 1925.

Meehan, M. J., *The Guianas, United States Department of Commerce, Bureau of Foreign and Domestic Commerce, Trade Information Bulletin No. 516,* Washington, 1927.

Moon, P. T., *Imperialism and World Politics,* New York, the Macmillan Co., 1926.

Moreno, L. Andelino, *Historia de las Relaciones Interstatuales de Centroamerica,* Madrid, Compañía Iberoamericana de Publicaciones, 1928.

Munro, Dana G., *The United States and the Caribbean Area,* Boston, World Peace Foundation, 1934.

Nearing, Scott, and Freeman, Joseph, *Dollar Diplomacy,* New York, Viking Press, 1925.

Paxson F. L., *The Independence of the South American Republics,* Philadelphia, Ferris and Leach, 1916.

Peck, A. S., *Industrial and Commercial South America,* New York, T. Y. Crowell Co., 1927.

Pitman, F. W., *The Development of the British West Indies,* New Haven, Yale University Press, 1917.

Ragatz, Lowell Joseph, *The Fall of the Planter Class in the British Caribbean, 1763–1833,* New York, Century Co., 1928.

Reynolds, Philip Keep, *The Banana,* Boston, Houghton Mifflin Co., 1927.

Rippy, James Fred, *Historical Evolution of Hispanic America,* New York, F. S. Crofts and Co., 1932.

————, *Latin America in World Politics,* New York, F. S. Crofts and Co., 1928.

Robertson, W. S., *Hispanic-American Relations with the United States,* New York, Oxford University Press, 1923.

————, *History of the Latin-American Nations,* New York, D. Appleton and Co., 1925.

Root, Elihu, *The Military and Colonial Policy of the United States,* Cambridge, Mass., Harvard University Press, 1916.

Ruhl, Arthur B., *The Central Americans,* New York, Charles Scribner's Sons, 1928.

Shanahan, E. W., *South America,* New York, E. P. Dutton and Co., 1927.

Shepherd, W. R., *Latin America,* New York, Henry Holt and Co., 1914.

Sherwell, G. Butler, *Budgets of Latin American Countries, United*

States Department of Commerce, Bureau of Foreign and Domestic Commerce, Trade Information Bulletin No. 281, Washington, 1924.

Stuart, Graham H., *Latin America and the United States* (2nd ed.), New York, Century Co., 1928.

Thomas, D. Y., *One Hundred Years of the Monroe Doctrine,* New York, the Macmillan Co., 1927.

Thompson, J. E., *Our Atlantic Possessions,* New York, 1928.

United States Department of Commerce, Bureau of Foreign and Domestic Commerce, *Caribbean Markets for American Goods, Trade Information Bulletins No. 329, 342, 357, and 402,* Washington, 1925–26.

United States Department of Commerce, *Caribbean Markets for American Goods, Trade Information Bulletin No. 352,* Washington, 1925, Part IV.

United States Tariff Commission, *Sugar,* Washington, 1926.

Verrill, A. H., *Getting Together with Latin America,* New York, E. P. Dutton and Co., 1918.

Warshaw, Jacob, *The New Latin America,* New York, T. Y. Crowell Co., 1922.

Webster, Hutton, *History of Latin America,* Boston, D. C. Heath and Co., 1924.

Whitbeck, R. H., *Economic Geography of South America,* New York, McGraw-Hill Book Co., 1926.

Wilgus, Alva Curtis, *A History of Hispanic America,* Washington, Mime-o-form Service, 1931.

Williams, Benjamin H., *Economic Foreign Policy of the United States,* New York, McGraw-Hill Book Co., 1929.

Williams, Mary Wilhelmine, *The People and Politics of Latin America,* Boston, Ginn and Co., 1930.

Winkler, Max, *Investments of United States Capital in Latin America,* Boston, World Peace Foundation, 1928.

Current developments are covered in a number of publications including:

Bulletin of the Pan-American Union, Washington.
Current History, New York.
Foreign Affairs, New York.
Foreign Policy Reports, New York.
World Affairs, Washington.

Central America, General

Corliss, James C., *Latin American Budgets: Central America and Panama, United States Department of Commerce, Bureau of*

Foreign and Domestic Commerce, Trade Information Bulletin No. 564, Washington, 1928.

Domville-Fife, C. W., *Guatemala and the States of Central America,* London, F. Griffiths, 1913.

Koebel, W. H., *Central America: Guatemala, Nicaragua, Costa Rica, Honduras, Panama and Salvador,* New York, Charles Scribner's Sons, 1917.

Munro, D. G., *The Five Republics of Central America,* New York, Oxford University Press, 1918.

Palmer, Frederick, *Central America and Its Problems,* New York, Moffat Yard and Co., 1910.

Putnam, G. P., *The Southland of North America,* New York, G. P. Putnam's Sons, 1913.

Thompson, Wallace, *Rainbow Countries of Central America,* New York, E. P. Dutton and Co., 1926.

Villacorta, C. J. Antonio, *Curso de Historia de la America Central,* Guatemala, Tipografia Sanchez y de Guise, 1928.

West Indies, General

Araquistain, Luis, *La Agonía Antillana,* Madrid, Espasa-Calpe, 1930.

Aspinall, A. E., *A Wayfarer in the West Indies,* Boston, Houghton Mifflin Co., 1928.

————, *The British West Indies,* Boston, Little, Brown and Co., 1912.

————, *The Handbook of the British West Indies, British Guiana and British Honduras,* London, West India Committee, 1926.

Beckwith, Martha Warren, *Black Roadways,* Chapel Hill, N. C., University of North Carolina Press, 1929.

Bell, Archie, *The Spell of the Caribbean Islands,* Boston, L. C. Page and Co., 1926.

Cestero, Tulio Manuel, *Estados Unidos y las Antillas,* Madrid, Compañía General de Artes Gráficas, 1931.

Cudnall, Frank, *Jamaica in 1928,* London, the Institute of Jamaica, 1929.

————, *Studies in Jamaica History,* London, the Institute of Jamaica, 1900.

————, and Pietersz, Joseph L., *Jamaica Under the Spaniards,* Kingston, Jamaica, the Institute of Jamaica, 1919.

Davis, William Morris, *The Lesser Antilles,* New York, American Geographical Society, 1926.

England, George Allan, *Isles of Romance,* New York, Century Co., 1929.

Foster, Harry La Tourette, *Combing the Caribbees,* New York, Dodd, Mead and Co., 1929.

Freeman, Lewis Ransome, *Afloat and Aflight in the Caribbean,* New York, Dodd, Mead and Co., 1932.

Gardner, W. J., *A History of Jamaica,* New York, D. Appleton and Co., 1909.

Harlow, Vincent Todd, *A History of Barbados, 1625–1685,* New York, Oxford University Press, 1926.

Hassam, John T., *The Bahama Islands,* Cambridge, Mass., John Wilson and Son, University Press, 1899.

Henderson, John, *Jamaica,* London, A. and C. Black, 1906.

Inman, Samuel Guy, *Trailing the Conquistadores,* New York, Missionary Education Movement, 1930.

Jamaica, Register General, *Census of Jamaica and Its Dependencies Taken on the 25th of April, 1921,* Kingston, Jamaica, 1922.

Jordan, William F., *Crusading in the West Indies,* New York, Fleming H. Revell and Co., 1922.

Lewis, Matthew Gregory, *Journal of a West Indian Proprietor,* Boston, Houghton Mifflin Co., 1929.

MacGowan, H. P., *Markets of the Dutch West Indies, United States Department of Commerce, Bureau of Foreign and Domestic Commerce, Trade Information Bulletin No. 405,* Washington, 1926.

Marden, Philip Sanford, *Sailing South,* Boston, Houghton Mifflin Co., 1921.

Ober, Frederick Albion, *Our West Indian Neighbors,* New York, James Pott and Co., 1904.

Pitman, Frank W., *The Development of the British West Indies,* New Haven, Yale University Press, 1917.

Shattuck, George Burbank, *The Bahama Islands,* New York, the Macmillan Co., 1905.

Sinckler, E. G., *The Barbados Handbook,* London, Duckworth and Co., 1914.

Stowell, Jay Samuel, *Between the Americas,* New York, Missionary Education Movement, 1930.

Treves, Sir Frederick, *The Cradle of the Deep,* New York, E. P. Dutton and Co., 1925.

Van Dyke, John Charles, *In the West Indies,* New York, Charles Scribner's Sons, 1932.

Verrill, Alpheus Hyatt, *Isles of Spice and Palm,* New York, D. Appleton and Co., 1915.

————, *In the Wake of the Buccaneers,* New York, Century Co., 1923.

————, *Jamaica of Today,* New York, Dodd, Mead and Co., 1931.

————, *The Book of the West Indies,* New York, E. P. Dutton and Co., 1917.

————, *West Indies of Today,* New York, Dodd, Mead and Co., 1931.

Williamson, James A., *The Caribbee Islands under the Proprietary Patents,* New York, Oxford University Press, 1926.

Wright, James Martin, *History of the Bahama Islands with a Special Study of the Abolition of Slavery in the Colony,* Baltimore, Friedenwald Co., 1905.

Wrong, Humphrey Hume, *Government of the West Indies,* New York, Oxford University Press, 1923.

Colombia

Bell, P. L., *Colombia, A Commercial and Industrial Handbook, United States Department of Commerce, Bureau of Foreign and Domestic Commerce, Special Agents Series, No. 206,* Washington, 1921.

Bingham, H., *The Journal of an Expedition Across Venezuela and Colombia, 1906–7,* New Haven, Yale Publishing Association, 1909.

Cunninghame-Graham, R. G. B., *Cartagena and the Banks of the Sinu,* London, 1920.

————, *The Conquest of New Granada: Being the Life of Gonzalo Jiminez de Quesada,* Boston, Houghton Mifflin Co., 1922.

Du Bois, J. T., *Colombia's Claims and Rights,* 1914.

Eder, P. J., *Colombia,* New York, Charles Scribner's Sons, 1913.

Escobar, Francisco, *Colombia and her Commercial Opportunities,* New York, 1915.

Freehoff, J. C., *America and the Canal Title,* New York, published by the author, 1916.

Humbert, Jules, *Histoire de la Colombie et du Venezuela,* Paris, Alcan, 1921.

Lévine, V., *Colombia,* New York, D. Appleton and Co., 1914.

Martinez, Abraham, *Colombia Yearbook,* New York, F. Mayans, 1925–1926 and 1927.

McFee, William, *Sunlight in New Granada,* Garden City, N. Y., Doubleday, Doran and Co., 1925.

McQueen, C. A., *Colombian Public Finance, United States Department of Commerce, Bureau of Foreign and Domestic Commerce, Trade Information Bulletin No. 417,* Washington, 1926.

Niles, Blair, *Colombia, Land of Miracles,* New York, Century Co., 1924.

Perez-Sarmiento, J. M. (ed.), *Colombia, 1789–1917: obra de propaganda arreglada y editada,* Cádiz, 1917.
Petrie, Francis L., *The Republic of Colombia,* London, 1906.
Rippy, J. Fred, *The Capitalists and Colombia,* New York, Vanguard Press, 1931.
Scruggs, W. L., *The Colombian and Venezuelan Republics,* Boston, Little, Brown and Co., 1900.
Taylor, Hannis, *Why the Pending Treaty with Colombia should be Ratified,* 1914.
Thomson, Norman, *Colombia and the United States,* London, N. Thomson and Co., 1914.
United States Department of Commerce, *Colombia and Venezuela, Trade Information Bulletin No. 524,* Washington, 1928.
Uribe, Antonio José, *Colombia y los Estados Unidos de America,* Bogotá, Imprenta Nacional, 1931.
Veatch, A. C., *Quito to Bogota,* Garden City, N. Y., Doubleday, Doran and Co., 1917.

Costa Rica

Calvo, J. B., *The Republic of Costa Rica,* Washington, United States Government Printing Office, 1894.
Fernández Guardia, Ricardo, *Cartilla historica de Costa Rica* (5th ed.), San José, Libreria Lehmann, 1927.
————, *History of the Discovery and Conquest of Costa Rica,* New York, T. Y. Crowell Co., 1913.
Guerrero, José, *Alfabetismo y Anafabetismo en Costa Rica según el censo general de población de 11 de Mayo de 1927,* San José, Alsina, 1928.
Jones, Chester Lloyd, *Costa Rica and Civilization in the Caribbean,* Madison, Wis., University of Wisconsin, 1934.
Merz, Carlos, *El Comercio internacional de la república de Costa Rica,* San José, Imprenta Nacional, 1929.
Soley Güell, Tomas, *Historia monetaria de Costa Rica,* San José, Trejos Hermanos, 1926.
Thiel, Bernardo A., *Viajes a varias partes de la república de Costa Rica,* San José, Trejos Hermanos, 1927.

Cuba

Aimes, H. H. S., *A History of Slavery in Cuba, 1511 to 1868,* New York, G. P. Putnam's Sons, 1907.
Atkins, E. F., *Sixty Years in Cuba,* Boston, Houghton Mifflin Co., 1926.

Beals, Carleton, *The Crime of Cuba,* Philadelphia, J. B. Lippincott Co., 1933.

Benton, E. J., *International Law and Diplomacy of the Spanish-American War,* Baltimore, Johns Hopkins Press, 1908.

Bigelow, John, *American Policy,* New York, Charles Scribner's Sons, 1914.

Buell, Raymond L., *Sugar and the Tariff,* New York, Foreign Policy Association Information Service, 1929.

Callahan, James Morton, *Cuba and International Relations,* Baltimore, Johns Hopkins Press, 1899.

Chadwick, F. E., *The Relations of the United States and Spain,* New York, Charles Scribner's Sons, 1911.

Chapman, C. E., *A History of the Cuban Republic,* New York, the Macmillan Co., 1927.

Draper, Andrew S., *The Rescue of Cuba,* Boston, Silver, Burdett and Co., 1910.

Edwards, Paul L., *Economic Conditions in Cuba, United States Department of Commerce, Bureau of Foreign and Domestic Commerce, Trade Information Bulletin No. 159,* Washington, 1923.

Everett, Guerra, *Trading Under the Laws of Cuba, United States Department of Commerce, Bureau of Foreign and Domestic Commerce, Trade Information Bulletin No. 343,* Washington, 1927.

Forbes-Lindsay, C. H. A., *Cuba and Her People of Today,* Boston, L. C. Page and Co., 1911.

————, and Winters, Nevin O., *Cuba and Her People of Today,* Boston, L. C. Page and Co., 1928.

Gonzalez, N. G., *In Darkest Cuba,* State Co., Columbia, S. C., 1922.

Guggenheim, Harry F., *The United States and Cuba,* New York, the Macmillan Co., 1934.

Hill, Robert T., *Cuba and Porto Rico, with the Other Islands of the West Indies,* New York, Century Co., 1898.

Jenks, L. H., *Our Cuban Colony,* New York, Vanguard Press, 1928.

Johnson, Willis Fletcher, *The History of Cuba* (5 vols.), New York, B. F. Buck and Co., 1920.

Livengood, C. A., and Coombs, Frank E., *Cuban Economic Improvement, Trade Information Bulletin No. 191,* Washington, 1925.

Meehan, M. J., *Caribbean Markets For American Goods: III—Cuba, Trade Information Bulletin No. 346,* Washington, 1925.

Musgrave, G. C., *Cuba, the Land of Opportunity,* London, Simpson, Marshall, Hamilton Kent and Co., Ltd., 1919.

Parker, William Belmont (ed.), *Cubans of Today,* New York, G. P. Putnam's Sons, 1919.

Porter, Robert P., *Industrial Cuba,* New York, G. P. Putnam's Sons, 1899.

Reno, George, *Cuba,* Havana, Bureau of Information, Department of Agriculture, Commerce and Labor, 1915.

Robinson, A. G., *Cuba and the Intervention,* New York, Longmans, Green and Co., 1905.

———, *Cuba, Old and New,* New York, Longmans, Green and Co., 1915.

Rubens, Horatio Seymour, *Liberty—The Story of Cuba,* New York, Harcourt, Brace and Co., 1932.

Stuart, G. H., *Cuba and Its International Relations,* New York, Institute of International Education, 1923.

United States Department of Commerce, Bureau of Foreign and Domestic Commerce, *Cuba and Other West Indies: A Current Business Analysis, Trade Information Bulletin No. 15,* Washington, 1922.

United States Department of Commerce, Bureau of Foreign and Domestic Commerce, *Cuban Sugar-Crop Financing, Trade Information Bulletin No. 29,* Washington, 1922.

United States Department of Commerce, *Cuban Readjustment to Current Economic Forces, Trade Information Bulletin No. 725,* Washington, 1930.

United States Tariff Commission, *Differences in Costs of Production of Sugar in the United States and Cuba,* Washington, 1926.

Verrill, A. H., *Cuba, Past and Present,* New York, Dodd, Mead and Co., 1914.

Wright, Irene A., *Cuba,* New York, the Macmillan Co., 1910.

———, *Early History of Cuba, 1492–1586,* New York, the Macmillan Co., 1916.

Wright, Philip G., *The Cuban Situation and our Treaty Relations,* Washington, Brookings Institution, 1931.

Dominican Republic

Albrecht, C. H., and Henry, F. A., *Development of the Dominican Republic, United States Department of Commerce, Bureau of Foreign and Domestic Commerce, Special Consular Reports No. 65,* Washington, 1914.

Dominican Customs Receivership, Annual Report, Washington, 1908 to date.

Final Report of the Transactions of the Dominican Customs Receivership under the Modus Vivendi, April 1, 1905 to July 31, 1907, Santo Domingo, 1907.

Inman, Samuel Guy, *Through Santo Domingo and Haiti,* New York, Committee on Coöperation in Latin America, 1919.

Knight, M. M., *The Americans in Santo Domingo,* New York, Vanguard Press, 1928.

Pan-American Union, *The Dominican Republic,* Washington, the Pan-American Union, 1924.

Schoenrich, Otto, *Santo Domingo,* New York, the Macmillan Co., 1918.

Stoddard, T. L., *The French Revolution in Santo Domingo,* Boston, Houghton Mifflin Co., 1914.

Ureña Henriquez, Max, *Los Yanquis en Santo Domingo,* Madrid, M. Aguilar, 1929.

Verrill, A. H., *Porto Rico Past and Present and San Domingo of Today,* New York, Dodd, Mead and Co., 1914.

Welles, Sumner, *Naboth's Vineyard: The Dominican Republic, 1844–1924,* New York, Harcourt, Brace and Co., 1928.

Guatemala

Domville-Fife, C. W., *Guatemala and the States of Central America,* London, F. Griffiths, 1913.

Winter, N. O., *Guatemala and Her People of Today,* Boston, L. C. Page and Co., 1909.

Haiti

Annual reports of the American High Commissioner at Port-au-Prince, Haiti, Washington.

Balch, E. G., *Occupied Haiti,* New York, Writers Publication Co., 1927.

Beauvoir, Vefort, *Le controle Financier du Gouvernement des États-Unis d'Amérique sur la République d'Haiti,* Paris, Sirey, 1930.

Bird, M. B., *The Black Man; or Haytian Independence,* New York, published by the author; trade supplied by the American News Co.; 1869.

Buell, Raymond L., *The American Occupation of Haiti,* New York, Foreign Policy Association Information Service, 1929, Vol. V., Nos. 19–20.

Dashiell, H. H., and Honaker, S. H., *Trade Financing and Exchange in Porto Rico and Haiti, United States Department of Commerce, Bureau of Foreign and Domestic Commerce, Trade Information Bulletin No. 595,* Washington, 1929.

Davis, H. P., *Black Democracy,* New York, Dial Press, Inc., 1928.

De La Rue, S., *A Review of the Finances of the Republic of Haiti, 1924–30,* March 3, 1930.

Franklin, James, *The Present State of Haiti,* London, John Murray, 1828.

Haiti: Annual Report of the Financial Adviser-General Receiver.

Haiti: Blue Book, New York, Klebold Press, 1920.

Hazard, Sam., *Santo Domingo Past and Present with a Glance at Hayti,* New York, S. Low, Marston, Low and Searle, 1873.

Inman, S. G., *Through Santo Domingo and Haiti,* New York, Committee on Coöperation in Latin America, 1919.

Kuser, John D., *Haiti: Its Dawn of Progress after Years in a Night of Revolution,* Boston, R. G. Badger, 1921.

Leger, J. N., *Haiti, Her History and Her Detractors,* New York, Neale Publishing Co., 1907.

Marshall, Mrs. Harriet (Gibbs), *The Story of Haiti,* Boston, Christopher Publishing House, 1930.

Memorandum of Accomplishments of the Customs Receivership of the Republic of Haiti—by the General Receivers of Customs, Port-au-Prince, 1924.

Millspaugh, Arthur Chester, *Haiti Under American Control,* Boston, World Peace Foundation, 1931.

Niles, Blair, *Black Haiti,* New York, G. P. Putnam's Sons, 1926.

Prichard, Hesketh, *Where Black Rules White,* New York, Archibald Constable and Co., 1900.

St. John, Sir Spenser, *Hayti or the Black Republic,* London, Smith Elder and Co., 1889.

Seabrook, W. B., *The Magic Island,* New York, Harcourt, Brace and Co., 1929.

Steward, T. G., *The Haitian Revolution, 1791–1804,* New York, T. Y. Crowell Co., 1914.

Stoddard, T. L., *The French Revolution in Santo Domingo,* Boston, Houghton Mifflin Co., 1914.

Treudley, Mary, *The United States and Santo Domingo, 1789–1886* (Ph.D. thesis), Clark University, Worcester, Mass., 1916.

United States Department of Commerce, Bureau of Foreign and Domestic Commerce, *Haiti: An Economic Survey, Trade Information Bulletin No. 264,* Washington, 1924.

United States Department of Commerce, *Trade Financing and Exchange in Porto Rico and Haiti, Trade Information Bulletin No. 595,* Washington, 1929.

Vandercook, John W., *Black Majesty,* New York, Harper and Brothers, 1928.

Verrill, A. H., *Porto Rico Past and Present and San Domingo of To-day,* New York, Dodd, Mead and Co., 1914.

Waxman, Percy, *The Black Napoleon,* New York, Harcourt, Brace and Co., 1931.

Wirkus, Faustin, and Dudley, Taney, *The White King of La Gonave,* Garden City, N. Y., Doubleday, Doran and Co., 1931.

Honduras

La République de Honduras; notice historique, géographique et statistique, Anvers, 1898.

Lazo, Hector, *Honduras, United States Department of Commerce, Bureau of Foreign and Domestic Commerce, Trade Information Bulletin No. 193,* Washington, 1924.

Squier, E. G., *Honduras,* London, Truebner and Co., 1870.

Nicaragua

Brief History of the Relations Between the United States and Nicaragua, 1909–1928, Washington, United States Department of State, 1928.

Cox, Isaac J., *Nicaragua and the United States, 1909–1927,* Boston, World Peace Foundation, 1927.

Cumberland, W. W., *Nicaragua, an Economic and Financial Survey,* Washington, Department of State, 1928.

Nicaragua, Report of the Collector General of Customs, Managua. (Annual)

Playter, H., and McConnico, A. J., *Nicaragua: A Commercial and Economic Survey, United States Department of Commerce, Bureau of Foreign and Domestic Commerce, Trade Promotion Series, No. 54,* Washington, 1927.

Stimson, H. L., *American Policy in Nicaragua,* New York, Charles Scribner's Sons, 1927.

Panama

Abbot, W. J., *Panama and the Canal,* New York, Syndicate Publishing Co., 1913.

Bakenhus, R. E., Knapp, H. S., and Johnson, E. R., *The Panama Canal,* New York, John Wiley and Sons, 1915.

Bishop, Farnham, *Panama, Past and Present,* New York, Century Co., 1916.

Bunau-Varilla, P., *Panama, Creation, Destruction, and Resurrection,* New York, Robert M. McBride and Co., 1914.

Edwards, Albert (pseud. for Ballard, Arthur), *Panama, the Canal, the Country and the People,* New York, the Macmillan Co., 1914.

Freehoff, J. C., *America and the Canal Title,* New York, published by the author, 1916.

Johnson, E. R., *The Panama Canal and Commerce,* New York, D. Appleton and Co., 1916.

Johnson, W. F., *Four Centuries of the Panama Canal,* New York, Henry Holt and Co., 1909.

Root, Elihu, *Panama Canal Tolls,* Boston, World Peace Foundation, 1913.

Smith, D. H., *The Panama Canal,* Baltimore, Johns Hopkins Press, 1927.

White, T. R., and Tower, Charlemagne, *Our Duty Concerning the Panama Canal Tolls,* Boston, World Peace Foundation, 1913.

Puerto Rico

Annual Report of the Governor of Porto Rico, Washington, 1900 to date.

Capó, Claudio, *The Island of Porto Rico,* San Juan, the Globe Publishing Co., 1925.

Clark, Victor S., and associates, *Porto Rico and Its Problems,* Washington, Brookings Institution, 1930.

Dashiell, H. H., and Honaker, S. H., *Trade Financing and Exchange in Porto Rico and Haiti, United States Department of Commerce, Bureau of Foreign and Domestic Commerce, Trade Information Bulletin No. 595.* Washington, 1929.

Diffie, B. W. and J. W., *Porto Rico: A Broken Pledge,* New York, Vanguard Press, 1931.

Dinwiddie, William, *Puerto Rico; Its Conditions and Possibilities,* New York, Harper and Brothers, 1899.

Fernández y García, E., *The Book of Porto Rico,* San Juan, El Libro Azul Publishing Co., 1923.

Fleagle, Fred K., *Social Problems in Porto Rico,* New York, D. C. Heath and Co., 1917.

Mixer, Knowlton, *Porto Rico; History and Conditions,* New York, the Macmillan Co., 1926.

Ober, F. A., *Porto Rico and Its Resources,* New York, D. Appleton and Co., 1898.

Rowe, L. S., *The United States and Porto Rico,* London, Longmans, Green and Co., 1904.

Van Deusen, R. J. and E. K., *Porto Rico, A Caribbean Isle,* New York, Henry Holt and Co., 1931.

Verrill, A. H., *Porto Rico, Past and Present and San Domingo of Today,* New York, Dodd, Mead and Co., 1914.

Von Middledyck, R. A., *The History of Puerto Rico from the Spanish Discovery to the American Occupation,* New York, 1903.

Salvador

Martin, Percy F., *Salvador of the Twentieth Century,* New York, Longmans, Green and Co., 1911.

Venezuela

Arcaya, Pedro Manuel, *Estudios de Sociología Venezolana,* Madrid, Editorial América, 1924.

————, *Notes on Political History (of Venezuela),* New York, Carranza and Co., 1924.

Bates, John, Jr., and Lindon, W., *The Path of the Conquistadores,* London, 1912.

Beebe, William, *Jungle Days,* New York, G. P. Putnam's Sons, 1925.

————, *Jungle Peace,* New York, Henry Holt and Co., 1918.

————, *The Edge of the Jungle,* Garden City, N. Y., Garden City Publishing Co., 1925.

Bell, P. L., *Venezuela, A Commercial and Industrial Handbook, United States Department of Commerce, Bureau of Foreign and Domestic Commerce, Special Agents Series, No. 212,* Washington, 1922.

Bingham, H., *The Journal of an Expedition Across Venezuela and Colombia, 1906–7,* New Haven, Yale Publishing Association, 1909.

Bowen, H. W., *Recollections Diplomatic and Undiplomatic,* New York, Frederick H. Hitchcock, 1926, Chaps. XXIII and XXIV.

Cleveland, G., *Presidential Problems,* New York, Century Co., 1904.

Dalton, L. V., *Venezuela,* New York, Charles Scribner's Sons, 1912.

Dewey, D. R., *National Problems (1885–1897),* New York, Harper and Brothers, 1907, pp. 297–313.

Drago, L. M., *La República Argentina y el caso de Venezuela,* Buenos Aires, Imprenta y Casa Editorra de Coni Hermanos, 1903.

Edgington, T. B., *The Monroe Doctrine,* Boston, Little, Brown and Co., 1904, Chap. XVI.

Fried, A. H., *Die Zweite Haager Konferenz, ihre Arbeiten, ihre Ergebnisse u. ihre Bedeutung,* Leipzig, 1908.

Hale, Albert, *South Americans,* Indianapolis, the Bobbs-Merrill Co., 1907.

Henderson, J. B., *American Diplomatic Questions,* New York, the Macmillan Co., 1901, pp. 411–450.

Hull, W. I., *The Two Hague Conferences,* Boston, Ginn and Co., 1908.

MacVeagh, Wayne, Bowen, Herbert W., and Penfield, Wm. L., *Great Britain, Germany and Italy Against Venezuela,* Internal Tribunal at The Hague, 1903.

Mallarmé, A., *L'Arbitrage Venézuélien devant la Cour d'appel de La Haye (1903–1904),* Paris, 1906.

Martens, F., *Par la justice vers la paix,* Paris, H. Charles-Laranzelle, 1906, annexe: "Doctrine de Drago."

Moulin, Henri A., *La doctrine de Drago,* Paris, A. Pedone, 1908.

Mozans, H. J. (pseud., Zahn, J. A.), *Up the Orinoco and Down the Magdalena,* New York, D. Appleton and Co., 1910.

Ralston, J. H., and Doyle, W. T. S., *Venezuelan Arbitrations of 1903,* Washington, United States Government Printing Office, 1906.

Rowe, L. S., and Borges, E. Gil., *Venezuela, American Nation Series, No. 21,* Washington, Pan American Union, 1928.

Scott, J. B., ed., *The Texts of the Peace Conferences at the Hague, 1899 and 1907,* Boston, Ginn and Co., 1908.

Scruggs, William L., *Fallacies of the British "Blue Book" on the Venezuelan Question,* Washington, McGill and Wallace, 1896.

————, *The Colombian and Venezuelan Republics,* Boston, Little, Brown and Co., 1900.

Spence, J. M., *The Land of Bolívar,* London, S. Low, Marston, Searle and Rivington, 1878.

United States Department of Commerce, *Commercial and Industrial Development of Venezuela, Trade Information Bulletin No. 783,* Washington, 1931.

Virgin Islands

Booy, T. H. N. de, and Faris, J. T., *The Virgin Islands,* Philadelphia, J. B. Lippincott Co., 1918.

Brock, H. G., Smith, P. S., and Tucker, W. A., *The Danish West Indies, Their Resources and Commercial Importance, United States Department of Commerce, Bureau of Foreign and Domestic Commerce, Special Agents' Series, No. 129,* Washington, 1917.

Tansill, Charles Callan, *The Purchase of the Danish West Indies,* Baltimore, Johns Hopkins Press, 1932.

Tucker, R. S., *Economic Conditions in the Virgin Islands, Senate Documents No. 41 and 110,* Sixty-ninth Congress, First Session, Washington, 1926.

United States Census Bureau, *Census of the Virgin Islands of the United States,* 1918.

Virgin Islands, Governor of the, *The Virgin Islands of the United States,* Washington. (Annual)

Westergaard, W. C., *The Danish West Indies Under Company Rule, 1671–1754,* New York, the Macmillan Co., 1917.

Zabriskie, L. K., *The Virgin Islands of the United States,* New York, G. P. Putnam's Sons, 1918.

Index